MILITARY INTELLIGENCE BLUNDERS

Colonel John Hughes-Wilson is one of Britain's leading military historians, and a well-reviewed author and commentator on a wide range of intelligence and military historical subjects. He was awarded the International Napoleonic Society's gold medal for his ground-breaking work, with Scotland Yard, on 'Who really killed Napoleon?', and was later selected to be the author of the Imperial War Museum's *A History of the First World War in 100 Objects* for 2014, the centenary of the start of the Great War. He also wrote the original *Military Intelligence Blunders and Cover-Ups*, which was found at Osama bin Laden's bedside after his assassination and has become a CIA textbook. Colonel Hughes-Wilson has been a frequent broadcaster for BBC television and radio, and worked alongside Huw Edwards and David Dimbleby providing live TV commentary for events including the annual Cenotaph ceremony and the twenty-fifth anniversary of the Falklands War. He qualified as an NBC officer during the Cold War. During his twenty-five years in the Intelligence Corps and as a special forces operations officer, he saw active service in the Falkland Islands, Cyprus, Arabia and Northern Ireland, as well as in the dangerous jungles of Whitehall and NATO. His *JFK: An American Coup d'Etat*, a remarkable new study published to mark the fiftieth anniversary of the events in Dallas, Texas, of November 1963, was acclaimed in the US. His latest book for John Blake Publishing is *Eve of Destruction* (2021), a critical study of nuclear accidents. He admits to having assisted in a number of cover-ups of embarrassing blunders during his service in intelligence, and to committing several personally.

MILITARY INTELLIGENCE BLUNDERS

COLONEL JOHN HUGHES-WILSON

REVISED AND UPDATED EDITION

First published in the UK by John Blake Publishing
an imprint of Bonnier Books UK
4th Floor, Victoria House
Bloomsbury Square
London WC1B 4DA
England

Owned by Bonnier Books
Sveavägen 56, Stockholm, Sweden

www.facebook.com/johnblakebooks
twitter.com/jblakebooks

First published by Robinson in 1999; revised edition 2004
This revised and updated edition first published in paperback in 2023
by John Blake Publishing

Paperback ISBN: 978-1-78946-669-0
Ebook ISBN: 978-1-78946-676-8

British Library Cataloguing-in-Publication Data:
A CIP catalogue record for this book is available from the British Library.

Design by www.envydesign.co.uk

Printed and bound in Great Britain by Clays Ltd, Elcograf S.p.A

1 3 5 7 9 10 8 6 4 2

Every reasonable effort has been made to trace copyright-holders of material reproduced
in this book, but if any have been inadvertently overlooked the publishers would be glad
to hear from them.

John Blake Publishing is an imprint of Bonnier Books UK
www.bonnierbooks.co.uk

For
Victor Andersen†
of the British intelligence services
and
Val Heller†
of the US Defense Intelligence Agency
and
Corporal Sarah Bryant, Intelligence Corps†
and
General Sir James Glover, KCB, MBE†,
all of whom made it possible.

CONTENTS

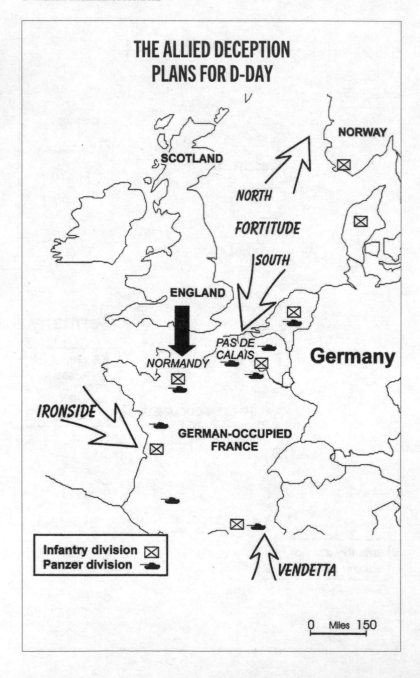

THE ALLIED DECEPTION PLANS FOR D-DAY

NORWAY

SCOTLAND

NORTH

FORTITUDE

SOUTH

ENGLAND

NORMANDY

PAS DE CALAIS

Germany

IRONSIDE

GERMAN-OCCUPIED FRANCE

Infantry division ⊠
Panzer division

VENDETTA

0 Miles 150

OPERATION BARBAROSSA
22 JUNE 1941

MALAYA AND SINGAPORE, 1942

THAILAND

Singora

South China Sea

Kota Bharu

Alor Star

Penang

Kuala Trengganu

Taiping

MALAYA

Slim River

Kuantan

Prince of Wales
& Repulse sunk
10 Dec 1941

Selangor

Kuala Lumpur

Endau

Malacca

SUMATRA
(Dutch East Indies)

Batu Pahat

Johore

SINGAPORE

——— Major routes
—·—·— National border

0   Miles   100

BATTLE OF MIDWAY, 1942

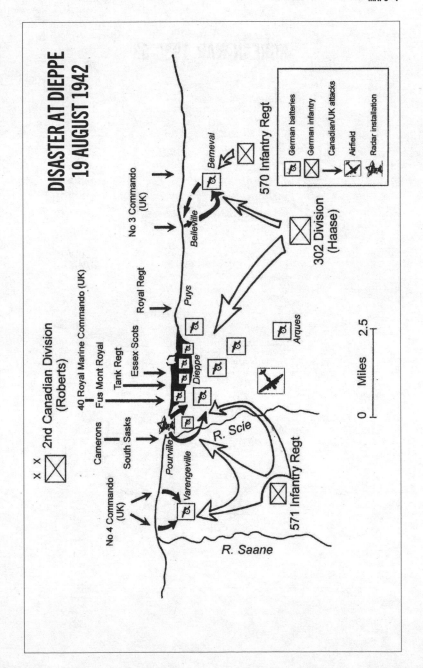

DISASTER AT DIEPPE
19 AUGUST 1942

KOREAN WAR, 1950-53

THE VIETNAM WAR 1956-75

NORTH VIETNAM

Dien Bien Phu

Hai Phong

Hanoi

GULF OF TONKIN

LAOS

THAILAND

Ho Chi Minh trail

17th parallel

Khe Sanh

Hue

Da Nang

CAMBODIA

SOUTH VIETNAM

SOUTH CHINA SEA

Saigon

Miles

0   300

THE TET OFFENSIVE
SOUTH VIETNAM
30-31 JANUARY 1968

NORTH VIETNAM

Demilitarized Zone

Quang Tri

Hue

Khe Sanh

Da Nang

THAILAND

LAOS

0   50
Miles

Dak To

Kontum

Pleiku

Qui Nhon

CAMBODIA

Tuy Hoa

SOUTH VIETNAM

Tay Ninh

Bien Hoa

Can Tho

SAIGON

South China Sea

Major Tet attacks

"GREATER ISRAEL" 1967-73

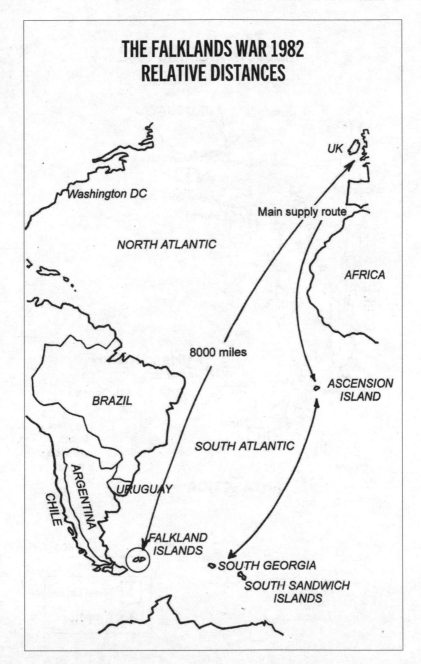

THE FALKLANDS WAR 1982
RELATIVE DISTANCES

THE SOUTH ATLANTIC 1982

CHILE

ARGENTINA

Santiago

Concepcion

Cordoba

URUGUAY

Buenos Aires

Montevideo

Mar del Plata

Bahia Blanca

Comodoro Rivadavia

Falkland Islands
Stanley

South Georgia

Punta Arenas

Rio Gallegos

Ushuaia

**South
Sandwich
Islands**

ANTARCTICA

0   400
Nautical miles

⚓ Naval bases

✈ Airfields

THE GULF WAR 1990-91

AFGHANISTAN, 2001-21

RUSSIAN INVASION OF UKRAINE, 2022

PREFACE

'Intelligence' has several meanings. This is a book about military and political mistakes rooted in intelligence.

Military Intelligence Blunders was first published in 1999 and, with a revision in 2004/5, became a bestseller and a textbook for the CIA and many academic institutions, as well as garnering praise from numerous senior intelligence professionals. (The Canadian Head of Service Intelligence described it as 'required reading for intelligence professionals and military historians alike…' and 'this is a well-written, easy-to-read book that provides an excellent review of intelligence practices that have had an historic impact on our world.') 'This has become an important addition to my library…' wrote Professor M. R. D. Foot, a distinguished academic on intelligence. Osama bin Laden kept a copy by his bedside.

So this book is more than a rehash of old wine in new bottles. It includes much new material, as well as three new chapters analysing the American triumph (and Japanese intelligence disaster) at Midway; the myopic use of intelligence in Korea; and the strange debacle of Afghanistan. It even tentatively examines the possible outcome of Russia's on-going war in Ukraine, a hostage to any author's fortune and events if ever there was one.

The result is effectively a new book, drawing on the old plus much new material. Because, as the headlines show us daily, 'intelligence' matters…

One of the very first things the President or the Prime Minister sees every morning is the daily intelligence update.

'Intelligence' is one of the most important things that governs our lives: but we are usually totally unaware of its existence. Yet we, the taxpayers who have bought all this expensive effort, very rarely get to see what we have paid for.

Following the World Trade Center disaster, the US-led coalition's invasion of Iraq in the spring of 2003; the blatant shenanigans over the British Joint Intelligence Committee's flagrant distorting of the truth; and the long debacle of Afghanistan, intelligence assumed a prominence in the headlines rarely seen before. Russia's clumsy mishandled invasion of Ukraine emphasises the point.

The public discovered for the first time not only just how important intelligence really is in determining government policy but also how intelligence works. Many people were astonished and shocked to discover just how governments try to manipulate or ignore intelligence that doesn't fit in with their policies at the time. Intelligence, normally a subject kept in the shadows, has been forced onto the front pages and into the public consciousness as never before. This is a book that tries to give a view of some recent events, all within living memory, from this different angle: intelligence. And not just 'military intelligence' either, because the distinction between military and political intelligence is usually a false one. Pretty much all intelligence is *government* intelligence; it tends to become a military problem only when it goes horribly wrong.

Most of us have read press accounts and books about the events that unfold on these pages. But very few of us have seen the events from the *inside*. The inside implies knowledge; and knowledge means *power*. By 'inside', I do not mean the insider views of politicians or the other self-satisfied classes like ex-government aides or even very grand journalists who often write along the lines of, 'Well, as the President said to me in confidence…' implying that they were really the only ones in the know.

The real 'insiders' knowledge' however is always the intelligence that was available to the politicians and decision makers *at the time*. It is easy to forget it was really this secret intelligence that lay behind the headlines that shaped events. It was intelligence that made the people who took the decisions at the time to appear as heroes or villains to later generations. Any writer can be correct in hindsight.

This book tries to lift the veil on what really happened behind the scenes in the intelligence world at the time during some of the most well-known events of the last half of the twentieth century and the first two decades of the twenty-first, from the Second World War to today's War on Terror. It tries to show why decisions were made, for good or ill, by a number of famous and not so famous characters, based on the intelligence and the secrets they had to work with at the time.

The book concentrates on intelligence mistakes and blunders for the very simple reason that they are more interesting than the far more numerous successes of intelligence that must remain secret so they can be repeated if necessary. And in many cases the intelligence blunders have usually been *very* carefully concealed from the taxpayer who paid for them. For example, the Japanese people only found out that Midway had been a complete failure months after their defeat.

The book therefore identifies numerous lies and cover-ups. Not all these deceptions were committed to deceive the enemy, which will not make the stories outlined in the following pages universally popular. For example, the real story behind the Dieppe Raid and the then Vice Admiral Lord Louis Mountbatten's role in that disastrous adventure, in particular, have aroused strong emotions. But the recorded facts are clear and truth will out. Turning over stones invariably lets a hard sunlight onto some areas that many would prefer to remain hidden or forgotten. Mountbatten is not alone. There are many other government officials and intelligence officers, in all regimes, who would much prefer to remain creatures of the shadows and keep their blunders and bad decisions secret, if only to protect their reputations, careers and pensions. Secrecy in intelligence matters is not always for the highest motives.

Secrecy is also a dangerous ally of those very senior civil servants of every country's administration who thrive and prosper in the sure and certain knowledge that control of intelligence secrets gives them the ultimate benefit of the harlot: the decision-maker's ear and power without responsibility. Good intelligence officers should always have the moral courage to take responsibility for the advice they give – good or bad – to their political masters. Intelligence is, after all, about predicting the most likely future and not just regaling today's worried decision-makers with yesterday's facts. CNN, Sky and BBC Television can do that far better, which is why there is always a television set in every government minister's private office.

The various case studies in this book are intended to provide a readable narrative of the events they describe, accompanied by some professional intelligence insights of how those events came about and unfolded at the time. Wherever possible I have tried to avoid 20/20 hindsight judgements. That is neither fair to the individuals concerned, nor honest guidance to the reader. Everyone can be clever after the event.

Since the first edition there has been an understandable demand from the academic world for much more detail on the sources and background to many of the chapters. This is always a tricky area in a book which is primarily intended for general popular reading. To keep everyone happy I have tried to tread a delicate path between the laboriously footnoted detail, which will satisfy my friends in academia, and 'popular history', by including a more comprehensive list of sources for each chapter at the back of the book for those who would like to delve into the stories more thoroughly. Where possible, quotations are clearly indicated in the text. The result is, I hope, a book that enjoys a grudging degree of academic acceptability while at the same time being 'a good read'.

JOHN HUGHES-WILSON
North Cyprus, 2023

1
ON INTELLIGENCE

'Speak truth unto power'
BAYARD RUSTIN, 1942

'Military Intelligence', runs the old saying, 'is a contradiction in terms.' This weary old joke has about the same impact on professional intelligence officers as jokes about striking oil have on drilling dentists. It is a commonly held view, however, because history is littered with disastrous intelligence mistakes. From the earliest recorded times down to the Gulf War, soldiers of all kinds have been taken by surprise. How could the military be so stupid?

Yet surprise is one of the cardinal principles of war. Every military academy and staff college in the world teaches the need to achieve surprise – and to guard against it – to every single student of the military art. Despite this, the military appears to have been caught out with almost predictable regularity. Is the failing one of endemic stupidity or of an opponent's cunning?

The answer is both. Just as every military commander hopes not to be taken by surprise, potential adversaries strive equally hard with every trick and resource to mislead, to deceive and to catch their enemy unawares. To avoid being surprised, commanders rely on intelligence and their intelligence staffs to warn them. Sometimes they are successful, sometimes not. On the success of intelligence hinges a military commander's decisions and his reputation; and very often the future of his country and its population as well.

Therein lies our fascination with the decisions of the military professional, and the difference between his and other callings. Military decisions simply carry more weight and potential disaster than those of other professions. Think Stalingrad?

For while other professionals in a host of occupations make key decisions, none of them, with perhaps the exception of a politician in war, carry such an awesome responsibility. If a banker makes a fatal error, economies crash and people lose their savings and jobs. If a surgeon makes a dreadful mistake, a patient dies. But when a general, admiral or air marshal blunders, soldiers and civilians alike die, sometimes in appalling numbers. To take just one example: Hitler and Paulus sent no fewer than a quarter of a million men to their doom around Stalingrad. Of that number, only 5,000 broken men ever came back from Russia. Would Hitler have ordered the 6th Army to stand fast had he had accurate intelligence about the Soviet generals' plans?

Although intelligence can help, it cannot make a commander's decisions for him. Even when confronted with crystal-clear reports, accurate, up to date and supported by first-hand evidence, history has shown us over and over again that a stubborn, ambitious or misguided commander will simply ignore the cast-iron proof before him. We do not have to go very far to find an example. MacArthur, 'the American Caesar', stands as a prime example.

A more blatant attempt to disregard unpalatable intelligence can be found in the disaster at Arnhem. In September 1944, General 'Boy' Browning disregarded Major Brian Urquhart's black-and-white aerial intelligence photographs clearly showing the presence of German SS panzer divisions refitting near Arnhem. Not only that; a furious Browning promptly dismissed his unfortunate intelligence officer on the grounds that 'he had potentially compromised the whole mission and was mentally disturbed by stress and overwork'. Urquhart was escorted out of the headquarters by a grim-faced Director of Medical Services and sent off on convalescent leave. Days later, the paras dropped.

The consequences of Browning's orders led to the catastrophic loss of the British 1st Airborne Division on the ill-fated Operation Market Garden. It need never have happened but for Browning's decision, which seems to have been based primarily on a desire not to be left out of the action when the war's end was thought, wrongly, to be in sight. The soldiers of the British and Polish airborne brigades paid a terrible price for the conceit and arrogance that motivated Browning's refusal to acknowledge the accurate information put before him by his intelligence staff.

Ironically, years later, when Urquhart was the senior adviser on security operations as Secretary-General of the United Nations, he recounted the story of that fateful wartime autumn in sad, almost humorous terms, ending with, 'But I don't really blame General Browning; in his shoes, what else could he have done?'[1]

Worst of all, arguably, was Stalin, who just ignored intelligence he didn't want to hear. By and large, military commanders are not stupid. Even the most intellectually challenged general has always understood that war is a matter of at least two sides and wants, understandably, to be on the winning team. Victory will bring him honours, riches, rewards and the applause of his countrymen. Why then, with such incentives, do approximately 50 per cent of them get it so consistently wrong?

In the great majority of cases, defeat can usually be traced back to a lack of knowledge of the enemy. Whether from overconfidence, ignorance, gullibility or just a failure to comprehend the facts, military defeat is almost invariably associated with an intelligence defeat caused by an underestimation of the enemy. In Malaya in 1941, British and imperial commanders believed that the Japanese were puny little Asiatics, incapable of fighting in the jungle let alone operating modern combat aircraft, who posed little or no threat at all. They were wrong.

It is hard in hindsight to grasp how such misjudgements ever became part of a nation's military policy. We must therefore look closely at the actual mechanisms of intelligence itself, long regarded as a black and mysterious art practised by anonymous men and women far from the limelight. Are their failings and failures the true reason behind so many military blunders? How can 'intelligence' ever get it so badly wrong?

We should not be too surprised. Considering how important good intelligence is, the military has traditionally not been lavish in its support for a staff speciality that can sometimes save an army's skin. In many an army, navy or air force, the intelligence staff is often a Cinderella organization. The problem is that the path to military glory invariably lies in the field of operations. Shooting down aeroplanes, sinking ships, destroying enemy brigades or being

---

1 Personal exchange with the author, 1975

a victorious operational commander is the sure path to recognition and high command in all military organizations. The result is that, with its fellow battle-winning partner, logistics, intelligence is often treated like a backwater or a mysterious haunt of clever but difficult individuals. Yet ironically, both intelligence and logistics are acknowledged by every staff college in the world as two of the fundamental keys that can guarantee a commander's success on the field of battle.

The realization that intelligence can be disregarded or challenged as being unpalatable or inaccurate has forced modern intelligence services to make their intelligence ever more robust. The aim is to force their 'customers', be they military or political, to acknowledge the truth staring them in the face. To achieve this, military intelligence nowadays has been turned into a system designed to reduce error and anomaly, a kind of simple system that aims to transform information into intelligence, despite the attempts of academics to promote their own complex views of a very straightforward problem. Here is an example of that type of academic approach:

- FORESIGHT, the ability to understand trends that present threats or opportunities for an organization;
- VISIONING, the ability to conceptualize an ideal future state based on foresight and create a process to engage others to implement it;
- SYSTEM THINKING, the ability to perceive, synthesize and integrate elements that function as a whole to achieve a common purpose;
- MOTIVATING, the ability to motivate different people to work together to implement a vision. Understanding what motivates people is based upon another ability, personality intelligence.

What on earth use this is to the professional is ignored, or hidden in a maze of linguistic mumbo jumbo. This kind of jargon and theorizing helps the aspiring academic to 'publish or perish', but is of little practical use to a hard-pressed intelligence officer busy on a problem at the coalface. What is much more important for us to understand are the basic processes of the intelligence world. And how it really works – or should work. Only then can we understand what went wrong in the past, and why.

Intelligence is nothing more or less than information that has been systematically and professionally processed and analysed. There are many definitions of intelligence, but every professional intelligence officer understands precisely what he or she is required to deliver. For the professional, intelligence is simply defined as 'processed, accurate information, presented in sufficient time to enable a decision-maker to take whatever action is required'. These intelligence principles are understood by every trained intelligence officer worldwide.

The intelligence cycle is usually presented graphically as a circular process, as in figure 1 below. Inaccurate information speaks for itself; no one gets credit for wrong facts. Even junior reporters are fired for failing to check their sources. Equally, to shout 'Look out!' *after* the piano crashes to the ground is hardly timely intelligence. But the intelligence officer confronts another, more subtle, problem: that of capabilities versus intentions.

UNDERSTANDING CAPABILITIES VERSUS INTENTIONS

Understanding the difference between a potential enemy's *capabilities* and his *intentions* is crucial to understanding the difficulties facing the purveyor of intelligence. For example, if I have a gun gathering dust in a drawer, then I have a potential capability for violent action. But there is no evidence of intention. I pose only a potential threat, based solely on my possession of an object designed for killing.

If, on the other hand, I have a sharpened pencil, but I am waving it in front of your face, absolutely determined to stab you in the eye, then I am an extremely dangerous individual. Despite an apparently limited aggressive capability (every household, school or office has a pencil or two), my intention makes me a major threat. Capabilities and intentions are very different things.

This problem of separating intentions and capabilities will recur throughout our examination of intelligence failures. The intelligence cycle makes an effort to separate the two, though how successfully is open to question. But the distinction is clear.

The best way to understand how intelligence works is the intelligence cycle. This starts with **DIRECTION**, where the commander or political leader states his *intelligence requirement*, usually in the form of a question. This is then put out to **COLLECTION**, which is broken down into **intelligence requirements**.

THE INTELLIGENCE CYCLE

DIRECTION

The commander or political leader states his *intelligence requirement*, usually in the form of a question.

COLLECTION

The intelligence staff convert the commander's intelligence requirement into a series of essential elements of information (EEIs) and task the intelligence agencies using a *collection plan.*

COLLATION

The intelligence staff collates all the information from the various sources into a readily accessible database. It is essential that all the information collected can be *retrieved.*

DISSEMINATION

Dissemination can take any form: a written brief, an urgent signal, a routine intelligence summary, or, more usually in urgent cases, a verbal brief to the political leader or commander.

INTERPRETATION

Interpretation is where the collated information is analyzed and turned into intelligence. This is usually done by asking the key questions: Who is it? What is it doing? What does it mean?

Intelligence Requirements

In order better to understand the intelligence process, we must go first to our military commander or politician and his wishes. The first stage of the intelligence cycle is the definition by the commander of his intelligence requirements. What precisely does he want to know?

Surprisingly, many commanders have been unclear about this vital aspect of their task. It is often as if their potential adversary and the whole business of intelligence can be disregarded as a mere impediment to their own impressive plans. At Waterloo, even Napoleon and Wellington, two of the greatest captains in history, both ignored their opponent's intentions and wider dispositions, concentrating only on fighting their own battle, despite Machiavelli's advice 300 years earlier: 'Nothing is more worthy of the attention of a good general than to endeavour to penetrate the designs of the enemy.'

However, with prompting, most sensible generals will usually come to address this vital question. For example, 'Will the Argentines invade the Falkland Islands? If so, when, where and in what strength?' is a classic and clear example of a commander's intelligence requirement, enabling the intelligence cycle to begin. If the British Joint Intelligence Committee (JIC) had debated these particular questions in such clear terms in late 1981, the Falklands War might never have erupted in the way it did.

The intelligence staff convert the commander's intelligence requirement into a series of essential elements of information (EEIs) and task the intelligence agencies using a *collection plan*.

The reason is simple. Capabilities are relatively easy to measure – anyone can count tanks or aeroplanes – but determining an adversary's true intentions is fiendishly difficult to quantify. A man's intentions can change like the weather. Even the most sophisticated intelligence breaks down when confronted by the vagaries of the human mind. Just what were Saddam Hussein's real intentions before he invaded Kuwait in 1990? What was Hitler actually thinking before he reoccupied the Rhineland, or Putin before invading Ukraine? Intentions are everything.

In fact, the classic Cold War intelligence briefing invariably centred on the issue of Soviet capabilities (lots of tanks and missiles) versus Soviet intentions for their use. During the Cold War, the 'bean counters' (that is, the capabilities men) ruled the intelligence roost with a vengeance. For the first time in history, technology enabled intelligence organizations to collect information on a massive scale. Intelligence was reduced to the acquisition of huge quantities of information, lovingly – and expensively – stored on shiny new computers often in very expensive and career-enhancing ways, and then drawing dubious conclusions from the evidence.

This was summed up elegantly in a NATO intelligence briefing in 1979, packed with pictures of Soviet tanks and guns and ships and aeroplanes and missiles. It concluded with the Supreme Allied Commander saying 'So we're outnumbered, then' to the young intelligence briefing officer.

'Yes, sir!' he replied enthusiastically.

'Will they use them?' came the quiet question.

Crestfallen, the briefing officer replied, 'We don't have that information, sir.' Then he brightened up. 'But they could do, sir!'

Sometimes it is hard not to feel some sympathy for a commander confronted with this level of advice. Capabilities are not always intentions.

The Collection Plan

The various detailed intelligence requirements are then tasked to the various collection sources and agencies as part of a *collection plan*. To construct a collection plan, it is essential that the intelligence users understand the strengths and weaknesses of all the various agencies involved.

For example, 'humint' (human intelligence, the business of running agents, traditionally the province of the CIA, MI6 and the James Bonds of fiction) is good at reporting on an enemy's *intentions*, whereas satellite photography (the province of the USA's National Reconnaissance Office, or NRO) can count an enemy's *capabilities*, measured in tanks or rockets. Both agencies would find it difficult, if not impossible, to do it the other way round, given their sources of information. Plainly, it makes little sense to task an intelligence source or agency with a job for which it is ill-suited. No one would expect a maritime search radar to provide up-to-date intelligence on a land-based nuclear research programme.

An intelligence collection plan works as follows:

An Intelligence Collection Plan

A Commander's Intelligence Requirement:

- Does the enemy intend to invade or not? If so, when, where and in what strength?
- What are the essential elements of information?
  - Enemy force dispositions?
  - Readiness states?
  - Exercises and training?
  - Pattern of air and maritime activity?
  - Civil mobilization?
  - Logistic preparations?
  - Stated intentions?

The detailed intelligence collection plan is prepared by the Intelligence Staff and tasked to as many different sources and agencies as possible. Not all the information collected will be secret: what is vital, however, is that the very secret information is kept separate ('compartmentalized') and that a time limit is placed on the agencies for reporting back. The collection programme is monitored and managed on a regular basis. 'Hot' items are usually reported immediately.

An intelligence collection plan's requirement can be broken down into even more specific 'essential elements of information', as shown in the figure overleaf.

As information is collected, it is then stored and **COLLATED.**

The intelligence staff collates all the information from the various sources into a readily accessible database. It is essential that all the information collected can be *retrieved*.

COLLATION – PUTTING IT ALL TOGETHER

Collation can be laborious and unglamorous, but the greater part of the intelligence operative's work is taken up with collating a mass of information rather than collecting it. Nowadays, collation systems and records data rely heavily on computerized systems. Digitization and artificial intelligence have revolutionized collation systems from high-speed banking transmissions to

An Intelligence Collection Plan's Essential Elements of Information

SOURCES & AGENCIES / ESSENTIAL ELEMENTS OF INFORMATION (EEIs)	HUMINT e.g., SIS/MI6 CIA, KGB	SIGINT e.g., NSA (US) GCHQ (UK)	IMAGERY e.g., NRO (US) JARIC (UK)	DIPLOMATIC e.g., Foreign & Commonwealth Office, including attachés	MILITARY e.g., DIS (UK) DIA (US) GRU (Russia)	ALLIES e.g., UK/US Treaty, or NATO	OPEN SOURCES e.g., CNN BBC, media, newspapers
Where are the enemy's attack aircraft?			✓	✓	✓		
Is there any evidence of ammunition being out-loaded?	✓		✓				✓
Are the attack pilots away for the weekend?	✓	✓	✓	✓		✓	✓
Are the marines embarking on ships?		✓	✓	✓	✓		
What is their government's official line?		✓		✓			✓
Is there any evidence of civilian mobilization?	✓	✓	✓	✓		✓	✓

stock control in supermarkets. Military intelligence analysts can now find obscure data as quickly as they can push a button. Like so much of the digital age, the algorithm is king: although not always for the better, as many an unhappy currency trader will testify.

Collation is important for another reason. In today's technical age it is, perhaps for the first time, possible to overload an intelligence system with *too much* data. For example, in the Vietnam War the Americans famously held drawers full of unlooked-at aerial photographs. This 'foot-drawer of photographic intelligence' became a derisive symbol of the failure of US military intelligence to cope with the mass of information available, let alone present it to their masters. There simply was not the time or the manpower to look at every single image. And – who knows? – perhaps the vital piece of intelligence that could have alerted the USA to an important event and saved lives in Vietnam was never looked at.

Collation is the province of the clever and industrious clerk and is far removed from the exciting world of guns and missiles. In Napoleon's day they relied on quill pens and good memories…

Interestingly, Hitler's prime expert on the Soviet Army, Colonel Gehlen of Fremde Heere Ost, or Foreign Armies East, who had painstakingly collated the best card index on the Red Army and records on the Eastern Front, was promptly recruited by the US Army at the end of 1945. Gehlen went on to found West Germany's new Secret Service, the BND. A unique intelligence database can overcome almost any scruples.

There is another problem, too. Security professionals are often plagued by two fundamental security challenges: first, maintaining and managing IT systems, and second, 'alert fatigue'.

Over time, IT systems make attractive targets for attackers because they become increasingly difficult to maintain. It's hard to justify replacing a system that continues to work well and perform all the functions you need it to. But as time goes by, these systems depreciate and are superseded by modern technologies that are more efficient and effective. Security becomes ever more important. Operator fatigue doesn't help. Tired, over-taxed operators often miss important items because of the nature of their boring work, staring at computer screens and failing to spot anomalies.

Technology can overwhelm resources. Modern police surveillance cameras suffer from the same problem: too much information. So a collation system must have a 'rapid retrieval response capability' to be immediately accessible to users when they need to get at data, for it to be of any real value. For the collator, the cardinal sin is to have vital evidence and not know it or be able to find it in order to interpret it.

INTERPRETATION

Interpretation is where the collated information is analysed and turned into intelligence. This is usually done by asking the key questions: Who is it? What is it doing? What does it mean?

Once collated, information then has to be interpreted or processed. This means that it is compared with all other existing information to answer four basic questions:

- is it true?
- who is it?
- what is it doing?
- what does it mean?

On the objective answers to these deceptively simple questions, the whole expensive intelligence effort can stand or fall. Maddeningly for the technocrats, the human factor, with its flair, expertise, experience and intuition, cannot be bettered. Interpretation remains firmly the province of the intelligence subject expert.

DISSEMINATION – TELLING THE BOSS

This final part of the intelligence cycle is perhaps the most fraught. Although the days of killing the bearer of ill tidings are long past, no bureaucracy relishes the prospect of passing on unwelcome information to its political or military masters. Intelligence officers are as human as the rest of us, and the temptation for the nervous, ambitious or sycophantic officer to tailor the story to suit a superior's wishes or avoid his displeasure can be very strong. Who would relish saying to Winston Churchill or any other strong-willed prime minister or president, 'I'm afraid you are wrong...'

Interpretations can be and often are twisted to suit political preconceptions with no basis in fact, as happened to the Israelis in 1973 with their mantra 'no attack is possible without full Egyptian mobilization'. Even worse, intelligence reports can be blatantly excluded altogether. In 1916 and 1917, General Sir Douglas Haig's intelligence chief, John Charteris, smoothly ordered his junior staff not to report bad news or intelligence that contradicted the British C-in-C's assessment of the German Army: 'We shouldn't upset the Chief with this sort of stuff... it merely increases his burdens and makes him depressed.' Willoughby, MacArthur's G2 in Korea, got round this problem by simply corrupting or hiding unpalatable information. Against this sort of bureaucratic manipulation there is little defence. In a university, such behaviour could be airily dismissed as 'intellectually dishonest'. In the two world wars it led to the slaughter of hundreds of thousands of men. Military decisions carry a grimmer responsibility than a discredited academic thesis.

Dissemination, then, should be accurate, timely and clearly distinguish intelligence *fact* from interpretative *comment* or assessment. It should also be secure and free from prying eyes. (If the enemy knows what you are up to, he will probably change his plans.) Above all, it should be brutally honest and objective. These are easy sentiments; but who in reality really likes to confront an all-powerful politician or general with the knowledge that their best-laid plans are either nonsense or soon will be because the enemy refuses to co-operate?

Hitler, the supreme warlord who dictated both the strategic and the tactical dispositions of the German Army in the Second World War, could fall into towering rages when contradicted by his staff. On one occasion before the final Russian attack at Stalingrad, a brave intelligence officer briefed him on the growing Soviet capability in the Don Bend. The Führer exploded with rage, shouting, 'I won't have that sort of talk in my headquarters... ridiculous pessimism!', then physically attacked the unfortunate individual before his astonished generals and had him sacked from his staff. As every intelligence officer has known throughout history, unpalatable intelligence can sometimes be a *very* bad career move. Telling the truth to the powerful can be fraught with danger...

I&W: BEATING THE PRE-CONCEIVED MIND?

The pinnacle of the whole intelligence process is often a device called the I&W Display. 'Indicators and Warning' is the most important way of keeping track of an enemy's capabilities and intentions. It effectively fuses all known intelligence into an easily read matrix, usually coded like a traffic light's green, amber and red for danger. Black usually means unknown. It is really nothing more than a comprehensive all-source collection chart. Technically developed governments like the USA and high-tech agencies such as North American Aerospace Defense Command (NORAD) rely nowadays on highly sophisticated computer-driven I&W displays to display and react to fast-changing events. Traditional, politically conscious organizations (such as the mandarins of Britain's Foreign & Commonwealth Office or the Joint Intelligence Committee) have tended to look down on such an obvious technical tool as 'too mechanistic,' or lacking the intellectual subtlety of the more elegant 'diplomatic assessment'.

However, the deceptively simple I&W display can be relied on by military and political planners far more than the vagaries of individual minds, however brilliant or experienced, because it applies ruthless academic discipline that cannot be denied. For example, if in the Cyprus crisis of late 1974 the British Foreign Office had asked the key questions 'Are the Turkish Air Force's aircraft at flight dispersal or not? Are they bombed up? Are the Turkish pilots at readiness or away for the weekend?' they might have been better served. If the Foreign Office had listened to the Ministry of Defence's political-military I&W assessment of the Turkish government's intentions over Cyprus in late 1974, which was based on answers to these simple questions, it need never have embarrassed the Foreign Secretary and forced an apology at Cabinet level, a fact which is still concealed with some embarrassment.

I&W, done properly by objective third parties, and using rigorous techniques of critical source analysis, can successfully fuse intelligence from all sources to give realistic estimates of a potential enemy's capabilities and intentions. Even where it cannot, a good I&W display will highlight even for the most obtuse minister or commander precisely which critical elements of information are needed to make up the full picture.

Armed with a better understanding of the mechanics of the intelligence process, and able now to discern the true role of 'intelligence', we can look more closely at the truth behind some of the intelligence blunders that have shaped armies, wars and the destinies of nations. From George Armstrong Custer at the Little Big Horn to the Battle of the Bulge, ignorance of the enemy has invariably invited disaster – and will continue to do so. This book breaks down intelligence failures into modern case studies and examples can be grouped under the headings of the intelligence process itself: failures of collection, of collation, and of interpretation with a particular hell being reserved for failures to disseminate intelligence to those who really needed it. (It is impossible not to feel some sympathy for those unfortunate commanders who just didn't know, *because someone with the information deliberately failed to pass it on.*)

For our first foray into the murky world of poor intelligence, it is reasonable to start with a genuine error: those unfortunate intelligence officers in the run-up to D-Day who were deceived by the evidence they had so conscientiously collected and collated, and who failed to interpret it correctly – the *misinterpreters*.

They undoubtedly did their job; they just didn't do it very well.

THE MISINTERPRETERS – D-DAY, 1944

'Well, is it or isn't it the invasion?'

**ADOLF HITLER TO FIELD MARSHAL WILHELM KEITEL
ON 6 JUNE 1944**

If the D-Day landings had failed, then the rest of the twentieth century would have been very different. If there was one event in the Second World War that could possibly have changed the course of history more than any other, an Allied repulse on the Normandy beaches would have had cataclysmic consequences. The German generals would have been unlikely to risk their bomb assassination plot against a triumphant Adolf Hitler. Hitler could have redeployed east and bought time, new secret weapons would have become available and Stalin's Soviet Army would have faced the full might of a rearmed and victorious Wehrmacht, equipped with the greatest outpourings of German industry so far. (German arms production peaked in September 1944.)

Today we take it for granted that D-Day, codenamed Operation Overlord, was a success. At the time, however, there was a real fear that the landings might fail and that the Germans would be waiting to hurl the invaders back into the sea, as they had done at Dieppe in 1942. Churchill himself feared another first day of the Somme with its 60,000 casualties. We even know that on the morning of 6 June 1944, Eisenhower secretly began to draft a signal beginning 'The landings in Normandy have failed', just in case the invasion was the disaster it could so easily have been.

And if German intelligence had interpreted the evidence they had collected correctly, Eisenhower might well have gone down as a defeated and disgraced commander. However, blinded by the greatest deception operation in history, the German intelligence staff was confused, misled and tricked into a calamitous misinterpretation of Allied intentions. To the key *intelligence requirement* questions of 'Will the Allies invade? If so, when, where and in what strength?' the baffled German intelligence officers and their masters got three out of four answers wrong.

It was not as if the Germans failed to realize the Allies were coming; on the contrary, they expected an invasion. To prepare for any invasion, in 1942 Germany began construction on the Atlantic Wall, a 1,670-mile network of bunkers, pillboxes, mines and landing obstacles along the French coastline from the border with Spain, and continuing along the coastlines of Belgium, Germany, Denmark and Norway. But without the money and manpower to install a continuous line of defence, the Nazis focused on likely ports. From the start, the main threat of an Allied invasion was believed to be Calais, only twenty-one miles across the English Channel from Dover.

Early in January 1944, the Chief of Fremde Heere West (Foreign Armies West, or FHW), Colonel Baron Alexis von Roenne, received a crucial signal from one of the German military intelligence service's secret agents in England, telling him that General Eisenhower was expected back in Britain. After the catastrophic German defeat in North Africa in 1943, such an appointment could only have one significance: 1944 was expected to be the year of the Second Front and Ike was to command the invasion forces in the West. Von Roenne would have been less pleased had he realized that the signal from his agent had in fact been dictated by Agent Tate, an MI5 double agent.

The German C-in-C West, von Rundstedt, and his Atlantic Wall deputy, Rommel, commander of Army Group B, also understood the dangers of invasion only too well. The key question was where the Allies would strike. On the other side of the Channel, von Rundstedt and Rommel's dilemma was unsurprisingly also the key topic of conversation among the Overlord planners. Even if the Allies could not hide that an invasion was imminent, they were determined to sow as much confusion in the German intelligence service as possible. The organization charged with the crucial task of deceiving the German High Command was a unique group, the Allied Deception Staff, better known by its cover name of the London Controlling Section or LCS (aka 'the Dirty Tricks Committee'). The LCS's primary task was simple: to deceive and confuse the German High Command, and Hitler himself, as to the Allies' intentions over the D-Day landings.

LCS was a remarkable organization. As befitted its extraordinary task – to 'puzzle and defeat' the German intelligence staff – it was staffed by some remarkable men. In Colonel John Bevan, its leader, supported by men like Dennis Wheatley, the novelist, Sir Reginald Hoare, the banker, and Bevan's brilliant multilingual deputy, Lieutenant Colonel Sir Ronald Wingate, the LCS boasted one of the most high-powered collections of talent on any wartime staff. More importantly, LCS's members had an extraordinary network of personal contacts and links with nearly every centre of power and influence in the Allied camp. As a result, and perhaps most important of all, LCS enjoyed the complete confidence of the Allied Chiefs of Staff, even Churchill himself and the War Cabinet. This trust was crucial, because at times LCS was effectively co-ordinating and directing the efforts of nearly all the argumentative and competing Allied intelligence and security agencies in their own intelligence attacks on the Germans' indicators and warning system.

Hitler was keenly aware that the Allies' first priority was to deceive him. In March 1944, he told his commanders in the West, 'Whatever concentrations of shipping exist, they cannot, and must not, be taken as evidence or any indication that the choice has fallen on any one sector of the "Long Western Front" from Norway to the Bay of Biscay.' Like many a commander before and since, the Führer believed that he was his own intelligence officer and he was determined to dictate terms to his intelligence professionals.

Hitler and his military experts were, however, convinced of one thing: in order for a successful invasion to work, the Allies would need to seize a port on landing. This preconception, based on sound German naval advice and the experience of the Allied raid on Dieppe in 1942, was to seriously distort any objective intelligence assessment. Across the other side of the Channel, an ingenious plan had been drawn up with the sole purpose of feeding these German preconceptions: Plan Bodyguard.

Bodyguard was the Allied cover name for a comprehensive range of strategic deceptions aimed at using the German intelligence system to pass false messages. It had two clear aims: first, to weaken Hitler's forces by making him spread his key divisions and armies throughout Europe, from Norway to the Balkans; and second, to delay any German reaction to the invasion for as long as possible by keeping the German planners unsure whether the first landing was just a feint.

In order to do this, Bevan's LCS proposed an extraordinarily wide-ranging series of deception operations to feed the German intelligence staff with exactly the information they were seeking. Moreover, by using real intelligence as far as possible, Bodyguard would even offer Colonel von Roenne of FHW a reasonably accurate picture of Allied troop strengths. The real subtleties lay in clever distortions designed to mislead the German staff about the exact time and place of the landings and the size and dispositions of Allied units. These reports were embedded in a huge mass of conflicting information that was to be pumped directly into the German intelligence system. Some of it, astonishingly, was true. The only problem for the German planners was, which parts? To use the modern language of intelligence, LCS's aim was to overwhelm the German intelligence services' I&W display with 'noise'.

The sheer scope of the Bodyguard plan was vast, and in Anthony Cave Brown's words, 'resembled nothing less than a large-scale corporation fraud'. Bodyguard was split into sixteen main stratagems or intelligence areas, each designed to feed the Germans' known intelligence collection plan, from humint to electronic warfare, from bombing target analysis to French resistance activity. In this the British were helped immeasurably by Ultra, the highly secret code-breaking operation at Bletchley Park that enabled the British to read Hitler's most secret Enigma-enciphered messages, sometimes even before the intended Nazi recipient had seen them. Using Ultra, the Allies were able to discover precisely what information the Germans were looking for and then, obligingly, to provide it for them; suitably doctored to mislead and misinform, of course.

Enigma turned out to be a remarkable coup for the British and a triumph of secrecy. Even so, the story of the breaking of the Enigma machines has probably had more nonsense written about it than almost any other event of the Second World War. For a start, the Enigma story was *not* a triumph of British skill and intellect: the Poles broke Enigma, and the French gave it to the British.

The true story of the Enigma machine, or 'Secret Numbers Machine' to give it its proper title, goes back to the end of the Great War. In 1919, the mechanical cipher machine, looking like a heavy typewriter in a wooden box, was developed from a Dutch invention by a German, Arthur Scherbius, and sold openly as a commercial venture at the International Postal Union Congress in 1923. Scherbius didn't sell many and became disenchanted, but in 1926 the German Navy bought a number of Enigma machines and modified them for military use.

In 1929, an alert Polish customs officer in Warsaw intercepted a crate allegedly containing radio equipment addressed to a German company. On making the usual checks, an excited official appeared from the German Embassy claiming that there had been a terrible mistake, and that the crate should be returned to Germany immediately. Intrigued, the customs officers decided something odd was going on, but as it was a Friday they agreed to deal with the matter first thing on Monday morning. Over the weekend the Polish General Staff, having been tipped off by the now thoroughly suspicious customs men, covertly opened the crate and copied its contents with drawings and photographs.

The crate contained a secret Enigma cipher machine for the German Embassy. Realizing the potential of their find – if they could make it work – the Poles began the laborious job of 'reverse engineering' to recreate an Enigma and, more importantly, work out how to read its traffic. The Poles had a powerful motivation; between 1928 and 1932 all Germany's armed forces and its Foreign Service adopted the Enigma machine as their principal encoding device on the grounds that it was completely unbreakable.

In 1932 Captain Bertrand, Chief of the French Cryptographic Department, recruited a German called Hans Schmidt. Schmidt's claim to fame was that he worked in the German Military Cipher Department. As agent 'Asche' ('H') he supplied secret German code and cipher manuals to French Intelligence, handing over 303 secret documents, including at least one long enciphered Enigma message and several sets of cipher keys, possibly on behalf of Moscow Centre for whom he was also an agent. The French directed Bertrand to offer this intelligence to the British and Poles, friendly nations equally worried by Hitler's rise to power. On the instructions of the Foreign Office, the British turned agent Asche's intelligence material down.

However, the Poles gratefully accepted H's windfall and gave it to a brilliant young team of mathematicians from Poznan University, where the first courses in code-breaking were now on the syllabus. In co-operation with the French, and armed with brand-new, legally acquired commercial Enigma machines and H's sets of keys, Marian Rejewski and two assistants in a secret team codenamed BS-4 broke the secrets of Enigma. By the mid-1930s they had begun reading 'up to 80 per cent' of some secret German military traffic. By 1937 the Polish mathematical team had even managed to build a rudimentary mechanical computer – which they called a *bombe* – to replace their earlier methods of using punched cards and long paper 'keys'.

Once Sudeten Czechoslovakia had fallen to Hitler after Munich in 1938, the Poles knew that a war with Germany could not be avoided. In January 1939 they held a secret intelligence conference in Paris to discuss code-breaking with the British. According to Meyer, the head of Polish Intelligence, the disappointed Poles offered little to the British because it was 'obvious they knew little about Enigma' and quite clearly had 'nothing to offer in the code-breaking of Enigma in return'. (This was not strictly true; the British had begun to read some low-level Enigma traffic from Germany's Kondor Legion in 1938 during the Spanish Civil War and were intrigued by the potential for code-breaking.)

By July 1939, the situation had changed completely. The Poles were no longer able to read Enigma traffic because the Germans had increased the number of rotors on their service machines. With war now inevitable, the Poles had not the time to start another mathematical logic hunt for the new cipher keys. So, on 16 August 1939, nineteen days before war broke out, Captain Bertrand of French Signals Intelligence personally handed over a Polish-built copy of an Enigma machine together with documents, keys, ciphers and even technical drawings of the first-ever secret Poznan computer to an astonished – and grateful – British Secret Services Liaison Officer from Bletchley Park. The British had been given their war-winning weapon on a plate *by the Poles*. Armed with this invaluable tool, suitably developed and refined to meet the changes that the war brought about, the British deception service could not only feed the Germans false information, but their intelligence services could also monitor whether their enemy had taken the bait.

London Controlling Section was also keenly aware of another vital fact: few intelligence organizations believe easily won information. Just as a wealthy collector may resolutely refuse to believe that an expensive painting could be a fake, so intelligence officers tend to believe that the most hard-won secrets are more likely to be true than easily gathered information. This is of course nonsense, but Bevan and his staff prepared a series of inspired leaks that would come to Colonel von Roenne and his staff only by the most roundabout – and sometimes expensive – means: through obscure agent runners in Madrid, the Swedish stock exchange and hastily suppressed 'leaks' in the neutral press to name but three.

In all this, Bevan was aided by a remarkable humint coup. Since 1940, the British Security Service, MI5, had effectively been running and controlling every known German agent in the UK. Instead of executing the majority of the lacklustre, even amateur, spies sent by the Abwehr, the German military intelligence bureau, in 1940 and 1941, a special British MI5 team had arranged for them to be picked up shortly after landing and 'turned' them to work for the British by sending false messages to their former masters. Faced with the choice between a firing squad in the Tower of London or a spell of warm, safe house arrest, three square meals a day, with a radio to send fake messages to expectant German controllers, most agents became extremely co-operative.

Using MI5's network of long-established double agents, the Double Cross Committee, headed by Sir John Masterman, could send the Germans whatever lies the Bodyguard plan required. Agent Tate's message about Eisenhower's arrival in England was merely the first of an elaborately conceived series of half-truths and lies that would continue until well after the D-Day landings. At least six other trusted Double Cross agents pumped messages direct to their Abwehr controllers in Hamburg or Madrid, giving such details as unit badges, tank and infantry landing-craft concentrations and sightings of troops.

In Operation Fortitude North, one of Bodyguard's major sub-plans, a phantom 'British 4th Army' was reported around Edinburgh in Scotland, painstakingly recorded by two Double Cross agents, 'Mutt' and 'Jeff'. These were in fact loyal Norwegian patriots who had defected to the British immediately on landing. From their mythical network of contacts and sub-agents, the two Norwegians informed Hamburg about 4th Army's new 'commander', Lieutenant General Sir Andrew Thorne, deliberately chosen because he was well known to Hitler personally as the British Military

Attaché in Berlin before the war. For good measure they also threw in local Scottish newspaper reports of civilian welcome committees and military traffic accidents. Meanwhile the Germans themselves could log 4th Army's ceaseless administrative local radio chatter. In fact '4th Army' never amounted to more than about forty staff officers and a few heavy-handed wireless operators diligently churning out a tightly controlled script.

These wireless operators were the next stage in Colonel Bevan's complex deception. Knowing that the German Staff would, like any professional intelligence operation, look for 'collateral' (reports from other sources, confirming the humint agents' information), the ever-helpful Bevan thoughtfully provided von Roenne and his people with just the material they were seeking. The fake '4th Army' headquarters and its busy sub-units transmitted and received a stream of credible messages for the excellent Abwehr Signals Intelligence or Y Service to intercept and plot. Here an officer – easily checked against the Army List – would be sent on compassionate leave; there an irate quartermaster would be indenting for quantities of missing ski equipment.

Whatever the variations, the messages, when carefully collated by the diligent Abwehr intelligence staff, all indicated that there was a major British Army assembling in Scotland, preparing for a campaign in mountainous or arctic terrain. Allied to the dangerous RAF photo-reconnaissance flights over the fjords and the increased Royal Navy destroyer activity off the Norwegian coast, it could only mean one thing. Hitler was eventually to tie down no fewer than twelve much-needed divisions in Norway against an invasion that never came, from an army that never existed.

These humint and sigint (signals intelligence) reports had to be complemented by other sources that LCS knew the Germans would use. While photographic reconnaissance was unlikely to be able to check the Fortitude North dispositions around Edinburgh – few German planes had the range, service ceiling or speed to survive after a long flight across the North Sea – in the south of England it was another matter. Specially equipped very high-flying Luftwaffe PR planes could easily overfly Kent. Bodyguard decided, as part of Operation Fortitude South, to offer them suitable 'targets' to feed into the Abwehr collection plan. Ever mindful of German nervousness about an invasion across the short sea crossing against the Pas de Calais, Bevan's team decided to strengthen the image of an army group massing in the south-east. This would have the effect of diverting attention away from Normandy and reinforcing the Germans' anxieties about the Calais area, an area that the Germans deemed most likely for the shortest route to cross the Channel.

A massive dummy oil depot was built on the coast near Dover, complete with pipes, valves, storage tanks and even well-publicized inspections by King George VI. From 34,000 feet the German aerial photographs could not reveal that what they were recording was a wooden fake whose building had been directed by the illusionist Jasper Maskelyne and Sir Basil Spence. The photographic interpreters could not spot that the hundreds of tanks parked in the Kentish orchards were really nothing more than inflatable rubber Shermans. One farmer even saw his bull charge a 'tank' and watched in astonishment as the pierced dummy slowly deflated. And the lines of landing craft moored in the Medway, with their sailors' washing hanging on the lines, looked real enough.

When the evidence of aerial photography was added to agent reports, analysis of signals traffic (which showed that all over Kent, Essex and Sussex well-known US Army radio operators were transmitting) and the well-publicized presence of General George Patton in the area, German intelligence analysts received a clear message. Patton's 1st US Army Group (FUSAG) did exist, and it was poised in the south-east of England just across from the Pas de Calais. Masterman's double agents Brutus and Garbo enthusiastically reported every fictitious detail, while the ever-loyal Tate faithfully confirmed their reports in his own radio messages from Wye in Kent. 'Something big is building in the Dover area,' he told his controller. It was; Bevan and his LCS were building an illusion that would pin down the bulk of German panzer divisions in France 150 miles to the east of the real invasion site.

By now the fastidious and aristocratic von Roenne had the key components of his collection plan collated: humint, reporting a massive build-up; sigint, confirming new formations arriving in the UK; and imagery intelligence, whose aerial photographs clearly indicated an enormous concentration of troops and materiel in the south-eastern corner of England. All now depended on von Roenne and his experts' evaluation and interpretation of the mass of intelligence reports they were studying. Were they true? Which units were they? What were the Allies doing? And what did it all mean?

Von Roenne's personal assessment was vital because he, unlike many of Hitler's inner circle of senior army officers, was implicitly trusted by the Nazi dictator. But von Roenne was fighting *two* enemies as he sat in his Zossen office trying to interpret the intelligence in front of him: the Allied deception staffs, clever, well resourced and playing him like a fish on the hook; and, amazingly, his own side – specifically the Sicherheitsdienst, or SD, the Nazi Party's own security service, now firmly in control of all Germany's intelligence services.

In early 1944, the head of the military intelligence bureau, the Abwehr, Admiral Canaris, had been quietly retired by Hitler and pensioned off. Wilhelm Canaris was a complex character and one of the real enigmas of the war. The Director of the British Secret Intelligence Service (SIS, popularly known as MI6) later described him as 'a damned brave man and a true patriot', an unusual accolade from an enemy. Was Canaris a leader of the anti-Nazi resistance and a British spy? It seems an astonishing question, and highly unlikely, and yet there is enough circumstantial evidence that he was in contact with Sir Stuart Menzies, the Director of SIS, to raise serious doubts about his role in the mysterious intelligence exchanges that seem to have taken place between the British and those Germans who abhorred the Nazi Party. The role of these murky links between the Abwehr and the SIS may well have influenced the outcome of D-Day.

Canaris had been a resourceful and gallant naval officer in the Great War, escaping from the doomed SMS *Dresden* off Chile in 1915 and making his way overland to Buenos Aires and back home to Germany in a series of adventures that read like a Hornblower novel. Once back he was awarded the Iron Cross and seconded to secret intelligence duties in Spain. (Interestingly, one of the British agent handlers in Spain at this time was a young British MI6 officer, Stuart Menzies.) Escaping a British plot to kill him, Canaris fled Spain and ended the war as a successful U-boat commander in the Mediterranean where he sank eighteen enemy ships.

After the war, Canaris dropped into the shadowy world of the post-Versailles Reichswehr and its unofficial secret service. In 1934 the new

Chancellor, Adolf Hitler, offered him the job of head of the Abwehr with the words, 'What I want from you is an intelligence service like the British Secret Service.' Canaris was no Nazi, however, and when war broke out a series of mysterious intelligence coups helped the British. For example, packages of priceless technical information turned up anonymously on the doorstep of the British Embassy in Oslo, among other places. (The information was so good that the British didn't believe it at first.) As the war developed, the leaks and links between the Abwehr and its opposition became too obvious.

A suspicious Hitler finally pensioned off Canaris and gave his responsibility for intelligence to his arch rival and Party stalwart Obergruppenführer (General) Walter Schellenberg, the head of the SD. Canaris's discredited Abwehr was merged with Schellenberg's SD to form a single unified Nazi intelligence organization, the Reich Security and Intelligence Service, firmly under party control. Even in the middle of war, the inevitable bureaucratic turf battle now broke out between the SD's Nazi ideologues and the remnants of the Abwehr as each side tried to keep control of their own area of expertise. In the event the military intelligence professionals were consistently overruled or taken over completely.

However, the Amt Mil or military section of the new service was still – just – under General Staff control. Its British Area intelligence officer was a cheerful extrovert called Oberstleutnant Roger Michel, who like all his brother officers heartily detested his new Party bosses. Worse, Michel was labouring under a particular handicap. Whenever he submitted an order-of-battle estimate to headquarters, it was invariably sanitized and diluted by the SD officials above him. They halved every estimate he made of Allied strength in Great Britain. For any professional intelligence officer to have his reports altered on ostensibly political grounds is like a red rag to a bull. It impugns his professional capabilities, integrity and objectivity. The hot-blooded Michel was no exception.

Colonel von Roenne, however, had devised a way for his frustrated subordinate to thwart their Nazi masters tampering with, as they saw it, perfectly good intelligence assessments. If the new SD was going to halve their estimates, what could be easier than *doubling* them in the first place? So, in the spring of 1944, von Roenne and Michel began to multiply their assessments of Allied strength by a factor of two, secure in the knowledge that the SD would then halve their figures, thus ensuring that the report which went to Hitler's desk was an accurate reflection of the General Staff's original estimate. To add verisimilitude to this breathtaking scheme, the two plotters uncritically accepted the flood of Fortitude reports about the British 4th Army in Scotland, Patton's FUSAG and the military build-up in the south-east of England. Ironically, von Roenne and Michel needed the LCS's flood of false evidence almost as much as the Allied deception staff needed to send it. Only the false Fortitude reports could be relied on to satisfy the Germans' desperate need for every scrap of collateral about troop dispositions in Britain to support their inflated figures.

In May, von Roenne's crucial pre-invasion 'FHW Assessment of the Enemy's Order of Battle' (ORBAT) was published. To his horror, this time the SD did not halve his estimate of Allied strength. The reason was simple: the SD officer who had been cutting the estimates had been posted. Von Roenne's assessment was sent out as the official secret combined intelligence ORBAT to all Wehrmacht formations and headquarters in the West. Von Roenne dare not admit the deception – to do so would invite summary execution in the fevered atmosphere of suspicion and intrigue surrounding Hitler's court in spring 1944 – and so he had to accept that the influential report issued under his name had effectively doubled the true known strength of the Allied forces in Britain from forty divisions to over eighty. It was a deception that would ultimately cost von Roenne his life.

Colonel Bevan's ever-resourceful LCS intelligence hoaxers had one final trick up their sleeve. How much better, they reasoned, if a trusted *German* general could himself corroborate the mass of false reports they had fed into the German intelligence machine. And, as chance would have it, the British just happened to have a spare German general. General Hans Cramer had been captured in May 1943 as the Axis forces collapsed in Tunisia. As a prisoner of war in England his health had deteriorated, and in May 1944 the Red Cross arranged to repatriate him back to Germany in a neutral Swedish ship. Bevan's staff ensured that the general did not go empty-handed. His drive to the docks took him through some of the heaviest troop concentrations in southern England, ending up at Patton's 'HQ' for his last night before embarkation. General Cramer hadn't the faintest idea where he had been; but was dined out as a military courtesy to a sick man by Patton himself. He also met some of Patton's 'divisional commanders' who were cool and correct to an enemy general officer, however ill, but gossiped away among themselves about 'Calais'.

The ruse worked. By 24 May, only thirteen days before D-Day, General Cramer was back in Berlin faithfully reporting to General Zeitzler, Chief of Staff of the Wehrmacht, everything that he had seen and heard in England. Unsurprisingly, his information tallied with everything the Germans had collected and provided further collateral for von Roenne's intelligence estimate. So, in the final days before the landings, the great LCS deception plan had, remarkably, become the basis for the German intelligence appreciation. Even Hitler himself, despite an almost feminine intuition that suddenly swung him towards Normandy at the last moment, forbore to change his dispositions. Of the German Army's 300 divisions, only sixty were active in the West: less than 20 per cent. And of those, only eight divisions were in place to oppose the Allies directly as they came ashore. The remainder were spread between the Balkans, Italy, Russia, the south of France, Denmark, the Netherlands, Norway and, most important of all, the Pas de Calais. From their reading of the decrypted Ultra intercepts on 1 and 2 June, Bevan's delighted staff could read that Baron Oshima, the Japanese envoy in Berlin, was reporting to Tokyo that no less a person than Adolf Hitler himself had assessed that the likely attack would fall in the Pas de Calais, with feints elsewhere.

For Bevan and his LCS, it had been an intelligence triumph. A small, highly talented and influential staff had successfully orchestrated the most complex deception in history against an alert and highly competent adversary. One slip, one mistake in the script, one piece of the story that did not quite fit, could have unravelled the whole fraudulent network that was Bodyguard, Fortitude and their interlocking layers of hoaxes. By complete understanding of the Germans' professional intelligence methods, and aided by the ability to read the Enigma traffic, LCS had effectively hijacked the German intelligence staff assessment for D-Day and forced von Roenne and the whole German intelligence machine to do precisely what the Allies wanted. The final German intelligence summaries for the end of May 1944 read like a catalogue of errors:

the Germans were convinced that the Allies would attack in good weather, in the dark near a large port and at high tide. They also assessed that there would be *several* feint landings designed to draw German reserves away from the true landing site – the Pas de Calais.

Astonishingly, the deception operations continued well after the Allied troops came ashore on 6 June 1944. During 9 and 10 June, a fresh wave of resistance attacks, heavy air raids and an unheard-of tempo of offshore preparations hit the Calais area. Masterman's ever-faithful Double Cross agents sent extensive humint 'collateral' explaining that the Normandy landings were merely a diversion and the real blow – the landing of Patton's FUSAG – was just about to fall on the Pas de Calais.

Von Roenne, who had by now probably begun to believe his own inflated assessments, accordingly sent out an intelligence summary to all Wehrmacht Western Front headquarters and formations: 'In all probability major enemy landing expected Belgian coastline from 10 June.' To compound his misinterpretation and after consultation with Marshals Keitel and Jodl of Führerhauptquartier, von Roenne then added a fatal *operational*, not intelligence, assessment: 'Withdrawal of [German] forces from the Pas de Calais/15th Army Sector unwise.' Intelligence assessments should *never* include operational recommendations.

To further compound this catalogue of errors, von Roenne personally contacted Hitler's intelligence liaison officer, one Colonel Krummacher, and reinforced FHW's written intelligence estimate by insisting that any diversion of forces from the Pas de Calais to Normandy would be a mistake, as 'von Roenne personally had definite intelligence that a new invasion was about to fall on the 15th Army Sector, beginning with a wave of resistance attacks starting on the night 9/10 June'. Armed with this highly unusual special pleading from a senior staff intelligence officer, Krummacher agreed to represent FHW's view at Hitler's crucial midday situation and planning conference.

At that conference, Marshal Jodl reported FHW's assessment to Hitler and added to it the weight of General Kühlentahl's latest secret radio message from his ever-diligent agent Garbo, giving fresh collateral for an imminent main force attack on Calais by Patton's non-existent FUSAG based in Kent. Kühlentahl was the senior agent controller in Portugal and Spain. Hitler took the bait. At the midnight staff conference on 9/10 June, the Supreme Commander of the Armed Forces abruptly ordered a halt to any movement from the Pas de Calais to Normandy. Not only that, but the Führer ordered extra divisions to the 15th Army Sector and not to the hard-pressed Wehrmacht battlefront in Normandy.

Hitler might have been less happy with his decision and with the FHW/Kühlentahl intelligence assessment had he realized that Garbo's radio message had taken *two hours* to send. The critical question why the extremely efficient British Signals Security Service had failed to pinpoint a two-hour transmission and catch the illegal sender never seems to have occurred to the gullible Kühlentahl and von Roenne. Intelligence officers need a highly developed critical factor, and never more than when their prejudices are being pandered to so obligingly.

Back in London, the delighted Bevan and his LCS saw the map lines heading towards Normandy suddenly stop, and over the following days coalesce into the Pas de Calais. Fortitude and Bodyguard had worked. Even then, the great intelligence deception was not over and continued well into July. In addition to the mock invasion off Calais on 10 June, as late as the last week in June there were more Allied spoof airborne and naval operations off Boulogne and Dieppe. These feints were successful enough for Hitler to personally authorize an order (a full month after D-Day) for all divisions still held back in the Pas de Calais to go on full anti-invasion alert for 8 July. For Bevan and his LCS, it had been a triumph of deception; for von Roenne's FHW and the German High Command, it had been an intelligence disaster.

Was von Roenne an incompetent intelligence officer? Far from it. His track record before 1944 had been outstanding. His mistake was probably to allow his belief in his own system to overcome his doubts and to forget the need for critical analysis. The old intelligence assessment of source material – Is it true? Is it credible? Is it confirmed by other sources? – seems to have either broken down or just been saturated by an enemy deception operation that knew, thanks to Enigma, just how FHW's intelligence system worked and how to fool it. Faced by the key questions of 'Will the Allies invade? If so, when, where and in what strength?', the German intelligence staff got it completely wrong. It was a mistake that was to end in the ruins of Berlin and the collapse of the Third Reich. Rarely can a mistaken intelligence estimate have had such catastrophic consequences.

The D-Day intelligence deception story has a postscript that elegantly sums up Bevan's cunning, Masterman's professionalism and the German tragedy. At 3 a.m. on the morning of D-Day, Masterman's trusted double agent, Garbo, frantically signalled his German controllers to inform them that one of his 'network of agents' had reported that the Allied troops had left camp, complete with sea-sickness bags. Only by dawn did the message get through to Berlin, by which time the Allies had begun to land, thus boosting Garbo's credibility as an agent without damaging Allied operations. Bitterly, Garbo castigated his German controllers: 'I sent you this priceless information and it makes me seriously question your professionalism and responsibility.' Two months later, Garbo received a message awarding him the Iron Cross by Hitler's command.

Von Roenne was not so lucky. He was arrested in the aftermath of the bomb plot against Hitler of 20 July 1944. He was joined later by his old boss, Admiral Canaris, who may well have been a party to some of the deceptions and was almost certainly in touch with the British. For the Nazis, the final straw over the intelligence duplicities of the Abwehr appears to have been a mysterious journey that Canaris undertook to France in June 1944. His replacement Schellenberg knew that Canaris had been talking to a number of the generals who were later implicated in the plot. Three days later Canaris was arrested by Schellenberg and his men. 'Hello,' said the little admiral to his arresting officer, 'I've been expecting you.'

On 11 October 1944, Colonel Baron Alexis von Roenne, lately Chief of Foreign Armies West of the German General Staff, was executed by the Nazi authorities for treason in the bloody aftermath of the bomb plot on Hitler's life. Rarely can an intelligence officer have paid such a high price for getting it so badly wrong. Canaris, whose role in the whole D-Day deception has never been clear, was to follow. An SD search of the old Abwehr offices revealed records and diaries that implicated the admiral and his staff as having been in the know about many things he should have reported. The last head of the Abwehr was finally condemned for contact with the enemy. In vain, Canaris protested that contact with the enemy was the job of a secret intelligence service, and that he was a loyal German and no traitor to the Reich. It was to no avail; he was imprisoned, and as the Reich crashed around the deranged dictator, Hitler finally ordered him killed.

Canaris's end was not easy. After being beaten by SD thugs, and with blood dripping from a smashed nose and jaw, he was slowly strangled by hanging from a meat hook on 9 April 1945 at Flossenbürg, a lonely sacrifice to Nazi vengeance. In their own way, the two German intelligence officers, von Roenne and Canaris, were both among the final victims of the successful Allied deception on D-Day.

3

'COMRADE STALIN KNOWS BEST' – BARBAROSSA, 1941

*'The German Wehrmacht must be prepared to crush
Soviet Russia in a quick campaign...'*
ADOLF HITLER; FÜHRER DIRECTIVE 21, DECEMBER 1940

At 01.45 on the morning of 22 June 1941, a Soviet train steamed up to the frontier post on the Russian-German border at Brest-Litovsk, loaded with 1,500 tons of grain. The trucks were part of the 200,000 tons of grain and 100,000 tons of petroleum products delivered to the west *every month* for the German war economy by Stalin, keeping his word to Adolf Hitler under the Nazi-Soviet non-aggression pact's 'co-operative economic ventures'. The scene at the border was of routine, calm and order. The Union of Soviet Socialist Republics and the Nazi Party's Greater German Reich were allies, by solemn treaty.

An hour and a half later, the all-conquering Wehrmacht burst east across that same bridge in yet another ferocious blitzkrieg, to begin the invasion of communist Russia. 'We just need to kick in the door,' the Führer boasted to his inner circle, 'and the whole rotten edifice of the Bolshevik regime will come crashing down.' The Nazi leadership, in a phrase that has eerie echoes, believed that it would all be over by the autumn, let by alone by Christmas.

By 1941, the Soviet Union had the largest, most efficient and best-informed intelligence service in the world. Under the leadership of the revolutionary founder of the Soviet Secret Service, Felix Dzerzhinsky, by the 1920s the Soviet intelligence service had grown both in size and scope until it reached into every aspect of Russian life as well as overseas communist parties and foreign chanceries. Using a vast network of agents and sympathizers, little went on in the rest of the world that did not find its way back to the seat of the communist revolution in Moscow. Comrade Stalin, General Secretary of the Communist Party of the Soviet Union, was determined that in the historic clash of ideologies between capitalism and communism, the heirs of Marx and Lenin would not be found wanting.

Yet just before dawn on 22 June 1941, over 3 million men and 3,350 tanks of the armies of the Greater German Reich invaded the Soviet Union and took its unprepared western border defences almost completely by surprise. How on earth could such a failure of intelligence, which led to the most destructive war in human history, have happened apparently without warning?

The answer is simple. The dictator of the Soviet Union refused to acknowledge a truth presented to him over and over again: Nazi Germany was going to invade the Union of Soviet Socialist Republics. There was abundant evidence. Stalin is the prime cause of the intelligence disaster that befell Soviet Russia in 1941. His obsession with avoiding a war with the Third Reich, coupled with his persistent refusal to acknowledge clear intelligence that the Germans were about to invade, were to ensure that his country suffered a catastrophic defeat as Operation Barbarossa pushed the Russians back to the gates of Moscow itself.

Stalin's motives were complex but seem to stem from an overriding desire to buy time and a successful intimidation of the USSR's neighbours. Despite a supposedly slavish following of Marxist theory, Stalin was really intent on power – and his own survival. In 1939, on the eve of the Second World War, Stalin and Germany's dictator Adolf Hitler signed the Nazi-Soviet Non-Aggression Pact. Stalin then proceeded to annex parts of Poland and Romania, as well as the Baltic states of Estonia, Latvia and Lithuania. He also launched an invasion of Finland. That winter campaign showed the Red Army at its worst.

Stalin therefore knew better than anyone just how unprepared the Red Army was for war, and he seems to have been prepared to ignore the most accurate reports of trouble in a vain attempt to convince himself that it couldn't happen, or in a feeble attempt to appease the German leader. Stalin expected and was terrified of a war with the Nazis although, in the analysis beloved of Marxist–Leninists, a final clash between communism and capitalism was a 'historic inevitability'. Stalin's problem was he was not yet ready for this particular stage in the unfolding of the Hegelian-Marxist dialectic. For just three years before, he had wrecked – deliberately wrecked – his own nation. The Great Purge of the 1930s was all-encompassing and cowed its survivors into fear and a dog-like obedience to Stalin's orders. 'In some cases, a quota was established for the number to be executed, the number to be arrested,' says Stanford University history professor Norman Naimark. 'Some Party officials over-fulfilled as a way of showing their exuberance.'

The effect on Stalin's Red Army and the consequences were only too clear later, in the Winter War disaster in Finland.

In the spring of 1937, as part of what became known as the 'Great Terror', Stalin had moved to purge the Red Army of 'internal enemies'. During the next three years he executed most of his senior military commanders on trumped-up charges. The cull was horrific: seventy-five of the eighty members of the 'Military Soviet' were killed; every commander of every military district; two-thirds of the divisional commanders, half the brigade commanders and over 400 of 456 staff colonels were 'liquidated'. Stalin effectively sliced the head off the Red Army.

Hardly surprisingly, the Red Army's invasion of neighbouring Finland in the winter of 1939 turned into a military debacle. Little Finland's 200,000 defenders sliced the million-strong Red Army to pieces, inflicting nearly a quarter of a million casualties on the Russians before finally being ground down by superior numbers. David had not only thrashed Goliath but shown him to be a sluggish incompetent, a fact of which Stalin was now only too well aware. Suddenly the cunning Georgian crook realized that he needed to buy time.

It is to the inner recesses of Stalin's secretive, fearful and cunning psyche that we must turn for the truth behind the surprise attack known as Barbarossa. Stalin may have wielded supreme authority in the USSR, but at heart the Russian dictator was terrified – paranoiac, even – of losing power. While he could master events inside the Soviet Union by killing off his enemies, real or imagined, outside it one man and his all-conquering army posed a potentially mortal threat to the communist regime and leader.

In this light, many of Stalin's actions become not only understandable but also strangely rational. By the bizarre standards of paranoic ideological dictators, Stalin's behaviour makes a kind of curious sense. He felt he had at all costs to prevent a war which could destroy him until he was ready for the final historic combat between the great ideologies. If we understand this *Weltanschauung*, or world view, then Stalin's attempts to ignore and suppress unequivocal intelligence warnings of a German attack seem almost logical. At worst they offer the ultimate nightmare for the intelligence officer: a commander who chooses to ignore and suppress the very best intelligence handed to him because he has his own agenda, and is prepared to go to any lengths to suppress the truth becoming known, much less acted upon. Stalin was not the first or the last commander to utter the immortal words, 'I am my own intelligence officer!' He just wasn't a very good one, as events proved.

The facts speak for themselves: between late July 1940 and 22 June 1941, no fewer than 105 separate, unequivocal warnings of an impending attack on the Soviet Union were passed to Stalin. In every case they were professionally collated, evaluated, interpreted and briefed to Stalin as supreme commander. So far as we know, none of them was disseminated further. As a direct consequence of this intelligence failure, the USSR lost 4 million soldiers – including over 2 million prisoners of war – 14,000 aircraft, 20,000 guns and 17,000 tanks in the battles from the frontiers to the outskirts of Moscow between June and December 1941 at the hands of the German invaders.

To understand how this came about, we have to go back three years to Munich. The Munich Agreement of 1938 had come as a great shock to the Soviet Union. Convinced by Marxist dogma of the historic inevitability of another Franco-German capitalist war (from which there could only be one beneficiary – the Soviet Union), and still trusting in the international system of 'collective security' to contain Hitler's resurgent Germany, for the USSR, Munich spelled a new and dangerous Europe. The Soviet Ambassador in London, Ivan Maisky, warned Moscow that 'International relations are now entering an era of brute force, savagery and the policy of the mailed fist.' Further Soviet analysis of the USSR's position in the post-Munich world spelled out British and French policy in brutally stark terms: '[British] Foreign Office policy now has only two aims: peace at any cost, and secondly, collusion with aggressors at the expense of third countries to grant the aggressor concessions.'

Such a policy of colluding with Hitler was seen by Stalin and his advisers as both fundamentally anti-communist and anti-Russian, and therefore a serious threat to the USSR. For, looming ever larger in Soviet official thinking, was the not unreasonable belief that Britain and France would be only too happy to use a conflict between Germany and the Soviet Union to divert Hitler's rapacious attention away from themselves.

Alan Clark's telling phrase about Hitler's advisers, 'vanity and self-delusion are among the lesser vices of despotic courts', applies equally to the Byzantine post-revolutionary circle of Stalin and his Bolshevik cronies, where paranoia and conspiracy were the norm. Any objective analysis of events was further distorted by communist prejudices and dogma, plus a fear of capitalist plots to snuff out the fledgling Soviet Union, both of which led to a ruthless search for internal traitors and counter-revolutionaries.

The problem of deciding what was reality in Moscow was further hindered by Stalin's decision to kill his intelligence analysts. Like the Red Army, the NIO (the Foreign Intelligence Service) and the NKVD/NKGB (the State Security Intelligence Apparatus) had both been ruthlessly purged between 1937 and 1939. Maxim Litvinov, the architect of the failed collective security foreign policy, was removed and replaced by a Stalin-led committee early in 1939 after Munich. Although, surprisingly, Litvinov survived, his staff did not. Many diplomats and foreign service officers tainted by association with 'counter-revolutionary elements' disappeared overnight, 'liquidated' in the purges that reached into every aspect of Soviet life in the years immediately before the Second World War.

In these circumstances, it is hardly surprising that Stalin lacked sound and informed foreign policy advice in the months after Munich. Most of those who understood what the British and French might do were dead or dying off in the slave camps of the Gulag, enjoying the delights of 'honest proletarian labour'. Those who survived were keeping their heads well down in a personal survival policy based on the well-known Soviet adage 'sniff out, suck up, survive'. Only a brave man or a fool was going to gainsay Comrade Stalin's interpretation of events in 1939–40.

The irony was that the post-Munich period really marked the *end* of appeasement by the French and British. Hitler's cynical invasion of the rump of Czechoslovakia in March 1939 had in fact strengthened Allied resolve and convinced hitherto timid politicians that an Anglo-French and German clash was inevitable. The Soviets read it differently. From Stalin's perspective, the USSR now had a hungry fascist wolf loose on her unprotected western border, aided and abetted by perfidious capitalist democracies. An accommodation with Germany had therefore to be sought: Stalin believed he had to buy Hitler off at all costs. If the road from Munich steeled the Western democracies for a war with Nazi Germany, then, paradoxically, the road from Munich led Stalin directly down his own path of appeasement to the Ribbentrop-Molotov Pact of August 1939.

With Soviet policy bent on avoidance of war with Germany, Britain and France became secondary players. The Soviet leadership believed the USSR was now isolated and alone in a dangerous world. Almost in desperation, Stalin ordered Molotov to seek an alliance that would bind their potential enemy, Germany, into a non-aggression pact. Hitler's peremptory rupture of the Peace of Munich in March 1939 merely accelerated the process. However, before approaching Germany direct, Stalin tried the Western Allies one last time, although he believed that neither Britain nor France was in any position to protect their new eastern clients, Poland and Romania. In April 1939, Stalin proposed a new triple treaty based on a collective defensive alliance against Hitler, consisting of Britain, France and the USSR, to protect eastern Europe and by definition the USSR.

Whether this was to put pressure on Hitler, buy time or, most likely, merely to keep Stalin's options open, the French and British response to the proposal was both lukewarm and ambiguous. They counter-proposed a military pact where Russia would come to *Britain and France's* aid if Poland was attacked. As every intelligent observer in Europe knew that Poland was next on Hitler's list of territorial aims, and that neither France nor Britain was capable of protecting that isolated and encircled nation in the event of a Nazi attack, the Anglo-French proposals looked not unnaturally to Stalin like a cynical ploy to suck the USSR into Hitler's coming war with Poland; the very thing he was determined to avoid. Nonetheless, desperate for an accommodation, he dispatched emissaries from his new, purged Foreign Ministry to woo the Poles and their new allies. If and when war came, Stalin had no intention of fighting the Germans alone.

The negotiations for the triple alliance dragged on through the summer of 1939. Unfortunately, the French and British saw the talks as a political exercise designed to frighten Hitler and apply pressure to Berlin. The British in particular dragged their feet and played for time. The French, correctly, feared that if the talks were unsuccessful, Stalin might feel that he had no choice but do a deal with Hitler. Stalin himself viewed the discussions differently. Low-level Franco-British delegations without authority to sign agreements gave the Russian dictator no comfort and merely confirmed his suspicions of capitalist duplicity. He needed a result, and he needed one quickly.

Exasperated by the lack of progress in the triple-alliance talks, and receptive to German counter-approaches designed to give Hitler the free hand he needed to deal with Poland, in August 1939 Stalin decided to make a pact with his potential arch-enemy. In an astonishing volte-face, he authorized face-to-face negotiations between Molotov and Ribbentrop. This time, to ensure success, the negotiations were conducted by the secret police, the NKVD (the fiefdom of Lavrentiy Beria, Stalin's security chief) and not by the purged and cautious diplomats.

On 23 August, to the surprise of non-diplomatic observers, Ribbentrop flew to Moscow. The Nazi-Soviet Pact was signed the very next day, on 24 August, just eight days before Hitler's invasion of Poland. This unholy alliance of tyrants was a diplomatic coup that, in the words of one seasoned reporter, 'stupefied the world'. At a stroke, Hitler was given a free hand to attack Poland; and for his part, Stalin had his cherished guarantee of peace. As the German delegates left, a relieved Stalin announced, 'The Soviet Government takes [this] new pact very seriously… The Soviet Union will never betray its partner.' He meant it. The price was that over the next eighteen months, he steadfastly chose to ignore the mass of indications that his partner was about to betray *him*. Whether this was calculation, wishful thinking or just fear we will never know. The seeds of the Barbarossa disaster were sown.

Having signed his treaty, Stalin determined to keep his word. The most striking feature of the Soviet leader's appeasement of Germany was now a series of political and economic gestures designed to conciliate Hitler. Some of these were pure theatre, as when Stalin bear-hugged the embarrassed German Ambassador at Moscow's railway station and swore eternal friendship. History doesn't recall what the fastidious von der Schulenburg said in reply to this very public display of Georgian emotion.

Others were more devious, as the Tass official denial on 8 May 1941 of any German troop concentrations on the Russian border showed. There was a mass of evidence to the contrary, of which Stalin was well aware. Even overt German photo-reconnaissance flights were studiously 'overlooked', despite at least one crash at Rovno on 15 April 1941 of a Luftwaffe plane laden with incriminating exposed intelligence films in the wreckage. Soviet anti-aircraft defences were specifically ordered not to open fire on German aircraft, even if they strayed into Soviet airspace. Apparently no humiliation was too much for Stalin in his desire to avoid provoking the Germans and to prevent an outbreak of war between autumn 1939 and spring 1941.

It is not difficult to understand the workings of Stalin's mind in this period. According to Churchill, the Soviet leader later claimed ruefully, 'I thought I could gain another six months or so,' and there is plenty to suggest that Stalin's aim was to delay war until the Soviet Union was prepared for one, perhaps in 1942. Unfortunately, Stalin believed that he alone could effect this. Any adviser bringing him a contrary view was dangerous, not just to Stalin's perceived – and obsessive – beliefs, but also to 'peace'. The unenviable task of being one of Stalin's intelligence officers in the spring of 1941 was thus fraught with danger. The last thing Stalin wanted was objective and honest reporting that would compel him to take action.

It is against this twisted logic that the failure of Stalin to heed the intelligence warnings of an impending German attack should be viewed. And there was no shortage of intelligence warnings. As early as the end of June 1940, information about Hitler's future intentions had already been passed to Moscow. Where this came from is obscure, but it was subsequently reinforced by no fewer than 105 factual reports – accurate, credible and in many cases confirmed by other sources – between July 1940 and 22 June 1941. How Stalin could dismiss some of the intelligence that was passed to him personally almost beggars belief. For example, on 25 December 1940, the Soviet Attaché in Berlin passed on a résumé of Hitler's Führer Directive 21 of 18 December 1940, the operation order for Barbarossa. And on 1 March 1941 in Washington, Sumner Welles, the US Under-Secretary of State, formally summoned and briefed the Soviet Ambassador with the full details of a forthcoming German attack. His source was the junior US Commercial Attaché in Berlin, Sam E. Woods. Woods had been briefed by a disgruntled anti-Nazi official in the Berlin Trade Ministry on detailed German plans for an invasion of the USSR planned for spring 1941.

The stunned Soviet Ambassador heard that the American attaché had learned of the details in *August 1940*. The American authorities were so concerned to ensure that the reports were accurate before passing them on that they had turned them over to the FBI in January 1941 for critical evaluation. After exhaustive cross-checking, analysts confirmed that the intelligence appeared to be accurate and confirmed by other sources. Welles gravely informed the Soviet Ambassador that the evidence was 'so overwhelming it should be passed to Foreign Minister Molotov immediately'. Konstantin Umansky, the ambassador, 'turned very white', according to Welles. Stalin's reaction on being told was different. He ignored the US reports and in the Russian phrase 'safed it in the wall'. And 'safed' the intelligence stayed.

The reason Stalin could do this was simple: like many dictators and supreme commanders, he allowed an intelligence organization to grow up around him that reflected his own prejudices. Only the 'right' intelligence could be passed to the great man, if intelligence officers wanted to survive. Being human, General Golikov, his chief intelligence officer, an efficient if doctrinaire operations officer, with no reputation as an intelligence analyst but a commendable political loyalty to the Communist Party line, made sure that any intelligence reports reaching his master were carefully sorted into 'reliable' and 'not confirmed'. As the Kremlin definition of 'reliable' in early 1941 seems to have embraced any information that agreed with Comrade Stalin's analysis of the politico-military situation, Stalin's propensity for self-delusion was powerfully reinforced.

Golikov's promotion as head of the GRU (Soviet Military Intelligence) in 1940 must have wrung sad farewells and tears over the vodka from his colleagues rather than the congratulations that accompany the usual office party. The seven previous incumbents of the post had all been shot on Stalin's orders.

Yet Golikov survived, even though his two immediate successors were also shot by Stalin, doubtless anxious to re-establish his track record for consistency in these matters. Quite why Golikov survived is a curiosity. After the German attack he was even transferred to England in late 1941 in order to run the GRU's agent network from a safe overseas base – a fact that the British have been reluctant to advertise. We now know from GCHQ's Venona decrypts that there were at least *thirty-three* British-based traitors working for Moscow, including some very senior figures, in addition to the 'famous five' usual suspects – Philby, Burgess, Maclean, Blunt and Cairncross. The Soviets must have been very confident of their British spy network to have allowed the head of their Military Intelligence Service to run it from London.

Golikov was certainly in Stalin's confidence; in December 1940, on Stalin's direct orders, he had secretly briefed the twenty-five most senior officers of the GRU, 'that the Nazi-Soviet Pact, which was a product solely of the political genius of Comrade Stalin, was no more than a temporary expedient', and that 'Hitler would never dare to attack Russia as he was not unbalanced, and to a realist such a course would be suicide.' This was, of course, little more than wishful thinking at best, and at worst, pure self-delusion on Golikov's part. However, to survive and prosper as Chief Intelligence Officer amid the murderous intrigues of Stalin's court, sycophancy was the norm, and the 'Great Leader's Party Line' the only true guide to accurate intelligence assessment.

Golikov died in his bed in 1980. Only then did the truth come out. Far from being a simple son of peasant stock, as his revolutionary biographers claimed, like many others he had lied about his origins and even his age to survive the Revolution. He had attended the Tsarist Cavalry Academy before the Great War in 1911 (which would have been difficult for an alleged eleven-year-old) and had won his party credentials by being a ruthless killer in the repression of the peasants and kulaks after 1918. Stalin had chosen him to bear the poisoned chalice of the GRU in July 1940 precisely because he trusted Golikov's slavish devotion to the party line and to his leader personally. He could rely on comrade Golikov to follow his orders without question.

The result was that, with the military commanders Timoshenko and Zhukov, Golikov conspired with Stalin to ensure that the Soviet intelligence apparatus turned a blind eye until the Germans struck on 22 June 1941. On 20 April 1941 he had brandished the latest intelligence warnings of the impending German invasion in front of a group of GRU officers and parroted the very words Stalin had just screamed at him: 'This cannot be true. It is an English provocation! Investigate!'

Golikov was not alone in this. His counterparts, Vsevolod Merkulov, the Georgian head of the NKGB, and Pavel Fitin, the head of the International Department, the INU, adopted a similar survival strategy. Both of them also backed down from any confrontation over the intelligence flooding in about Barbarossa. Even when Fitin took his courage in his hands and suggested they sign a joint warning to Stalin, a frightened Merkulov flatly refused, saying, 'No – up there at the top [Comrade Stalin] knows far more about intelligence than we do. Comrade Stalin knows best.' For the chief of a national intelligence service this is a remarkable statement.

Faced with cowed intelligence advisers like these, Stalin was easily able to delude himself about German intentions. When Churchill (armed with hard Enigma decrypts that elite Nazi divisions were in Cracow, Poland, and not in the Balkans) decided to alert Stalin with a personal message from a 'trusted agent' in April 1941, Stalin is alleged to have scrawled 'Another English provocation!' in the margin before filing it, and took no action. Churchill's accurate and timely warning was by no means the only one. With the advantage of the 20/20 vision conferred by history, we can today see clearly both sides of the intelligence build-up to Barbarossa, and, equally clearly, Stalin's blind refusal to countenance it. It makes astonishing reading.

As early as 22 July 1940 (*before* the Battle of Britain had reached its peak) the German Army's Chief of Staff, General Franz Halder, noted that Hitler wanted now to 'begin planning for an attack on Russia'. A week later, Jodl and Hitler are both on record as saying that Russia must be smashed. On 9 August 1940, the German High Command issued the directive for 'Otto', the preliminary planning for an attack in the east set for spring 1941. And on 8 September 1940, the Wehrmacht's new Quartermaster-General at Zossen took over a draft operation order for the invasion of Russia in his safe. There is ample evidence that Stalin was made aware of these German intentions.

On 1 July 1940, Churchill wrote personally to the Soviet dictator warning him of Hitler's intentions. Although the British prime minister's letter appears not to have been based on any specific hard intelligence, he was the wrong man to alert Stalin and, considering Britain's post-Dunkirk plight, it was the wrong time. Stalin read it merely as a feeble attempt to involve the USSR in Britain's lost war and, coming as it did from the arch anti-Bolshevik Churchill, just another clumsy provocation. Amazingly, he passed the message directly to the German Ambassador, von der Schulenburg, as yet another example of perfidious Albion. No one was going to accuse Comrade Stalin of breaking faith over the Nazi-Soviet Pact with his valued ally, Herr Hitler.

To add to this catalogue of ignored warnings, Stalin's intelligence service was feeding him with high-grade human intelligence from a number of trusted agents deep within the combatants' war machines. For example, John Cairncross (later revealed to have been the KGB's 'Fifth Man' in Britain) was Private Secretary to Lord Hankey, the minister responsible for the British intelligence services in Churchill's government. (Between 1941 and 1945, Cairncross supplied the Soviets with 5,832 documents, according to Russian archives. In October 1944, Cairncross wrote to his Soviet leaders in foreign intelligence that, 'I am delighted that our friends found my help worthy of attention, and I am proud that I contributed something to the victory, which led to the almost complete cleansing of the Soviet land from the invaders.')

We do not know in detail what Cairncross passed to his masters in Moscow, but Oleg Gordievsky has claimed that there were literally 'tons of documents' in the KGB archives sourced from Cairncross after his recruitment in September 1940.

The intelligence from Britain was confirmed by other reports: the Schulze-Boysen spy network based in the German Air Ministry, the Trepper 'Red Orchestra' from Switzerland and the German traitor Rudolf von Scheliha in the German Embassy in Warsaw all contributed to the flow of alarming reports landing on Golikov's desk in Moscow. They confirmed one clear and constant trend: Hitler and his generals were planning an attack on the USSR in spring 1941.

In all fairness, Barbarossa, like any thorough military operation planned by the German General Staff, had a substantial deception plan. Indeed, its deception measures were the biggest the Wehrmacht ever used; only the Allied plans for D-Day were more all-embracing. The major thrust of the deception effort was the pretence first that Hitler was covering the Balkans (where

Mussolini was in deep trouble fighting the Greeks and Albanians), and second that the movement of troops to the East in winter 1940–41 was a ruse to fool the British into thinking that Operation Sea Lion, the German invasion of England, had been cancelled. The massive Barbarossa troop redeployments were represented as *a deception plan for an invasion of Britain.*

Even though the German General Staff operation order on deception for Barbarossa closes with the plaintive words, 'The stronger our troop concentration in the East, the harder [it will be] to create uncertainty about our plans... Suggestions and proposals by subordinate units are desired,' the overall deception plan worked, despite the numerous accurate warnings that presaged it. Stalin's ears were sealed and his eyes were blind; a therapist today would say that he was 'in denial'. However much evidence he was given, Stalin just ignored it, believing only reports that coincided with his own perception of intelligence. Anything that did not fit was dismissed as provocation or disinformation. Even though some of the reports flowing to him were amazingly precise, in the end Stalin believed only what he wanted to believe. Early in June 1941, the German Ambassador, the ever-sympathetic von der Schulenburg, briefed the new head of the Soviet International Affairs Department that 'I am going to tell you something that has never been done in diplomacy before... Germany's state secret number one is that Hitler has taken the decision to begin war against you on 22 June.' Stalin's indignant response to the Politburo was that 'Disinformation has now reached ambassadorial level!'

Looking now at the sheer mass of intelligence presented to the Russians, it seems incomprehensible that Operation Barbarossa would have taken them by surprise. And yet it did. Stalin even ignored the detailed intelligence on Barbarossa from Richard Sorge, the NKGB's prized agent in Japan, to such an extent that the communists' most trustworthy and accurate spy was reduced to weeping 'Moscow doesn't believe me' in his mistress's arms. Stalin had rejected Sorge's warning of 19 May 1941 that nine German armies with 150 divisions were massing against the USSR. Stalin angrily denounced Sorge as 'a little shit who has just set himself up with some good businesses in Japan'.

Stalin also chose to overlook news of Luftwaffe and panzer units relocating to Poland; a personal statement by Hitler to his ally Prince Paul of Yugoslavia that he would invade the USSR in mid-June; a copy of the outline Barbarossa operation order from an agent; massive German railway traffic to the east; German General Staff requests for thousands of copies of maps of the Baltic States and the western USSR; Wehrmacht defectors giving precise details of their targets and objectives and, last but not least, on 9 June 1941, precise details of the instructions to Ambassador von der Schulenburg to 'burn all documents' and prepare to leave Moscow. The number and detail of the Soviet reports read like an intelligence officer's indicators and warning textbook and cover every available intelligence source and agency.

Some of the warnings were positively bizarre. The case of the drunken professor is one of the more remarkable and reads more like a film script than reality. At a diplomatic reception on 15 May, Professor Karl Bömer, the head of Dr Goebbels's Foreign Press Department, 'waving a glass', announced to the astonished throng of diplomats and journalists that 'he would soon be leaving his post as *he was being promoted to become Gauleiter of the Crimea after the invasion of Russia on 22 June.*' As Bömer was known to enjoy a good party and was notoriously indiscreet with journalists, this drunken boast by a senior Nazi official should have been taken seriously, especially as Bömer was promptly relieved of his post and arrested by three large Gestapo men in leather coats.

Another more serious report was of an exchange at the farewell party for the American Embassy's First Secretary at the end of April in Berlin. Secretary Patterson introduced his Soviet diplomatic counterpart to a Luftwaffe major in uniform, who revealed (rather more soberly than Dr Bömer) that his squadron had just been secretly redeployed from Rommel's command in North Africa to Lodz in Poland. 'I know I shouldn't be telling you this,' the German added, 'but I'd hate anything to happen between our two countries.' The startled Russian transmitted this to Moscow where it was doubtless filed away as 'another provocation'.

Stalin ignored all these reports. Worse, he suppressed them to such an extent that in the final days before war he even ordered German deserters coming across the border bringing precise details of their units' Barbarossa objectives to be shot as *provocateurs*. Not a word reached his generals. Neither Timoshenko at the Defence Commissariat nor Zhukov at the General Staff saw any data or hard intelligence of the impending German attack. Golikov, with Stalin's approval, 'safed' his intelligence away. To compound their difficulties, by spring 1941 the Russian generals' own subordinates in the frontier military districts were warning them from below. German troop and aircraft movements on the scale of Barbarossa could not be entirely concealed. Pleas for contingency plans to relocate forward Soviet units to better defensive positions began to flood into Moscow in late May and June 1941. In desperation, the Soviet marshals turned to their intelligence staffs on the High Command for accurate assessments.

The fact that they did not get them can be attributed to two other factors, in addition to Stalin's suppression of the truth. First, there was the German deception operation designed to mask their build-up in the East. Many of the individual incidents of German activity reported to the Soviet commanders on the western border were undoubtedly capable of ambiguous interpretation. However, although the deception arrangements made by the Germans to disguise Barbarossa were both professional and comprehensive, it is doubtful whether they would have worked as well as they did without the dead hand of Stalin's self-deception. There were simply too many reports, and the Soviet intelligence system was simply too thorough to be deceived. But Stalin made it otherwise.

A second reason, which we may find hard to credit today, was that Stalin may have believed there could be no war without an *ultimatum*, a view shared by the diplomatic community of the time. There was a misplaced but obstinate belief that any crisis must start with a German ultimatum. This pre-Pearl Harbor outlook coloured all intelligence assessments, and not just in the Kremlin. As a result, the whole thrust of Stalin's policy of appeasement towards the Nazi regime in 1941 seems to have been designed to prevent any situation that could have led to a German ultimatum. If we accept the fact that *no pretext for war was to be offered under any circumstances*, then Stalin's deliberate suppression of unwelcome intelligence makes sense. The more unwelcome and forceful the intelligence, the more danger it posed to Soviet policy. Like a puppy fearing a beating, Stalin was rolling on his back, determined not to provoke Hitler at all costs.

In its final days, the prelude to Barbarossa saw perhaps one of the most bizarre events of the Second World War and one that muddied the waters hopelessly against any Russian perception of British good faith over the final warnings of German intentions. On 10/11 May 1941, Hitler's deputy, Rudolf Hess, unexpectedly flew to Scotland in an Me-110 long-range fighter. Even today, the mysterious circumstances of his flight remain unexplained. Hess appears to have acted for his own reasons, in a desperate last-minute attempt to negotiate peace with Britain to avoid Germany's long-standing nightmare of war on two fronts.

Whatever Hess's motives, Soviet suspicion of both the flight itself and the British government's reaction fatally skewed his perceptions of the subsequent British warnings over Barbarossa, however accurate and urgent. Stalin's greatest fear – an Anglo-German negotiated peace, thus freeing Hitler to turn all his victorious legions east – suddenly looked frighteningly possible. Every British action over the next month was weighed in the Kremlin against the belief that the British aim was to do everything in their power to provoke a Soviet–German clash. Even Anthony Eden's personal warnings (2–13 June 1941) of the impending Nazi onslaught were dismissed by the Soviet Ambassador in London as merely part of Hitler's 'war of nerves to wring concessions from the USSR without a fight'. The stage was set for Barbarossa.

So it was that on the night of 21/22 June 1941, trains full of wheat, tungsten and oil were still being dispatched west by the Soviets. The grain shipment at the bridge over the River Bug at Brest-Litovsk was the last of many. Nazi customs officials solemnly cleared the train and its cargo, which then steamed slowly across the bridge and into the Fatherland, to add to the thousands of tons of *Soviet* food and petrol with which Hitler, with calculated effrontery, would supply his invasion of the USSR.

As it crossed west on to Polish soil, the train snaked between batteries of German artillery massed in the darkness, where sweating gunners stockpiled ready-use shells in the short humid night. An hour and a half later they were in battle, part of the huge barrage that flamed into action at 03.15 along the 1,250 miles of the whole Eastern Front from the Baltic to the Black Sea. It launched the biggest invasion in history and the bloodiest campaign of the Second World War. Barbarossa had begun. Its first casualty was a German communist, Private Alfred Liskow, who deserted on 21 June to alert the Russians. He was shot immediately on Stalin's orders.

The shock of the attack in Moscow was total. Marshal Zhukov's memoirs, although written cautiously as befitted a canny survivor of the Communist Party's purges, give clear indications that in the Kremlin, Comrade Stalin had the equivalent of a nervous collapse. The Great Leader disappeared to his dacha at Kuntsevo. His train was ordered to be ready to evacuate Stalin. A shaken Molotov went on the radio to break the news to the Soviet people. Stalin was stunned and panicky, telling his family to 'flee to the Urals with all their children'.

Stalin was not to regain his composure for several days. Everything for which he had deceived, killed and suppressed apparently lay in ruins. We can even speculate that he may have felt his own position was at risk as a result of his denial and misreading of intelligence vital to the state. He had, after all, ordered others shot in the gloomy dungeons of the Lubyanka for much less. Fortunately for the Russian dictator, the Kremlin had more pressing concerns in those confused days of the last week of June 1941. After three days a delegation from the Politburo learned that the great leader was skulking in his dacha, where they found him slumped in an armchair. 'Why have you come?' he asked nervously. Mikoyan realised that Stalin suspected that they were about to arrest him, and so explained the urgent need for a State Committee of Defence. Stalin asked: 'But who's going to head it?' Molotov suggested that only the Soviet leader could be the chairman of the committee. An obviously relieved Stalin said: 'Me? Good.' For the USSR and Stalin's survival it was business as normal.

Across the years we can ask ourselves how such an obvious military build-up could have been ignored. How could seasoned intelligence professionals allow such an intelligence disaster to happen? In all fairness, many of the warnings were *not* ignored. They were misinterpreted: as political pressure, as relocations of units for other purposes, as part of Hitler's wider ambitions in the Balkans and eastern Mediterranean. Stalin was not alone in his misinterpretation of the available intelligence. Even the British Joint Intelligence Committee was ambivalent in its conclusions until the end of May 1941 and only confirmed the Germans' final intention to invade early in June.

In the final analysis, the failure to anticipate Operation Barbarossa must stand as one of the greatest intelligence disasters in history, and there can be no doubt that the blame must be laid squarely at Stalin's door. Harrison Salisbury, who was in Moscow at the time, sums up the Soviet dictator's intelligence failure thus in his book *The 900 Days*:

> Neither quantity nor quality of intelligence reporting determines whether national leaderships act in a timely and resolute fashion. It is the ability of that leadership to comprehend what is reported, to assimilate the findings of spies and the warnings of diplomats. Unless there is a clear channel from lower to top levels, unless the leadership insists on honest and objective reporting, and is prepared to act on such reports, regardless of preconceptions or prejudices... then the best intelligence in the world goes to waste – or even worse, is turned into any agency of self-deceit. This was clearly the case with Stalin. Nothing in the Bolshevik experience so plainly exposed the defects of the Soviet power monopoly as when the man who held that power was ruled by his own internal obsessions.

Stalin's fatal misinterpretation and denial of the clear intelligence he was given was to cost the Soviet Union 20 million dead, 70,000 cities, towns and villages laid waste, and changed the map of the world for ever.

With potentially the best intelligence service in the world at his beck and call, Stalin blew it. There can be no other judgement. Although he may have bought a little time for the USSR, he did not even prepare the Red Army for invasion, with the result that Soviet losses in 1941 were far worse than they needed to be. In 1941 alone, Mother Russia – to which Stalin now desperately pleaded in Churchillian rhetoric for his own and his regime's survival – suffered nearly 2 million casualties, many of them avoidable as the Red Army's trapped forward divisions were encircled and annihilated by the scything Nazi panzer thrusts.

Stalin was indeed his own intelligence officer – and a thoroughly bad one at that. We are still paying the price for his mistakes today in our post-Cold War world.

'THE FINEST INTELLIGENCE IN OUR HISTORY' – PEARL HARBOR, 1941

*'I fear all we have done is to awaken a sleeping giant
and fill him with a terrible resolve'*
ADMIRAL ISOROKU YAMAMOTO

If D-Day was a triumph of deception over an efficient intelligence service, and Barbarossa the neutralization of an outstanding intelligence service by a dictator's stupidity, then Pearl Harbor represents the consequences of a nation not having a proper intelligence service at all.

For the intelligence analyst Pearl Harbor deserves particular attention because it was the classic case of a nation actually having nearly all the key intelligence indicators of an impending attack, but failing to recognize them or act upon them as clear warnings. As a result of poor intelligence the course of world history was altered irreversibly and the new dominance of the USA confirmed four years later in the world's first atomic bomb. That mushroom cloud over Hiroshima has cast a shadow over world affairs to this day, and yet without Pearl Harbor the USA would have been reluctant to become involved in Japan's war in the Pacific.

The disaster at Pearl Harbor on Sunday 7 December 1941, when eighteen major fighting ships were sunk (including four out of eight battleships), 188 aircraft destroyed and 2,403 Americans killed by the Japanese Imperial Navy in a surprise dawn air attack, came as a huge shock to the American people. Every American of that generation could remember where they were the day war broke out. President Roosevelt called it 'a day that will be remembered in infamy'.

The irony was that most informed commentators were expecting war at some point with Japan. Even by the standards of the time, there was ample evidence that a Pacific war was not only inevitable but imminent. How then did the US government fail to prepare for what was recognized at the highest levels as 'a clear and present danger'? To understand how such a disaster could befall a great nation, we have to go back to the beginning of the Second World War.

The USA of 1939 was a world power; economically, politically and in terms of sheer size. Paradoxically, with the exception of her navy, she exhibited few of the trappings of a major global force. Her army was tiny, she was not even a member of the League of Nations (the forerunner of the United Nations) and both government policy and public mood were fiercely isolationist. Not only did America lack an integrated intelligence organization, but she steadfastly refused to create one. Secure behind her ocean barriers, continental America wanted nothing more than peace and a return to prosperity. In 1940, Washington was absorbed by the presidential election and domestic politics.

This attitude was understandable. The Great Depression of 1931–38 had hit the USA harder than any other democracy. With millions unemployed, food queues and the near collapse of what was effectively unregulated capitalism, the American economy in the thirties had come much closer to a meltdown of society than is realized today. Only unprecedented political and economic measures by the new president, Franklin Delano Roosevelt, some of them of dubious constitutional legality, had enabled the Union to survive. Economically and socially, the America of 1936–38 was a traumatized country.

The advent of yet another European war was in many ways an unmitigated blessing for the United States. Provided the country could stay out of the conflict, rich economic pickings could be made out of the misfortunes of others. For example, US unemployment plunged by nearly three-quarters of a million in the autumn of 1939 as the value of the great defence stocks – chemical, aircraft, steel, shipbuilding and auto-manufacturing companies – soared following Hitler's invasion of Poland. Industry and the economy boomed; in the words of the old Depression song, 'Happy days are here again!'

In this atmosphere there was little incentive for the US political authorities to do anything that might endanger the USA's domestic economic recovery. While President Franklin D Roosevelt's enemies claimed that he was trying to drag the USA into an unwanted war, the facts seem to indicate that FDR, although not unaware of the long-term threats posed by fascism and communism, wanted nothing more than to keep the US economic recovery going.

Despite some claims by conspiracy theorists, the path to Pearl Harbor is not littered with deep plots to involve the USA in a major war or some cunning Churchillian scheme to lure the USA into rescuing Britain in her darkest hour. Rather, the more one examines the build-up to America's greatest intelligence disaster, the more it becomes clear that like most accidents there was a chain of errors, some big, some small, all contributing to a fatal climax. Hindsight is a fairly exact science. Today with the benefit of the evidence, we can examine in some detail those links in the chain that brought America so disastrously to war. In the cumulative sequence of US miscalculation, however, the one clear and constant failure was of intelligence; of that there can be no doubt.

For the professional intelligence analyst the factors that led to the failure at Pearl Harbor are fairly clear:

1. No national intelligence organization
2. Total underestimation of the Japanese as potential enemies
3. No single analysis of all the available evidence
4. Under-resourcing of the various providers of intelligence
5. Failure to understand the significance of intelligence provided
6. Competition between intelligence agencies
7. Ignorance of senior officers
8. Lack of any warning system
9. Inter-service rivalry for political-military power and influence
10. Lack of trained intelligence analysts
11. No sense of urgency

Alarming as this list of intelligence mistakes is, it could be longer. But it makes the point: in December 1941, the USA was not taking the possibility of a war with Japan seriously and was certainly not organizing her intelligence services, such as they were, to provide a priority warning of war. In retrospect the intelligence picture seems blindingly obvious, but then most disasters are only really obvious after they have happened.

One unusual feature of the Pearl Harbor story is that we can identify almost precisely the catalyst that triggered the Japanese attack on the sleeping US fleet. The story of the slippery slide to war really begins with an *American* action. By July 1941, Imperial Japan's policies of militarism and expansion, and the invasion of her neighbours, had finally caused the exasperated Allied powers to act. After the brutal invasions of China and Manchuria, the Japanese seizure of southern Indochina in 1941 was the final straw. In retaliation, the United States, followed by Britain and the Dutch colonial government in the East Indies, imposed a strategic embargo on any exports of oil or steel to Japan in a move designed to force the Japanese to the negotiating table. Japan's ability to make war and indeed to survive economically depended on the oil and other crucial raw materials such as rubber from the Dutch East Indies and British Malaya. Surely, reasoned the far-off politicians in their committee rooms, the embargo would bring the aggressor to its senses. In fact, for Premier Tojo's Japan, there was another policy option. As any knowledgeable adviser on Japanese culture and thought at the time could have explained, the American diplomatic pressure left only one real choice open to the proud, fiercely independent and irredeemably martial heirs to the Samurai: to fight, and to seize what Japan needed, despite efforts to deny access by the Americans and their friends. From July 1941, certainly in Japanese minds, force was the only real option.

It was even possible to work out the timing of any likely attack. In the summer, American planners had calculated, correctly, that Japan had stockpiles of aviation spirit for only another six months. Surely then, reasoned the policymakers in Washington, by December 1941 the Japanese would be forced to come cap in hand to the Allies. Would not the Japanese have no choice but to agree to demands for a withdrawal from their illegal conquests in South East Asia, if they wanted to get their hands on the precious stocks of oil and strategic materials they so desperately needed?

Unfortunately, the Japanese planners saw the ticking clock started by their American counterparts in July of 1941 rather differently. From the Japanese perspective at the time they really had no choice but to seize by force what the US and Allied embargo was denying them. And, calculated the Japanese planners, their seizure had to be made before the end of December 1941 when their existing stocks of strategic war supplies would begin to run out. Not for the first time in intelligence matters, two opposing sets of planners looked at identical information and came up with diametrically opposed conclusions. Therein lie the real roots of the blunder and the fascination of the disaster at Pearl Harbor.

Despite having naively miscalculated probable Japanese intentions, the US administration was not completely unaware of Japanese policy and military thinking. By a triumph of code-breaking that paralleled Britain's Ultra operation to break the German Enigma traffic, by 1941 the USA could read Japan's most secret codes and ciphers. Every high-level Japanese diplomatic message could, theoretically, be 'unbuttoned' and made available to defence planners from the president downwards. The code name of this priceless intelligence advantage was, appropriately enough, Magic, and through the labyrinth of this shadowy code-breaking world, many of the secrets of Pearl Harbor were to be revealed in advance.

The US record in signals intelligence was unusual. In 1929, America's original team of diplomatic code-breakers, MI-8, led by the legendary Herbert Yardley, was summarily disbanded by Secretary of State Henry Stimson because, as he said later, 'Gentlemen don't read each other's mail.' This astonishing act of political self-denial may not have been quite as high-minded as history likes to make out. For at the very time that Yardley's MI-8 closed, its work was being discreetly transferred to yet another branch of the US bureaucracy, the Army's Signal Intelligence Service (SIS) under William F. Friedman. Friedman, brilliant, dedicated and giant among cryptographers, now took on the task of deciphering the Japanese diplomatic codes.

To complicate the picture further, yet *another* American signals intelligence (sigint) organization was successfully reading Japanese radio traffic. In Washington, the US Navy had established its own highly secret code-breaking organization known as OP-20-G, under a quiet naval lieutenant, Laurance Safford. Laurance F. Safford was known as the 'father of US Navy cryptology', and established the naval cryptologic organization after the First World War, heading the effort more or less constantly until shortly after the Japanese attack on Pearl Harbor.

There is no evidence that any of these signal intelligence organizations' activities were coordinated. By an even more ironic stroke, SIS and OP-20-G were only one block apart in Washington, DC. Safford's Navy team were diligently going about their mysterious trade in the Navy building on Constitution Avenue; up the road in the Munitions Building, Friedman's Army SIS group was equally enthusiastically attacking Japanese diplomatic cables.

By 1941 both groups were heavily overworked. For the Navy, OP-20-G had obtained almost complete access to day-to-day Japanese naval traffic, which was code-named Orange. Breaking the Magic Japanese diplomatic traffic, known as Purple, was the responsibility of SIS. Neither Army nor Navy agency fully trusted the other or shared its information. Naval secrets were for the Navy and Army secrets were for the Army. Therein lay yet another seed of disaster. You need to see *all* the pieces in the box to complete the jigsaw.

If this bureaucratic mismanagement were not enough, the deal struck between OP-20-G and SIS late in 1940 is beyond belief. Safford, the head of OP-20-G, recorded: 'We agreed [with SIS] to divide all Japanese Diplomatic processing on a daily basis, the Navy taking the odd days' traffic and the Army the even days' traffic… later Naval Intelligence and Army G2 arranged for dissemination of the Japanese Diplomatic [take] to the White House and State Department on a monthly basis, Navy taking the odd months and Army the even months.'

So, to further confuse the intelligence picture, not only were the US Army and Navy failing to co-operate on collection targets, traffic analysis or technical breakthroughs, they were also refusing to share interpretation successes. And to compound it all, they were both competing to disseminate any intelligence gleaned separately to their political masters. In today's world, where knowledge is a valuable commodity, the ability to gain a monopoly of access to a politician's ear is rightly hailed as a bureaucratic triumph. Astonishingly, for many months in 1940 and 1941, the US Army and Navy intelligence chiefs refused to tell even the president of the United States vital intelligence that was being made available to their own service chiefs.

Their motives appear complex and seem primarily to be based on a deep and not unreasonable suspicion that Washington's party politicians could not be trusted to keep their mouths shut with real secrets. There were probably other, less clear motives. Both General Marshall, the Army Chief of Staff, and

Admiral Stark, the Chief of Naval Operation, shared a mistrust of the political advisers surrounding the president. Not everyone trusted Roosevelt's New Deal administration to behave in the national interest. As a result, both Army and Navy restricted the 'read' lists for Magic to the bare minimum, using the fiercest need-to-know criteria. Only Roosevelt, his Secretary of State for War, Stimson (who appears to have overcome his previous aversion to reading other people's mail by 1941), the Secretary for the Navy, Frank Knox, and Cordell Hull, the Secretary of State, appear to have had access to the secrets of Magic, and even then on a severely restricted basis.

By December 1941, the US intelligence services had between them managed to read both the Japanese naval operations code, JN-25, and most of the Japanese government's high-level diplomatic traffic. They therefore possessed the capability to decipher and read the Japanese intentions before Pearl Harbor. Unfortunately what the Americans had also done was to allow their sigint units to grow in a fragmented and uncoordinated fashion and so weaken their code-breaking efforts. They had also failed to establish an intelligence coordinating staff. Last, but by no means least, in order to keep a great deal of their strategic intelligence out of the hands of their service rivals and the loquacious Washington politicians, they were only showing some of the intelligence to some of the decision-makers *some* of the time. Suddenly, the disaster at Pearl Harbor becomes a little more understandable.

There is much more to Pearl Harbor than a confused and incompetent misuse of sigint, however. The intelligence analysts, indicators and warning board for December 1941 flashed red and amber for a large number of other significant indicators as the build-up to Pearl Harbor continued. Sigint alone cannot be held responsible. The American authorities had access to plenty of other evidence from a variety of other sources.

In Chapter 2, we saw how Sir John Masterman's Double Cross Committee had used MI5's turned Abwehr agents and then played them back against their former masters. If bureaucratic Washington is to bear the principal burden of the Pearl Harbor debacle, it is only just to include the Director of the Federal Bureau of Investigation, J. Edgar Hoover. He appears to have disregarded, on grounds of prejudice, a vital warning about Pearl Harbor given by one of MI5's prize double agents.

As part of the complex game of playing the Abwehr's agents, 'Tricycle', Dusko Popov, a Yugoslav, was dispatched by the British to the neutral USA via Lisbon in late summer 1941. Popov's value was twofold: first, he could help to educate American counter-intelligence chiefs in what Britain was achieving by 'doubling' agents and playing them back; second and perhaps more important, Tricycle had received one of the Germans' new microdots with clear instructions from his official Abwehr masters on their collection priorities. Tricycle had, in fact, the Abwehr's collection tasking for the USA, in the form of a long questionnaire. This revealed a great deal about the Axis alliance's intentions, obsessions and preoccupations.

The Nazi preoccupations in the questionnaire contained, among a mass of other questions, some revealing queries. One whole section was devoted to Pearl Harbor, its layout, dispositions and defences. Armed with this, double agent Popov met the FBI Bureau Chief in late August 1941 in a hot and humid Washington.

The meeting was a disaster. Hoover's dislike of the louche Balkan playboy was manifest. MI5's codename for the Yugoslav is alleged to have originated as a dry joke based on Popov's liking for two girls at a time in his bed, but any idea of using such a 'corrupt degenerate' as agent Tricycle was dismissed out of hand by the sexually fastidious and xenophobic Hoover. Even the significance of such items in the long German questionnaire as 'What is the progress of the dredger at the entrance to [Pearl Harbor's] East and South East Loch?' was ignored or overlooked by him. Tricycle was banished and the whole security liaison effort between the successful British and the arrogant Hoover never materialized. Hoover did not bother to inform the Navy or the State department of the questionnaire, preferring instead to gloat in his memoirs later that he had personally interviewed a 'dirty Nazi spy... and sent him packing'. Yet, sadly, Hoover had held a vital piece of the Pearl Harbor jigsaw in his hand that hot August day: since 30 January 1941, the Japanese had agreed to coordinate their collection efforts in the USA with their Italian and German allies. Popov's Abwehr questionnaire was in reality partly a *Japanese*, not a German, collection plan. But J. Edgar Hoover never knew; more importantly, he never cared.

Whatever one thinks of Hoover or Popov, one inescapable fact emerges:

if the FBI had compared Tricycle's Abwehr questionnaire with the Navy's existing intercepts of the Japanese J-19 and PA-K2 messages, then the significance would probably have struck them like a thunderbolt. The Japanese intercepts and Popov's questionnaire were nearly identical. Someone really did want to know about every tactical detail of Pearl Harbor; the only questions were who and why?

In 1941 no one in Washington coordinated intelligence, no one assessed all source material at the highest level, and there was no way that J. Edgar Hoover was going to share his information with the armed forces, even though he must have known that his own head of station in Honolulu would have been *very* interested in Popov's questionnaire and anything else that gave an indication of Japanese intentions on the islands. For the FBI was responsible for security and counter-intelligence on Hawaii, and the Japanese Consul-General was using a similar questionnaire to Popov's. Another piece of the Pearl Harbor jigsaw was not just overlooked, but thrown away in Hoover's inimitable mixture of conceit, prejudice and arrogance.

Even the crown jewels of intelligence, the Magic intercepts of the Japanese Purple code, were nearly compromised. On 5 May 1941, a worried Tokyo signalled their embassy in Washington, 'According to reliable information, it appears that Washington is reading some of your coded messages.' The precise source of the leak has never been established, but Ambassador Nomura was probably being tipped off indirectly by another Axis source, possibly the Abwehr in Berlin. However, the Japanese investigation came up with no hard evidence of compromise, and so, on 20 May, Nomura signalled Tokyo admitting that perhaps some low-level material was being read, but not the high-level diplomatic traffic. The Japanese were aided in this judgement by a mistaken belief that Japanese was too difficult for foreigners (a not uncommon Oriental conceit), and the somewhat sad conviction that the Purple code, like the Enigma machine, was unbreakable. The Washington siginters could breathe again.

As the countdown to war continued, the indicators of approaching hostilities intensified. During 1941, signals were intercepted from Bangkok, Berlin, Buenos Aires, Batavia (in the Dutch East Indies), London, Moscow, Rome, Shanghai and Singapore. All confirmed the same simple message:

Japan was preparing for war. Ironically, even Stalin's Russia helped to build the picture of Japanese preparedness. As part of the Soviet dictator's desperate attempts to avert a war on two fronts, Stalin signed a Japanese-Soviet neutrality pact on 13 April 1941. This freed the Soviets to concentrate on their western border and the looming Nazi threat; but the pact equally released Japanese forces for deployment elsewhere than Siberia. The US I&W board – if such a thing existed – was beginning to fill up with indicators, and nearly all were red.

The relatively moderate Ambassador Nomura in Washington was reluctantly dragged into the picture yet again, with a peremptory order from his Foreign Minister, Yosuke Matsuoka, to 'set up a [clandestine] intelligence organization in North America for the purpose of being prepared for the worst'. American service intelligence staffs faithfully reported the message, but in the absence of a joint national assessment staff, the significance of the warning was lost in the welter of background noise and contradictory signals.

With hindsight we can see that it was not war in itself that came as such a traumatic shock to the United States. The real surprise was the way war erupted, and where. But even here the US authorities should have been more alert. Not only did they have the intercepted Japanese Navy questions about Pearl Harbor and the discarded collateral of Tricycle's Abwehr questionnaire, but they were also being fed a daily diet of bellicose Japanese intercepts from all over the Far East. Many of these pointed to American possessions as a potential target.

As the year progressed, further confirmation of Japan's warlike intentions came with the so-called 'Canton' signal intercepted in mid-summer 1941 which spelled out the target list for what was to become notorious later as Japan's Greater East Asia Co-Prosperity Sphere. While not denying its provenance, the US Office of Naval Intelligence (ONI) dismissed its contents as a mere Japanese wish list, an 'expression of Tokyo's wishful thinking' and not a possible warning of targets for attack – which in fact it was. The weight of intelligence flooding in from other sources was equally significant. For example, British intelligence in Manila (MI6) is on record as passing a warning of the Japanese build-up to 'Chiefs of American Military and Naval Intelligence, Honolulu' on *3 December* stating clearly the British assessment that the US was 'a likely target for early hostilities'.

Reviewing the evidence, we must ask ourselves two questions. First, did the available intelligence up to 6 December 1941 identify Pearl Harbor as a definite target? Second, was Pearl Harbor prepared for trouble, and if not, why not? (The second question is not strictly a matter of intelligence interest, but is crucial to the American reaction to the Japanese threat and to the final stages of the disaster.)

It is important to remember that, especially to the Japanese strategic planners, Pearl Harbor was merely a sideshow. It was intended as nothing more than a surprise aerial blitzkrieg, designed to neutralize the American fleet on the flank of the *real* Japanese attack. The prime strike was designed to seize Japan's key economic objectives in South East Asia. Hard though it is to accept, Pearl Harbor was not the main Japanese target on 7 December 1941. The merest glance at the balance of Japanese forces deployed in the Pacific during the first week of December 1941 shows that only a fraction of Japanese power was dedicated to neutralizing the US fleet. *Politically* the Pearl Harbor strike was every bit as important as the attack on Malaya and the Philippines; however, in strictly military terms, it was a sideshow.

This fact comes as a slightly shocking revelation to many observers. After all, was it not Pearl Harbor that dragged the USA into the Second World War and turned an essentially European quarrel into a global conflict? The judgement is easily supported by the evidence, however, not just of the balance of Japanese forces deployed but also in the Japanese staff planning for the 7 December attacks. The greater part of the Japanese planning effort was focused on *economic* targets for strategic occupation. This was inevitably reflected in the number of messages intercepted by the Americans and British. The greater part of the traffic was taken up with events in the South-West Pacific and Asia, and staff interest in the US fleet anchorage appeared to be minimal or non-existent.

This balance of strategic priorities was strongly felt in Japan's councils of war. For example, the Japanese Naval Staff in particular was initially highly sceptical of Admiral Yamamoto's plan for Pearl Harbor. Admiral Nagano, the Chief of Japanese Naval Staff, only authorized the attack on condition that it could be cancelled at any time and *would not interfere with or jeopardize other, more important strategic operations.* So, while there was a wealth of evidence that Japan was going to assault the Far East, the signals for any activity at Pearl Harbor were essentially secondary to the main assaults being planned. This balance of operational priorities was mirrored in the balance of intelligence received by the Allies and reflected in their assessments.

The salient fact about the intelligence disaster at Pearl Harbor is that most of the evidence was hidden by a blizzard of other information at the time. This masking of vital indicators in an overall level of other signals is called 'noise' by professional intelligence officers. Quite simply, the clamour of other voices drowned out the Pearl Harbor material. After any surprise attack it is relatively easy to go back over the evidence and pick out the crucial indicators; and thus it proves with Pearl Harbor. But at the time they were competing for attention with other, more likely, events.

There is another factor. By the end of November 1941, almost every informed commentator had realized that the diplomatic policy of bringing Japan to her knees was failing and that the Japanese were preparing to go to war. This is easily confirmed from a selection of the Hawaiian newspapers of the time. During the last two weeks before Pearl Harbor they included the following headlines:

- US-JAPAN TALKS BROKEN OFF
- US REJECTS COMPROMISE
- HAWAII – TROOPS ALERTED
- JAPAN GIVES TWO MORE WEEKS FOR NEGOTIATIONS – PREPARES FOR ACTION IN EVENT OF FAILURE
- PACIFIC ZERO HOUR NEAR: JAPAN ANSWERS THE US

The problem was that although everyone recognized the gravity of the crisis, equally every informed commentator focused on Thailand, Malaya, Burma and the Dutch East Indies as the most likely targets for any Japanese onslaught. Even so, there can be no doubt that the USA took the situation very seriously. Secretary of War Stimson, acting for Roosevelt while the president was on holiday in the last week of November 1941, actually signed a war alert to all US commands on 27 November, during the period of the headlines above. The US Navy's OPNAV version of this signal of 27

November, sent by the Chief of Naval Operations to his fleet commanders in both the Atlantic and Pacific theatres, could not be more specific:

> This dispatch is to be considered a war warning… an aggressive move by Japan is expected within the next few days.

Crucially, the signal goes on:

> The… organization of naval task forces indicates an amphibious expedition against either the Philippines or Kra Peninsula [Thailand] or possibly Borneo.

There was no mention of Pearl Harbor.

Both Stimson's and the OPNAV message were received by their respective services in Hawaii. Astonishingly, both were effectively ignored in that neither commander in Hawaii, Army or Navy, put their forces on full alert. Peacetime routines, albeit enhanced ones, continued. Apparently the Japanese threat did not involve Pearl Harbor. Another weak link in the chain had been forged.

So, of the two key questions, the first is clearly answered: by December 1941 the balance of evidence is that everyone who counted knew that war with Japan was imminent, but there was little unambiguous intelligence available to commanders that *Pearl Harbor* was a definite objective, even though US territories might well be a target. The focus of our investigation now homes in on the second question: were the US commands on Hawaii prepared, and if not, why? More ink has been spilled on this issue than almost any other. Nowadays Pearl Harbor stands as a model of the surprise attack, with innocent sailors preparing to go to church on a Sunday morning being slaughtered by a perfidious hail of bombs and high-explosive raining without warning from a clear blue sky. No fewer than six separate inquiries have examined the disaster at Pearl Harbor, although only one appears to have been privy to all the available intelligence.

In this climate of recrimination and accusation it is hardly surprising that conspiracy theories have flourished. The usual suspects in the Pearl Harbor conspiracy stakes are, predictably, Roosevelt and Churchill. Roosevelt, it is claimed, knew only too well that the attack on Hawaii was imminent but deliberately refrained from alerting his hapless commanders in order to drag the USA into a war against the wishes of his countrymen. Churchill, more sinister still, is alleged not only to have known the attack was coming but also to have suppressed any warnings to Washington in order to suck the USA into a war for survival that Britain was losing. Even Stalin gets a mention: some conspiracy commentators allege that the USSR knew all about Pearl Harbor but kept the information to itself in order to ensure that the Japanese would embroil themselves in Pacific adventures. The threat to the Soviet Union's exposed eastern possessions in Siberia would thus be lifted.

None of these conspiracy claims stands up to close scrutiny. Roosevelt and his advisers knew that something was going to happen, but they didn't know what until it was almost too late to save Pearl Harbor. Churchill and British signals intelligence (GCCS), particularly their Far East Combined Bureau, shared the bulk of their relevant operational intelligence with their American counterparts. They passed across much more than any nation at war would normally pass to a neutral country. No one disputes Churchill's relief at the involvement of the USA in the war or his delight at Hitler's ill-judged declaration of war on the USA. There is no evidence, however, that Churchill deliberately misled his American colleagues or knew more about the Pearl Harbor attack than Roosevelt, although both parties knew a great deal of what was going on in Japanese official thinking.

Part of the problem facing commentators both today and the intelligence analysts of 1941 is that the sheer volume of high-level signals intelligence often exacerbates the problem. Given complete transparency of the twists and turns of an enemy's internal policy debates, the analyst often becomes a party to the discussion, if only as an invisible observer. But detailed knowledge of the policy background is not the same as access to a clear copy of the final chosen course of action, the resulting operational plan and, crucially, its executive instructions with locations, timings and code words. This was really the position that the American commanders at Pearl Harbor faced in the first week of December 1941. They knew a Japanese strike was imminent, *but they never appreciated that it might also fall on them.*

The reasons for the detailed operational and tactical failures at Pearl

Harbor on the ground on the morning of 7 December 1941 are therefore neither military nor strategic. The intelligence failures *before* Pearl Harbor were undoubtedly failures at a national, governmental level. The issue of the commanders' 'preparedness' in Hawaii *on the day* cannot be ascribed to Roosevelt, Churchill or any other Machiavellian conspirator; the failure at Pearl Harbor lies squarely at the feet of the respective local commanders and their immediate supervisors.

To understand this we have to be clear about the status of the US Hawaii Commands in 1941 and see the world as it was then, far from modern military practice of unified command structures, joint service organization and the like. The first and most striking fact is the plural, 'commands'. Hawaii was a divided US defence responsibility: the US Navy, under its C-in-C Pacific Fleet, Admiral Kimmel, was responsible for the fleet, its operations in the Pacific and its fleet anchorage at Pearl Harbor. The US Army, on the other hand, under Lieutenant General Short, was responsible for ground security of all the Hawaiian Islands, defence against invasion and counter-sabotage (there was no separate US Air Force until 1946). The sad fact is that the US Army and the US Navy did not work together in 1941. They were two entirely separate and competing organizations. Relations between the two commanders and their staffs were distant. The US Navy regarded itself as the premier service and saw Short and his forces as little more than a high-ranking garrison commander ashore for their naval base. There were no joint staffs and no effective liaison between the Navy's intelligence assets on the islands and the Army's.

Another factor intrudes, hard for us to judge across the years but one that is instantly understandable. Rather like Cyprus for the British and Tahiti for the French, Hawaii was the classic 'cushy billet' or soft posting. The islands' reputation for sun, sand and the other recreational delights of a semitropical paradise were as strong in 1941 as they are today. For the Navy, 'Pearl' was where you docked after tough sea duty, went ashore and relaxed while the ship was refitted. For the Army, 'The Army's Hawaiian Command was a perpetual happy hour,' in the words of Colonel Henry Clausen, the lawyer appointed to conduct the definitive secret US Department of Defense investigation into the debacle.

The state of affairs in Hawaii before Pearl Harbor is reinforced by a damning and little-known report by a Colonel H.S. Burwell into the Hawaiian Command, dated July 1941 and prepared for Lieutenant General Short, the Army's new commanding general for the islands. It identified a number of important deficiencies in his Command, in particular:

- A dangerous lack of awareness of the possibility of a surprise enemy attack in the event of 'an abrupt conflict with Japan'
- Complacency at all levels based on 'the ingrained habits of peacetime'
- Lack of 'aggressive attitude' and 'unconcern for the future'
- 'Inattention accorded in peacetime to intelligence functions'
- Failure to implement joint planning sufficiently with other services

Short was not alone in his problems. The US Navy in Hawaii, under Admiral Kimmel, almost intentionally cut off the Army from the deliberations of the Fleet and its staff. For example, there was, according to the subsequent inquiries:

- No joint planning staff on the islands
- No joint air or radar surveillance of the waters around Hawaii
- No official liaison staff between Navy and Army
- A deliberate C-in-C Pacific Fleet policy to withhold signals intelligence from the Army, especially the decision by Admiral Kimmel or his staff not to pass on the final Japanese alert for war, the so-called 'Winds Code' messages
- Squabbles between Navy and Army over who should be in command of outlying islands such as Guam and Wake

Admiral Kimmel failed to even contact his Army counterpart to discuss their problems as the clock ticked on. In his damning testimony to the subsequent Naval Court of Inquiry, the admiral's peacetime failure to comprehend the need for joint command rings clearly:

I tried to inform the Commanding General of everything I thought might be useful to him. I did not inform the Commanding General of my proposed plans... I saw no reason for taking the additional chance of having such information [further] divulged... by any agency who would have no part in the plan.

Faced with a divided command, no real liaison, a reluctance to share vital intelligence and a peacetime lack of urgency at all levels in the islands, it is hardly surprising that the US forces on Hawaii were unprepared.

As the final days of the tragedy unfolded, US and Allied intelligence staffs went into overdrive. Early in December 1941, traffic analysis correctly spotted the build-up of the Japanese attack fleets for Batavia, Thailand and Malaya. The timing of any attack then became the key requirement. The 'essential element of information' or prime intelligence requirement came down in the end to one simple question: when?

The Japanese had gone to considerable lengths to prepare their embassies abroad for just such a contingency. Having elected for a surprise attack, they had also decided to give their ambassadors just enough time to hand-deliver a message to their host governments. Timing, like the attacks themselves, would be crucial not only for the victims but also for the attacker. This traffic was a specific weakness in Japanese security, but they could not simply abandon their embassies and diplomats. Naturally, for the intelligence analyst, these sorts of signals are crucial indicators on any indicators and warning board.

On 19 November, Tokyo issued a specific warning to its Washington Embassy to listen out for a special radio broadcast 'in case of an emergency (cutting off diplomatic relations) and the cutting off of international communications'. This would be done by inserting a coded personal message into the daily Japanese international short-wave news broadcast. The messages were to be disguised as meteorological reports (hence the name 'Winds Code') with 'East Wind, Rain' standing for a breach with America and 'West Wind, Clear' for a break with the British Empire. The instruction went on to order all low-level secret diplomatic codes and ciphers to be destroyed and for the diplomatic staffs to prepare for war.

The message was duly intercepted and read by all the Allied intelligence staffs. Needless to say, from that moment on, the number one priority of all US and Allied intelligence staffs was to listen for the 'Winds Code' message.

It was to become the intelligence obsession of the Pearl Harbor story, and the mystery as to whether the message was ever sent endures to this day.

Alert to the deteriorating situation, and fully aware of the significance of events, the Office of Naval Intelligence and the War Department in Washington stepped up their vigilance. They were rewarded by two damning intercepts that, more clearly than anything else, indicated war was now imminent. On 3 December, the Washington Navy Bureau alerted Admiral Kimmel in Hawaii with two crucial signals:

> Highly reliable information has been received that categoric priority instructions were sent yesterday to Japanese diplomatic posts at Hong Kong, Singapore, Batavia, Manila, Washington and London to destroy most of their codes and ciphers at once and to burn all other confidential and secret documents.

The second message from Washington to C-in-C Pacific Fleet at Hawaii should have rung even more alarm bells.

> Tokyo One December ordered London, Hong Kong, Singapore, Batavia and Manila to destroy 'machine'. Batavia 'machine' already sent back to Tokyo. December second Washington also directed to destroy all but one copy of other systems and all secret documents.

When an embassy is ordered to destroy all its codes and ciphers and, more importantly, its code *machines*, there can be only one explanation: the embassy is about to be withdrawn and diplomatic relations broken off. Once the code machines have gone, there can be no turning back. Destruction of code and cipher machines is one of the intelligence analyst's ultimate warnings of war.

We know from the record that the Hawaiian naval intelligence staff received this intercept. Sadly, there is no evidence that Admiral Kimmel passed on this vital information to his Army counterpart, the man responsible for the defence of Hawaii, General Short. Joint command and mutual co-operation were conspicuous by their absence amongst the US forces on Oahu in the first week of December 1941.

Across the years separating us from Pearl Harbor there seems to be an almost tragic acceleration towards disaster in the last days. The US Navy, aware but not alert, struggled with the problem of what to do. It was not just an academic problem. A naval alert in Hawaii in 1941 had certain practical limitations. The manning for the ships in port was regarded as an individual captain's responsibility. Already naval families were complaining bitterly about the burden of their husbands doing extra ship duty in harbour unnecessarily. The Executive Officer of the USS *Indiana* 'thought that he might have trouble from the wives ashore unless he eased the watch bill for the crew in port'.

In their barracks ashore, a peacetime Army garrison decided that there were not enough specialists to man the new surveillance radars for more than three hours a day. They also planned to lobby Washington for more specialist manpower to be posted to the Hawaii establishment in order to start up a low-level liaison staff with the Navy. As an interim counter-sabotage measure, all the aeroplanes at Hickam Field airbase were drawn up wing tip to wing tip so that they could be better guarded. The effect was to create what a later generation of military planners would call a 'target-enriched environment' for the Japanese planes when they swooped down on Hickam Field a few days later.

There was one final chance that Hawaii could be saved from the Japanese combined fleet, which had sailed in secret from northern Japan on 26 November and was now closing on the Hawaiian Islands from the fog-shrouded waters of the North-West Pacific. Arrival was timed for Hawaiian dawn, 7 December 1941. If the USA could only see clear intentions of the Japanese attack in time, Hawaii could still be warned.

Fortunately for the intelligence specialists, one clear political indicator of the likely course of events was becoming ever more significant. The Japanese had been given a final set of diplomatic proposals for a peaceful solution by the USA, and their reply, when it came, would be crucial. It would only be a yes or no: peace or war. All efforts were diverted to listening for and unbuttoning any Japanese reply. Once again the aptly named Magic code-breakers did not fail.

The US authorities were alerted by their siginters that the Japanese Embassy in Washington was to receive a long fourteen-part top-secret message from the Japanese Foreign Ministry on or about 6 December 1941. The message was to be handed formally to the US authorities as Japan's reply to their proposals. The timing for precise delivery of the reply was to be sent in a separate message. The US code-breakers, using their Magic access to the top-secret Japanese diplomatic codes, could now intercept and read Japan's reaction as it came in. American foreknowledge of its contents might buy a few vital hours.

What happened next was the final link in the chain of mismanagement, bad organization, bureaucratic wrangling and chronic understaffing that characterized the whole story of Pearl Harbor. By 6 December it became apparent to Washington that the Japanese reply to the American proposals was being transmitted. It was duly intercepted by both Army and Navy (despite the agreement to break codes on odd and even days), and the Navy took the lead in unbuttoning and translating the signal. Unaware of the secret parallel excitement in downtown Washington, so did its official recipients, the Japanese Embassy.

About 22.00 Washington time, a Navy courier took the first thirteen parts of the Japanese reply to President Roosevelt, who read it with his aide, Harry Hopkins. Both men read the English text carefully, and Roosevelt Commented, 'This means war.' The naval courier, Lieutenant Commander Kramer, then hand-carried the highly sensitive signal around late-night Washington to a number of other senior naval officers. Eventually, seeing no sign of the fourteenth part of the signal on his return to the Navy sigint office, he went home to his bed at about 01.00 on Sunday 7 December, after a twelve-hour working day.

Across at G2 (Army) Intelligence, the same message was getting the Army treatment. This time the signal was unbuttoned and the two Army Intelligence watch officers, Colonel Rufus Bratton, Chief of the Far Eastern Section, and his deputy, Lieutenant Colonel Clyde Dusenbury, waited impatiently for the full text to arrive. By 21.30, as with the Navy, the crucial fourteenth piece had still not arrived. Unlike his naval counterpart, however, Bratton was not prepared to drive around the Washington dinner circuit late on a Saturday night. Bored and tired, for he had been working long hours as the Japanese crisis developed, Bratton went home to bed enjoining his deputy to make sure he 'showed the whole signal to General Marshall [the Army's Chief of Staff]'.

Sometime around midnight on 6/7 December 1941, Dusenbury received the final, fourteenth part of Tokyo's secret instructions to their Washington Embassy. It ordered the Japanese Ambassador to break off relations with Washington at precisely 13.00 Eastern Standard Time, which meant at 07.00 in Hawaii.

Having at last received the final part of the long-awaited message, Dusenbury tried to contact Marshall. He could not be located and so a weary Dusenbury himself decided to go to bed at about 01.30, intending to deliver the full message to the interested parties later on Sunday morning. Across town in the Navy office, the fourteenth part of the Japanese message was also sitting in Lieutenant Commander Kramer's in-tray. It, too, could be delivered in the morning. While Washington slept, nine precious hours of warning time were lost.

Early on Sunday morning the truth dawned on the key players. In the Navy building, Admiral Stark, C-in-C of the Navy, was reading the final part of the message. Colonel Bratton was frantically trying to deliver the whole fourteen parts of the Japanese reply to his Army Chief of Staff, General Marshall. President Roosevelt read the fourteenth section, given to him by the Navy, and said, 'So it looks as if the Japanese are going to break off negotiations.' But that was all.

But the fourteenth section was both damning and final. It read: 'The Imperial Japanese Government regrets to have to notify hereby the American Government that in view of the attitude of the American Government it cannot but consider that it is impossible to reach an agreement through normal negotiations.' Fortunately, the president's service chiefs were not so casual about a message which effectively gave the USA a blunt reply involving sex and travel, albeit in the language of diplomacy. The significance of the 13.00 Washington deadline was immediately obvious to both Admiral Stark and General Marshall. After urgent discussions with his colleague, the Army Chief of Staff drafted a warning to be sent priority to Hawaii as well as to all other Pacific commands. The agreed text read: 'The Japanese are presenting at 1 p.m. (13.00) Eastern Standard Time, today, what amounts to an ultimatum. Also they are under orders to destroy their code machine immediately. Just what significance the hour set may have we do not know, but be on alert accordingly.'

Now a message like this from a national command authority is not just an umbrella against any future Board of Inquiry. A regional C-in-C can use a signal like this to take whatever steps he deems appropriate, particularly at a time when even the open press is headlining a war as imminent. The message from Washington effectively devolved complete freedom on a fighting commander to act: 'be on alert accordingly'. The Fleet could have been prepared for sea; the Army could have gone on red alert and issued ammunition. Indeed, in the judgement of professional officers ever since, that is precisely what they would have done on receipt of such a message from the C-in-C to a commander in the field, given the international tension at the time and their existing knowledge of events.

Unfortunately, the message was not sent in time. Marshall released the signal to the Comms Room at about 11.30 Washington time (H hour minus one and a half hours for the Japanese attack), but the War Department message centre could not raise Hawaii on their secure radio. As a result, Colonel French, the senior signals officer, ordered Marshall's crucial warning to be sent, suitably encoded, as a civilian Western Union cable to San Francisco and thence by RCA commercial radio to Honolulu. The message was logged at 12.01 Washington time (06.01 in Hawaii). By the time Marshall's warning actually reached Hawaii, the air raids had already started and it was finally delivered by a motorcycle messenger to General Short's HQ at 11.45 Hawaii time, 17.45 in Washington. Apparently the RCA courier apologized for taking longer to deliver a cable than was normal but said that he had been obliged to 'take shelter from an air raid'.

The chain of intelligence warnings had failed completely, and despite futile last-minute attempts to alert Hawaii, the Japanese fell on to an unprepared US Fleet and land bases. Asked later by the Congressional Inquiry why he hadn't simply telephoned Hawaii, given the time constraints and the urgency on the morning of 7 December, Colonel French replied that the telephone was never used by the Message Center for overseas calls; it was considered insecure. 'If senior officers wanted to use the phone,' said French, 'then that was up to them.'

As the shock waves of the Japanese attack reverberated around the Pacific, some other fairly obvious indicators suddenly assumed a new significance.

Why they were ignored at the time remains a mystery to this day. What happened to some of those warnings remains an even bigger mystery. On 2 and 3 December, a liner, the Matson shipping company's SS *Lurline*, had been routinely monitoring the radio frequencies in the empty northern Pacific as she ploughed a lonely passage to the west towards Honolulu, outbound from San Francisco. Suddenly, on 2 December, her radio operator had been blasted by powerful signals in Japanese naval code on the lower maritime frequency. The signals were so lengthy and powerful that the ship's radio operator was able to identify the Japanese Navy's HQ call sign ('JCS') and to take bearings on them over the next two days. The radio operator plotted the signals along a bearing that placed a powerful Japanese naval force transmitting somewhere north-west of Hawaii and moving slowly *eastwards*.

When the liner docked at Hawaii two days later, the two merchant marine radio operators, like the conscientious professionals they were, went immediately to the US Naval Intelligence Office at Admiral Kimmel's Pacific Fleet HQ, turned over their logs to the duty officer and briefed him on what they had heard. The logs have never been seen since and there is no record of the warning ever having been received by the US Navy.

Another curiosity is the story of the long-awaited 'Winds Code' message, which everyone was looking out for. Usually, as the bombs finally rain down and the fighting erupts, *all* the lights on a modern electronic indicators and warning board are flashing red, like the control panel of a stricken aeroplane. Ironically, as the Japanese Navy's aircraft hurled themselves on Pearl Harbor, the most sought-for indicator of all remained stubbornly *green*. The famous 'Winds Code' message, the sure-fire sign of an impending Japanese attack, appears never to have been sent according to the documentary evidence. As with so much of the Pearl Harbor story, however, even this has been muddied by time and conflicting testimony.

Sometime before dawn on 4 December, a US Navy radioman, Ralph Briggs, a qualified Japanese-speaking radio intercept operator working at the Navy's signals intercept station, picked up the Japanese telegraphic code for 'East Wind, Rain' (*Higashi no kaze ame*) in a routine official naval weather broadcast. He dutifully logged it and transmitted it down the secure TWX circuit to Commander Safford's Fleet Intelligence Office at Pearl Harbor.

Briggs was subsequently given four days' leave by the US Navy, his reward for being the 'first man to intercept the Winds Message'. This is confirmed by the fact that Briggs was at home in Cleveland, Ohio, when the Japanese attacked. Briggs is also on record as saying on 7 December that 'the Japanese must have received a terrific surprise, as Pearl Harbor knew that they were coming'.

Across the passage of time it is impossible to follow the paper trail of Briggs's discovery. Both Safford and Briggs were adamant that they had received and reported the vital 'Winds Code' message, but in that dreadful week after the Japanese attack, some unknown agency (probably on the orders of the Director of Naval Intelligence) destroyed a significant number of vital documents in what looks suspiciously like a panicky attempt at a cover-up. An unknown number of highly classified documents were mysteriously removed in silent hours from safes on the 'second deck' of the Navy Building.

It is possible, indeed likely, that Safford's copy to Washington of the message from Hawaii found itself there, among those sensitive documents, but got no further. It could have been one of the embarrassing messages sitting in the safe of an ONI officer. We shall never know. The official Washington inquiries denied any evidence of any 'Winds Code' message and concluded, despite Safford's vehement assertions to the contrary, that the latter's memory was faulty and that he was confused by the passage of time. However, Briggs undoubtedly got his four days' home leave; if not for the 'Winds Code' message, then for what? But none of the official inquiries seem to have questioned Ralph Briggs.

One other curious mystery about Pearl Harbor has never been satisfactorily resolved. As the prospect of war loomed ever closer, the Allied intelligence services around the Pacific began to forge ever closer informal links with each other, for obvious reasons. The British intelligence services, particularly the Far East Combined Board (FECB), an out-station of the Government Communications and Cipher School (GCCS), increased their US liaison efforts, as did their co-belligerents, the Dutch. With the Netherlands overrun by the Germans in May 1940, the Dutch East Indies kept an effective independent colonial administration up and running. More importantly, it had diplomatic accreditation as representing the Dutch government in exile, now based in London.

One of its officers was a Captain of the Royal Netherlands Navy, Johan Ranneft. Captain Ranneft's duties as the Dutch Naval Attaché in Washington were to ensure that the Netherlands benefited from his presence in the USA. His main preoccupation was selling 40 mm Bofors anti-aircraft guns to the US Navy. This, while infuriating Bofors AG (the Swedish patent holders), would at least bring revenue to their co-manufacturers, the Dutch company Signaal. The US Navy was delighted with their new AA gun and afforded Ranneft all the easy, informal access that valued attachés strive so hard to achieve but so rarely obtain. For Ranneft was not only a valued friend, he was also, in the eyes of the US naval officers based in Washington, a colleague, a senior officer, a friend to US interests and overall a 'regular guy'. As a result, the Netherlands Naval Attaché often saw much more than would be normal for a foreigner. Ranneft also kept an official diary. His record is interesting.

On 6 December 1941, Captain Ranneft called at the Office of Naval Intelligence, on the 'second deck' of US Navy Headquarters. A spirited discussion was going on over the location of the Japanese combined carrier fleet. Ranneft, who knew that the Dutch East Indies were a likely Japanese target, and who regularly shared intelligence acquired from Batavia and the Dutch East Indies with his American counterparts, rapidly became absorbed in the professional discussion of Japanese intentions.

Several days before, during an earlier routine visit to the 'second deck', Ranneft had been shown the track of a Japanese carrier force in the northern Pacific by two relatively junior ONI officers. To his surprise, the plot showed them *east* of Japan and heading towards Alaska and the Aleutian Islands. Ranneft was startled and noted in his official office diary, 'ONI. They show me on the map the position of two Japanese carriers. They left Japan on an easterly course.'

Now, a few days later, Ranneft rounded on Admiral Wilkinson, the head of US Naval Intelligence: 'What about those two carriers? Where are those fellows?' Someone (Ranneft didn't remember who) pointed to a position on the chart about 400 miles *north* of the Hawaiian Islands. Ranneft was stunned, but assumed that, in the words of his official diary entry for 6 December 1941, 'I myself do not consider it, because I believe that everyone in Honolulu is 100 per cent on the alert just as everyone is at ONI.'

Ranneft reported on the same day (6 December) by official cable what he had learned to the Dutch government in exile in London. At no point was Ranneft's testimony ever read into any of the subsequent official US inquiries into the disaster at Pearl Harbor. ONI Washington resolutely denied that it ever knew where the Japanese carriers were. Certainly there is no record that they ever informed Admiral Kimmel that a powerful Japanese carrier force had been plotted 400 miles to the north of the Pacific Fleet's main base.

What makes this story all the more tragic is that Kimmel, a highly professional two-star admiral, who had only recently been promoted to acting four-star admiral (an unusual jump), actually discussed the location of the Japanese carriers with his staff on 2 December. On being informed that the Hawaiian-based Fleet Naval Intelligence Staff had no idea of the carriers' location, Kimmel dryly observed, 'So they could be rounding Diamond Head [the entrance to Pearl Harbor] at any moment?' A member of his somewhat embarrassed staff is on record as replying that 'they hoped that they would locate them before that, Admiral.' In the circumstances this exchange takes on a particular poignancy.

Years later, in 1960, the now retired Admiral Ranneft attempted to raise the subject with Admiral Stark (the senior US Naval officer in Washington during Ranneft's 1941 tour of duty) while on a valedictory visit to Washington from NATO. When Stark realized why Ranneft wanted to see him, he abruptly cancelled the meeting and refused to see the Dutch officer. No explanation was ever given.

To round off this series of mysteries about Pearl Harbor, finally we have the curious testimony of a newspaper boy. Early on Sunday 7 December 1941, sixteen-year-old Tom Nichols dropped off a copy of the Sunday edition of the *Washington Times-Herald* to one of his regular customers, the Japanese Naval Attaché, on the top floor of 3601 Connecticut Avenue, Washington, DC. To his surprise, two burly uniformed US Marines were standing guard on the attaché's door and took the newspaper from him. No one has ever explained who ordered a special US Marine guard on the Japanese Naval Attaché at dawn, Washington time, Sunday 7 December 1941; or, perhaps more significantly, *why* a guard was ordered. Even the president hadn't been shown the fourteenth part of the crucial diplomatic signal at the time the youngster delivered his papers. Only the US Navy and Lieutenant Commander Kramer of ONI in particular had that intelligence. However, US *Marines* are routinely tasked by the US Department of the *Navy*. No explanation has ever been offered for this curious side-tale to the events of 7 December 1941.

For the intelligence analyst, Pearl Harbor is unique. It presents a story of opportunities missed, intelligence ignored and bureaucratic bungling across a broad and tragic canvas. The whole mystery is also spiced by a slim, but persistent, possibility of conspiracy or cover-up. No fewer than six major national inquiries crawled over nearly every detail of the tragedy for the US authorities, all with a broadly similar aim: who knew what, and when? The inquiries were:

1. The Roberts Commission (1941) (Roberts was a Supreme Court Justice)
2. The Hart Inquiry (1944) (Hart was a senior admiral)
3. The Army Pearl Harbor Board (1944)
4. The Navy Court of Inquiry (1944)
5. The Congressional Inquiry (1945–46)
6. The Clausen Inquiry (1945)

Of these, only the top-secret Magic inquiry by Colonel Clausen, a lawyer in civilian life, had access to all the facts and, most important of all, to the surviving sigint traffic. It is hardly surprising therefore that Clausen's conclusions differ radically in a few areas from the thrust of the earlier service and political inquiries, which seem to have been primarily designed to assign blame or find scapegoats. Unfortunately, as with so much of signals intelligence during the Second World War, the real facts remained highly classified until Clausen broke his fifty-year silence in 1992.

Clausen based his post-war criticisms on a very clear understanding of who had really known what and when. By meticulously piecing together the story in 1945, mainly by flying all over the world with a live document destruction charge strapped to his body, and by shoving the top secret sigint intercepts under the noses of startled 1941 staff members, Clausen discovered that people had known much more than they admitted to the various official inquiries, *most of which had not been cleared for sigint.*

Congress, smelling a whitewash, then ordered the Army and Navy to make formal inquiry of the indicted officers. Boards were named in each of the two services and the inquiries were conducted. The Boards reported to their Army and Navy Secretaries in November 1944. The reports were suppressed by the president on the pretence to 'military security'. Now, nine months later, President Truman released the reports when he realized that an angry Congress was about to demand them. The reports had been subjected to political alterations and deletions. Kimmel and Short were again smeared and with them Hull, Marshall and Stark.

One of the biggest dangers of the secret world is excessive secrecy. Not for nothing are intelligence staffs, especially those cleared for exclusive information and locked away behind closed doors, visited only by high-ranking commanders, often known derisively as 'the secret squirrel club' by those without access to the information. The principle of need to know, designed to keep access to delicate information very tightly controlled, is a vital part of security but can also be highly dangerous, for two main reasons.

First of all, decision-makers can be denied access to information on the grounds that they have no need to know. So it was with Lieutenant General Short on Hawaii in 1941; he was not cleared for all available sigint and certainly did not know that the Navy was reading Japanese intentions. This ignorance *must* have affected his decisions before 7 December 1941. Short didn't know what he didn't know. Equally, Admiral Kimmel's refusal to show Navy intelligence to his co-commander on the island becomes understandable. Short was not cleared for the Navy's most sensitive secrets in the competitive struggle for Congressional tax money between the US armed services. Worse, Kimmel himself wasn't seeing everything the Navy was intercepting. His personal Magic code-reading machine had been removed earlier in 1941 as part of a highly secret sigint exchange deal with the British. It is clear that both senior commanders on Hawaii were blindsided to a significant degree by inter-service rivalry.

The problem was compounded by the uncoordinated organization of US national intelligence at the time. There was no national intelligence assessment staff reporting to the president. No single agency saw everything or reported the significance of the intelligence. Everyone had their own piece of the jigsaw, but no one was making them put all their pieces on the table to complete the whole puzzle. In the circumstances it seems harsh to put all the blame on the two commanders in Hawaii. Although Clausen compares them to 'sentries who fell asleep on watch', it is hard not to feel some sympathy with Kimmel and Short, who were both subsequently disgraced and took the bulk of the blame for the debacle.

Second, and much more serious, the 'secret squirrel mentality' can sometimes be used to conceal errors. There seems to be little doubt that in the aftermath of Pearl Harbor, secrecy prevented an honest and thorough evaluation of the facts. Much of the real truth never came out in the earlier inquiries. The question is whether 'national security' was used as a cloak to hide war-winning secrets from an enemy (that America could read the Japanese codes) or as an excuse to conceal embarrassing and politically explosive mistakes. The answer, unhelpfully, is probably both.

There is another, perhaps psychological reason for the disaster. In 1941 every expert *knew* that Pearl Harbor could not be attacked. The US Pacific Fleet's base was simply too far from Japan or any other likely enemy, the anchorage too secure and well guarded, and the surrounding hills and shallow anchorage made any torpedo attack a technical impossibility. The received wisdom of the day was that Pearl Harbor was invulnerable.

Unfortunately, what had been true in 1939 was no longer valid in 1941. On 11 November 1940, the Royal Navy, in one of the most successful and least acknowledged actions of the Second World War, caught the Italian battle fleet at anchor at Taranto in southern Italy. Eleven special torpedoes from obsolescent Swordfish biplanes sank or disabled three Italian battleships and two heavy cruisers and effectively neutralized Mussolini's Navy in a daring night attack launched from British carriers off the coast.

An abiding American trait, often remarked upon by friends and enemies alike, is the 'not invented here' syndrome. With the confidence of youth and the limitless power of the most developed, innovative and successful economy in history, Americans tend only to trust American ideas and developments and tend to ignore or resent others' achievements, be they weapons, consumer goods or even TV shows.

The US Navy virtually ignored the lessons of Taranto. The Imperial Japanese Navy, on the other hand, recognized it as the remarkable strategic victory it undoubtedly was, and set out to recreate the British success in their own doctrine. In the words of the Japanese Naval Staff, 'Taranto made Pearl Harbor feasible.'

In particular, the Japanese naval aviators were curious as to just how the Royal Navy had been able to air-launch torpedoes to run in such a shallow anchorage. By trial and error the Japanese discovered that aerial torpedoes can be modified to surface immediately and not 'dig deep' after dropping provided they are rigged with special hydrofoils or fins. The superlative Japanese torpedoes, already the best in the world, were rigged with special fins like the British ones for air-dropping in late 1941 and tested for shallow launch. They worked, and suddenly the attack on the anchored fleet in the shallow waters of Pearl Harbor became a practical possibility. This was one piece of techint (technical intelligence) that the USA didn't discover until it was too late, although, ironically, it was freely available from the Royal Navy had they only been asked. But then, in the complacency and insularity before Pearl Harbor in 1941, the US Navy felt that it had little to learn. Not so the Japanese.

Whatever the psychology of technical surprise in 1941, it is possible to dissect the attack on Pearl Harbor by straightforward reference to the intelligence cycle which we laid out in Chapter 1 as a tool for approaching intelligence in a calm and logical way. Analysis of this basic planning system shows clearly the deficiencies of the US intelligence and warning system in 1941, and is worth a careful study.

Was there an overall US national intelligence requirement?

No. Although all the players knew that war with Japan was either a possibility or imminent, and each organization appears to have been busy collecting intelligence on its own, there is no evidence of any coordinated *national* collection requirement.

Was there a collection plan?

Again, no. Within the single service preoccupations (naval intelligence was interested in the Japanese fleet, the FBI was looking out for Japanese spies ashore, etc.) there was obviously planned and tasked collection. But it was never integrated and assets were duplicated or wasted.

Were collection assets coordinated and tasked?

No. Each service or agency did its own thing without reference to others. For example, in 1941 the FBI's Chief of Station on Honolulu was one Robert L. Shivers. His primary interest was security: spies, sabotage and subversion. With a large Japanese population on the Hawaiian Islands this was a task the FBI took very seriously, despite Hoover's disregard for agent Tricycle's Abwehr questionnaire. To ensure smooth working arrangements, Shivers established weekly liaison with his service counterparts on the islands, Commander Joe Rochefort of the US Navy and Lieutenant Colonel George Bicknell of Army G2. Shivers was particularly interested in the Japanese Consul-General on Hawaii and so he was excited to learn that US Navy Intelligence had been secretly tapping the consul's office telephone for over a year. As wire taps were officially within the remit of the FBI, Shivers decided to add his own line into the Japanese Consul-General as well. Unfortunately, the telephone company immediately informed the original 'bugger', Captain Mayfield of the US Navy, that another federal agency wanted to get in on the act. Worried about the breach of security and concerned for the political repercussions if the Japanese discovered they were under surveillance, on 2 December 1941, Mayfield decided to bail out and ordered an immediate halt to any US Navy taps on the Japanese Consul-General. No one told Shivers of this, however, and none the wiser he then decided not to proceed with the FBI tap. As a result, in the critical last week before the attack, no US agency was bugging the Japanese diplomats on Hawaii, and no one realized it had stopped.

Was intelligence collated in an accessible and ready format?

Again, no. Single services and agencies squirrelled away their own precious nuggets with no regard for the wider picture and reported independently, if at all, to their masters. In the modern jargon of intelligence there was no 'integrated all-source database' on the Japanese.

Was the available intelligence interpreted correctly?

The answer to this is both yes *and* no. For example, the Magic sigint take was correctly assessed and interpreted as leading to war with Japan. Although the location of the Japanese combined carrier fleet was either ignored, suppressed or misunderstood by ONI, the majority of intelligence received was understood correctly. The problem appears to have been that although its meaning was understood, its *implications* were ignored or overlooked. The whole institutional psychology at the time must also have been influenced by the pervasive contempt for the Asiatic Japanese as any kind of credible enemy. The American interpreters of intelligence – at all levels, from the president downwards – completely underestimated the Japanese both technologically and as warriors.

Was the interpreted intelligence disseminated to decision-makers in a timely fashion?

The answer to this must be an emphatic no, from top to bottom. Thus the president and decision-taking Washington were not alerted to the fourteen-part message from the Japanese Foreign Ministry in time to act upon it; Admiral Kimmel and Hawaii were left unwarned at the last minute; vital naval operational indicators disappeared between Hawaii and the Navy Department; and the unfortunate Army commander in Hawaii seems to have been kept in the dark throughout. The dissemination of intelligence before Pearl Harbor was not just a sorry tale: it was *appalling*. There was no all-source integration of material, no all-source assessment and no briefing to those with a need to know.

If there is any single factor that links all these failures of US intelligence in 1941, it lies in the phrase 'all-source integration'. Nowadays it is axiomatic that a single assessment and tasking staff must coordinate and integrate a nation's intelligence effort at the highest level like any other scarce resource. This principle is easy to state, but desperately difficult to achieve. Every agency has its own special monopoly of secrets, and equally, every agency is reluctant to tell its colleagues, for two reasons, one good and one bad. The laudable reason is invariably security. A secret shared with another agency, without the strictest need-to-know criteria, is usually viewed as a potential loss of control of a vital source and thus of secrecy. The second reason is less edifying but understandable. Any bureaucratic agency holding a monopoly of a secret source can usually guarantee for itself access to politicians, power and resources. In the constant US bureaucratic battle for political advantage, agencies are reluctant to share their victories with others and only too keen to seize more offices and better budgets in the corridors of power.

This puts an enormous responsibility on the ultimate decision-makers, usually the politicians, for they are the only people with the authority and control of national resources to command the agencies to work together. Even if this means a specialist assessment staff (like the UK's Joint Intelligence Committee or JIC) *above* competing agencies, someone has to integrate the effort. In the final analysis politicians have to knock civil servants' and military heads together.

In December 1941, the one clear omission in Washington was of a national intelligence assessment and briefing staff, with access to all available intelligence from every source. With the lunacy of the Navy briefing on odd days and the Army on even days, Roosevelt was effectively cast as his own co-ordinator and tasker of political-military intelligence. It is a job he did very badly which, given his other responsibilities and lack of understanding of the Japanese, is hardly surprising. He was not equipped as an analyst of the Japanese military mind and he never knew just what was *not* being shown to him. His service chiefs failed him. And in their turn, the service chiefs' specialist intelligence staffs failed their masters too. The truth is that they, and the nation as a whole, consistently underestimated both the capabilities and intentions of the Japanese as a potential adversary.

Whatever the excuses, and whatever the failings of subordinates at all levels, the brutal fact remains that the USA had ample and timely intelligence of a Japanese surprise attack somewhere in the Pacific and probably on Pearl Harbor from a wide variety of indicators and sources. Because the nation's chief executive failed to establish an integrated national intelligence organization in time and to control the Washington bureaucracy, over 2,000 US servicemen died and America was plunged into a war which might have been avoided.

The final judgement on Pearl Harbor must be that the president and US government of the day were to blame, aided and abetted by their senior advisers. Kimmel and Short, the 'fall guys', seem to be as much victims as those killed and wounded on 7 December 1941. There was no conspiracy to drag the USA into a world war, although Churchill was undeniably delighted to welcome the USA as an ally in Britain's struggle. (As, ironically, was Adolf Hitler: in a strange echo of Churchill, Hitler expressed himself delighted at Japan's entry into the war. Indeed, his jubilation may explain his misreading of the real significance of America's involvement and his rash declaration of war on the USA. On hearing the news of Pearl Harbor, the Führer rushed in to see a Nazi Party crony, Walther Hewel, and exclaimed, 'Now we have an ally who has never been vanquished in 3,000 years!')

At the end of the day, Pearl Harbor stands as an awful warning of the ultimate intelligence blunder perpetrated by a badly organized and uncoordinated group of parochial intelligence providers who had the tools but didn't know how to do the job properly. In the words of the 1946 Congressional Inquiry, 'With some of the finest intelligence in our history, with the almost certain knowledge that war was at hand, with plans that contemplated the precise sort of attack that was executed on the morning of 7 December 1941 – why was it possible for Pearl Harbor to succeed?'

5

'THE GREATEST DISASTER EVER TO BEFALL BRITISH ARMS' – SINGAPORE, 1942

'The city of Singapore must be converted into a citadel and defended to the death. No surrender can be contemplated, and the Commander, Staffs and principal officers are expected to perish at their posts'

WINSTON CHURCHILL

The British loss of Malaya and the fall of Singapore in 1941–42 were consequences of perhaps the most dangerous intelligence vice of all: underestimating the enemy.

Winston Churchill described it as the 'greatest disaster ever to befall British arms'. On 15 February 1942, the British imperial garrison of the supposedly impregnable bastion of Singapore, on the southernmost tip of Malaya, surrendered to a numerically far smaller Japanese assault force. Some 130,000 well-equipped British, Australian and Indian officers and soldiers, with ample battle stocks, capitulated to just 35,000 hungry, exhausted Japanese front-line combat troops, almost out of ammunition and at their last gasp. The Japanese were astonished at the ease of their victory. In the brief but martial history of the British Empire, no greater military humiliation can be found.

Only 9,000 of the total of 60,000 Japanese soldiers became casualties in the whole Malayan campaign. The British-led force lost 146,000, of which over 130,000 surrendered. Many of those Allied prisoners of war later died in appalling conditions in Japanese captivity. We have to go back to the Athenian defeat at Syracuse in 415 BC to find comparison for the debacle at Singapore: both effectively marked the beginning of the end of a great maritime empire.

The root cause of the British defeat was, like so many defeats, to be found in poor intelligence. Combined with the Western underestimation of the Japanese as a potential adversary was the breathtaking smugness and complacency of successive British governments and the colonial regime in Malaya, which appears to have sleepwalked into a major war in the Far East sure in the knowledge that 'it can't possibly happen to us'. Only on Sunday, 15 February 1942, as the victorious Japanese rounded up the tens of thousands of demoralized, drunk and deserted British and Indian troops, ad hoc Royal Navy shore parties, fleeing RAF ground staff, thousands of drunken and mutinous Australian deserters (many of whom had basically 'withdrawn their labour' in a kind of military strike in the last days) and the rest of Lieutenant General Percival's humiliated command on Singapore – only then did it really dawn on the British in Malaya that their world was gone for ever.

If they were in any doubt, numerous bayonetings and rapes by the Japanese of the terrified civilian population put them absolutely in the picture. The day of unquestioned rule by the white *tuans* in Asia was ended, and their long nightmare of three and a half years of captivity at the hands of the Japanese was about to begin. The wretched inhabitants of Malaya had merely swapped an Asian colonial occupying force for the British, but the myth of white superiority in Asia had been exposed once and for all as fiction. Things would never be the same again.

For years before the outbreak of the Second World War, the British had watched the rise of Imperial Japan's maritime power in the East with mounting unease. During the First World War the Japanese had actually been allies of the British in their long hunt to sweep the Pacific free from German surface raiders. Yet the Versailles peace treaty of 1919 had come as a bitter disappointment to at least one of the supposedly victorious powers. Although Japan was given a mandate over some German colonial territories, the Japanese felt that their contribution to the war had not been sufficiently recognized. This resentment at being deprived of the spoils of victory sharpened after the Washington Naval Conference of 1922 when Japan was theoretically locked into an inferior maritime position in the Pacific by a new treaty favouring the United States.

Japan had only been opened up to Western influences in the late 1850s. The medieval political mechanisms within the Shogunate state were, by Western democratic standards, primitive and more akin to today's developing world, where the power of the military often permits a disproportionate influence on politics. As the global economic stresses of the late 1920s and 1930s swirled round Japan, the military seized political power and began a policy of armed expansion to guarantee Japan access to the economic riches and raw materials of the East, readily available to those prepared to seize them for itself by armed force. In 1931, the Army Party engineered an invasion of Manchuria, thus lighting the fuse for the long sequence of military and political expansion that would finally explode at Pearl Harbor and Malaya a decade later, on 7 December 1941.

The British colonies in Malaya were a particularly tempting target for Japanese economic aggrandizement. During the 1930s, Japan had managed to secure a plentiful supply of coal by conquest from China, but she still lacked other vital raw materials, especially iron, tin, oil and rubber. Further attempts to go north had been decisively crushed by the Soviet Army at the Battle of Khalkhin Gol on the Mongolian border in 1939. Japan turned south. By 1940, in response to Japanese expansion into French Indochina, the USA had slowly begun to apply political pressure to freeze out Japanese imports and other economic activity from the US and its territories. The result was that by mid-1941, the Japanese Economic Planning Board could forecast, fairly accurately, the moment when Japan would no longer be able to function owing to lack of raw materials. The Japanese planners also predicted (with a chilling clarity unusual among government planners) that 'it will be impossible to obtain oil… by peaceful means.'

In Japanese eyes, the only answer to pressing shortages of strategic supplies now lay far to the south: the prosperous, ill-defended and peaceful colonies of British Malaya and the Dutch East Indies. Malaya with its tin and rubber was regarded as little more than a cash cow by the British, earning a fortune in dollars every year for the City of London and helping to subsidize the war against Hitler in Europe and the Middle East. The defeated government of the Netherlands, now in exile in London, was effectively sustained by the rich outpourings of the Royal Dutch Shell oil wells in the East Indies. Possession of these two colonies would enable Japan to become industrially independent; and neither Britain nor the Dutch seemed to be capable of defending their assets to any marked extent.

To protect their economic empire in the East after the Great War, successive British governments had established a fleet anchorage and naval bastion based on the harbour and island of 'Fortress Singapore'. The intention was clear: to provide a fixed defended point that could hold out, whatever happened, like some embattled medieval castle until the Royal Navy could send a fleet from Britain to relieve the beleaguered fortress and sweep away the importunate invaders. The British were deceiving the Empire, despite bold words in Parliament. But as the Romans had proved over many centuries, nearly 2,000 years earlier, the only way to defend a far-flung empire was to have a strong mobile force able to deploy rapidly using internal lines to any threatened point on the perimeter. When war did come later and Britain was pinned down fighting in Europe, this was the one thing that Churchill could never guarantee. The Western Desert campaign, Crete and Greece in 1941 all siphoned off any resources that could have protected Britain's Eastern Empire.

In cold print, this imperial policy looks remarkably suspect as a strategic concept, posing as many questions as it answers. For how long would the naval base have to hold out? What size of relieving force would be required? How many days would it take to assemble a fleet and sail it to the Far East? Why was Britain spending a fortune on *Singapore* when the real colonial asset that needed protecting was the extraordinary wealth of the *Malay Peninsula*, producing over 60 per cent of the world's rubber and tin? How was it to be paid for? With Malayan colonial money or by the straitened taxpayers of the 'Great White King across the sea', who were already feeling the pains of the Great Depression?

Armed with these doubts and a cunning Treasury that used the government's policy of 'no war within the next ten years' as a device for avoiding expenditure, Britain brought the allegedly impregnable fortress of Singapore into being slowly and inefficiently during the 1920s and 1930s at enormous cost and without a single integrated defence plan. In 1924, Winston Churchill had become the Chancellor of the Exchequer. In setting budget priorities, Churchill made deep cuts to the Royal Navy, confident that the US's involvement in the Washington Treaty would help keep Japan in check. He was mistaken. In fact the final product was anything but impregnable.

The main approach through the Malayan forests to the north was virtually ignored by the planners, despite warnings, and the airfields built all over Malaya by the fledgling RAF were constructed without consultation with the Army's tactical needs for ground defence. Even so, the illusion of security was there.

Although the great base and its peacetime garrison provided little or no real defence at all, the expatriates living their comfortable peacetime lives in Malaya and the cinema-going audiences in the West genuinely believed the propaganda they were shown on the screen: that Singapore was one of the greatest fortifications the world had ever seen. This might explain the curious lack of concern when the Japanese did finally invade northern Malaya. Singapore was impregnable. It might also explain the subsequent panic and loss of nerve when it looked as if the unbelievable was actually happening and the 'Gibraltar of the East' was about to fall in February 1942.

The one consistent voice in the planning for the defence of Singapore between the wars is a surprising one: Winston Churchill. He had been the Chancellor of the Exchequer in 1928 who had starved the project of building funds, and he had been one of the arch-advocates of the defence policy that based all expenditure on 'no war within the next ten years'; a risky approach to international security. With megalomaniacs like Hitler roaming loose, events such as policy shifts happen very quickly. Churchill's record was damning on Malaysia and Singapore. As a former First Lord of the Admiralty, he had also argued passionately *against* the Royal Navy's coldly realistic estimate of the true cost of a genuinely defensible naval base in Singapore; and finally, as prime minister he was ultimately responsible for the disastrous defence of Malaya between 1940 and 1942.

Despite the myth of Churchill the great war leader, Singapore was most definitely not Winston Churchill's finest hour. This may well be the reason that no parliamentary inquiry was ever held on the debacle, although Churchill had ordered an inquiry into the disaster in Crete in May 1941 with commendable alacrity. It may also be why so many of the official government files on the Malayan campaign remain closed to this day. If there is a single individual responsible for the debacle of Singapore then the most likely candidate is Winston Spencer Churchill. Even he acknowledged his failure, growling privately to the editor of *The Times* in early 1942 that he might lay down his premiership: 'I am an old man. No man should have to bear the disasters I have had.' He also – not unreasonably – blamed the army.

The top brass agreed with their despairing leader. Wavell wrote to the War Office that 'the real trouble is that we have lost a great deal of our hardness and fighting spirit… '.

Alan Brooke added that, 'the real reason is directly due to a low standard of discipline and morale… among Britain's citizen army.' Britons just didn't want to fight, as Singapore proved.

The Australian government was especially wary of Churchill by 1941. The relationship between the two countries was politically ambiguous and both sides had based their defence needs before the war on a series of highly suspect guarantees and false premises. To Churchill, Australia was little more than a potential base in the East and a ready supply of fresh Commonwealth divisions to eke out Britain's small army. Any promise or reassurance that could lock Australia into this relationship and prise more manpower out of the dominion was freely given. For example, when he was First Lord of the Admiralty, Churchill went to great lengths to reassure the Australian minister, Richard Casey, in late 1939 that Britain was even prepared to abandon the Mediterranean should it become necessary to save Australia. This was a promise he could not honour.

Not all the deceit was on the British side, however. In peacetime it had suited Australian governments to ignore defence and pretend that the old country would pay for Australian security. Military spending was thus kept at less than 1 per cent of the government's budget during the 1930s. Australians were fed on the fiction that the British were primarily responsible for their defence and would automatically come to their rescue if the worst happened. This arrangement was encouraged by Australian politicians ever mindful of the American saying that 'there ain't no votes in bullets', even though a moment's sober reflection might have led them to wonder why the British should be able to send a fleet in war when they had never been able to dispatch one in peacetime. But no one asked awkward questions like that. It was all too politically convenient to get someone else to pay for your defence, however false the premises.

When Churchill finally took over the premiership from Neville Chamberlain in May 1940, he had eyed events in the Far East and the Japanese threat with growing concern. Fine speeches and rhetoric were no substitute for a credible and well-resourced imperial defence policy. The year of 1941 was to expose his strategic reassurances as dangerous gambles with the security of Australia and the East, concentrating on the war in North Africa and aid to a beleaguered Soviet Union.

As the year 1941 opened, and after their decisive rebuff by the Soviets at Khalkhin Gol had blocked expansion north into Siberia, the Japanese turned their attention to the south. In early summer, Thailand, directly to the north of Malaya, had a brief war with the Vichy French regime in Indochina over a border dispute. By June 1941 the Japanese, under the guise of mediating between the combatants, had established a formidable military presence in Indochina (one estimate is 200,000 troops) and were pushing hard for a military presence in, and transit rights through, Thailand. For the first time, northern Malaya was directly threatened. The subsequent Japanese move into the airfields of southern Indochina suddenly brought their bombers well within range of the Malay Peninsula.

British intelligence had followed these developments with increasing interest and growing alarm. The British were hampered in their intelligence efforts, however, by four fundamental problems: a complete underestimation of the Japanese armed services as effective fighting forces; fragmentation and lack of any real intelligence co-ordination in the Far East; a serious shortage of local resources for collecting intelligence; and finally a dangerous lack of any influence in the war councils of the civil and military staffs in Malaya.

Of these, without doubt the worst failing was the first: the underestimation of the Japanese as a viable adversary. In many ways this is surprising, given that Japan was a warrior nation with an impressive track record. They had trounced the Russians in the Far East in 1904–05, possessed a large and modern fleet, and had been successfully fighting a major ground war in China and Manchuria since 1931. To understand quite why this dramatic underestimation of an enemy came about it is necessary to enter the mindset of the white colonial world before the shocks of 1941.

Britain was not alone in her contempt for 'Asiatics' as little more than clever natives. Even in America, which had a large Japanese immigrant population, on the eve of Pearl Harbor the Japanese were generally seen in a similar light. The myths of racial superiority were not confined to Hitler's Nazi Germany in the 1930s. The British view is best summed up by the then C-in-C Far East, Air Chief Marshal Sir Robert Brooke-Popham, on a visit to Hong Kong in December 1940:

> I had a good look at them [the Japanese guards on the frontier] close up across the barbed wire, of various subhuman species dressed in dirty grey uniform... If they represent the average of the Japanese army, although the problems of their food and accommodation should be simple enough, I cannot believe that they would form an effective fighting force.

At the time it was genuinely believed that the Japanese were physically small, buck-toothed, had poor eyesight and were incapable of fighting in the dark or operating sophisticated machinery. White men were inherently superior. The feeling was widespread. One naval expert even wrote, 'Every observer concurs... that the Japanese are daring but incompetent aviators... they have as a race defects in the tubes of the inner ear, just as they are generally myopic. This gives them a defective sense of balance.' The Japanese 'could not fire rifles because they could not close only one eye at a time'. An otherwise serious writer on aviation matters observed that 'nothing is much more stupid than one Japanese, and nothing much brighter than two.' There was a view that 'terrified Japanese would flee at the first sight of a white soldier'. The commanding officers of two British infantry battalions in Malaya are on record as saying to their generals that they hoped 'we aren't getting too strong in Malaya... as it might deter the Japs from a fight'. Perhaps most arrogant of all is the remark by *another* CO: 'Don't you think my soldiers are worthy of a better enemy than the Japs?'

This was dangerous nonsense. The reality of operations against Japanese imperial forces came as a profound shock to all the Allied combatants, on the ground, in the air and at sea. The Australian Russell Braddon looked aghast at the first Japanese bodies he came across in Malaya, 'not a specimen under six foot tall, with not a pair of glasses or a buck-tooth between them'. And as for

Japan's alleged technical deficiencies, while the British did not have a single tank on the Malay Peninsula, the Japanese, despite their supposed inability to operate machinery effectively, had managed to land armour in the north and used their light tanks to great effect against the static British defensive positions on the main roads.

The dismay at GHQ Malaya was profound: everyone knew – it was a matter of British operational doctrine – that tanks could *never* be used in the jungle. Anyway, Intelligence had assured successive British planners that there was absolutely no armoured threat from the Japanese. Now there was a Japanese combined infantry and tank assault slicing straight through the British jungle defences and heading south for Johore and Singapore.

The Japanese had also developed new tactics (the majority of the battles in 1941–42 in Malaya were fought not in thick jungle but in primary forest or rubber plantations with good spaces between the trees and visibility, akin to a beech wood) that involved thrusting hard and swiftly down the main axes of of the modern Malayan roads. Once they were halted, the Japanese infantry deployed swiftly into the trees on either side, firing as they went and outflanking the dug-in defensive positions blocking the track. By using these so-called 'fishbone' tactics, they consistently outflanked the bewildered and static imperial heavy infantry, forcing a perpetual morale-sapping retreat on the increasingly exhausted and despondent Australians, British and Indians.

The baffled defenders trudged wearily back through the January monsoon rain to the next roadblock to the south, leaving a trail of abandoned equipment, guns, stores and wounded comrades in their wake for the Japanese to do with as they chose. To make things worse, the retreating foot soldiers often saw the Japanese using *bicycles* to cycle past them through the trees, making their lightly equipped troops significantly more mobile than the encumbered imperial infantry. British intelligence knew nothing of these 'secret weapons' until the after-action reports were collated in India after the disaster.

In the air, the same tale of underestimating the potential enemy unfolded. It was thought that Japanese pilots – even if their aviation industry had been able to provide them with sophisticated modern aircraft that were mechanically efficient – would be quite incapable of operating them to Western standards as 'Japanese aircrew could not withstand the rigours of high G forces'. As the first bombing raids thundered down on the RAF's airfields, the derisive British airmen poured scorn on the so-called 'diarrhoea' bombing tactics where tight formations of bombers dropped their loads simultaneously on to an area target. This was not the individual precision bombing operation the RAF trained for.

The raids were remarkably successful, however. Using tactics developed in four years of area raids on targets in China, the Japanese aircrew knew their business. On the order to release from a master bomber, Japanese bombs fell in a broad pattern that turned out to be a highly effective tactic for airfield denial, ensuring that some damage was *always* done to the target. And, in a curious development that puzzled the air staff in Malaya, the Japanese bombers always seemed to know just when and what to strike.

Another unpleasant surprise in the air, unforeseen by air intelligence, was the high-performance capability of Japanese aircraft, especially the Navy '0' fighter, the Zero. Dismissed as little more than an 'unarmoured, under-armed light sports plane with a 1,000 horse-power engine on the front', in the words of one American analyst, the Zero's dragonfly manoeuvrability came as a traumatic shock to Allied pilots unaware of its phenomenal dogfighting capabilities. The crews of the outnumbered and obsolete Brewster Buffalo fighters of RAF Malaya swiftly learned that they were outclassed.

Although a little later than the Singapore story, perhaps the best example of this underestimation of the Japanese in the air is the contact between the 'Darwin Wing' ferrying new American P-40 fighters out to the Far East and the Zeros escorting a Japanese bombing raid on Australia's Northern Territories in early 1942. The action was a memorable one, and not for reasons that the seasoned Battle of Britain fighter squadrons newly arrived in Australia wanted to remember. As the experienced British pilots broke into the diving Zeros (as was their successful operating procedure with the Luftwaffe's Messerschmitt 109s), the Japanese pilots promptly turned expertly inside them and effortlessly shot down eleven out of twelve P-40s inside five minutes with only one loss to themselves. This humiliation was not lost on the British and for the rest of the Pacific war *all* Allied pilots, both British and American, learned to rely on the superior diving speed and firepower of their fighters and never to try to out-turn the lightweight Zero in a turning dogfight.

In fact RAF intelligence in Malaya had known all about the Zero and its fighting capabilities long before the war. In May 1941 the Chinese had downed one of the new Japanese fighters near Chungking and produced a comprehensive air intelligence report warning of its fighting potential. This intelligence eventually got to London where the Air Ministry passed it to the co-ordinating staff for all intelligence in Malaya, the FECB or Far East Combined Bureau. In Malaya, despite its clear significance – of all the services, aviation depends on technical superiority more than any other – the information was not just ignored: the Secret Air Staff Technical Intelligence report disappeared!

This is not to say that the FECB failed to alert the services in Malaya to the overall Japanese threat. An accurate and clear General Staff Malaya intelligence memorandum exists from mid-1941 that spells out the Japanese order of battle and weapons capabilities in some detail. The problem was that the information, even when it was supplied, appears to have been largely ignored by the operational staffs, the units and particularly the politicians. So much so that the day before war broke out, one of the military staff officers on the GHQ staff said publicly that he 'couldn't understand why the Governor had got the wind up and mobilized the local volunteer forces'. Even the day before the Japanese invaded, the politicians vacillated. The unfortunate C-in-C Brooke-Popham, on asking if he should execute Operation Matador (an advance into Thailand to block off the narrowest part of the Kra Peninsula), was met with the reply from London on 6 December 'that he could act at his discretion'. His Chief of Staff, contemplating his troubled chief, said dryly, 'They've made you personally responsible for declaring war on Japan, sir.'

If the British and their intelligence service underestimated the threat from Japan, then the Japanese did not make the same mistake about the British. Japanese intelligence efforts for their campaign in Malaya before the war were comprehensive, thorough and well resourced. The aggressor always has the initiative, even in intelligence, and for more than ten years the Japanese intelligence service had been able to build up a sophisticated intelligence organization largely based on the numbers of legitimate Japanese companies and business activities trading in Malaya, with their 7,000 Japanese residents and visitors. In addition, there was a steady commercial sea traffic in small boats along the eastern coast; many of the Japanese craft included naval officers on reconnaissance missions. It was later claimed that even the official photographer to the Singapore naval base was a serving Japanese intelligence officer, Colonel Nakajima.

This Japanese intelligence activity was well known in Malaya. The head of the Straits Settlement Police, writing after the war, claimed that the extent of Japanese espionage had compelled him to recommend to the Governor that at least half of any Japanese company's workforce must in future be non-Japanese labour. Nothing was done. The policy from London was to do nothing that might antagonize the Japanese, in case it provoked them to attack.

Sometimes Japanese spying was so blatant that it became farcical. In late 1940 the Japanese Press Attaché in Singapore, Mamoru, was arrested in flagrante and eventually jailed by the British authorities for three and a half years for openly running espionage agents in Malaysia (including a British Army corporal) and in particular for offering *guided tours of British barracks and military installations* to Japanese army officers visiting Malaya. The most blatant examples of all were the unauthorized mooring of two Japanese submarines in the Malayan harbour of Endau, which was owned by a Japanese mining company, and the remarkable testimony of Captain Collinge of the Straits Volunteers. In September or October 1940, he saw a Japanese officer, in full Japanese Army uniform, observing a squadron of British armoured cars on exercise before coolly embarking on a motor boat and heading out to sea in the gathering dusk, 'presumably to rendezvous with a Japanese ship offshore'. When he reported this, Collinge was told by two British civilians on the Governor's staff not to make an issue of it, 'as the policy of H.M. Government… was to appease the Japs and to avoid provoking an incident at all costs'.

Across the years we can only imagine the fury of the helpless FECB officers in Malaya collating this intelligence and vainly trying to warn the military authorities at GHQ. The greater the truth, the greater the potential provocation, made worse by the peaceful languor of colonial life in a humid semitropical paradise where the Governor, the Colonial Civil Service and the old Malaya hands ruled supreme. No one, and certainly not the white *tuans* out to make their commercial fortune in Malaya, wanted to prepare for the worst. Malaya was a long way from the war, and life, for the Colonial British, was good. Raffles Hotel reported booming business; civilians still packed the cricket club bar and girls would dance with punters for 6d a time. The war and the Japanese could have been miles away.

They weren't. If the British were unprepared for a war in Malaya, then the Japanese most certainly were not. We are fortunate that the chief operational planner of General Yamashita's victorious 25th Army, Colonel Masanobu Tsuji, Imperial General Staff, has left a full account of the planning for the seizure of Malaya. Planning for the invasion began on 15 September 1941 and was accompanied by an intensive programme of aerial reconnaissance. As the date of the invasion drew nearer the busy Japanese pilots conducted ever more blatant overflights of RAF airfields and installations, many of which were detected by the British. On one flight on 22 October 1941, Tsuji actually went along himself in a Japanese Type 100 'Diana' reconnaissance aircraft as it flew directly over the sites of the landing beaches at Kota Bharu and the RAF base at Alor Star at only 6,000 feet. Many of these flights were noticed by the RAF but no action was taken.

A second, even more thought-provoking example is the story of Air Technician Peter Shepherd, then eighteen years old, who was serving as an RAF aircraftsman at the forward airfield of Sungei Petani in northern Malaya in December 1941. Shepherd, a highly trained RAF Halton apprentice, was one of the numerous intelligent, well-educated young men who were attracted before the war by Lord Trenchard's vision of a new technical elite for Britain's youngest armed service.

On 4 December 1941, Shepherd was ordered to fly as stand-in crew on a Dutch East Indies civilian Lockheed Hudson as the Dutch technician had been taken ill. In his own words:

To my surprise we landed in Cambodia on a private landing airfield in the south at a place near Kampot. As French Indochina was virtually in Japanese hands at the time, this made Cambodia a pretty dangerous place for a Dutch plane to land. The French authorities were of course liberally sprinkled with pro-Vichy elements and so no friends of the British in 1941.

My own position as an RAF serviceman in civilian clothing was therefore highly dangerous. To make things worse, on the way north, the Dutch pilot divulged that the real purpose of the trip was to collect a single British passenger under cover of what sounded to me like a clandestine commercial flight smuggling contraband. To me this looked like a combination of agent-running and smuggling. I had been told none of this before we took off. I thought we were going to Thailand, which was neutral, not to Cambodia, so I was extremely unhappy as you can imagine. I decided to stay out of the way on the ground.

Later in the day the pilot took me to a restaurant to eat. There were only the two of us. The pilot went off into the back of the kitchen to do some business, probably about the cargo. I was only eighteen and stranded in a strange country in civilian clothes. I thought I could be shot as a spy, so I was fairly frightened as you can imagine, and kept my head well down.

At the restaurant, an Oriental came up to me and offered me some of his Tiger Balm for my mosquito bites, which were pretty bad. He started to talk, but I could hardly understand a word. I gathered from his mixture of broken English and sign language that he was a Jap civilian and some sort of aircraft engineer himself. After all, 'engineer' sounds the same the whole world over. He thought I was a *French* aircraft engineer. He seemed very pleased about something and kept trying to talk to me. He was pretty drunk, mainly on cognac. We communicated in a weird mixture of sign language and place names and eventually he pulled out his diary and a map and tried to tell me where he had been and what he was doing there.

He indicated that he had sailed on an aircraft carrier from Japan to Hitokappu Bay north of Japan and had seen a huge armada assembled there. On 24 November, he had been flown south to Phu Quoc Island to supervise some urgent operational modifications on the bomb racks of the Japanese planes based in southern Cambodia.

He seemed very proud of what he was doing and what he had seen and indicated that we were the only people who knew about the fleet, and that it had been planning to sail on 26 November to obliterate the US fleet in Pearl Harbor and to launch a simultaneous invasion of Malaya and Singapore. He explained this with lots of signs and 'boom, booms'. When I indicated surprise, he dragged out a kind of diary book and even showed me a few rough sketches of some of the naval ships that he said he had seen moored the week before to convince me.

I realized it was important, so when he staggered out to the lavatory, I stole the drawings from his book. He got even more drunk after he came back, and when the pilot told me it was time to go I left my new friend vomiting over the verandah rail.

On returning to Malaya the next day, 5 December, I immediately reported all I had been told to the RAF Station intelligence officer. Later that morning I was flown down to Kuala Lumpur where I was interrogated by two civilians whom I took to be intelligence officers. I handed over the sketches that the Japanese engineer had drawn and went through all the details yet again. During the course of my interview I said that I believed the Japanese to have been telling the truth as he saw it, and we agreed that *if* all the details of his story were true, then the time of the supposed attack would probably be in three days on 8 December [7 December Hawaii time, because of the International Date Line]. I flew back north to Sungei Petani that afternoon with strict instructions to keep my mouth shut once I got back to the station.

Nothing happened after I got back. Despite the state of emergency the airfield never even went on full war alert, much to my surprise, and the next thing I knew was when a bomb blew me through the concrete doorway of the aircraftsmen's showers at 7 a.m. on the morning of 8 December during a surprise Japanese air raid.

As a result of my serious injuries I was evacuated from Malaya to Batavia and then Karachi and didn't pay much attention for the next two years while my wounds healed. Then I was invalided out of the RAF back in the UK in early 1944.

I often wonder what happened to the information I gave to those intelligence officers at Kuala Lumpur. To this day I can't understand why Malaya Command didn't go on a war alert that morning, let alone attack the Jap shipping which we all knew had been detected offshore.

Peter Shepherd's story has since been told in detail and is merely one dramatic example of the mass of intelligence warnings that were flooding in to the British authorities in Malaya in the month before the invasion. The Japanese appear to have provided plenty of last-minute signals and indicators of attack for the British intelligence staff; the only mystery is why they were not acted upon.

To understand this, we have to look at the second fundamental problem that hampered British intelligence in Malaya: poor organization. The British approach to the management and co-ordination of intelligence in the Far East seems to have been remarkably fragmented. It is easy to understand that at the height of a war for survival against a ferocious and dangerous enemy like Nazi Germany, the British would give priority to the immediate danger on their doorstep and worry less about the Far East. That is logical. What is less easy to understand is the apparent disorganization of the intelligence effort in Malaya itself. The reason appears to be both lack of organization and shortage of resources.

The structure of intelligence in Malaya was thin, to say the least. The key body was the Far East Combined Bureau (FECB) which was theoretically charged with co-ordinating intelligence from the three services, sigint sources and sometimes SIS reports, providing the authorities with up-to-date, accurate summaries of the threat to British interests. In fact its prime role was as an outstation of Bletchley Park's Ultra code-breaking operation. Very little has been written about the activities of FECB in comparison with its Whitehall-based controllers, the Joint Intelligence Committee (JIC) and the Government Code and Cipher School (GCCS). It most certainly did not occupy anything like the same authoritative place politically in the Far East as its Whitehall cousins. It was more a collection agency than a co-ordinating body or filter. What is clear is that FECB was relocated from Hong Kong to Singapore in 1939.

FECB was effectively GCCS's outpost in the Far East. As such its role of sigint kept it 'in the corner'. We do know that FECB was not a respected voice in the war councils of Malaya. If anything, it was excluded from them and because of the requirements of tight security (FECB was evacuated before the fall of Singapore to prevent its secrets falling into Japanese hands) was unlikely to be heard in the more rarefied civil and military committees responsible for the defence of the peninsula. The truth seems to be that no organization was co-ordinating intelligence in Malaya in 1941.

Part of the fragmentation problem was a lack of understanding about what intelligence could and should do. Military intelligence was only a small and subordinate staff within the bureaucracies that ran the Malayan colonies and was largely ignored by 'real intelligence'. This seemed to stem from ignorance on the part of the colonial regime and an outdated belief that intelligence and the secret services were one and the same thing in some curious John Buchan or Bulldog Drummond view of the 'Great Game'. The whole of the Far East Command seems to have been permeated with the belief that the Secret Intelligence Service (SIS, or MI6) and espionage collection was what intelligence was *really* all about; the rather more mundane intelligence cycle of collection, collation, interpretation and dissemination seems to have been ignored or unknown. Vital assets like the services' signals intelligence units, which were breaking Japanese codes and reading Japanese messages, seem not to have had any great influence on events before spring 1942; or if they had, intelligence secrets were not put to work for operations or GHQ.

To compound this unworldly unprofessionalism was another agency's jealously guarded monopoly of *counter-intelligence* through the so-called Defence Security Officer (DSO). The British Security Service (MI5) has always seen itself as the service with prime responsibility for espionage, sabotage and subversion within British Crown Territories and for their security, an arrangement which continues to this day. But MI5, as ever, lacked operators. Fragmentation was further increased by the variety of secret political police officers (the so-called Special Branches) of the several police forces in the Malayan colonies. The result was that intelligence co-ordination in the Far East was effectively non-existent, and endless squabbling between agencies was the norm.

To add to the confusion, many of the individuals in charge of the various intelligence departments got on so badly on a personal level that co-operation between their offices became impossible. In just one case, MI5's DSO in Singapore, retired Colonel Hayley Bell, was not on speaking terms with the head of the Japanese Section of the Singapore Police Special Branch (SB). Relationships were so poisonous that Major Morgan, the SB chief, flatly refused to tell the DSO (who was Chairman of the Governor's Security and Intelligence Committee) precisely what he knew about Japanese espionage *on the grounds of security.*

Eventually the row between the two came to the attention of the military. There is a fascinating note in the files of the man who surrendered Singapore, Lieutenant General Percival, from the days when he was the Chief Staff Officer in 1937 about the secret policeman Morgan: 'It is not possible to feel any confidence in Major Morgan. His statements and views… convey a strong impression of an eccentric mentality, ill-balanced judgement, muddled thought and uncalled-for reticence.' A sardonic view might be that this is merely the inevitable *déformation professionnelle* and descent into paranoia of any secret policeman anywhere who has spent too long inside the secret world, but Percival – who many feel was a much more incisive staff officer in 1937 than he was a commanding general in 1941–42 – goes on, 'Morgan is clearly lacking in ability and not fitted for the appointment he holds… and this view is supported… by his past history and antecedents.' However, like all good civil servants, Major Morgan was well able to escape the consequences of his actions, particularly from a mere soldier. Percival goes on sadly, 'On the other hand, he appears to be on a seven- to ten-year [Civil Service] contract, so there may be some difficulty in removing him.'

With men of Morgan's calibre looking for spies, it is no surprise that British counter-intelligence had a poor record of protecting the colony from the disaster which was to befall it. Morgan and his colleagues would have had a fit had they realized that there was a major Japanese military espionage operation active in Malaya in 1940–41. *It was run by a serving British Army officer.*

Captain Patrick Heenan was probably recruited as a spy by the Japanese Military Intelligence Service during a visit to Japan in the winter of 1938. He was unpopular with fellow officers in his battalion, the 3/16th Punjab Regiment in Malaya, so much so that he was posted out as an Air Intelligence

Liaison Officer. AILO was never going to be a good career move for an infantry officer, but it did provide Heenan with the agent-runner's dream: access to military secrets. As an AILO, Heenan now had access to all Malaya Command's orders of battle and the types, dispersal locations and weapon states of every RAF aircraft on the peninsula, together with contingency battle plans.

One of the great mysteries of the Malayan campaign was the uncanny ability of the Japanese to hit RAF airfields so accurately and at a time that guaranteed maximum loss to the British. 'It was almost as if they knew our plans,' in the words of one RAF NCO of the time speaking long after the campaign. They did.

Heenan supplied the Japanese with everything he knew, and in particular probably provided accurate detailed plans of RAF Alor Star, the key airfield in the north. Alor Star was neutralized in a devastating series of air raids early on, thus virtually guaranteeing the Japanese air superiority for the rest of the campaign. Worse, Heenan almost certainly passed on top secret British codes and ciphers, enabling the Japanese sigint service to read all the Army and RAF traffic throughout the battle.

Heenan was careless. He had attracted attention and suspicion before the war within the military, but nothing was done. However, on 10 December 1941, he was arrested after what looked like a botched attempt to murder his section head, Major France, and his quarters were searched. He was found to be in possession of unauthorized classified maps, operation orders and codes, and two disguised transmitters and a code book to encipher transmissions. Among other espionage equipment, he reportedly had a Morse code transmitter operated by an alphanumeric keyboard – similar to a Traeger Transceiver – which was disguised as a typewriter. In the exigencies of wartime a full counter-espionage security inquiry into Heenan's contacts was impossible; but it soon became quite clear that he was heavily implicated not only in his own direct espionage activities but also in running a network of agents in Malaya before the war.

Heenan was moved south under escort with the retreating British armies and taken to Singapore in January 1942 to be court-martialled for espionage, in that 'he wilfully communicated information of value to an enemy while on active service in Malaya in December 1941'. He was found guilty and sentenced to death. Heenan was not alone in the intelligence he supplied. The British discovered to their horror after the war that the Japanese had also seen all the most secret traffic between Churchill and the War Cabinet in London and the Commander-in-Chief in Singapore in 1941.

To ensure that the most secret and the highest-level documents of all were not hazarded or compromised by transmission or by aircraft overflights, Whitehall dispatched direct correspondence by a fast merchant ship, the 7,500-ton MV *Automedon*, to Singapore in late September 1940. On board was a weighted sack containing 'most secret' operational plans for the Far East together with an extremely pessimistic British Chiefs of Staff appreciation of Britain's real ability to defend Malaya. The *Automedon*'s Master, Captain McEwen, and the diplomatic courier Captain Evans both had strict instructions to drop the sack over the side should anything go wrong.

It did. In November 1940, the *Automedon* was intercepted on the last leg of her journey off the Nicobar Islands as she swung north through the Indian Ocean by the disguised German surface raider *Atlantis*, which had been reading British merchant codes. At 300 yards' range – *Atlantis*'s resourceful Captain Rogge had disguised some of his crew as women and run up a Dutch ensign – a hail of twenty-eight 5.9-in shells smashed the *Automedon*'s radio room, disabling the Master, Evans the diplomatic courier and the radio.

The leader of the German boarding party, an English-speaker called Mohr, could not believe his luck. The delighted Germans found that they were now in possession of a weighted British diplomatic courier mailbag containing the top-secret personal correspondence and intelligence crown jewels for the Far East, together with all the new British maritime code books, *and the British did not know*. The Admiralty assumed that *Automedon* had been torpedoed and sunk by a submarine, as the victims of surface-raider attacks were usually able to get off a signal; but not this time.

The Germans were not much concerned with the details of British plans in the Far East – although the new British maritime (BAMS) codes were another matter – and so they passed all the relevant Far Eastern documents to their ally, Japan. The British did not know that early in 1941 the Japanese had copies of the highest-level policy between London and Singapore and in addition could read almost all the British secret maritime radio traffic. By the time London found out, it was too late.

The *Automedon* affair was the biggest British intelligence loss in the Far East. One of the recurring mysteries, given its importance to Britain's enemies, is why no real mention of the *Automedon* or the loss of its priceless cargo is made in the official history, *British Intelligence in the Second World War*. It is clear, however, from the change in Japanese thinking and planning *after* they had been given their copy of the British Chiefs of Staff report by the Germans, that the *Automedon*'s haul was one of the primary catalysts that steered Japan towards ever-bolder planning to strike at Pearl Harbor and Malaya. If there can be any doubt about the significance of the *Automedon*, after Singapore surrendered in 1942, Kriegsmarine Kapitän Rogge of the *Atlantis* was presented with an antique samurai sword from the emperor of Japan's own hands; a Japanese honour almost impossible for any Westerner to comprehend, and the real mark of Japanese appreciation for an intelligence coup of extraordinary magnitude.

As if superior Japanese military intelligence and British incompetence, underestimation of the enemy and poor organization were not enough, the British in Malaya were hampered in all their efforts by a self-inflicted wound: a divided and weak command. The final ingredient in the loss of Malaya and Singapore was provided by the fragmentation of the colonial government itself. Just who was really running the Crown Colonies in Malaya as they prepared for war in 1941 is open to question. It was most certainly not the armed services, neither before nor, more seriously, after the Japanese invaded.

The problem lay firmly with the colonial government itself. Under the leadership of Sir Shenton Thomas, the Governor since 1934, the Straits Settlements of Singapore and Malaya had slipped into a colonial torpor more concerned with the status quo and the social life of the colony than with harsh external realities. Described by a contemporary American observer as 'a [pompous] slave to British civil service values [...] living in some kind of dreamworld where reality seldom enters and where the main effort is to restrict the entrance of anything disturbing', Governor Thomas seems to embody the worst characteristics of early twentieth-century effete British social values.

Much of the blame for the debacle in Malaya has been laid at his door, especially by the defeated British armed forces. The Governor may have been at least partly a victim of poor leadership himself, however. Churchill's War Cabinet had given him strict instructions on Malaya's prime role in Britain's second great war with Germany, which was not to prepare for a war with Japan but to make as much money as he could for the Empire by selling rubber to the Americans.

In this atmosphere the main priority was undoubtedly economic. It therefore followed that anything that impeded the production and sale of tin and rubber – such as calling up local defence volunteers for guard duty or military training – was a costly distraction from Malaya's principal task. Despite this, Thomas *did* direct that considerable civil effort was put into assisting the armed services by helping to construct camps, build airfields and redirect labour, although in the case of the last of these without any great success. Like the careful civil servant he was, Thomas devoted much of his *apologia* after the war to his bureaucratic struggles over the costing details of native labour in the colony in 1941 and how it was impossible to pay realistic wages for war workers without more government money. This begs the real question in 1941: whether Malaya was on a war footing or running a civil economy, being run by the military or by the old colonial administration? The answer seems to be both, and neither was doing it particularly well.

Perhaps the true reason for Malaya's problems, including its incompetent intelligence organization, can be found in this schizophrenic rule. Faced with a mortal threat to the colony, the patterns of peacetime social and civil service life nevertheless seem to have continued unchanged. Imperturbability in the face of deadly danger is a quality much admired by the English.

In Singapore in 1942 it found its limits.

Not all Britons were as complacent and confident as the Governor and his herbivorous civil service. At least two men made sound intelligence predictions of the real threat to Singapore: Lieutenant General Percival, when he was a staff officer in 1937, and the one man who sounded a really accurate alarm before the war, C. A. Vlieland. Unfortunately Vlieland was a civilian and a member of Governor Thomas's staff. Appointed Secretary for Defence Malaya in 1938, he was eventually to resign after some curious backstairs political intrigue in 1941 before war broke out. Before then, however, Vlieland had predicted in great detail and with uncomfortable accuracy the probable route and outcome of any likely Japanese invasion from the north through Siam and Malaya. Equally accurately, he outlined the need for strong defences in the forests to the north of Singapore and virtually dismissed the notion of any assault from the sea. He even claimed that 'Fortress Singapore' was a complete white elephant and pointless to Malaya's real defence priorities. This was not a view likely to endear him to the collective mandarins of official British policy or the combined services.

Vlieland's real tragedy was to get caught up in the bureaucratic power play between the Governor, the Army, the RAF and the new Commander-in-Chief, General Bond, when he arrived in August 1939. Bond, a powerful and opinionated figure, promptly set about regaining control of the defence strategy of his command from 'a bunch of damned civilians'. Bond's particular obsession was with Singapore Island, and he would have no truck with a mere colonial civil servant meddling in matters of defence policy, especially one offering his own intelligence appreciations; the clash was inevitable, as was the outcome. Outmanoeuvred by the services and abandoned in committee by his boss – and theoretically the Commander-in-Chief, the Governor – an embittered Vlieland eventually resigned as Secretary for Defence in early 1941. Once back in England he was to suffer the worst torture of all: seeing all the bitter predictions of his 1940 military appreciation for the defence of Malaya and Singapore being successfully put into action by the Japanese.

Perhaps this civil-military clash ensured the fall of Malaya more than any other factor, more so than poor intelligence and underestimation of the enemy. The infighting and lack of a clear command structure meant that no organization, from intelligence operations to civil defence, could survive the endless wrangles over who was in charge. Given the other weaknesses of British intelligence and Japan's ability to get inside the British operational information flow, it is hard to see how the British could have succeeded, even if Malaya and Singapore had been run as a battle zone and not as a supposedly peaceful colony right up to the very last days of the siege, as the Japanese closed in and finally invaded Singapore Island.

Even as the final convoys of reinforcements poured into Singapore Harbour in late January and early February 1942, it was already too late to save the campaign. To the Australian government's dismay they found that their final reinforcements for the 8th Australian Division, disembarking in Singapore as late as 24 January 1942, were little more than more fuel for the fire. The pasty newcomers were unfit after months at sea and only half trained. The battle for Malaya was as good as lost.

The discovery that Churchill had been contemplating diverting the *British* 18th Division on the high seas and sending it to the Middle East instead of embattled Singapore turned out to be the last straw for the Australian prime minister. John Curtin had already seen Churchill sacrifice Australian troops twice in 1941 in Greece and Crete, and he was alert for any backsliding or evidence of duplicity from the British. In January 1942, he cabled Churchill as part of a surprisingly bitter and acrimonious exchange, baring the tensions between the two leaders and exposing their different strategic interests. In January and February 1942, Churchill's interest in the struggle against Japan was focused on protecting India and keeping the route to China open through Burma. By February he was even prepared to leave Singapore and the troops to their fate. Curtin's focus was on defending Singapore, saving Australian lives and maintaining Australia's forward defence. He warned Churchill that any attempt to divert the British 18th Division from reinforcing the garrison in Singapore would be, in Australian eyes, an 'inexcusable betrayal'. Churchill backed down and sent the last drafts of the 9th, 11th and 18th Divisions virtually straight into captivity, to join their Australian comrades in the last days of the doomed colony.

These troops could have been needed elsewhere, as retreat and panic spread throughout the Far East. Subsequent Japanese air raids on Darwin in 1942 spread even more dismay and panic as far away as the isolated population of northern Australia. After the worst raid, when all the ships in the harbour were either hit or sunk, hundreds of Australians deserted and joined the headlong flight south in what became known as the 'Great Darwin Handicap' as vital Air Force technicians and their families headed for the safety of the interior. Fortunately for Australia, the Japanese were at the limit of their resources and never did invade. But the events of early 1942 stand as an inglorious chapter in Australian history. The atmosphere of the time was one of flight, despair and the end of an era.

Two stories sum up the atmosphere of those last days in Singapore more than any other. As a tired British infantry battalion began to dig its fire trenches for the final defence of Singapore on a golf course, 'a colonial planter of the worst type' came up quivering with rage and demanded to know what was going on. On being told by the young officer in charge, he stormed off 'apoplectic with rage, shouting that the Golf Club was private property and threatening to tell the Governor to get this nonsense stopped, and full compensation'.

The second story is the popular canard that it was really lack of water that finally persuaded Lieutenant General Percival to capitulate. When the local civil works engineer said that nothing could be done about Singapore's water supply, the Army's Commander Royal Engineers countered that, with a few trucks and a work party of a hundred men, he could repair and maintain the reservoirs and pipelines, and guarantee water for as long as it was needed. He never got them: not from the hundreds of thousands of desperate civilians nor from the thousands of drunken, defeated deserters roaming the streets amid the flames and chaos of the doomed island on that terrible Sunday of 15 February 1942.

Amid the uproar of the last days, one grim final act was played out. On 'Black Friday', 13 February 1942, the convicted traitor Captain Patrick Heenan of the Punjab Regiment was, officially at least, executed by firing squad. Rumour has it that what really happened amid the smoke and explosions was that he was dragged on to the dockside between two sergeants during a Japanese air raid. An enraged Military Police sergeant, who had won the right (by cutting cards) to kill the traitor before the Japanese arrived, then blew Heenan's brains out with a revolver at point-blank range before kicking the body into the dock and melting back into the crowds of deserters, drunks and terrified civilians trying to fight their way on to the last boats out.

It took the victorious Japanese Army to restore order and calm to the imperial garrison. They did so quickly and efficiently in their own brutal way, proving once again that it had been a very serious mistake to underestimate them, even up to the very end. Perhaps Churchill was wise after all not to have convened a parliamentary inquiry into the blunders and mismanagement that led to the fall of Singapore, the 'impregnable fortress'.

Churchill called the shameful fall of Singapore to the Japanese the 'worst disaster' and 'largest capitulation' in British military history.

Lord Moran, Churchill's physician, wrote: 'The fall of Singapore on February 15 stupefied the Prime Minister.' In particular, the surrender of the British troops bewildered him. How came 100,000 men (half of them of our own race) to hold up their hands to inferior numbers of Japanese? Though his mind had been gradually prepared for its fall, the surrender of the fortress stunned him,' wrote Moran. 'He felt it was a disgrace. It left a scar on his mind.'

Some disasters are so shameful that they are best quietly ignored: but their lessons should not be forgotten.

Singapore was not Churchill's finest hour…

MIDWAY – AMERICA'S TRIUMPH OF SIGNALS INTELLIGENCE

'The disintegrating effects of victory...
were soon observed'

C. S. FORESTER

After their swift conquest of the British and Dutch empires' cash cows of economic domination of South East Asia, the Japanese Empire had attained its initial strategic goals quickly and with consummate ease. The Dutch East Indies (modern Indonesia) with its vital oil resources meant that the problem of Japanese national oil supplies was now solved; and even the partially successful secondary attack on America's Pearl Harbor in the Hawaiian Islands was a mere sideshow to Tokyo's grand design for empire.

With the main objectives seized, the question now for Japan was, what to do next? Victory brought new problems and new challenges.

Because of this, preliminary planning for future operations only began as late as January 1942. Planning was not helped by a basic strategic disagreement between the Imperial Army (IJA) and Imperial Navy (IJN). A bitter power struggle surfaced between the all-conquering Navy's Combined Fleet and the Imperial Japanese Army, hopelessly bogged down in its long war in China and still licking its wounds after defeat in the Battle of Khalkhin Gol on the Mongolian border by the Red Army in late 1939. The IJA had priority, but after the defeat by the Soviets the army needed to find an Eastern strategy to replace its expansionist – and defeated – 'Western Strategy'.

Only in April 1942 was a follow-up strategy finally agreed when Admiral

Yamamoto finally won the bureaucratic struggle with a thinly veiled threat to resign, after which the Navy's plan for the Central Pacific was adopted.

As an interim measure the Japanese carrier fleet was sent on a raiding foray into the Indian Ocean in April 1942 with the aim of threatening Ceylon. Across the years it is hard for us to grasp the profound shock that the sinking of HMS *Prince of Wales* and *Repulse* by Japanese land-based aircraft had caused back in December 1941: it was the proof that aircraft, and aircraft carriers, would now dominate the oceans. For the first time in naval history, aircraft had sunk battleships manoeuvring over the horizon at sea. As the May 1941 battle off Crete with its heavy losses had confirmed, the Royal Navy and surface ships had no real defence against air power.

In the Indian Ocean the IJN's aircraft quickly sank the Royal Navy's old carrier HMS *Hermes*, plus two heavy cruisers and a score of merchant ships. Admiral Somerville prudently fled west from Ceylon with his ageing, slow battleships as far as East Africa. Admiral Nagumo's Combined Striking Fleet and its aircraft had swept the Indian Ocean bare of the British Empire.

With the British no longer any threat, the IJN's priority now became the elimination of America's carrier forces, which by being at sea had escaped annihilation at Pearl Harbor. Yamamoto now regarded these leftover carriers as the principal threat to any Japanese follow-on operations in the Central Pacific. To emphasize the point, the Doolittle Raid on Tokyo by USAAF B-25 bombers on 18 April 1942 came as a 'WTC moment' to the Japanese and shock to Tokyo; the Americans could now reach and bomb God's islands! Yamamoto saw no alternative to starting to plan to ambush and sink the remaining US carriers in the Central and Western Pacific as a matter of urgency.

But first the Navy had to accommodate the army's ambitious plans for Australia. Yamamoto had to deal with the IJA General Staff, who were wary of the Navy's cautious plan to seal off the open flank of the new Japanese Empire to the south.

The navy wanted the army to invade India and even northern Australia. Already burdened with its heavy commitments in China, Manchuria and South East Asia, and never an enthusiastic supporter of wider naval strategy at the best of times, the Japanese army pointed out that this strategy was beyond its resources. Instead, it agreed to a compromise, whereby there was to be a joint operation to block off and isolate communications between the United States and Australia, the UK and India. The new plan called instead for a land invasion of New Guinea to be covered by the IJN's carrier planes moving into the Coral Sea.

In mid-February a 'local agreement' was reached by the army and navy to implement Directive #47. The plan was for a joint effort to seize Port Moresby in early March and cross New Guinea north to south. In the centre, Japan's commander, Admiral Yamamoto, mistakenly believed that the Doolittle raid on Tokyo must have taken off from Midway Island, 1,300 miles west and north of Hawaii. He never considered the raid was launched from a US carrier, USS *Hornet*. In revenge, he determined to attack and seize Midway Island with a four-carrier task force, once his southern flank was secure. He believed he could ambush and defeat the US Navy's three Central Pacific carriers in a decisive engagement, occupy the island and dominate the Central Pacific. That would threaten Pearl Harbor and Hawaii, and keep the US forces at bay.

Yamamoto's plan was a typically overcomplicated one, more redolent of a staff college war game than the simplistic demands of battle. It relied on no fewer than six separate task forces operating under radio silence and centred on a core of battleships, ready to fight a naval gun battle like Jutland. The Japanese had learned little from their original campaign.

In the euphoria of their victories, the Japanese disregarded the possibility that any power or weapon could derail their intentions. Unlike Pearl Harbor, they made little attempt to train or practise for Midway. This meant that they had not practised the difficult sequencing of preparing aircraft for attacking land or sea targets. Today this is achieved by multi-mission aircraft. Back then, aircraft were single mission, with one piece of ordnance per aiming point, land or sea. New targets meant the ability to change ordnance – quickly. This was to prove crucial off Midway.

But first the IJN had to find and neutralize the American carriers. And in this hunt for the enemy, the Japanese were short of a key capability: intelligence.

The key to intelligence in the war in the Pacific was the interception and reading of radio traffic. In early 1942, sigint involved collecting intelligence from radio traffic and providing it to the US Navy's operations staff for them to plan and take action.

Electronic interception was not new.

The Imperial Russian Navy had experimented with wireless communications as early as 1900. The birth of signals intelligence dates to the Russo-Japanese War. In 1904, the British ship HMS *Diana*, off Suez, was able to intercept Russian naval wireless signals and reported:

> An intelligence report on signals intercepted by HMS *Diana* at Suez shows that the rate of working was extremely slow by British standards, while the Royal Navy interpreters were particularly critical of the poor standard of grammar and spelling among the Russian operators.

Sigint was here to stay.

But signals intelligence is very much a two-edged weapon. Signals *can* give an unrivalled insight into an enemy's intentions and plans – provided that the opposition believes their radio transmissions to be secret. Yet sigint works both ways. If the sender knows an enemy is reading his signals, the possibilities for fake traffic, deception and misinformation are boundless. Not for nothing did the Germans very early on label Marconi's wireless as a dangerous threat, pointing out that 'transmission is treason'.

Sigint for the US in the Pacific by 1942 was complicated by the fact that not only was the information in a foreign language (Japanese) but was protected by codes and other security measures. The US sigint staff had to collect, find the heavily encrypted original text, translate it, and only then understand the information, interpret it, and get it to the 'customers' in time for them to take action.

Phase I of Yamamoto's plan brought about the Battle of the Coral Sea north-east of Australia. This was the first time since the Japanese attack on Pearl Harbor that their advance met real opposition and was the first major US Navy fleet action against Japan. Coral Sea was also a historic milestone, being the first naval engagement in history in which the participating ships never sighted or fired directly at each other. Carrier-borne aircraft were now the mobile artillery of this new warfare.

The Japanese plan was for combined army and naval forces to push south-east from the Solomons, capturing and garrisoning Tulagi in the Solomons and Port Moresby, New Guinea, along the way. Secondary objectives were the Gilbert Islands north-east of the Solomons, to secure their vital phosphate resources, essential for Japanese agriculture.

From 29 April to 4 May, Japanese forces attacked, invaded and occupied Tulagi, although several of their warships were surprised and sunk or damaged by aircraft from USS *Yorktown*. Alerted to the presence of US carriers nearby, the Japanese Carrier Strike Force deployed towards the Coral Sea with the intention of finding and destroying the Allied naval forces. Beginning on 7 May, the two sides exchanged clumsy air strikes over the next two days. Both sides traded losses and the battle ended inconclusively with tactical errors and missed opportunities on both sides. Japan lost a carrier and the Americans lost another, USS *Lexington*; the carrier USS *Yorktown* was put out of action with serious battle damage.

It was time for Phase II of Yamamoto's strategic master plan. Unfortunately, it was flawed from the start: the Japanese secret naval signals were being read by the Americans.

America's concerns over Japan were well founded. By 1931, when the Japanese invaded Manchuria, it was clear that Japan's intentions were expansionist. Collection of Japanese intelligence became a US national priority: and both sides now squaring off in the Pacific faced the same problem: intelligence.

Land warfare can rely on a wide mix of sources for intelligence – humint and spies; stolen documents; local radio traffic; known movements; loose-tongued diplomats; and even civilian and open sources. Across the watery wastes of the Pacific, however, only radio traffic was available quickly enough for useful intelligence. The area to be covered was huge (7,000 x 7,000 miles).

The vast chessboard of the Pacific could only be monitored by radio transmissions, but the US was in a better position than many realized. The US had, despite Secretary Stimson's self-denying ordinance of 1929 (see page 77), in fact cobbled together a very sophisticated and competent strategic sigint capability, more by accident than design, by 1940. The

American sigint effort had begun in the early 1930s as tension mounted with Japan. A cryptological genius, William Friedman, put together an organization that would strip Japan's most secret codes naked. Friedman was the first to describe 'cryptanalysis' and wrote many monographs on cryptography, which later expanded to become the first textbook on the subject.

Realizing that mathematical and language skills were essential to America's 'Secret Intelligence Service's' work, Friedman managed to get authority to hire a team of top mathematicians as well as Japanese linguists. It is no exaggeration that Friedman's work in America equalled anything that Alan Turing and the British code-breakers managed at Bletchley Park – and all without the help of Polish 'cribs'.

In this he was a colleague of Laurance F. Safford, the 'father of US Navy cryptology', who had established the naval cryptologic organization after the First World War, and headed the effort more or less constantly until the start of 1942. The Navy opened HF/DF (High Frequency Direction Finding) stations mainly on the Atlantic Coast after the start of Hitler's war in 1939. The first operational radio intercept actually came from what would later be called Station CAST, at Cavite in the far off Philippines. By December 1940, the Navy's communication organization, OP-20-G, had used HF/DF on German surface vessels and submarines. Training continued and co-operation with the British began as early as January 1941, and in April the British (who were specializing in traffic analysis to locate German U-boats) gifted the US Navy a sample of their latest HF/DF set.

By early 1942 the post-Pearl Harbor guilt felt by the Pacific sigint community at their failure to warn of the Japanese attack was replaced by a determination to keep tabs on the Japanese navy as never before. In this they were helped by the Japanese radio operators who were sometimes sloppy to the point of carelessness with their Naval Code (JN-25), believing their language to be too difficult for mere foreigners, so they did not take the full measure of precautions. Transmission really *was* treason…

Key to this attack on Japanese secret codes was the head of Station Hypo, Commander Joseph Rochefort. Rochefort, who was both a Japanese linguist and a cryptanalyst, was trained at OP-20-G by Laurance Safford and the brilliant Agnes Driscoll.

Station Hypo, correctly known as Fleet Radio Unit Pacific (FRUPAC), was the United States Navy signals monitoring and cryptographic intelligence unit in Hawaii during the Second World War, based at Pearl Harbor. The station took its initial name from the phonetic code at the time for 'H' for He'ia, Hawaii radio tower. Crucially, Hypo was under the control of the OP-20-G Naval Intelligence section in Washington.

Highly regarded by Safford, Rochefort was a graduate of a programme that detailed dozens of officers to study Japanese language and culture in Japan during the interwar years. At one time he had actually been head of OP-20-G with its overall responsibilities for communications intelligence. Rochefort and Commander Edwin T. Layton, the chief intelligence officer for the Pacific Fleet, who was also a Safford-trained cryptanalyst, enjoyed a close working relationship and a strong friendship begun years before when they were both language students in Japan. Lacking such a close working relationship with anyone in Washington, which had no intelligence requirements to which it could conceivably respond, it was natural for Rochefort to consider CINCPAC in Hawaii as Hypo's day-to-day boss, not far-off OP-20-G on America's east coast.

In 1942, Rochefort and his staff slowly began to make progress against JN-25, one of the many challenging Japanese command codes. JN-25 was the Japanese Navy's top secret operational cipher. If it could be broken, Rochefort would be able to provide Nimitz, his C-in-C, the information he needed to make key decisions for the admiral's deployment and dispersal of his precious warships.

The prize for success was beyond a commander's dreams. By intercepting, deciphering and translating the Japanese Navy's messages that contained their order of battle, the communications analysts were beginning to strip away any veil of secrecy over Japan's plans. The timetables for their military operations at Port Moresby, the Aleutians and Midway, plus a myriad of vital details concerning their most secret plans and intentions, were suddenly available to the US admirals.

Key to this was the breaking of the JN-25 code. This proved a daunting task. The code consisted of approximately 45,000 five-digit numbers, each number representing a Japanese pictogram of a word or phrase. For transmission, the five-digit numbers were then super-enciphered again, using another code. Breaking through to the real code meant using mathematical analysis to strip off the added cover code, then analysing traffic patterns over time to unravel the original five-digit numbers. This complex process presented a major challenge, but Rochefort and his team were able to make progress because the system called for the repetitive use of the add-on cover cipher. This exposed the code's vulnerability to decryption. Even so, the work was painfully slow. Before Pearl Harbor, only 10 to 15 per cent of the traffic was being read. By June of 1942, however, Rochefort's staff were able to break key messages and to assess the Japanese fleet's most likely next move. Yamamoto's long-term aim had always been to force the US to sue for peace before its industrial might could be directed against Japan. As a young officer he had travelled extensively in the United States and was well aware of America's industrial potential. His short-term aim was to lure the American Navy into a decisive battle, in which it would be forced to deploy its remaining assets, thus providing his forces an opportunity to administer one final knockout blow and bring America to its knees in the Pacific. Then he hoped a deal could be struck.

While Yamamoto plotted to bring a quick end to war in the Pacific theatre, the United States Navy in the Pacific, led by Admiral Chester Nimitz, was desperately trying to anticipate Japan's next move. Nimitz had no room for error. At the time of the battle, his fleet with its three aircraft carriers were all that lay between Hawaii and the American West Coast and a large Japanese Fleet that could muster eleven carriers if necessary. Nimitz would have one shot at the enemy. Any miscalculation on where Yamamoto would strike next would be disastrous to the Allied war effort in the Pacific.

In order to prevail, Nimitz had to have some sense of Japan's intentions. The task of obtaining the critical information required to turn the tide in the Pacific fell to OP-20-G, the Navy's overall radio intelligence organization in Washington, tasked with providing communications intelligence on the Japanese Navy. They in turn 'subcontracted' the task to the Pacific and to station Hypo.

After the attack on Pearl Harbor, Japanese Navy operational radio traffic increased. This increased volume of signals traffic helped the code-breakers to make progress against it because more signals equalled more mistakes and more chance to break in. By May a clear option was emerging for any forthcoming Japanese attack. Hypo assessed a move against the Central Pacific: opinion at OP-20-G, backed by Washington, favoured a move against the North Pacific, perhaps in the Aleutians.

This disagreement was not helped by the reorganization of OP-20-G in February 1942. In the new organization structure, a new branch called 'Combat Intelligence' was created and designated OP-20-GI. This element produced little original current intelligence. Tasked to disseminate the various translations to the commands and field elements along with its own analytic reports, OP-20-GI became in effect just another competing intelligence centre in Washington. Until 15 May, however, it continued to publish its own translations and sporadic reports based on the sigint product of Hawaii, Corregidor and Melbourne, which further muddied the waters. Hypo was now but one of several reporting agencies.

Inevitably there was disagreement. By late April, Rochefort's team assessed that the Japanese were planning major operations against the Central Pacific or the Aleutians, but which? The key issue by late May was the real target for the Japanese fleet and invasion force, identified as 'AF' in the Japanese coded messages: where exactly was 'AF'? The various intelligence agencies disagreed and were clamouring for their master's ear. OP-20-G were all for Alaska and the Aleutians: Hypo remained firm that the target was Midway Island in the Central Pacific. As June 1942 approached, Hypo was under extraordinary pressure, and there are tales of thirty-six-hour stints, of Rochefort working in his bathrobe and appearing for briefings late and unshaven. This effort climaxed in the last week of May with the decryption of enough JN-25 traffic to understand the Japanese attack plan at Midway in some, but not complete, detail.

In this argument Hypo was favoured by a ruse to identify the true Japanese objective. In May, Hawaii decided upon a clever method to settle the identity of 'AF' once and for all by faking a water shortage on Midway, sending a message *in clear* asking for more water tanks, radioing on 22 May: 'Refer this unit's report dated 19th, at the present time we have only enough water for two weeks. Please supply us immediately.'

To Hypo's delight, two days later the Japanese reported in code that 'AF' was short of water. So the target 'AF' *was* Midway; no doubt about it now. Thanks to sigint, the American commander had a priceless advantage: he could see his opponent's hand. He knew where Yamamoto intended to strike. Pacific Fleet intelligence officer Lieutenant Commander Edwin 'Eddie' Layton presented the fruits of Hypo's and Rochefort's work on 27 May at the Pacific Fleet staff conference. In his own words:

> Summarizing all my data, I told Nimitz that the carriers would probably attack on the morning of 4 June, from the north-west on a bearing of 325 degrees. They could be sighted at about 175 miles from Midway at around 0700 local time.

This intelligence allowed Nimitz to order the carrier USS *Yorktown*, damaged at the Battle of Coral Sea, to be rushed back into action after forty-eight hours of frantic repairs at Pearl Harbor. This is still viewed by the US Navy as a minor engineering miracle, because it enabled the two US task forces to roughly match the 230 planes on board the Japanese carriers.

The irony is that the Japanese actually had begun to suspect that their secret plan had leaked. A few days before the battle, the Japanese naval leadership ashore suspected that the Americans were aware of the Midway operation and Admiral Nagumo, commanding the carrier group, was sent intelligence from Tokyo while en route to Midway. It was not relayed to the flagship. Nagumo's failure to anticipate the US ambush resulted not just from poor intelligence practices, but from inflexibility and institutional bureaucratic inertia. The rigid Japanese command and control practices forpassing on information were complex and slow and made it difficult for Nagumo to receive even urgent battle intelligence in a timely manner. They failed to alert Nagumo.

Not so the American admirals. Their two carrier task forces were commanded by two very different personalities: Rear Admirals Fletcher and Spruance. Spruance was a gun cruiser man, not an aviator. Nimitz put Spruance in place of Vice Admiral Halsey, an aviator, after the latter was bedridden with shingles. In the hyper-unionized US Navy of the time, surface line officers just did not command aircraft. Or carriers. Nimitz's choices were, however, inspired. Both men were very aware of the paramount need for reconnaissance and set out to pinpoint the Japanese. By giving Nimitz an accurate prediction of the enemy's position and intentions, they, and good intelligence, allowed him to gamble on the carrier ambush that resulted in the Battle of Midway, and what is generally agreed to have been the turning point of the Pacific war.

On the morning of the battle, as the initial American reports sighting the Japanese force began to trickle in, Nimitz remarked to Layton, Rochefort's boss, with a smile, 'Well, you were only five minutes, five degrees and five miles out.'

In this he was way ahead of Washington, where CNO Admiral King had just sent a pessimistic assessment to the Joint Chiefs of Staff. He attributed any Navy progress in the Pacific to the success it was having in obtaining timely information from the Japanese naval codes. Without this information, he said, 'disaster is probable'. He was overtaken by events at sea, when on 3 July, a reconnaissance Catalina spotted the forward elements of the Japanese carrier force and radioed its location to Nimitz.

At dawn on 4 July, battle was joined: at dawn the Japanese sent a major bombing raid against Midway and Midway retaliated with high-level bombing of the Japanese ships by US Army Air Force B-17 bombers. These were unsuccessful, but the surprise attack significantly disrupted Nagumo's decision-making and operations. In retaliation, the Japanese carrier bombing raid on Midway, to soften it up for the amphibious landing, caused serious problems for the US and knocked out most of the island's fighters.

The Japanese still didn't realize they had walked into an ambush until a series of low-level attacks by US Devastator[2] carrier-borne torpedo planes after 09.00 alerted them to the presence of US carriers nearby.

The American naval doctrine, learned at the Coral Sea, was 'git in fustest with the mostest' and waves of US low-level torpedo attacks started to arrive at the Japanese carriers from 09.18.

---

2   The slow, lumbering Douglas TPD Devastator was hopelessly outclassed in both speed and manoeuvrability by the Mitsubishi Zero fighters they faced; most of the force was wiped out with little consequence except to distract the Zeros from the US dive-bombers.

These attacks alerted Nagumo to the presence of American carriers, but he was still in the dark as to their location. The US ambush continued in a series of torpedo attacks by a mixture of various torpedo planes over the next hour.

The first attack began with fifteen Douglas TBD Devastator torpedo bombers of VT-8, led by Lieutenant Commander John C. Waldron from Hornet. As the planes bore in on their torpedo runs, all were shot down, leaving Ensign George H. Gay Jr. in the sea as the only surviving aviator.

Shortly afterwards, fourteen more Devastators from Torpedo Squadron 6 (VT-6) of the *Enterprise*, led by Lieutenant Commander Eugene E. Lindsey, attacked. The combat air patrol (CAP) Zeros launched by *Sōryū* at 09.45, shot down all but four of the Devastators, after Torpedo Squadron 3 (VT-3) from *Yorktown* was spotted. These attacks were a disaster. Despite the suicidal bravery of the aircrew, the slow-running and unreliable US torpedoes[3] were easily avoided and even those that hit failed to explode as the hapless, obsolescent Devastator aircraft were blown out of the sky by Zero fighters and anti-aircraft fire.

As the initial Japanese strike force against Midway began to return and land, two things happened to change the situation. First, the Japanese pilots were adamant: a second bombing raid on Midway was essential to finish the job of softening up the ground defences. This was at the very moment Admiral Nagumo was preparing his response to the reports of American carrier forces to the north-east. Nagumo then ordered the Japanese maritime strike force (preparing to set out to attack the American carriers) to swap its torpedoes for bombs, and target Midway instead of the unlocated US carriers. It was a fateful decision.

However, the various abortive US torpedo attacks had accomplished one thing; they diverted the Japanese CAP fighter defences just as US carrier-based dive-bombers arrived high overhead at the moment the Japanese carriers were most vulnerable while refuelling and rearming their planes.

The four Japanese carriers were a flurry of frantic activity as deck crews

---

3   American torpedoes were poor. Thanks to pre-war Congressional parsimony and a refusal to admit to error, the Mark 14 had four major flaws. It tended to run deeper than set. The magnetic exploder often caused premature detonation. The contact exploder often failed to detonate the warhead. Finally, it tended to fail to straighten its run once set on its prescribed gyro-angle setting, and instead, to run in a wide circle. (source: Wikipedia)

wrestled to remove live torpedoes and to reload HE bombs, while pumping petrol into the returned Midway planes at the same time. The hangar decks were a scene of disciplined chaos with piles of loose bombs, torpedoes and exposed aviation fuel hoses.

The US carriers' strike force of Douglas Dauntless dive-bombers arrived at 20,000 feet. Their air commander, Lieutenant Commander McClusky, had pinpointed the Japanese by following the arrow-like wake of a speeding destroyer, racing to catch up with the carriers.

Lieutenant Commander McClusky graduated from the United States Naval Academy in 1926 and was an experienced naval aviator. In 1940, he was assigned to Fighting Squadron Six (VF-6), based on USS *Enterprise*, and assumed command of the squadron in April 1941. McClusky decided to press on with the bombing group to the limit of his range. His decision to continue the search and his judgement, in the opinion of Admiral Nimitz, *'decided the fate of our carrier task force and our forces at Midway...'*

The Japanese carrier forces were now off-balance as Nagumo was preparing his response to the first reports, received at 08.20, of the sighting of American carrier forces to his north-east. Around 08.30 *Sōryū* had launched one of her Judy D4Ys on a recce mission to confirm the precise location of the American carriers. It was too little, too late. The Midway force began to return from 08.45 onwards.

The landed aircraft were quickly struck below, while the carriers' crews began preparations to spot aircraft for the torpedo strike against the American carrier forces. The preparations, however, were interrupted at 09.20 when the first American carrier aircraft to attack were sighted.

By 10.00, Nagumo's force was hotly engaged by torpedo bombers at sea level and looking out for more torpedo attacks. McClusky's thirty-one Dauntless dive-bombers from three American squadrons arrived overhead at 10.22 while the Japanese CAP fighters were directing their attention to the US torpedo attacks and were out of position, low down near the surface. The Japanese ships were sitting ducks, with bombs and torpedoes stacked around the decks, rather than stowed safely in the magazines, and live fuel hoses snaking across the decks. Like avenging hawks, the thirty-one Dauntless dive-bombers from the USS *Enterprise*, USS *Hornet* and USS *Yorktown* plunged down. The tight defensive anti-aircraft box of the three carriers presented what military jargon calls a 'target-enriched environment'.

First to be hit was *Akagi*. The fatal bomb was dropped by Lieutenant Richard Best, whose bomb landed by the middle elevator. The 1,000-pound bomb burst through the unarmoured flight deck, exploded in the upper hangar, instantly killing many Japanese crewmen working in the enclosed hangar and hurling everything from men to aircraft over the edge of the flight deck. The hangar, fuelled by aviation petrol hoses and exploding bombs suddenly became an inferno.

The most damaging hit came in the form of a near miss on the stern by Ensign Frederick Thomas Weber, which jammed the ship's port rudder, rendering her essentially uncontrollable. Burning from end to end, wracked by internal explosions and with no engines, *Akagi* began to sail in a circle.

When Captain Taijiro Aoki later abandoned the ship (he was the last to leave her), she had already been burning for nearly nine hours. He remembered later:

> The dive-bombers attacked my ship while we were still taking evasive action from the torpedo bombers. We were unable to avoid the dive-bombers because we were so occupied in avoiding the torpedo attacks...
> We only received two hits...

Initially refusing to leave *Akagi*, Admiral Nagumo was finally convinced by Captain Aoki to transfer his flag to another ship because it was impossible to command a fleet from a burning ship without a working radio. The emperor's portrait was reverently lowered and accompanied Nagumo aboard the light cruiser *Nagara*.

Next to go was *Kaga*. The other dive-bombers, some of which nearly collided with each other, scored at least four hits on *Kaga*. The first blew in the rear elevator and set the stern on fire. The next hit the forward elevator and penetrated the upper hangar, which became a nightmare of explosions and fires among the armed and fuelled planes packed on the deck. The third bomb hit *Kaga*'s island and exploded directly on the bridge, killing Captain Okada and all his command staff. The final blow was a

1,000-pound bomb direct hit amidships which added to the inferno of fires and explosions raging in the upper hangar. The explosions ruptured the ship's avgas lines. With burning avgas leaking everywhere and pouring on to the hangar deck, the fires detonated 80,000 pounds of bombs and torpedoes strewn across the decks in a series of catastrophic explosions that blew out the ship's sides. Worse, they knocked out all the fire suppression systems. With dead leaders, out of control and burning from end to end, *Kaga* was doomed.

Sōryū was next to go. She had begun recovering her Midway strike force at around 08.40 and finished shortly by 09.10. The landed aircraft were quickly struck below, while the carriers' crews began preparations to spot aircraft for the torpedo strike against the American carrier forces. The preparations were interrupted at around 10.25 when *Sōryū* was attacked by thirteen Dauntlesses from *Yorktown*'s Bombing Squadron (VB-3). The carrier received three direct hits from 1,000-pound bombs: one penetrated to the lower hangar deck amidships and the other two exploded in the upper hangar deck. The hangars contained armed and fuelled aircraft preparing for the bombing strike, resulting in massive explosions which ruptured the steam pipes in the boiler rooms. The result was the same as her sister ships. Within a very short time, the fires on the *Sōryū* were out of control. At 10.40 she stopped and her crew was ordered to abandon ship five minutes later.

Commander Hisashi Ohara, the *Sōryū*'s executive officer, later recalled:

Our planes were being made ready for a second sortie and were all lined up on the flight deck ready to take off. The planes in the hangar below decks were loaded with bombs and fuel, ready to be brought to the flight deck, so that the first bomb started all these planes burning. The bombs loaded aboard the planes went off one by one by induced explosions… Due to the large fires aboard the ship, the large gasoline storage area in the stern of the ship exploded, leaving only the bow afloat, after which the gasoline storage tanks in the forward part of the ship exploded and sank the ship.

The seamen who worked in *Sōryū*'s boiler room were all killed by superheated live steam, boiled alive as the pipes were burst by the explosions, which also immediately rendered the ship immobile. Stationary, on fire and without power, the order to abandon ship was given.

Hiryū, the only surviving Japanese carrier, had been outside the defensive box and was manoeuvring independently, so escaped the first American attacks.

A USS *Yorktown* scout plane finally located *Hiryū* and the US carrier launched a strike. In turn, *Hiryū* launched eighteen fixed undercarriage 'Val' D3As, escorted by six Zeros, against USS *Yorktown*.

It did not save *Hiryū*: she suffered the same fate as her sister ships as the remorseless American attack pressed home. She was struck by four 1,000-pound bombs, one on the forward elevator and three on the flight deck. The explosions started huge fires among the aircraft on the hangar deck and the forward flight deck collapsed into the hangar. The elevator was hurled against the ship's bridge. The ship was an inferno and a US bomber actually strafed *Hiryū*'s flight deck, killing several anti-aircraft gunners.

But *Yorktown* herself was in trouble. *Hiryū*'s strike force was already about to attack the US carrier.

The attackers had been picked up on *Yorktown*'s radar at about 13.30 and she cleared for action. Her returning dive-bombers were moved from the landing circle to clear the area for anti-aircraft fire. The Dauntlesses were ordered aloft to form a CAP.

Yorktown's fighters were vectored to intercept the oncoming Japanese aircraft. The Wildcat fighters attack broke up the Japanese formation. *'Planes were flying in every direction and many were falling in flames,'* according to Captain Buckmaster after the action. The leader of the 'Vals', Lieutenant Michio Kobayashi, was probably shot down in this battle.

Despite an intensive AA barrage and violent evasive manoeuvring, some Japanese got through. *Yorktown* was hit by three bombs. The third hit was the most damaging as a Val went out of control just as he dropped his bomb. Plane and bomb hit just abaft the starboard elevator and penetrated the hangar deck. The hangar deck officer ordered the emergency sprinkler system, quickly extinguishing the fire but blocking any aircraft operations.

The second bomb hit the ship on the port side, pierced the flight deck and exploded in the lower part of the funnel. This was a deadly hit as it fractured the air intakes for the ship's boilers, which were blown out. Without air, smoke and gases began filling the fire rooms. The men at number one boiler remained at their post trying to keep enough steam pressure to allow the auxiliary steam systems to function.

The third bomb and plane hit the carrier on the starboard side, pierced the side of number one elevator and exploded in the ship deep down in the fourth deck, starting a fire near the forward avgas bunker and the magazines. The area was promptly flooded with carbon dioxide which undoubtedly saved the ship from a disastrous explosion.

Yorktown lost power and slowed to 6 knots. At 14.40, about twenty minutes after the bomb hit that had shut down most of the boilers, *Yorktown* slowed to a stop, dead in the water. The damage repair teams worked furiously to get the engines restarted. At about 15.40, *Yorktown* prepared to get under way; and, at 15.50 was, astonishingly, once more ready for action.

She hauled down her yellow breakdown flag and hoisted a huge new (10 feet wide and 15 feet long) American battle ensign. Just in time: the battle was not over, because the ship's radar picked up yet another incoming air group at a distance of 33 miles. At 16.00, and manoeuvring sharply, *Yorktown* picked up speed, making 20 knots. The fighters she had launched and vectored out to intercept made contact with the enemy and reported that the incoming planes were 'Kate' torpedo bombers.

The Japanese attacks were pressed home with great bravery. *Yorktown* manoeuvred hard, avoiding at least two torpedoes before another two struck the port side within minutes of each other, at about 16.20. The carrier was mortally wounded; losing power and dead in the water with a jammed rudder and an increasing list to port.

As the ship's list progressed, with no engines, controlling the flooding looked impossible with all boiler fires out, all power lost, no electrics and a growing list to port. *Yorktown* was doomed.

The list continued to increase. When it reached 26 degrees, the captain agreed that capsizing was imminent and ordered abandon ship to save lives.

By nightfall the battle was over. Throughout the night of 6 June and into the morning of 7 June, *Yorktown* remained afloat and an attempt was made to salvage her. However, Japanese submarine *I-168* had discovered the disabled carrier and next morning launched a salvo of four torpedoes from the starboard beam. One torpedo hit USS *Hammann,* a destroyer stationed alongside, which sank quickly. Two of the torpedoes struck *Yorktown.* By 06.30 her list was rapidly increasing to port. Shortly afterwards, the ship turned over and at 07.00 finally sank.

Over the next two days, the US forces continued their attacks, forcing the Japanese to abandon the battle and retreat. Two of the fleeing Japanese heavy cruisers were sunk by follow-up carrier-launched air attacks. The Japanese defeat was crushing and total. They lost approximately 3,057 men, including many of their finest and most experienced aircrew, four carriers, three cruisers and hundreds of aircraft, while the United States lost approximately 362 men, one carrier, one destroyer and 144 aircraft. This critical US victory stopped the advance of Japan in the Pacific and allowed the United States to go on the offensive to begin shrinking the Japanese Empire through a long campaign of island-hopping invasions. Midway had huge strategic consequences and changed the tide of the Pacific war.

As dawn approached on the morning of 5 June, Midway itself was safe. At midnight the night before, Admiral Nimitz had sent his message congratulating his task forces:

'You who participated in the Battle of Midway today have written a glorious page in our history. I am proud to be associated with you.'

There can be no doubt of the importance of the US victory at Midway. The Japanese defeat changed the tide of war and history. Military historian John Keegan called Midway 'the most stunning and decisive blow in the history of naval warfare', and historian Craig Symonds called it 'one of the most consequential naval engagements in world history, ranking alongside Salamis, Trafalgar and Tsushima Strait, as both tactically decisive and strategically influential'. There can be no doubt that, in addition to the bravery of those who fought that day, intelligence was the real battle winner.

For example, Admiral Nimitz and his task force commanders had invaluable advantages at dawn on 4 June: thanks to sigint, the US had advance knowledge of the Japanese objectives and the Japanese Midway and Aleutian Strike Forces order of battle. They also had before them the composition of the Midway forces, the timetables for the enemy attacks and the axes of advance and planned routes. A commander could ask for little more: thanks to sigint, Nimitz was in the fortunate position of the card player who can see his opponent's hand.

The invaluable contributions made by communications intelligence were long afterwards recognized by senior naval officials in Washington and Honolulu. In their words, communications intelligence had given the United States a 'priceless advantage' over the Japanese which had been provided to the naval high command by the communications intelligence unit in Hawaii under the direction of Commander Joseph J. Rochefort.

However, the battle had two unpleasant consequences. Admiral Nimitz's final estimate of the make-up of the Japanese Midway Force fell into the hands of a reporter, Stanley Johnston, an embedded journalist for the *Chicago Tribune*, sailing back to San Diego with survivors from the battle. He had been sharing a cabin with the Executive Officer of *Yorktown* and had somehow seen a copy of a TOP SECRET-COMINT signal.

Sensing a scoop, the ambitious reporter filed his story. On 7 June 1942, five days after Johnston's arrival in San Diego and the day after CINCPAC's Official Communique appeared, announcing 'a momentous US victory', Johnston published his story stressing the US foreknowledge of Japanese forces and their plans. This was picked up by the *Chicago Tribune* and other newspapers in Washington and New York. The headlines that introduced the story in the *Washington Times-Herald* for 7 June 1942 revealed without a doubt that the author had been privy to secret material concerning Japanese intentions and strategy: '**US KNEW ALL ABOUT JAP FLEET. GUESSED THERE WOULD BE A FEINT AT ONE BASE, REAL ATTACK AT ANOTHER.**'

According to Admiral King's biographer, Thomas B. Buell in *Master of Seapower*, the Chief of the US Navy, a bad-tempered man at the best of times, 'was in a white fury' at his headquarters while his staff frantically tried to discover the source of the leak.

The result was the Battle of Midway continued long after the battle ended and the combatants retired. Because of the confusion that surrounded the US government policies governing secrecy and the need to know in 1942, the

Battle of Midway was refought in the newspapers and courthouses of three major US cities – New York, Chicago and Washington – for several weeks after the battle actually ended. The embedded reporter, Stanley Johnston, had deliberately compromised the US Navy's greatest secret. This was treason.

The argument centred on how the Navy knew of Japanese plans, how that knowledge came into the possession of a civilian newspaper reporter, and how the government should handle a serious security violation. The Navy wanted blood; the press hid behind the sacred text of the First Amendment, guaranteeing freedom of the press. In the end no one was ever formally indicted for revealing to the public – and the enemy – just what a vital role communications intelligence had played in the Japanese defeat. Doubtless the loose-lipped Johnston won a handsome bonus from his editor.

Ironically, no one was sure if the Japanese were fully aware that US cryptologists had successfully penetrated their most secret operational code, or even suspected the magnitude of the warning provided by sigint thanks to Johnston's treacherous article. The Navy's conclusion was that the damage done by the Johnston revelations was slow to emerge because the Japanese themselves did not initially change their procedures. At first it seemed that even the Japanese had not grasped what a vital role their compromised communications had proved. Nevertheless, it was no mere coincidence that within a few weeks of the compromising Johnston story, drastic changes were made in virtually all Japanese codes and ciphers. The Japanese Fleet General-Purpose System changed on 15 August, two months later, and complete communications changes were only finalized by October.

The second, and sad, consequence of the battle for Midway was an ugly piece of bureaucratic assassination by the Navy's communications staff. The old saying 'Victory has many parents – defeat is an orphan' was confirmed as OP-20-G tried to take all the credit for code-breaking before Midway. At its heart was who was really responsible for the code-breaking success that had made victory possible.

Rochefort had some powerful enemies who were only too happy to denigrate his role in the great victory. His titular boss was a Captain Redman, Officer Commanding OP-20-G in Washington. Redman's brother just happened to be the senior officer in charge of all radio communications for the US Navy. It was a deadly combination, because the Redman brothers, who were Rochefort's theoretical own bosses, felt as though Rochefort had ignored them and gone behind their backs with his assessment, made them look bad and, bluntly, they were jealous. They questioned Rochefort's fitness for an award.

Rochefort, in fact, was 'a total aristocratic, quiet, soft-spoken guy who did have a very acerbic wit, a sharp sense of humour... a workaholic' according to a contemporary. He worked himself and his crypto staff to death and was considered mildly eccentric. His contributions in radio intelligence were legendary among his colleagues in Hawaii and his services were so highly valued by the Commander-in-Chief of the Pacific Fleet, Admiral Chester Nimitz, that, after the American victory at Midway, he was recommended for a Distinguished Service Medal. He didn't get it.

In Washington, the CNO, Admiral King, denied the award on the recommendation of his staff. His chief of staff was Russell Wilson, whom Rochefort had encountered on the battleship *Pennsylvania* many years earlier. They did not get along. Russell Wilson recommended against the medal, quoting the Redman brothers, who were Rochefort's immediate bosses, both of whom felt humiliated by Rochefort's success. Admiral King tended to trust his immediate advisers and followed their advice.

The upshot was that in late October 1942, Commander Joseph Rochefort, USN, was removed from his job as officer in charge of the Navy's radio intelligence centre in Honolulu. Trained in both Japanese language and radio intelligence, he had been sent there a little over a year before by OP-20-G, the element in naval communications in overall charge of radio intelligence: now OP-20-G removed him. He was appointed to command a dry dock ashore in San Diego where the hero of Midway languished for the rest of the war.

Let the last word rest with Ensign 'Mac' Showers, who was the last surviving member of Layton's Pacific Fleet Intelligence Staff and who would later rise to the rank of rear admiral before his death in 2012: 'Rochefort was the origin of OPINTEL. No such systems existed prior to Pearl Harbor. No one told us to do it, or how to do it. Rochefort had the concept and Layton masterminded the execution.'

It was not until 1985 that anyone from the Pacific COMINT centres received any formal recognition for their contribution to either the Coral Sea or Midway victories. In 1985, in response to a widespread campaign and the combined efforts of his friends, the late Joseph Rochefort finally received the Distinguished Service Medal posthumously from the Secretary of the Navy.

UNCOMBINED OPERATIONS – DIEPPE, 1942

'There was mortar fire, and there were machine-gun nests in the cliffs which weren't seen by our intelligence people because they had them covered, and they had heavy six-pounder or more cannons shooting at us. We were sitting ducks'

DAVID LLOYD HART

On 19 August 1942, men of the 2nd Canadian Division based in Sussex, England, raided Dieppe, a small port on the northern coast of France. The landings were just after dawn in broad daylight and supported by thirty of the new, heavily armoured Churchill infantry support tanks. Five hours later the defeated invaders withdrew, having sustained the heaviest casualties of any Allied attack in the whole Second World War.

Of the 5,000 men who were in the force, 2,700 were killed, wounded or captured. As only 4,000 of the attackers got ashore, this meant a casualty rate of 60 per cent: worse even than that benchmark of loss, the first day of the Somme in 1916. The German defenders were astonished at the stupidity and temerity of their assailants. One German commentator wrote, 'This [reckless] affair mocked all rules of military strategy and logic.' Many myths and mysteries surround the Dieppe affair.

To some Canadian nationalists, Dieppe has become a defining myth of nationhood with brave Canadian soldiers being sold out by callous and incompetent British generals. To the British public, it was seen as a sacrificial political gesture to show Stalin that the British Empire really was trying to take the pressure off the USSR by opening up a second front; and to conspiracy theorists, Dieppe has even been represented as a cunning British plot to demonstrate to the American planners in Washington, new to the European war in 1942 and hot for some decisive action against the Nazis, that any premature cross-Channel invasion could only end in bloody failure.

All of these allegations have an element of truth: but no single one of them is the whole story. For, in one vital aspect, Dieppe is unique: it seems to have been the only major assault mounted by imperial forces without official authorization from the Combined Chiefs of Staff. It is the only *unrecorded* major Allied operational decision of the Second World War. Therein lies the mystery behind the myths about Dieppe.

Close analysis of the evidence reveals that Dieppe was nothing less than an *unofficial* attack that circumvented the chain of command. The attack on Dieppe went in without proper resources, lacked intelligence on many key aspects of the German defences and, last but by no means least, was not given the full support on the day by the British Home Commands, which had often been kept in the dark or just ignored. Worse, its planners deliberately chose not to alert the official intelligence organizations to the attack or its intelligence requirements. It was, as a result, a disastrous intelligence blunder.

If it seems bizarre that a commander could mount what was essentially a private attack against the Wehrmacht's Fortress Europe, then no less bizarre was the personality, ambition and track record of the man responsible for the Dieppe operation: Captain Lord Louis Mountbatten. At the end of 1941, Mountbatten was promoted from a ship's captain in the Royal Navy and appointed Chief of Combined Operations, with a seat alongside Field Marshal Sir Alan Brooke on the Chiefs of Staff. By March 1942, Mountbatten had been elevated *three grades* to become the youngest vice admiral in British naval history.

Mountbatten's principal claims to fame were three. He had shown himself to be a dashing captain of destroyers – his last three ships were rendered *hors de combat* under him in circumstances that his detractors, of whom there were many, claimed only demonstrated his recklessness and inexperience. Second, he was a master of personal public relations, projecting the image of a young, dashing and heroic commander able to carry the war to the Germans and lighten the gloom in a Britain weary of defeats. Last, Mountbatten was formidably well connected. A cousin of the King, confidant of the prime minister, personal friend of Noël Coward and able effortlessly to summon powerful friends from Hollywood and the British Establishment alike, Mountbatten was a public relations dream in the war-darkened Britain of early 1942. There was even talk among some Conservative politicians (almost certainly started by Mountbatten himself) that he should be elevated *over* the Chiefs of Staff in some capacity.

Mountbatten's carefully cultivated legend hid a ruthlessness and ambition that frequently accompany great men and their success. He was not averse to cheating during naval exercises to gain advantage over his brother officers, and he deliberately suppressed or falsified military records after the war when he felt that his carefully cultivated historical image was in danger. In the somewhat guarded words of even his *official* biographer, Mountbatten chose to 'rewrite history with a cavalier indifference to fact'.

Mountbatten's vanity knew few limits. In the midst of his wartime responsibilities he could be found posturing on the film set of *In Which We Serve*, a propaganda hagiography based on his own experiences in which the dashing destroyer captain was played by his close friend Noël Coward. Mountbatten actually wrote to Coward after the Dieppe raid saying, 'Your letter caught me on my busiest day… but since the matter… is so pressing, I am dealing with it before my service duties.' A normal commander would have been visiting the wounded and dying and debriefing the survivors.

Beaverbrook himself warned during the war, 'Don't trust Mountbatten in any public capacity,' knowing that Mountbatten's dark and untrustworthy side would brook no attack on his carefully managed reputation or self-image. Despite Beaverbrook's warning, the young, unscrupulous, vain and ambitious aristocrat had now been given a seat on the highest military council in the land, together with the resources and authority to attack the German-occupied coasts of Europe. Mountbatten's personality combined with his newly acquired power and ambition were to have tragic consequences.

That Mountbatten had much to conceal is no longer in doubt. After the war, the University of Southampton spent £2.8 million in buying the Mountbatten diaries and letters for the nation from the Mountbatten estate. As the author and literary agent Andrew Lownie discovered, however, in the course of writing his biography of Mountbatten, more than £1 million has since been spent trying to suppress them, although neither the Cabinet Office nor the Southampton University archive has so far answered questions about the cost of their litigation to keep the papers secret. The Mountbatten Dieppe papers remain buried by the UK government: why?

The roots of the 1942 attack on Dieppe are to be found twenty-four years earlier, in the attack on Zeebrugge on St George's Day 1918. Under the leadership of Admiral Sir Roger Keyes of the Dover Patrol, a raiding force of warships, marines and soldiers stormed the German submarine pens on the Belgian coast in a daring attempt to block the Kaiser's U-boats from access to the sea. The raid was partly successful and, despite heavy casualties, provided a much-needed boost to British morale, at the time reeling under the impact of the Germans' last ground offensive of the Great War. The Zeebrugge raid created an image of a brilliant military coup, causing serious damage at little cost – precisely the sort of indirect attack so beloved of British strategists over the years.

By 1940 Keyes was back, this time as Chief of Combined Operations with a remit to attack the victorious Germans around the coasts of Europe and repeat his success of 1918. Quite why the British felt that they had to raid the defended coasts of Europe is a question that seems rarely to have been asked – the Germans never felt a reciprocal urge to mount similar military adventures against the British coastline. In 1940, however, Britain's new Prime Minister Churchill was determined that even though British forces had been evicted from the Continent, the offensive must be maintained, not just to inflict casualties on the Germans but also as an act of faith with the suffering populations of occupied Europe, who in 1941 had no other hope of release. Apart from Bomber Command, it was the only offensive option at the time.

Combined Operations was a curious command. It was essentially an experimental tri-service co-ordinating and planning staff, put together as a result of wartime experience and designed to bring together the military assets of the three armed services to launch, as its name implied, combined operations against the enemy. By the time Mountbatten took over in late 1941 on the direct instruction of Winston Churchill, his orders were in Mountbatten's own words 'to continue the raids, so splendidly begun by Keyes, to keep the offensive spirit boiling... Secondly, to prepare for the invasion of Europe, without which we can never win this war.' Mountbatten also claimed that Churchill said, 'I want you to turn the south coast of England from a bastion of defence into a springboard for attack.'

This was heady stuff for a recently promoted 41-year-old naval captain whose next command was to have been one of the Royal Navy's new aircraft carriers. But Churchill had another, political agenda implicit in his choice of the dashing Mountbatten for such a high-profile appointment: the prime minister had to sell British aggressive spirit to the Americans, newly arrived in the war and sceptical of their ally's fighting capabilities. After the humiliations of Norway, France, Dunkirk, Greece, Crete, Malaya and Singapore, and Rommel's victories in North Africa, culminating in the surrender at Tobruk in June 1942, the Americans had every justification for their scepticism about the British Army's ability to fight. Even Churchill could not understand why the Army kept surrendering, saying plaintively on more than one occasion, 'Why won't our soldiers *fight*?'

Churchill had chosen well. Conscious of the effect of Mountbatten's charm, good looks and *beau sabreur* image on the Roosevelts, particularly Mrs Eleanor Roosevelt, the wily premier knew that if anyone could impress Britain's fighting spirit upon the highest councils of American decision-making, it would be Mountbatten. During visits to Washington the new commander of 'Combined Ops' won over all the Americans he met, including that doyen of republican military values and America's most powerful soldier, General George C. Marshall, who became a personal friend. The young hero had done his diplomatic PR work well, doing what he did so brilliantly, and at a time when it mattered for the rest of his countrymen, not just for himself. Churchill was justifiably proud of his protégé. Mountbatten himself appears to have been well aware of Churchill's wider intentions, boasting to a friend, 'Winston told me what he wanted and now it was up to me to carry it out.' Given this level of backing, it would have been difficult for the most humble personality not to have been tempted into delusions of grandeur, and Mountbatten's many friends had never accused him of excessive humility. In the words of the Canadian authority on Dieppe, Professor Brian Loring Villa, 'for thus turning Mountbatten's head, Churchill was in no small measure responsible.' There is even a case for seeing Mountbatten as a *victim* of an unscrupulous Churchill, manipulating the young admiral's weaknesses and vanity for his own ends.

Once Keyes had gone, Mountbatten lost no time in putting his own stamp on Combined Operations and was, like many others in his position, able initially to reap the rewards of his predecessor's efforts. Combined Ops basked in the glory of successful raids on Vaagso off Norway and the Parachute Regiment's first battle honour, the daring theft of German radar secrets from Bruneval in northern France. Even the St Nazaire raid of 27 March 1942, despite its cost (and five VCs), was counted a success because the destruction of the huge dry dock – the only one capable of servicing German battleships on the Atlantic – removed a major strategic pressure on the British. All these attacks were originally the fruits of Keyes's staff regime and planning.

For Combined Ops's new plans for 1942, Mountbatten's staff unveiled a wide-ranging schedule of attacks, ranging from the temporary seizure of Alderney in the Channel Islands to a hare-brained scheme for a raid on the Gestapo headquarters in Paris. The set piece was to be an attack on Dieppe in June, under the code name 'Rutter'.

The aims at Dieppe, despite later claims that it was the invasion of Europe gone wrong, or some kind of bluff to confuse the Germans and the French Resistance, were really quite straightforward: to see whether it was possible to seize and hold a major port for a limited period; to obtain intelligence from captured prisoners, documents and equipment; and to gauge the German reaction to a sizeable demonstration blow against the French coast.

The official Canadian war history covers the reason for a frontal attack on the town: '… it was feared that an attempt to "pinch out" a port by landings on its flanks might produce delays which would give the enemy time to demolish the harbour, whereas if the place could be seized by a blow into the centre the problem would be solved.'

There were other agendas at play, too. A small secret team from a new 'Intelligence Assault Unit' drawn from the recently formed Royal Marine Commandos, was intended to sneak deep ashore under cover of the main assault and, in the midst of the mayhem, were to make their way into town to a German naval headquarters housed in a hotel. Their prize was the Enigma cipher machines used to encode naval signals, as well as code books and lists of settings. In the team was Alan Saunders, a nineteen-year-old South Londoner who had signed up for 'special duties of a hazardous nature' and just completed six months of gruelling preparation in the Scottish Highlands.

Training for the operation was thorough and the intelligence very detailed. 'They knew exactly which room, the precise location of the safe and even what type it was,' recalls Alan's son, Ian Saunders. And at least one member of the team had an extremely unconventional background: he was an ace safe-cracker who had been released from prison to do his bit for King and Country.

Such material would be pure gold, in intelligence terms, to the code-breakers at Bletchley Park, who were engaged in a long-running battle to decode the U-boat signals traffic that could give the Navy an edge in its life-or-death struggle to keep the Atlantic sea lanes open.

In addition to these purely military goals, there were three other, less clear-cut agendas in play. The first was the wish of the Air Staff to draw the Luftwaffe in the West into a major air battle and inflict serious casualties on the German aircraft deployed in France; the second was the purely political goal of showing the USSR that Britain really was trying to get at the Germans' throats; and the third and most hazy agenda of all was the wish of the Canadian government to get more into the war.

The first of these was to play firmly into Mountbatten's hands later. Although the Royal Navy and the Army were wary of committing too many forces to Rutter, the Chief of the Air Staff, Air Marshal Portal, was only too keen to demonstrate the power of his vastly expanded fighter force in 1942 and bring the Luftwaffe to action in the hope of inflicting a crushing defeat on the Germans. A major fighter sweep over a port well within range of the southern English airfields would 'draw the Luftwaffe up'. As a result, the RAF became willing supporters of the plan whereas the other two fighting services were relatively lukewarm.

Churchill's political difficulties in the spring and summer 1942 had much to do with his backing for Operation Rutter in particular and Combined Ops activities in general. Any British victory in the West would be an important bargaining chip in the complicated manoeuvring that was taking place between the Allies. The need for decisive action had become more acute following a speech by Stalin in February 1942 in which he made what seemed to be an oblique offer to negotiate a separate truce with Hitler. A thoroughly alarmed British Foreign Office assessed the speech as an attempt either to negotiate a truce or to bring pressure to bear on the British to ease the pressure on the Russians. In any case, the USSR had to be reassured of Britain's determination to fight. A major attack in the West would do this, irrespective of its outcome.

As the summer wore on with its wearisome defeats in the desert and rumblings of political discontent with his leadership at home, Churchill became ever more depressed and desperate for a success – any success. With the fall of Tobruk on 21 June 1942, the political volcano in Westminster and Whitehall erupted as the murmurings against his wartime leadership surfaced. A torrent of political and press criticism burst over Churchill and his administration. A vote of no confidence was tabled in the House of Commons and, although the outcome looked suspiciously like a put-up job (the vote was 475 to 25 in his favour), Churchill was badly shaken. He admitted later that 'the only thing he ever feared was the House of Commons in full cry.'

Churchill needed a success to survive; and he knew it. Now he had a sceptical Parliament and Whitehall to battle with as well as the Germans and his strategic allies, Roosevelt and Stalin. The cautious and pragmatic Chiefs of Staff frustrated most of his military adventures as premature, content to build up Britain's military strength for the long haul. Churchill the politician, ever conscious of the need to keep the crowd entertained in a democracy, needed some short-term gains. Only Bomber Command under the pugnacious Harris and Combined Ops under the dashing Lord Louis Mountbatten seemed to share his values and be prepared to carry the fight to the enemy in the summer of 1942.

The third agenda for Operation Rutter was to have the greatest human consequences, but was the least practical of the attack's aims. It was the desire of the Canadian Expeditionary Force, after two and a half years of inactivity, to get into action. Since the outbreak of war, the Canadian prime minister, Mackenzie King, had followed a politically sensible but basically unsustainable policy. He had given the public appearance of vigorous Canadian support for the war but without committing his troops to actual fighting. Inevitably, with the raw aggression and justifiably famous fighting spirit of the Canadians, this policy could not last for ever. Although thousands of Canadians flocked to the colours, Mackenzie King knew that conscription, especially in French-speaking Canada, for service overseas was a recipe for political trouble and so he ensured that Canada's exposure to front-line combat was reduced to the minimum.

The political contradictions inherent in Canada's war policy gradually forced themselves upon the politicians back home in Ottawa. Having created a large, well-trained and well-equipped army and sent it to Sussex in England to prepare for battle, Canada's politicians discovered that their military machine had built up a momentum of its own. The Canadian Expeditionary Force's senior commanders in England, McNaughton, Crerar and Roberts, with two years of training under their belts, were pushing hard for a more active part in the fighting if only to give their bored soldiers something to do. As usual, this showed itself by a rising tide of indiscipline in which the Canadians stole, got drunk, fought and got up to the usual sexual shenanigans common to any large group of fit young men a long way from home with too little to do and too many available, lonely women on their own.

In vain the Canadian PR machine briefed that the Canadian Army's crime rate was no worse than any other. The grim and increasingly irritated citizens of Sussex counted the 3,238 Canadian courts martial up to August 1942 and hoped, like their high-spirited guests, that action would soon focus their minds on other things. In Lord Haw-Haw's mocking words from Berlin, 'If you really want to take Berlin, why don't you give each Canadian soldier a motorcycle and a bottle of whisky? Then declare that Berlin is out of bounds. The Canadians will be there in forty-eight hours!… that would end the war.' By 1942, the Canadians in Britain were the most exercised but least tried army in the war. The Canadians, and their commanders, wanted to fight. When Lieutenant General Harry Crerar, commanding the 1st Canadian Corps, was summoned to Montgomery's headquarters, South East Command, on 27 April 1942 and asked whether his Canadian soldiers would like to take part in a major attack on the French coast, his answer was brisk – 'You bet!'

On 13 May 1942, the Chiefs of Staff approved Operation Rutter. As it stood, the plan relied on a frontal attack across Dieppe town beach, supported by flanking attacks by commandos to knock out coastal batteries covering the approaches. In the air, a thousand RAF sorties would be flown to seize control of the sky and provide an umbrella of air superiority; and offshore, the Navy would bombard the town. Rutter was not a good plan. In the final planning stages the attack was considerably weakened. Alarmed by the risk of air attack on their warships, the Navy refused to provide a battleship or any other capital ship for fire support, and the RAF scaled down their plans for heavy bombing of the seafront at Dieppe to a series of fighter-bomber sweeps and strafing attacks, to avoid French civilian casualties. The Canadian 2nd Division would spearhead the assault and go on to seize a radar station and an airfield at Arques, three miles inland, for a limited period.

On 5 and 6 July, the Canadian troops embarked on their assault ships, but when the weather began to deteriorate they were ordered to batten down the hatches and ride out the weather at anchor. While the troops lay heaving with sea sickness in their small landing craft, two German bombers appeared over one of the Isle of Wight staging ports and bombed the flotilla, without significant result. As the Channel gale continued to blow, on 7 July the operation was cancelled and the troops disembarked to flood the pubs and billets of southern England with stories of the raid on Dieppe that never took place and the horrors of small landing craft in a storm. All concerned believed that 'Dieppe' was hopelessly compromised and now off for ever.

It was just as well. Neither the Army commander, Montgomery, nor the Naval commander at Portsmouth, Admiral Sir William James, really believed in the plan. The more Rutter had developed, the greater their concerns. As the Army commander, Montgomery was very uneasy about the whole idea of a frontal infantry attack, particularly without a proper bombardment by the RAF to soften up the opposition, which C-in-C Bomber Command was not prepared to provide. Bernard Law Montgomery had fought in the First World War and knew all about poorly prepared frontal attacks without proper fire support.

For their part, both the Royal Navy's commander in Portsmouth and the admiral commanding the amphibious forces were mindful of the fate of HMS *Prince of Wales* and HMS *Repulse* only six months previously off Malaya. They had no intention of risking battleships within five miles of an enemy coast and within striking distance of the Luftwaffe's bombers. The First Sea Lord, Admiral Sir Dudley Pound, agreed wholeheartedly. The professional military view was that the Rutter attack on Dieppe had been badly conceived, lacked sufficient fire support and was uncoordinated. Now it was off they could all breathe a sigh of relief.

What the Germans knew about an invasion attempt in the West after the aborted Plan Rutter, and how they reacted to it afterwards, remains a topic of some debate. Most theories do not stand up to rigorous examination of the documentary evidence. Well before August 1942, Hitler and the German High Command were aware of the increasing threat of an invasion and they undertook specific tactical measures to address it from December 1941 on.

What followed the cancellation of Rutter is the beginning of the mystery of Dieppe. Seething from the cancellation of a long-cherished project that would place his command – and himself – firmly in the public eye, and on the receiving end of a number of highly critical reviews of both the overblown organization of Combined Operations and its 'second-rate' planning procedures for Rutter, Mountbatten decided to act on his own. On 8 and 11 July, he called two meetings of the main staffs involved in the original operation and asked for their support to remount the raid. He did not get it.

As the second conference broke up on 11 July, a number of Mountbatten acolytes were quietly asked to remain behind after the main critics of the scheme (such as Rear Admiral Baillie-Grohman, the designated commander of Rutter's naval forces) had left the room. No one is completely clear what transpired at the closed meeting that followed, but from then on Mountbatten and his principal staff officer, Captain John Hughes-Hallett RN, were wholeheartedly dedicated to a substitute operation for Rutter. This was to be called 'Jubilee', and the target was to be Dieppe – again. The master plan saw 1,000 British troops from 3, 4 and 10 (inter-Allied) Commandos, plus fifty United States Rangers attached to No. 4 Commando and fifteen French Commandos attached to No. 10 Commando.

Any major operation to attack the continent of Europe needed the authority of the Chiefs of Staff. What followed that July is one of the more remarkable stories of the Second World War: the commander of Combined Operations, protégé of the prime minister and darling of the media, Lord Louis Mountbatten, set out deliberately to deceive the combined British Chiefs of Staff, the British intelligence co-ordination apparatus, the other armed services and most of his own staff officers. Mountbatten had decided to relaunch the aborted attack on Dieppe under another name and without formal authority. He admitted as much towards the end of his life, in a little-publicized interview with BBC Television in 1972: 'I made the unusual and I suggest rather bold decision that we would remount the operation against Dieppe.'

Even Captain Hughes-Hallett, who was closest to Mountbatten and a total accomplice in the scheme to remount the attack on Dieppe, was concerned at this lack of authorization from the top. He pointed out that as Combined Ops Principal Staff Officer he needed to quote some official authority on all the operation's paperwork and requisitions. Accordingly, on 17 July, Chief of Combined Operations formally minuted the Chiefs of Staff, asking the COS Committee for a specific decision to be included in the minutes of their next meeting that 'the Commander Combined Ops is directed to mount an emergency operation to replace Rutter... using the same forces.' The Chiefs of Staff did not agree, and the item was not recorded in the minutes.

Mountbatten was now getting desperate. He had another go at the Chiefs of Staff Committee on 25 and 26 July, this time asking for a blanket authority to conduct large-scale raids but without specifying the target every time. Already jealous of Mountbatten's rapid rise and privileged access, and highly suspicious of his personal ambitions and motives, the Chiefs of Staff were having none of it. On 27 July, they recorded a decision that merely widened his *planning* powers slightly, but specifically endorsed the existing need for Combined Ops to seek formal authority before embarking on any new operations.

That was enough for Mountbatten, however. Excited at getting his chance and chafing to do something, he gave direct orders for Captain Hughes-Hallett and a few trusted staff officers to proceed. No one knows precisely what he said to Hughes-Hallett, but there seems little doubt that he deceived him, probably by claiming that he had authority from the Chiefs to proceed with the new plan, Jubilee, under the blanket authority of the decision of 27 July widening his planning powers. Hughes-Hallett was a more than willing ally and believed what his charismatic master, a man who spoke directly to prime ministers, film stars and chiefs of staff, told him – which principal staff officer wishing to keep his job would not?

On 28 July, orders were issued to selected Combined Ops staff officers that Rutter was back on, under the authority of the Chiefs of Staff and with the code name Jubilee. New operational orders were issued to the raiding force headquarters on 31 July, and the whole planning frenzy for the aborted operation started again. On 12 August, the Chiefs of Staff noted that Mountbatten could, in principle, *plan* to mount a substitute raid for the abandoned Rutter. Dieppe as a target was not mentioned, nor discussed.

To the end of his days, Mountbatten used these broad planning directives to give the impression that he had received official backing for his second Dieppe raid. Interestingly, none of his colleagues on the Chiefs of Staff nor the Cabinet papers have ever supported this claim, either during or after the war. Even Churchill had great difficulty retracing the decisions for the Dieppe raid when he wrote his own history of the war, *The Hinge of Fate*, in 1950. Eventually, frustrated, he accepted Mountbatten's account and took responsibility himself: but we know from his correspondence that Churchill did so only because neither he nor anyone else could locate any substantive Cabinet documents to the contrary.

The fact was that there was no specific authorization to relaunch an attack on Dieppe and Mountbatten knew it. He got round the problem of the troops by telling the Canadian commanders to keep details of the new operation to themselves, 'in the interests of security'. A limited number of staff officers began to plan Jubilee in great secrecy. But not everyone was informed. Under the guise of 'security' (that invaluable military mantra for those hoping to conceal the unpalatable), several key agencies were deliberately kept in the dark. Rear Admiral Baillie-Grohman, the uncooperative naval commander, was excluded and Captain Hughes-Hallett offered the job by Mountbatten. Montgomery's army staff at GHQ were ignored as Mountbatten dealt directly and secretly with the Canadian Army's chain of command. Most dangerous of all, neither Mountbatten's own Chief of Staff nor the high-level intelligence liaison officer and his official deputy, Major General Haydon, were informed that Dieppe was back on. The nearest commercial analogy might be if the Chairman of Ford UK decided to invest in a new car in Britain but did not inform Ford HQ back in the USA and also did not tell the sales and marketing director or company secretary. As a planner one is left wondering how Mountbatten thought he could ever get away with it. Presumably he was gambling on a major success, in the knowledge that 'victory has no critics'.

The real danger to the revised operation lay in the intelligence world. While the logistics and administration will always give the game away that a military operation of some sort is afoot, they need not give the *objective*. The demands for intelligence will inevitably expose the target, however: Mountbatten's subterfuge needed maps, plans, pictures and information about Dieppe. Mountbatten, in fact, now had two threats to his security; not only did he need to keep his revised operation secret from the Germans, but he also had to keep it secret so far as possible from the Chiefs of Staff. The scale of the deception is breathtaking. But Mountbatten still needed intelligence – a lot of intelligence – to mount a successful assault on a defended port in occupied Europe.

Over the years, the British have shown considerable skill in the higher management and co-ordination of intelligence. Learning by mistakes and experience, they had refined a cardinal principle by the end of 1941; *all* operations were to be notified to the Inter-Services Security Board. The purpose behind this piece of bureaucracy was simple but profoundly important: the ISSB was the clearing house for deception planning. It alone coordinated the activities of the London Controlling Section, the highly secret British deception staff described in Chapter 2. The ISSB was also responsible for the security of operations. Only the ISSB knew what lies and what real secrets were being leaked to the Germans by various counter-intelligence and deception operations. Only ISSB was capable of evaluating the total security risk to any one operation.

Mountbatten deliberately chose not to inform the Inter-Services Security Board of Operation Jubilee. The official history, *British Intelligence in the Second World War*, is absolutely clear on the omission. Not only that, Mountbatten did not request any support from the major intelligence agencies like the Secret Intelligence Service, preferring to rely on the existing Rutter target dossiers. He updated this basic intelligence with an ad hoc series of low-level intelligence tasks put out to tactical photo-reconnaissance flights and small special signals units which could be tasked directly by Combined Ops without awkward questions being asked.

The dangers of this disregard of intelligence were serious. In the first place, Mountbatten risked not getting the very best intelligence for his troops as they went up the beach. In the second, he could not be sure how much the Germans knew of his plans. Dieppe was without doubt by now a deeply compromised target. Six thousand soldiers had been talking about the cancelled Rutter raid of 7 July all over southern England since they had disembarked. Why should they not? It was history now so far as they were concerned. Any real security about the Dieppe raid was long gone. To make matters worse, the London Controlling Section (about which Mountbatten knew little) was now busy passing carefully placed nuggets of information about the *old* Dieppe raid to their opposite numbers on the German intelligence staff. Now that Rutter was cancelled there were few restrictions on feeding really good titbits to the enemy in order to boost the credibility of MI5's turned Abwehr double agents.

The British Double Cross operation, using MI5's turned agents to send false messages back under control to their German masters, had a field day in the summer of 1942. As a result, the German intelligence service had at least four specific warnings about Dieppe from false agents whom they trusted in the UK. The Germans, in fact, were extremely well informed, so much so that some commentators have speculated that the second Dieppe operation was a deliberate deception operation offering a sacrifice to build up the reputation of MI5's false agents with the Abwehr. This seems far-fetched. The most likely explanation is that ISSB gave clearance to leak redundant secrets to the Abwehr after Rutter was aborted. The only problem was that they were *not* redundant secrets: Dieppe really was going to be attacked, but Mountbatten had chosen not to tell ISSB that the operation was back on again. The risks to Mountbatten's forces were horrific.

In one of those extraordinary twists of fate that happen in war, the German intelligence service in Paris never passed their warnings down to the local troops defending Dieppe. Although there was a practice alert on the French coast on 17 and 18 August 1942, and both Hitler and the German C-in-C West, von Rundstedt, warned that 'raids could be made against the French coast', there is no evidence that this was linked to any specific warning about an attack on the Dieppe area. There is no evidence that the Germans were reinforced and lying in wait for the Canadians. Neither Mountbatten's nor the Canadians' intelligence staffs could have known that, however. Mountbatten was lucky.

The intelligence requirements for Operation Jubilee were relatively straightforward. To attack a defended coastline, operations staffs require four specific kinds of information: the topography of the battlefield – beach gradients, currents, etc.; the enemy's strengths, dispositions and layout; enemy weapons, their locations and capabilities; and last, knowledge of the enemy's reaction plans – to fight, to reinforce or to withdraw.

None of these is particularly difficult in theory, but they all require access to the complete pantheon of intelligence sources and agencies. For example, beach composition and gradients may be laid out in pre-war books, but time and tide mean that a frogman has to double-check what the topography is really like as close to the time of the raid as possible. The enemy's strengths, dispositions and morale can be gleaned from a number of sources: photo reconnaissance, agent reports, sigint disclosures and even open-source material. Finding his weapons and their ammunition stocks is harder; once photo reconnaissance has shown where they are sited, only local information from agents, captured information or sigint will reveal the real details that flesh out the camera's pictures. Finally, knowledge of an enemy's plans and intentions will come only from humint, captured documents or sigint.

The point is that the whole of Britain's exceptional intelligence-collection armoury was needed to mount a successful operation of Dieppe's scale. It was available and perfectly capable of answering all the questions. But if Mountbatten asked for the full Joint Intelligence Committee support package for Dieppe, he knew that the JIC would alert the Cabinet Office and Chiefs of Staff to his scheme to remount the raid, and they might stop him. So, by bypassing the Chiefs of Staff, Mountbatten was forced to bypass the intelligence agencies.

By ignoring the intelligence community, Mountbatten was accepting the risk of deliberately keeping his troops in the dark about vital information. This failure to use the full intelligence resources available was to cause needless casualties. To give only two simple but deadly examples: the beach at Dieppe was too steep and too stony for loose-tracked tanks; second, there were artillery pieces hidden in the caves at either flank of the beach. On the day, the failure to identify these points would kill many Canadians. Both could have easily been answered by the Joint Intelligence Committee and its intelligence collection assets, had they known, but Mountbatten dare not risk asking for help from an outside and senior agency. He wanted to keep his private bid for glory secret.

Some of the other intelligence blunders at Dieppe were almost farcical. Combined Operations intelligence staff – in common with Military Intelligence – identified the Wehrmacht unit holding the area at Dieppe as the 110th Division. This would doubtless have pleased the sweating soldiers of that division greatly, had it been true: at the time they were trudging across Russia, 2,000 miles away, heading east in pursuit of the fleeing Soviets across the endless steppe.

The actual unit at Dieppe sampling the delights of the wine and French girls was in reality the 571st Infantry Regiment of the 302nd Division, a category two division consisting largely of Poles and middle-aged ethnic Germans equipped with a motley mixture of horses, bicycles, captured Czech and French guns and anything else that the harassed quartermaster staff at Wehrmacht GHQ West in Paris could scrounge from Berlin. Lacking weapons, ammunition and trained, fit manpower, the commander of 302nd Division wisely chose to concentrate his forces to cover the most likely and most dangerous enemy approach: the shingle beach at Dieppe. Equally wisely, he ordered a policy of not keeping his guns in the prepared emplacements in case they were spotted and attacked from the air. Combined Ops' tactical air reconnaissance flights were quite incapable of seeing *inside* the caves in the cliffs at Dieppe as they swept low along the beach. The wisdom of General-Major Konrad Haase's simple but effective divisional defence plan – from the defenders' point of view – came on the day, when the flanking fire from his concealed assortment of weapons and his single captured French tank, firmly cemented into the sea wall, slaughtered men and machines alike as the Canadians struggled up the steeply sloping stones of the beach.

If Mountbatten ignored the services of SIS and the SOE agent networks in France, his staff did at least try to involve the signals intelligence services at the tactical level if not at the strategic JIC level. This was as a result of the experiences of the raid on St Nazaire in the spring. If the command staff could listen to the enemy's reactions and countermoves as they actually occurred during a battle it would allow the Combined Ops force commanders to react accordingly. This was a sound tactical policy and actually worked on the day at St Nazaire far better than anyone at Cheadle (the intercept HQ) believed possible. Ironically, at Dieppe the Combined Ops HQ signals staff was completely flooded with tactical sigint and was unable to pass on any really timely intelligence to the air commander during the battle. However, the intention was sound.

As the day for the attack drew closer, concerns about the prospects for Jubilee's success and the security of the operation began to emerge. Security became the prime concern; after the cancellation of the first attack this seemed a bit pointless, but various scares over compromise and lost documents highlighted the need to keep the force secure from the British and the Joint Intelligence Committee, if from nobody else. Even the gung-ho Canadians had their doubts. Major General J. H. Roberts, commanding the 2nd Canadian Infantry Division, was uneasy about the plan but was gulled into an uneasy silence by the slick reassurances of Mountbatten and his staff at Combined Ops; after all, he reasoned, these were the experienced officers, not him. But many Canadians shared his unease.

The attack began to go wrong from the outset. The German Navy had a regular inshore milk run which tried to slip small merchant shipping along the French coast at night. This was well known to the Dover and Portsmouth maritime search radars, as was the Germans' general routine and timings for these little convoys. Precise intelligence on the convoy programme was held at the highest levels, however, as it would have come from sensitive strategic sources like the Enigma code-breaking operation. No one on Mountbatten's intelligence staff had asked for details of German Channel movements on the night of 18/19 August. To do so would have compromised the operation to the Joint Intelligence Committee and thus the Chiefs of Staff.

The result was inevitable. In the early hours of 19 August, as the convoy carrying the men of 3 Commando closed on the cliffs of Belleville and Berneval to the east of Dieppe, their escort blundered into a German coastal convoy in the dark. Despite two clear signals from the RN radars in England at 01.27

and 02.44 to the Force Commander aboard HMS *Calpe*, giving the German convoy's precise position, the warning was not passed on to the eastern flank naval escorts. Combined Ops planning had gone wrong from the outset.

The first the Jubilee attackers knew of the German convoy was when a star shell burst overhead and in the cold, wobbly light the German escorts opened fire, knocking out the vulnerable Steam Gun Boat Number 5 providing close protection for the eastern landing craft. A furious firefight developed with tracer streaming in all directions 'like a firework display' as other Royal Navy escorts joined in before the outgunned Germans were driven off with heavy losses. Jubilee was compromised. As dawn broke, the shocked occupants of the eastern landing craft closed on the coast in an eerie silence. As one of the sergeants in 3 Commando said, 'Through the binoculars you could see the bloody Germans watching *us* through binoculars as we ran in to the beach!'

At first light the various assaults got under way. Out to the east on the left flank, 3 Commando under the redoubtable Peter Young (who had watched in mounting horror from the very middle of the convoy firefight) climbed straight up the German barbed wire, 'which the Huns had so helpfully strung down the face of the cliff to help us ascend', and led the commandos in a successful assault that silenced the Goebbels artillery battery inland. By lunchtime Young was back in Newhaven, his battledress and his hands ripped to shreds. On the extreme western flank at Varengeville, Lord Lovat's disciplined 4 Commando destroyed the guns of the Hess battery in a textbook pincer movement assault.

These diversionary commando attacks to knock out the German guns covering the flanks were the only real successes of the day. The soldiers who landed on Dieppe's beaches walked into a nightmare. To everyone's surprise and horror, up on the cliffs on either side of Dieppe at Berneval-le-Grand and Varengeville, two well positioned artillery batteries accurately shelled the shoreline.

The guns had not been spotted by Mountbatten's air reconnaissance photographers in the lead up to the raid. More worrying still, both beaches seemed prepared for the attack. The CO of the 1st Battalion, Royal Hamilton Light Infantry, Lieutenant Colonel Robert Labatt, later said he saw recently placed German mortar range markers on the beach.

Closer in, on the eastern edge of Dieppe at Puys, the Royal Regiment of Canada was mowed down as the soldiers struggled to get ashore, suffering 225 killed and 264 prisoners. Only thirty-three wounded men survived. To the west of the town at Pourville, the South Saskatchewans and Cameron Highlanders of Canada got ashore without too much difficulty but were unable to cross the River Scie to get into Dieppe. David Lloyd Hart still remembers every detail of the bloody and chaotic scene on the beach during the ill-fated raid in 1942.

Hart, a communications operator, remembers being stuck on a crippled boat about five metres from shore, unable to swim for the beach because he couldn't leave the vessel's radio unit.

'The fire was terrible,' he said in an interview at his home in Montreal. 'There was mortar fire and there were machine-gun nests in the cliffs which weren't seen by our intelligence people because they [the Germans] had them covered, and they had heavy six-pounder or more cannons shooting at us.'

Of the 1,000 men in the two battalions, only 341 managed to get off; 144 were killed and the remainder went straight to German prisoner-of-war camps.

With both headlands covering the beach still firmly in German hands, the Canadian divisional commander, General Roberts, would have been wise to abandon the attack. But he was inexperienced, never having commanded a battalion attack before, let alone a divisional amphibious assault. He could not see the beach or the flanking headlands because of the thick smokescreen the attack force had laid down, and he could not talk to his commanders ashore because of communications failures. A tough-minded, decent soldier, who believed all the assurances Mountbatten and his staff had given him over the excellence of the Combined Ops plan, Roberts allowed the main frontal assault to go in on the beach as planned.

Somewhat surprisingly, the Royal Hamilton Light Infantry and the Canadian Essex Scottish got ashore in the centre without heavy casualties. Flights of cannon-firing RAF Hurricanes blasted the German defenders into momentary silence as the attackers closed the sea wall. Once the regrouped Canadians launched themselves across the wall and barbed wire into the buildings opposite, however, the full fury of the German defences shot them down in droves, with machine guns and mortars firing on fixed lines. Any officer or signaller was promptly sniped from the cover of the various buildings on the seafront, and the casino turned out to be a defensive strong point with arcs of fire covering right down the beach. The attack stalled, with the Canadians taking cover and the Germans firing at anything that moved.

Into this firefight lumbered the Churchill tanks of the Calgary Regiment. Under a hail of fire, which included the Germans dropping mortar bombs accurately into the landing decks of the ships, the LCTs closed the beach and disgorged their loads. Despite the damage and the difficulties, twenty-seven of the twenty-nine tanks got ashore but only fifteen managed to struggle up the smooth, grapefruit-sized pebbles of the beach gradient, slipping and sliding, to get on to the esplanade. And there they stayed; for the Germans had built tank traps for just such an occasion to keep any invading tanks from getting into the town. In the words of one Canadian trooper, 'We just went round in bloody circles, using up our gas and firing off all our ammo.'

One tank managed to push its way down to the western end of the beach and helped to shoot the infuriated Hamiltons into an assault on the casino, but that was the only success for the armour. If the intelligence for Dieppe had been properly coordinated, the planners at Combined Ops would have known that they had to deal with anti-tank walls more than six feet high and four feet thick protecting the exits from the esplanade. They were, after all, hardly secret, and every citizen of Dieppe knew just what they were and where they were. The agent-runners in SIS and SOE, the Special Operations Executive, handling the 'take' from French humint sources in the area, were equally aware of them; but no one asked or attempted to coordinate all the intelligence for Jubilee, and the tank traps had not shown up well on Combined Ops' last-minute photo-reconnaissance flights. The Canadians had been let down by a basic lack of intelligence. Even on the Somme in 1916 the assault troops had known the enemy positions in more detail.

The disaster was compounded at about 0700 hours. Desperately straining to make sense of the scanty and fragmented messages from ashore, General Roberts managed to pick up two clear pieces of information: the Essex Scottish were across the seafront and into the houses of Dieppe, and the casino had fallen. Roberts then took the only decision an attacking commander has left to him once his battle plan is in operation: to commit his reserve at a time and place of his own choosing. It was a defining moment for the stolid, steady-thinking Manitoban, who had won a Military Cross and been wounded as an artillery officer in the Great War. His soldiers' lives and his own career hung on his decision. He ordered his mobile reserves, the French-Canadian Fusiliers Mont-Royal and 40 Commando Royal Marines, to land on the beaches in the centre to reinforce what he took to be the success so far.

French-Canadian soldiers are a breed apart. Fired by some kind of North American version of the *furia francese* and a frighteningly fierce national pride, *Québecois* make formidable fighting soldiers. As the Fusiliers ran in, a storm of fire burst over their little vessels. One of the naval party counted over fifty bullet holes in his craft's White Ensign alone. Undeterred, the French-Canadians stormed ashore into six feet of water and 'a positive blizzard of firing'. Tragically, in the words of the official report, 'The Regiment Mont-Royal was unable to accomplish anything at all, except to add to the losses being suffered.' Within a minute of landing, the Fusiliers were shot down and reduced to 'shocked and dazed little groups, seeking only to survive'. Of the 600 men who landed, only 125 got back to England that night.

At 08.17 Roberts made his penultimate decision of the day and ordered 40 Commando to land on the very western edge of the town in a vain attempt to outflank the Germans. Lieutenant Colonel Joseph 'Tiger' Phillips, Royal Marines, had already tried once to sail his group into the harbour at Dieppe but had been driven back by the intensity of the German opposition. Phillips, a man who had bivouacked with his soldiers in the open all through the winter of 1941–42, 'to make sure we're all sharp and toughen us up', was not a man to quit lightly. He led the boats of 40 Commando Royal Marines in to the west edge of Dieppe.

As they broke from the cover of the smokescreen about 600 yards offshore into the bright sunlight, the terrible truth dawned on Colonel Phillips in the front boat; he was leading his men on to a shambles of a beach, swept by tracer bullets and dotted with dead men and the human remains of scores of Canadians blown to bits by the intensity of the fire. Despite his orders, Phillips was leading his commandos into what looked like another Charge of the Light Brigade. Even as he took stock, watched by the officers in the command group, a storm of small-arms fire cracked overhead and tracer began to rake the assault craft.

In an act of astonishing moral and physical bravery, and realizing the futility of further action, Phillips stood up on the stern of the command motor launch. In full view of the enemy he put on a pair of white gloves and signalled the following boats not to attack, but to turn back into the cover of the smoke. Seconds later he was shot down, mortally wounded. In the words of one of his officers, 'His final order undoubtedly saved the lives of over two hundred men.'

It was all over. At 10.50 Roberts gave the order to withdraw. The Navy managed to rescue only 300 men from the beaches. As the battered survivors of Jubilee limped home across the Channel, the firing gradually died down and stretcher-bearers and cautious Germans slowly put their heads up and began to help the moaning wounded. The remaining survivors surrendered. Jubilee was over.

The final cost was appalling: 1,027 dead and 2,340 captured and only Canadian pride on the credit side, together with a number of hard-learned lessons about invading Europe. To add insult to injury, overhead the RAF had suffered a major defeat, too. The new Focke-Wulf 190 single-engined fighter had come as a nasty shock to the RAF's overconfident fighter pilots with their older Spitfire Mark 5s. More than a hundred British aircraft were shot down, no fewer than eighty-eight of them fighters, and another hundred were damaged; the Luftwaffe lost only forty-six aircraft. The Navy lost a destroyer and thirteen major landing ships. For Combined Operations – and the Canadians – it was the worst day of the war.

Once the propaganda boasting was over, the world took stock. Churchill briefed the House of Commons, taking full responsibility, and saying that 'Dieppe had been a reconnaissance in force – to which I gave my sanction.' But he had not agreed, and he knew it. This was made quite clear in a private note dated December 1942 to General Ismay, the War Cabinet's representative on the Chiefs of Staff Committee. By this time the Chiefs of Staff had identified the duplicities behind the Dieppe operation and were taking steps to 'prevent a recurrence of these unfortunate breakdowns in procedures'. The finger pointed clearly at Combined Ops and a not particularly chastened Mountbatten. Churchill's note is worth quoting in full because it identifies the real mystery of Dieppe:

Although for many reasons everyone was concerned to make this business look as good as possible, the time has now come when I must be informed more precisely about the military plans.

In a torrent of questions that reveals just what Churchill did *not* know in 1942, he goes on:

Who made them? Who approved them? What was General Montgomery's part in it? And General McNaughton's [the senior commander of the Canadian Expeditionary Force] part? What is the opinion about the Canadian generals selected by General McNaughton? Did the General Staff check the plan? At what point was the Vice Chief of the Imperial General Staff [VCIGS] informed in the Chief of the Imperial General Staff's absence?

The last question was a shrewd and dangerous thrust to the heart of the matter. As Churchill almost certainly knew when he asked the question, the truth was that the VCIGS, General Nye, had known nothing about Operation Jubilee, even though he was the most senior military officer in the UK on the day of the attack.

On 2 August 1942, two and a half weeks before Jubilee, Churchill, accompanied by Field Marshal Sir Alan Brooke, the Chief of the Imperial General Staff, had flown to Cairo for wholesale sackings of his desert generals and then to Moscow for delicate political negotiations with the Soviets. In Brooke's absence the VCIGS, General Nye, an officer of formidable intellect and reputation, assumed responsibility for the chairmanship of the Chiefs of Staff. Now we know from no less a person than General Ismay that the first Nye knew of the Dieppe raid was on the morning of 19 August when he enquired what all the reports from C-in-C Portsmouth and Combined Ops were about. The embarrassed Ismay, who claimed to be equally ignorant, had to bear the full brunt of General Nye's rage at being kept in the dark.

If Churchill did not order the attack on Dieppe and the Chiefs of Staff, including the acting Chief of the Imperial General Staff on the day, were not consulted or advised, then just who did give the order to attack Dieppe? All roads seem to lead to Mountbatten. His sleight of hand in misrepresenting a Chiefs of Staff directive to widen his powers to make plans, and their later agreement that he could explore a substitute for Rutter, the aborted Dieppe raid of early July, is the key to the mystery. Mountbatten misrepresented these decisions to give his staff the impression that he *did* have official clearance for a second attack on Dieppe. After all, who was to gainsay the Commander Combined Ops? Senior commanders do not lie to their own staff.

This analysis is reinforced by Mountbatten's subsequent furtiveness in planning the second assault. It is clear that the only high-level staff informed of the new 'go' decision for Jubilee were Hughes-Hallett, the senior Canadian officers, the individual force commanders (one of whom was Hughes-Hallett, in place of Rear Admiral Baillie-Grohman who had not been kept informed after the secret 11 July meeting) and certain selected staff officers acting in good faith on the direct orders of their powerful new chief.

Any queries about the extraordinarily tight security for the operation were explained away by Mountbatten as special measures for a secret surprise operation, ordered personally by the PM himself. Only Mountbatten could have provided the necessary authority inside Combined Ops HQ for the way the operation was planned and handled. Only Mountbatten had the power and could have sanctioned the actions taken in his name and on his behalf, as he finally admitted in 1972.

Why did he do it? Ambition and vanity appear to have been the main driving force behind Mountbatten throughout the war. One friend wrote of him – presumably as a result of personal confidences – at this time, 'This operation [Dieppe] is considered very critical from the point of Commander Combined Operations' *personal career*… If he brings this off… he is on top of the world *and will be given complete control*.' The last statement is probably an allusion to Mountbatten's ill-concealed desire (expressed to Leo Amery, Conservative MP) for a post as *supreme commander* of all British forces reporting directly to Churchill. Mountbatten certainly did not lack ambition or self-belief. The view of Mountbatten at this time is given weight by other sources. At least one informed commentator has described him at Combined Ops as 'a master of intrigue, jealousy and ineptitude, [who]… like a spoilt child… toyed with men's lives'.

The implications of Mountbatten's 'vanity and conceit, and anxiety to steal the glory', in the words of the CO of 4 Commando, Lord Lovat, about his commander were profound. Operation Jubilee may well have been ill-conceived, poorly supported, lacking in basic intelligence and badly planned. There can be little doubt, however, that if only the mendacious Mountbatten and his dupes on his staff had been honest and asked for help from the official intelligence agencies, then his soldiers would almost certainly have known about the beach, the tank walls, the guns hidden in the caves and the need for overwhelming fire support from bombers and battleships to suppress the Wehrmacht's defences at Dieppe.

Certainly the Germans thought so. General Haase of 302nd Division, the victorious commander on the day, described the plan as 'mediocre, the timetable too rigid and the fire support entirely insufficient to suppress the defenders during the landings'. He paid tribute to the gallantry and determination of the Canadians, as did the 15th Army commander when he forwarded Haase's after-action report to von Rundstedt and Berlin. Field Marshal von Rundstedt added his own prescient postscript about the Dieppe landing: 'The enemy will not do it like this a second time.'

The raid was portrayed in the German media as a failed attempt at opening the Second Front. The propaganda value of its failure was immense and it was embraced wholeheartedly. Goebbels used every facet of his state-controlled media empire to heap ridicule on the Western Allies for their military incompetence and their abysmal failure to end the isolation of the Soviet Union as German forces continued their advance in southern Russia. The Dieppe raid also proved useful to Hitler and the Nazis in their efforts to bolster public support for the war and strengthen morale on the home front. German newspapers, specifically the *Völkischer Beobachter*, and newsreels hailed the Führer's 'strategic brilliance' in avoiding a two-front war.

We are indebted to David Ian Hall for his forensic analysis of Dieppe and particularly the Nazi reaction. Dr Goebbels's weekly newsreel of 26 August 1942 was nineteen minutes long. It began with an eight-minute feature on the Dieppe raid, using a map taken from a captured officer to explain the British plan and execution of the raid, the successful defence by the German coastal garrison, and ended with large columns of glum Canadian prisoners being marched off the beach and through Dieppe into captivity. Throughout the film report the cameras provided a panoramic view of the beach front revealing a large number of destroyed tanks and landing craft, and hundreds of discarded helmets, weapons and other equipment. Regardless of whether it was a raid or an invasion, the film images could not be denied; it was an unmitigated disaster for the British and their Canadian allies who provided the main body of troops for the attack. The next two features were very short scenes of the concrete fortifications and large coastal guns that were part of the Atlantic Wall, followed by scenes of workmen from the German Labour Front and Hitler Youth busy building bigger and better defences on the Channel coast. The Germans were very aware of the lessons of the debacle and their implications, however. Hitler cautioned his generals in September: 'We must realize that we are not alone in learning a lesson from Dieppe. The British have also learned. We must reckon with a totally different mode of attack and at quite a different place.'

In the series of lies, blunders and myths that have grown up around Dieppe, it is plain that intelligence failures take second place to, and were a direct consequence of, the basic lie by Mountbatten about the whole operation. It is equally clear that if he had used all the intelligence resources available to his command properly, many Canadian lives could have been saved. With proper intelligence, the operation might have been more successful and brought Lord Louis the adulation and further promotion he appeared so single-mindedly to crave. Certainly in many quarters he was never trusted again. However, the duplicitous Mountbatten was one of those unbelievably conceited individuals who genuinely believed that he had never made a mistake in his life.

His arrogance and vanity were pathological. 'It is a curious thing,' he is on record as saying, 'but I have been right in everything I have said and done in my life,' a statement of breathtaking arrogance. Canadians took a different view and Mountbatten became a despised and vilified figure. Historian of the raid, Alex Fitzgerald-Black, spells out the reasons:

For example, the Royal Hamilton Light Infantry committed 582 troops to this operation, and 82 per cent of them became casualties [killed, wounded or missing]. Most of that battalion was raised in Hamilton [Ontario] and the surrounding area. So the impact on Canada was huge. At the time, just about everybody knew someone who had a family member or a friend who was involved in some way. And there must have been a lot of angst in the first few weeks after the raid, waiting to find out what happened to your loved one, your friend, your family member.

The story has a footnote. On 3 September 1944, an irritated Montgomery demanded of Lieutenant General Crerar, the Canadian First Army's commander in Normandy, why he had seen fit to be absent from one of Montgomery's battle conferences. Having just taken the salute after the Canadian Army had captured Dieppe, Harry Crerar replied that there were *hundreds* of reasons why he had not been able to be at Monty's conference: the hundreds of Canadian graves he had just visited for the first time in the cemetery at Dieppe.

Montgomery, wisely, let his Canadian commander have the last word.

KOREA – IGNORED INTELLIGENCE AND MASSIVE EGOS

*'Eventually the Korean War will be understood as one of
the most destructive and one of the most important wars of
the twentieth century'*

BRUCE CUMING

If Midway 1942 showed American intelligence at its best, then Korea only eight years later showed it at its worst. The North Korean invasion of its neighbour in the summer of 1950 ranks as one of the most spectacular intelligence oversights in modern history because, thanks to a rogue general, it ignored the obvious evidence – twice.

If the first intelligence disaster was the failure to realize that North Korea was about to invade, the second intelligence failure was worse; it was nothing less than a blind refusal to accept clear evidence of a pending Chinese intervention. It was obvious that the Chinese were massing to come to the help of their ally and was happening before their eyes: a Chinese intervention that would inflict a crushing defeat and a rout of the US and UN troops.

The disasters were caused by a number of factors. Chief among them were a refusal to admit the truth; personal arrogance by the US commander-in-chief and his sycophantic intelligence officer; defence cuts by a tax-cutting post-war US Congress; and a mistaken view in Washington that Moscow coordinated all communist activity worldwide. But the main failing was a refusal to interpret the facts staring commander-in-chief Douglas MacArthur in the face. His arrogance and personal judgements were to cause the death of thousands of his countrymen and over a million Koreans.

In retrospect, the Korean War (1950–53) turned out to be a major event in the emerging Cold War conflict between Washington and Moscow. Suddenly the Cold War became very hot indeed, and mainly by failures of intelligence. Ironically, Korea's disastrous intelligence mistakes led to the creation of today's alphabet soup of competing American intelligence agencies.

However, the American intelligence failure in Korea was mirrored by a comparable intelligence failure by Moscow and Beijing. Communist China misunderstood and feared an American attack on mainland China, while the USSR sought to control events from 3,000 miles away. Both were ill-judged at best and merely prolonged the war.

The whole point of the North Korean invasion of the South on 29 July 1950 was to unite Korea by armed force. It failed. The war in Korea ended up by demonstrating the folly of constructing a foreign policy without good intelligence. Any ideas of a reunification of North and South Korea perished as China and the US faced off in a three-year struggle that would lead to no reunification on the Korean peninsula and merely confirm the ideological rivalry between the West and the Soviet Union. The result was that the impact of this unfinished struggle is still with us today. At the time of writing there is still no peace on the Korean peninsula. Instead, like the Cyprus war of 1974, there is merely a temporary cessation of hostilities and an armistice. Korea remains an unfinished war. The intelligence failures from Korea haunt our daily lives still, but neither they, nor those involved in the fighting of over fifty years ago, anticipated the actual course of the conflict nor the implications of its sterile outcome. Once again, intelligence and its failures would leave an indelible mark on history.

The Korean peninsula had for centuries been a bone of contention between Japan, China and Russia. Growing Japanese power after the Japanese victory in the Russo-Japanese War of 1904–05 left Korea as a protectorate of Tokyo and, in 1910, Japan annexed the peninsula as part of Japan. The unfortunate Koreans became Japanese vassals, like it or not.

Tokyo's sudden collapse and defeat in 1945 finally ended Japanese rule in Korea. The Koreans were for the first time in centuries suddenly free of foreign dominance and occupation. Many Koreans thought that with peace, political freedom was assured; they were to be sorely disappointed. However, the victorious allied powers were reluctant to grant the new Korea total political freedom. The sudden surrender of Japan left them unprepared as new political realities emerged.

Initially the US had no plans to occupy Korea after the Japanese surrender. However, the spectacular Red Army blitzkrieg in Manchuria and Korea in August 1945 sent ripples of alarm through Washington. Politics, like nature, abhors a vacuum, so events forced a hasty rethink to devise a US policy for Korea. The wartime allies had fallen out and although Korea initially held no strategic interest for the United States, the US was determined not to allow the peninsula to fall into communist hands.

As part of the peace settlement, Korea was divided into US and Soviet occupation zones using the 38th parallel as the arbitrary dividing line between the US and USSR spheres of influence. No one asked the hapless Koreans for their view on this high-handed division of their country.

This artificial division of the country at the 38th parallel caused some dangerous side effects. While the industrialized – now communist – north controlled the country's power stations and the mineral deposits (mainly coal) that produced the bulk of energy and manufactured goods for the south, it was the southern half that fed the country and produced food for the north.

This arbitrary division of the country produced other anomalies too. Although the south contained the capital and largest city, Seoul, South Korea was smaller than North Korea but, curiously, had a much larger population (21 million persons in the south against 9 million in the north).

In September 1945, General Douglas MacArthur took charge of the Supreme Command of Allied Powers (SCAP) and began the work of rebuilding Japan and its territories.

The victors quickly installed occupation forces in their own image. New governments turned the Korean peninsula into two very different countries, each reflecting Soviet and US priorities. The North became a totalitarian communist state ruled over by a former anti-Japanese resistance fighter named Kim Il-sung, a long-time Marxist. In December 1945, the Soviets installed Kim as First Secretary of the North Korean Bureau of the Korean Communist Party. The iron grip of totalitarianism and the Stalinist cult of personality would rule over the People's Republic of North Korea.

Meanwhile in the south, the United States tried to find a malleable puppet government that would follow Washington's instructions. Faced with a deteriorating political situation, America was unprepared for running the country whose history, culture and language were literally unknown to the US occupation forces. So, despite the initial plan of a unified Korea in the 1943 Cairo Declaration, Syngman Rhee, an opponent of communism, was backed and appointed by the United States as head of the provisional government, despite serious reservations about his curious brand of 'democracy' and known corruption. He won the first presidential elections of the newly declared Republic of Korea and began his own rule.

Both leaders promptly clamped down on any opposition, free speech or political rivals. Both had their own plans to unite Korea under their own leadership.

Ominously, North Korea's military was backed and heavily reinforced by the Soviet Union. However, South Korea's request for military support was initially denied by the United States.

The result was that by 1947 there were two very different Koreas, communist and capitalist, facing each other across the 38th parallel. Moscow pulled the strings in the north; Douglas MacArthur, C-in-C and effectively ruler of post-war Japan, oversaw South Korea as America's Imperial Vice Consulate in Tokyo.

At the time, neither the United States nor the USSR expected that the division of Korea would last for decades. Kim Il-sung had other ideas. He wanted to invade the south and force his own Stalinist regime on its people; Seoul in its turn was merely a satrapy, just a small part of Douglas MacArthur's sprawling Far Eastern responsibilities. And intelligence was not a priority.

In 1950, the Korean Military Advisory Group (KMAG), had no intelligence organization. This became the responsibility of the Korean Liaison Office (KLO), whose primary role was to monitor troop movements in the north and the activities of communist guerrillas operating in the south.

Inevitably, KLO was dependent on intelligence collected by the Republic of Korea (ROK), mainly through its agents in the north. This humint programme was of doubtful value. Although at the outbreak of war the

ROK had sixteen agents operating in North Korea, it was unable to infiltrate agents deep into the north and could not provide effective strategic intelligence or warnings.

The overall casualty rate for the several hundred agents overall dispatched into North Korea was a shocking 80 per cent. These KLO humint reports were considered unreliable by officials in Tokyo and Washington. Most of the KLO agents operating in North Korea disappeared almost immediately after the invasion.

A similar humint collection programme was conducted by the Office of Special Investigations (OSI) working to US-FECOM. However, their role was to target *Soviet* military capabilities in the Far East, not Korea.

The fledgling CIA at the time was just three years old and lacked resources and knowledgeable manpower. A newly declassified CIA memorandum from 13 January 1950 shows that the CIA had not fully understood what was happening in North Korea in the months preceding the 1950 invasion. In that memo, the CIA noted the gradual southward movement of the North Korean army but reported that it was probably 'a defensive measure to offset the growing strength of the offensively minded South Korean Army', That report concluded that an invasion of the South by the North was 'unlikely'.

'They didn't have the human capabilities or the technical collection capabilities to provide that kind of warning,' says CIA historian Clayton Laurie. 'That was something expected [by] the Truman administration, to prevent another Pearl Harbor, but nobody in the government had that kind of capability at the time.'

From Tokyo, MacArthur was equally determined to control all of the intelligence that was transmitted from his theatre to Washington and he refused to co-operate with the CIA. In fact he even refused them access to Korea; MacArthur only wanted intelligence that agreed with his personal views. Competing assessments could threaten his personal monopoly of intelligence. As early as June 1950, CIA director Admiral Roscoe Hillenkoetter warned of Chinese units massing just over the border. The Indians (who shared a common border with China in the Himalayas and had a close interest in matters military in Communist China) sent a specific alert to Washington to warn the US. Even when the occasional Chinese prisoner was captured in North Korea, they were dismissed as a few expert advisers. However, Willoughby's G2 staff in Tokyo identified the build-up of the North Korean army, as did the ROK government. The KLO produced dozens of analytical reports warning of a pending offensive in the year leading up to the invasion.

During this period, communications intelligence collection and processing activities for FECOM were managed by the Army Security Agency Pacific (ASAPAC), a regional command of the Army Security Agency (ASA). ASA was charged with collecting, processing and analysing signals intelligence *against the Soviet Union* and later the People's Republic of China and their allies or satellites. According to ASA's charter, their collection activities were focused almost exclusively on the USSR.

US and UN intelligence on Chinese and North Korean strategic intentions remained poor throughout the war, primarily due to the difficulty of running agents in the North and the lack of humint. The technical difficulties in collecting useful comint added to FECOM's woes. MacArthur, believing himself omniscient, ignored them all.

MacArthur was a complex figure.

In many ways he mirrored Mountbatten, another vainglorious figure, convinced of his own infallibility and with a breathtaking conceit that made him many enemies. Like Mountbatten he guarded his personal image and PR with obsessive care (pages 156–57). He was also, like Mountbatten, a liar and a man with an eye for the main chance, even in defeat. Skulking safely amidst the chaos of doomed Corregidor in early 1942 (where the troops derisively named him 'Dugout Doug'), he had somehow found time to check that his Filipino field marshal's pay was still being paid despite the Japanese siege, and that the $35,000 he had invested in the islands was being invested in blue-chip stocks. (By 1945 it made him a millionaire, war or no war.) And, just before the final surrender at Bataan, he fled to Australia. A US prisoner of war penned a scathing farewell from the hell of his Japanese prisoner-of-war camp:

> Let him run, let him run, we are the braver,
> Stain his hands with his blood and dye them forever,
> Recall, oh ye kinsmen, how he left us to die,

Starved and insulted by his infamous lie;
How he seduced us with boasts of defense;
How he cheated us with his tale of offense.

For such an unscrupulous personality to be made America's pro-consul and effective ruler of occupied Japan in 1945 was giving a greedy egomaniac free rein with which to indulge his dreams of glory. A personality that exulted in theatricality, pomp and grandiose gestures was handed supreme power by Washington and told to reform Japan. Only MacArthur had the final authority to make all decisions. It was an invitation to any egotist.

MacArthur did understand Asia (he had not been to the continental United States since 1937). Although the occupation was nominally an allied enterprise ('SCAP'), it was controlled by Washington – which meant MacArthur. As historian Michael Schaller noted:

> From its inception, the occupation be synonymous with its supreme commander. Although few Americans could name the man in charge of the occupation of Germany (General Lucius Clay) most could readily identify the top man in Tokyo.

And, to give him credit, MacArthur's record as effectively American Vice Consul in Japan after 1945 was highly successful.

In fact, most of the basic principles and policies for the occupation had been drawn up by planners in Washington in the last two years of the war. By implementing them skilfully, MacArthur helped a defeated and destroyed nation transform itself with remarkable speed.

MacArthur knew that ruling over such a large and militaristic nation was a serious challenge. He asserted his authority by modelling his 'reign' on imperial Japanese values. According to Masamune Komura, MacArthur was treated with great respect by the Japanese. He was known as gaijin shogun. It was a term of respect, since a shogun as supreme warlord is placed in a higher hierarchy than citizens, soldiers or almost everybody except the emperor. He capitalized upon this by shrewdly using the Japanese emperor to further America's aims.

Unlike the leaders of the other defeated Axis powers, Hirohito was allowed to keep his position as emperor. MacArthur realized that the best way to rule the people of Japan was to use their emperor as a mouthpiece. This excerpt from a declassified January 1946 telegram from MacArthur to General Eisenhower explains MacArthur's thinking. Replying to calls to prosecute the Japanese emperor as a war criminal:

[Emperor Hirohito's] indictment will unquestionably cause a tremendous convulsion among the Japanese people, the repercussions of which cannot be overestimated. He is a symbol which unites all Japanese. Destroy him, and the nation will disintegrate... it is quite possible that a million troops would be required which would have to be maintained for an indefinite number of years.

'Americans regard MacArthur as a conqueror of Japan but the Japanese did not take him that way. He was a liberator. Japanese regarded MacArthur as the highest human being, just below God,' notes Rinjiro Sodei, a biographer of MacArthur.

His carefully cultivated aloofness and haughty bearing, which so irritated his political enemies in the United States, struck the Japanese, with a long history of ruthless but distant military leaders, or shoguns, as normal and correct. He was an unapproachable ruler who shunned contact with ordinary Japanese, dealing only with Emperor Hirohito and a handful of elite politicians. Japanese policemen halted all traffic to speed the pro-consul's passage through the city. His status had reached legendary status in the minds of the Japanese and, worryingly, the American people, as well as himself. Tokyo became the centre of the world for him. As ruler he surrounded himself with a sycophantic military court and deferential Japanese politicians. Even a more modest man would have been hard-pressed not to have his head turned by the adulation: and no one had ever accused Douglas MacArthur of being modest.

He wielded power to such an extent that President Truman and the Joint Chiefs of Staff back in Washington were reluctant to clip the wings of a general who had, frankly, grown too big for his boots. This idea of his own infallibility was a major contributor to this first major geostrategic error. By 1950, the combination of MacArthur's arrogance and conceit, plus one of the worst intelligence officers ever to grace a US uniform, spawned a grotesque intelligence blunder.

In South Korea, intelligence operations were the responsibility of MacArthur's Intelligence Chief (G-2) Major General Charles A. Willoughby's organization. Willoughby had served as MacArthur's Intelligence Chief throughout the Second World War, where he had acquired a reputation for ensuring that his intelligence reports matched MacArthur's personal opinions. Willoughby's failings were well known. During the war, MacArthur said, 'There have been three great intelligence officers in history. Mine is not one of them.' John Ferris in his 2007 book *Intelligence and Strategy* calls this an 'understatement' and calls Willoughby a 'candidate for one of the three worst intelligence officers of the Second World War'.

To make matters worse, Willoughby had some extreme political views, being an open admirer of Franco and his brand of dictatorial fascist government, to such an extent that MacArthur referred to his G2 as 'my pet fascist'. Willoughby's 'vitriolic, paranoid and frequently fantastic' memos included anti-Semitic insults towards colleagues.

In the circumstances it is no surprise that Willoughby was later to downplay and even suppress reports of the Chinese army's (PLA) massing north of the Yalu. He had to keep his master happy. George Orwell's Winston Smith would have fitted nicely into MacArthur's intelligence staff.

MacArthur is on record as saying that if you 'control intelligence, you control decision-making'. With Willoughby in charge pandering to his boss's wanting and feeding him intelligence that reinforced his already held views, he could boast that 'he was his own intelligence officer'. The problem was that he wasn't a very good one. MacArthur wanted total control of the war and its execution, and no outside interference by Washington, especially by the White House and the Pentagon. If his Tokyo command headquarters were solely responsible for collecting and assessing intelligence on the enemy, then MacArthur alone could decide how big the enemy threat was and thus what to do about it. To him, Korea was seen as a small and unimportant sideshow.

US Secretary of State Dean Acheson (1893–1971) once said, 'If the best minds in the world had set out to find us the worst possible location in the world to fight this damnable war, the unanimous choice would have been Korea.'

To make matters worse, the American army in Korea, the Eighth Army, was poorly prepared for the war. While the North Korean combat veterans received equipment from China, with tanks, artillery and aircraft supplied by the Soviets, their rigorous training ensured North Korea's military superiority over the South. The ROK forces were lacking US heavy weapons such as tanks and heavy artillery. In early 1950, American advisers judged that fewer than half of the ROK infantry battalions were even marginally ready for war. The war began with 200,000 North Koreans fighting 100,000 South Korean personnel.

The US occupation troops in Japan who were rushed to the Korean front in August 1950 were not combat-ready, and many of the officers were too old for front-line battlefield conditions. Training was 'slipshod and routine'. This combination of unpreparedness, lack of armour, poor training and limited and contradictory intelligence combined to make the invasion not only a shock to the South Koreans and the US command in Japan, but a debacle on the ground.

The reason was the initial damning intelligence mistake: a failure to spot the growing threat of invasion from North Korea. In a secret report prepared for the White House on 12 October 1950, the CIA claimed it had seen 'no convincing indication' back in July that a Chinese intervention in the war was likely. Even after Chinese forces began moving into North Korea a few weeks later, CIA analysts failed to understand what that movement meant.

One explanation for the CIA's failure to predict neither the North Korean invasion nor the Chinese intervention in the war is that the agency, along with the rest of the US government, was paying attention primarily to Moscow's actions. They had reason. According to historian Kim Hakjoon, 'the many telegrams that Moscow and Pyongyang exchanged from January to June 1950, and, more important, the secret meetings between Stalin and Kim [Il-sung] in Moscow in April and Mao and Kim in Beijing during May, confirmed that the three Communist leaders were responsible for starting the Korean War on the morning of 25 June 1950.'

The US failure to see the significance of these meetings led to the major intelligence blunder on a par with the failure to foresee the Japanese attack on Pearl Harbor in 1941.

President Truman, upon learning of the North Korean invasion, decided it was a test case for the United Nations, which had been established just five years earlier. He asked Secretary of State Dean Acheson to ask for an immediate meeting of the UN Security Council, and within twenty-four hours the US ambassador, Warren Austin, was asking the UN to come to South Korea's defence.

A candid 2001 summary of pre-war Korea reporting, and published by the CIA's own Center for the Study of Intelligence, concluded that the agency's assumption that the Soviets controlled North Korean decision-making 'accounts for the failure to predict the North Korean attack'. The failure to predict China's October 1950 intervention in the war may also have been partly due to the agency's mistaken assumption that Moscow was calling all the shots in Asia.

That Kremlin-centred view characterized all CIA reporting from the time. A report, 'Current Capabilities of the Northern Korean Regime', issued just six days before the North's invasion of the South described the North Korean regime as 'a firmly controlled Soviet satellite that exercises no independent initiative and depends entirely on the support of the USSR for existence'.

'The belief here is that this is monolithic communism,' according to CIA historian Laurie, 'that things were being orchestrated worldwide by the Soviet Union, and that nothing is going to happen in Asia or Africa without the USSR saying, "This is permissible", or "Go ahead and do this".'

And as late as April 1951, Truman himself addressed the nation and portrayed it as being instigated from Moscow.

'The communists in the Kremlin are engaged in a monstrous conspiracy to stamp out freedom all over the world,' Truman said. 'If they were to succeed, the United States would be numbered among their principal victims.' According to General M. G. Parks of the South Korean Army, that was America's main concern well before the invasion of South Korea in 1950. Washington's (and MacArthur's) prime policy was to deter or contain worldwide communist expansion as they saw it. Washington regarded

Chinese intervention, even after the outbreak of war, as an attempt to accelerate the final unification of Korea. This thinking coloured all strategic intelligence assessments at the time.

An initially hesitant United States decided that it must take a stand against the North Korean armed aggression. The USSR's absence from its UN seat allowed the UN to intervene, and contingents arrived from nineteen countries to reinforce the beleaguered South Korean and US forces. American military intervention was ineffective at first, but by September 1950 the combined efforts of the US and ROK Armies, complemented by air and naval superiority, held the North Koreans in check at the Pusan Perimeter. It was a near-run thing. Chauncey E. Van Hatten believed part of the problem was that the United States government did not provide its troops with the equipment they needed to combat such a ferocious assault.

Philip Davis agreed that the Americans were woefully prepared for Pusan: 'We didn't have big bazookas, we didn't have flame throwers, we didn't have good ammunition… most all [of it] was duds.'

The battle-hardened North Korean forces equipped with Soviet weaponry – including T-34/85 tanks – quickly routed understrength US troops stationed there and South Korean forces. The North seized Seoul and bottled up UN forces on the south-eastern tip of the Korean peninsula, where they were in danger of being annihilated or pushed off the peninsula.

However, thanks to a stalwart ROK defence by six divisions, helped by US air power and naval gun support, the siege of Pusan turned out to be as far as the North Koreans would get. The Eighth Army, commanded by Lieutenant General Walton H. Walker, an experienced corps commander in Europe in 1944–45, and the ROK Army, led by Major General Chung Il-kwon, rallied and fought back with growing success.

The result was that, despite the original intelligence failure to predict the North Korean invasion of July 1950, the war in Korea had become a stalemate towards the autumn of the year. Although the North Korean army had initially overrun the south, and NK forces forced the UN and South Korean ('ROK') forces back to besiege them a tiny corner of the peninsula at Pusan, MacArthur planned a brilliant counterstroke.

It vindicates his claim as an attacking strategic general. He planned a risky amphibious landing, 120 miles behind the North Korean lines. It was a bold stroke, worthy of a Patton, Rommel or a Rokossovsky. It is difficult to envisage the staid Montgomery risking such a stroke after his stalemates at Salerno and Anzio, and defeat at Arnhem. MacArthur took a big risk.

MacArthur personally elected to land at Inchon, the port outlet of Seoul on Korea's west coast. A less ideal choice would have been hard to find; Inchon raised a number of serious challenges: a dangerous proximity to NVA reinforcements; an approach through a maze of shifting mudbanks and shoals; a tidal drop of seventeen feet; and a constricted landing zone.

Despite all these risks, MacArthur landed a Marine amphibious force at Inchon on 16 September 1950, hundreds of miles behind the communist lines to cut off the North Koreans. The North Vietnamese Army (NVA) was duped. One NVA commander, Lei Yingfu, Zhou's military adviser in Korea, did sense a trap and warned that MacArthur would attempt a landing at Inchon, 'because it was the least likely… '

The outcome was the swift collapse of the North Korean offensive, which had lost its base of operations literally overnight as they were cut off from the North and their supply lines. The invaders were routed and fled north back from Pusan in defeat and disarray. MacArthur and Syngman Rhee marched into the capitol building of Seoul and declared South Korea liberated.

US President Harry Truman applauded General MacArthur's 'brilliant manoeuvre' and called Inchon one of the best military operations in history. Syngman Rhee then showered praise on Truman and all Americans:

> Please accept… the deep gratitude of the Korean people for United States actions which now have led to the liberation of Seoul. The Korean people will always cherish the memory of your bold leadership in defence of liberty.

The Inchon landings were aided greatly by successful humint activities of the US KLO and ROK HID (Headquarters Intelligence Detachment). Both contributed decisively to the success of the amphibious action by operating well behind the lines and reporting accurate detail of local NK defences.

All this praise quickly went to MacArthur's head. Washington was uncertain about how to follow up Seoul's liberation, but MacArthur, flushed with victory, was determined to advance north to the Yalu River and the Chinese border. This was a dangerous development from the Chinese perspective. They began to reinforce their armed border with Korea.

This was when the malign influence of Willoughby was to really change history. Lieutenant Colonel John Chiles, X Corps' chief of operations, later wrote:

> MacArthur did not want the Chinese to enter the war in Korea. Anything MacArthur wanted, Willoughby produced intelligence for... In this case Willoughby falsified the intelligence reports... He should have gone to jail.

This is a devastating verdict on this gross misjudgement of Chinese intentions by a contemporary. It was to lead to the second disastrous mistake by MacArthur's intelligence staff.

Willoughby customized his reports in November 1950. He foolishly only forwarded those reports to support MacArthur's personal assessment that the Chinese would never dare to cross the Yalu. This was nonsense as all the indicators pointed to a possible Chinese invasion. There was ample evidence that Communist China was massing its forces north of the Yalu and preparing to rescue the beaten North Koreans. This occurred despite multiple intelligence sources reporting the presence of a Chinese intervention force ready to ambush UN forces and cut their supply line. Instead, ignoring the intelligence from outside his command, MacArthur ordered his UN troops all the way up to the Yalu River.

No one could claim that MacArthur was not warned of the impending storm about to break over the advancing US, UN and ROK troops as they continued their pursuit of a beaten enemy north to the Yalu.

Willoughby assured MacArthur that the Chinese would not invade the South, despite numerous alarms raised by then. By late autumn that year, Willoughby's office refused to believe or confirm reports that thousands of PLA troops were in North Korea. Willoughby 'doctored the intelligence *in order to permit MacArthur's forces to go where they wanted to go militarily, to the banks of the Yalu'*, ensuring that the contrary or dissenting voices in Tokyo or Washington didn't disturb his master. The Tokyo estimate of the number of Chinese forces in Korea was less than one-tenth the reality.

Once again the Indians sounded a warning. In September 1950, Ambassador Panikkar's contacts in Beijing began to warn him that the PRC would not sit still and allow the UN forces including the Eighth Army to march to the Yalu. Chinese military officials told him that Mao was prepared to risk nuclear war to stop those forces from advancing. The Indian embassy in Beijing reported that trainloads of PLA troops were moving to the border region, and the Indian government passed these reports on to Washington and London.

On 2 October 1950, Ambassador Panikkar was summoned at midnight to meet the Chinese Prime Minister Zhou Enlai, Mao's closest confidant. Zhou told Panikkar that if American troops crossed the 38th parallel, China would intervene. At 1.30 a.m., Panikkar cabled the warning to Nehru, who had it sent to the UN allies. Washington was sceptical. But the British were particularly alarmed by the Indian message, worried that provoking China could lead to a Chinese attack on Hong Kong. The stakes were high for London.

Truman called for a meeting at Wake Island in the mid-Pacific. The general told the president that the war would be over by Thanksgiving and most troops would be home by Christmas. When Truman asked, 'What will be the attitude of Commie China?', MacArthur said it would not intervene. Even if China tried, it could not get more than 50,000 troops across the Yalu River, MacArthur promised, citing Willoughby's G2 intelligence estimates. (In fact, by 19 October 260,000 PLA soldiers had already crossed into Korea.)

The CIA did prepare a National Intelligence Estimate, the collective opinion of the entire intelligence community in Washington, on 6 November 1950, titled 'Chinese Communist Intervention in Korea'; however, it assessed that there were only 30,000 Chinese troops south of the Yalu. An update on 24 November put the number at 70,000 in just four divisions, an estimate still wildly off the mark. MacArthur was informed and, true to form, ignored the Indian reports. And Washington's misgivings.

Even the first encounters with Chinese forces on the battlefield did not shake MacArthur and Willoughby's faulty intelligence estimate. As early as late October, the Eighth Army had fought a bitter and costly battle with PLA forces at Unsan in the North. The Americans were ambushed and routed, but then the Chinese pulled back. They wanted to entice the Eighth Army northward to trap it far from its supply lines and to isolate it near the Chinese frontier. Willoughby dismissed the Unsan battle as unimportant and continued to claim that the Chinese would not intervene in force. So did MacArthur. He ignored the prisoner-of-war evidence from the capture of the first Chinese PLA prisoner in the Korean War. In late October 1950, the prisoner revealed that there were 10,000 Chinese soldiers lying in ambush north of Unsan. MacArthur flatly refused to believe it.

MacArthur made one of his lightning-quick trips to Korea from Tokyo on 24 November 1950, telling the US ambassador in Seoul there were only 25,000 Chinese troops in Korea (there were 250,000). Then he had his return flight to Tokyo fly along the Yalu River, making possible a personal reconnaissance intended to impress the credulous media. He then flew back to Tokyo. (In the whole of the Korean War, 'Dugout Doug' never slept one single night in Korea.) His report to Washington dismissed any danger of Chinese intervention. What with the ROK estimates, the unequivocal Indian warning and the failure of humint, sigint and air photo reconnaissance, the stage was set for the second grievous failure of intelligence in Korea. Willoughby's failure was marked by ignoring – or hiding – the specific intelligence indicators freely available at the time, which were:

- The warning from Chou En Lai to the Indian ambassador that the Peoples Liberation Army (PLA) would respond if the UN troops extended their advance north of the 38th parallel to the Yalu river.
- Movement of two complete armies from the Formosa/Taiwan front to the Chinese border.
- A marked increase in public warnings and psyops broadcasts to the US troops not to advance further north.
- The appointment of General Peng te Huai, China's most successful general of the Second World War and the civil war, to command on the border.

- Movement of new air forces to the Yalu region.
- US humint sources warnings that the PRC was preparing to invade North Korea.

All were ignored by MacArthur and, three days later, Peng's armies struck the American forces as they were driving north to the banks of the Yalu River.

Bruce Ackerman remembered what happened next:

Well, the Chinese... surrounded us. We were totally surrounded. The only way out was to go out the way we came... As I was walking through, trying to get around [a] roadblock, I heard a BOOM. I don't know what it was, whether it was a mortar shot or a rifle grenade... It blew me up in the air, but I landed on my feet! And then my feet kept going. [I thought] this is it... my time has come... they'll read about me in the papers.

But miraculously, Ackerman survived.

MacArthur, in his relentless push into the north had ordered the ROK and US forces into a gigantic ambush. The surprised and shocked UN forces withdrew as fast as they could. It was nearly a rout.

From 24 November to 14 December, the Chinese battered the Allies all the way back to South Korea. Peng's Thirteenth Army Group split the UN forces and opened up a gap to the west. The US IX Corps and the ROK II Corps were isolated. The 1st Corps in the far north was nearly cut off as the Chinese Ninth Army Group's two armies surrounded the 1st Marine Division near the Chosin reservoir. Under the worst possible weather conditions, blizzards and under constant attack, the Marines retreated south and fought their way out, destroying seven Chinese divisions before reaching safety on the east coast at the port of Hungnam on 11 December. The 'Big Bugout' – as the retreat was called – covered some 120 miles in ten days and cost the lives of thousands of American and South Korean soldiers.

How did MacArthur blunder so badly? How could he miss more than 300,000 Chinese soldiers?[4] Once the intelligence finally came in loud and

---

4   By December 1952, the Chinese forces in Korea had reached a record high of 1.45 million men, including fifty-nine infantry divisions, ten artillery divisions, five anti-aircraft divisions, and seven tank regiments. Numbers remained stable until the armistice agreement was signed in July 1953.

clear, he and his staff of sycophants continued to dismiss it, suppress it or wilfully misinterpret its import. In so doing, they recklessly put tens of thousands of American, ROK and other United Nations troops in mortal danger. The result was catastrophic: one of the worst defeats and one of the most ignominious retreats in American military history. And all because MacArthur ignored the multiple intelligence warnings.

Carleton Swift, a CIA officer working at the US Embassy in Seoul, explains about Willoughby:

> It was as if he was always right, had always been right. Certitude after certitude poured out of him. It was as if there was an exclamation point after all of his sentences... Worse, you couldn't challenge him. Because he always made it clear that he spoke for MacArthur and if you challenged him you were challenging MacArthur... So that made it very hard for intelligence in the field to filter up to higher headquarters on something that he has made up his mind on.

MacArthur had also thwarted President Truman's attempt to negotiate a ceasefire when the general ordered his troops to invade North Korea and push the NKPA up way past the 38th parallel.

The general had assured a sceptical president that the American troops would be home by Christmas. However, when he continued to push the North Koreans further north and suggested bombing cities in China that were thought to be supporting the North Korean troops, a desperate MacArthur was risking propelling the US into a major war in Asia. But by early 1951, President Truman's main concern was saving as many lives as possible. He was determined to find a ceasefire.

MacArthur disagreed with his commander-in-chief, loudly and publicly. He thought a ceasefire was weak and argued that now was the time to crush the Chinese invaders. The two men clashed.

This was not the first time the general had ignored direct orders from his boss. MacArthur demanded that the US should bomb Communist China and use Nationalist Chinese forces from Taiwan against the People's Republic of

China. Truman flatly refused these requests and a public dispute broke out between the two men.

The final straw came when MacArthur called for the use of the atom bomb on the Chinese on the Yalu. This time MacArthur had overreached himself. Hubris and megalomania had done their corrosive work.

'MacArthur,' President Eisenhower once said, 'could never see a sun, or even a moon for that matter, in the heavens – as long as he was the sun.'

On 9 December 1950, MacArthur requested 'field commander's discretion' to employ nuclear weapons. On 24 December 1950, MacArthur submitted a list of 'retardation targets' in Korea, Manchuria and other parts of China, for which thirty-four atomic bombs would be required.

By the spring of 1951, Truman had had enough. MacArthur had gone too far. Let Truman's diary explain the reasons for the fall from grace of 'the American Caesar':

Friday, 6 April 1951 MacArthur shoots another political bomb through leader of the Republican minority in the House. This looks like the last straw. Rank insubordination. Last summer he sent a long statement to the Vets of Foreign Wars – not through the high command back home, but directly!...

I ordered the release suppressed and then sent him a very carefully prepared directive dated Dec 5 1950 setting out Far Eastern policy after I'd flown to Wake Island to see him and reach an understanding face to face.

He told me the war in Korea was over and that we could transfer a regular division to Germany on 1 Jan. He was positive Red China would not come in. He expected to support our Far Eastern policy.

... I've come to the conclusion that our Big General in the Far East must be recalled... [The JCS four] to meet again Friday afternoon and go over all phases of the situation.

Saturday, April 7, 1951 We met again this morning – Gen Marshall, Dean Atcheson [*sic*], Mr. Harriman and Gen. Bradley. It is the unanimous opinion of all that MacArthur be relieved. All four so advise. I direct that the order be issued...

On 11 April 1951, President Truman officially relieved Douglas MacArthur of his command. Despite demands from the Republican opposition to run for president, MacArthur, another failed would-be meddler in intelligence, finally bowed out, crushed by his own hubris, arrogance and failure to listen to intelligence. He had only himself to blame, having been responsible for two of America's worst intelligence blunders.

When a new American commander, General Matthew Ridgway, took over the war from Douglas MacArthur in 1951, he took a new broom to his intelligence staff. He brought in CIA analysts to scrutinize Willoughby's intelligence estimates.

The war had become a stalemate and bogged down into a battle of attrition. For different reasons both sides wanted the fighting to end.

After the US presidential election of 1952, the new president, General Eisenhower, decided to 'go to Korea'. On his return, Eisenhower began to publicly hint that the United States might have to make use of its nuclear arsenal to break the military stalemate in Korea. The president also put pressure on his South Korean ally to drop some of its demands and join in the emerging peace process.

By July 1953, all sides involved in the conflict were ready to sign an agreement ending the bloodshed. The armistice, signed on 27 July, established a committee of representatives from neutral countries. A new border between North and South Korea was drawn, which gave South Korea some additional territory and demilitarized the zone between the two nations. The war cost the lives of millions of Koreans and Chinese, as well as almost 40,000 Americans.

Many Americans questioned why the United States had not used its nuclear arsenal or expanded the war into China. However, as Washington was well aware, such actions could have led to World War III.

Finally, in July 1953, the Korean War came to an end. Some 5 million soldiers and civilians lost their lives in what many in the US refer to as 'the Forgotten War' for the lack of attention it received. Along with Cyprus, the Korean War is not finished: an armistice is just a war on hold. The peninsula remains divided on a war-like footing today.

The cost was grievous.

According to a North Korean census report found in Russian archives,

North Korea lost 20 per cent of its population during the Korean War of 1950–53. The 1953 figures of the Central Statistic Administration of the DPRK, obtained by the Center's Cold War International History Project (CWIHP), the country's population declined from 9,368,592 in 1948 to 7,425,939 in 1953. Official North Korean figures cite a total population in 1953 of 8,491,000.

The newly discovered census figures add important confirmation to Russian reports on the war recently published by South Korea's Ministry of National Defense. According to reports by Soviet ambassador and chief military adviser to the DPRK, Lieutenant General V. N. Razuvaev, compiled by the Ministry's Institute of Military History, there were a total of 1.2 million civilian casualties for North Korea, which include 282,000 killed in bombing raids and 796,000 fled to the South or missing. The remaining 800,000 population loss therefore represents the total deaths from combat and natural causes.

It would, however, take until September 1951 for Willoughby to share previous estimates and briefs on Korea with his civilian counterparts. Following that, the accuracy of intelligence that UN forces had access to markedly improved. The result was stark. Willoughby was dismissed from his post shortly afterwards.

Despite his role in the Yalu River disaster, US Army General Charles A. Willoughby was never officially reprimanded and controversy ensued as to what his real responsibilities were.

Willoughby was 'retired' from the Army on 31 August 1951. After his retirement, he became adviser to and lobbyist for the Spanish dictator Francisco Franco.

General Charles A. Willoughby died on 25 October 1972. Bizarrely, this fraudulent intelligence officer remains a member of the US Military Intelligence Hall of Fame.

Korea reshaped the post-war world. The decision of the United States to rearm as laid out in National Security Council Report 68 (NSC-68) (sitting on the shelf since April 1950) led to the United States rearming on a 'ready for war' basis and a global commitment to military assistance pacts and overseas basing. Perhaps most dangerous of all was an entrenched enmity between the US and the fledgling PRC. Korea poisoned relations between the United States and China for seventy years after Washington gave Taiwan a blank cheque to defend the last remaining bit of Nationalist China.

And all mainly because of a power-mad general and a sycophantic acolyte who lacked the most important virtue of any intelligence agency or intelligence officer: 'speak truth unto power.'

'I THOUGHT WE WERE SUPPOSED TO BE WINNING?' – THE TET OFFENSIVE, 1968

'The Tet Offensive failed because we underestimated our enemies and overestimated ourselves. We set goals which we realistically could not achieve'

NORTH VIETNAMESE GENERAL TRAN VAN TRA, WRITING IN 1978

If Pearl Harbor represents a salutary example of a great nation's failure to value intelligence properly, and suffering grievously as a result, then it must be said that America learned rapidly from its mistakes. With the astonishing energy and sense of purpose that characterizes the very best qualities of its people, the USA set about making sure that Washington would never again be taken by surprise by constructing a national intelligence service second to none.

The results were spectacular. By 1945 America had a fully developed worldwide signals intelligence capability, an international secret intelligence service, an effective clandestine operations capability and the best-equipped aerial reconnaissance capability in the world. These assets were reflected in the increased priority given to intelligence within the individual armed services and were backed by a formidable array of expensive technical aids and highly trained specialists to make the whole thing work. It was a staggering achievement.

In order to ensure that the mistakes before Pearl Harbor could never be repeated, a formal national intelligence assessment staff was activated with the prime task of ensuring that the president and his advisers would always have access to the best and most timely information, whatever the cost. Theoretically, by the early 1960s, only twenty years after Pearl Harbor, the US authorities were masters of the most sophisticated and certainly the best resourced intelligence service in the world.

When Professor C. Northcote Parkinson formulated his famous law that 'work expands to fill the time available for its completion', he applied it equally to corporate bodies and bureaucracies. Parkinson's experience of the post-war British socialist bureaucracy was both telling and depressing, and the professor never subsequently underestimated the ability of public servants to fight for power and influence among themselves in turf squabbles every bit as painful as the most savage corporate boardroom battle. It is, as Parkinson sadly observed, only human nature, and corporate organizations are but human nature writ large.

Bureaucratic Washington was no exception. Although the capability to provide intelligence had increased a hundredfold since Pearl Harbor, one unforeseen side effect was to increase the value of the prizes for the Washington bureaucrats to squabble over. New and powerful intelligence agencies attracted new and powerful budgets. The consequence was that by the 1960s the competition for power between the US intelligence agencies had become the new US intelligence problem.

The problems of having too little intelligence scattered around became the problem of having too much intelligence from competing organizations and the struggle for its control. Each agency clung jealously to its own particular monopoly and kept it tightly compartmentalized, with the CIA trying, unsuccessfully, to become the overall master of US intelligence. A kind of competitive market economy had begun to dominate America's secret world. Ideally, in intelligence matters, a strong executive would direct such matters without argument. However, the US Constitution is specifically designed to make central control of just about anything very difficult to achieve. Add to this the irresistible lure of defence contractors' dollars, the lobbying of elected politicians, regional demands for a share of the pork barrel of taxpayers' money, together with the competing demands of the armed services, and the internal battles over US intelligence become just another sad reflection of how Washington does business.

America's new intelligence capabilities were sorely needed. After the Second World War and the humiliating liquidation of financial support for Greece in 1947–48, British imperial power collapsed. In its place, in Sanche de Gramont's phrase, America embraced the 'struggle for the world' with commitment and enthusiasm, assuming the role of leader of the free world. The challenges of communist expansionism embodied in the Soviet Union and its revolutionary allies needed to be met, and America took over its new global responsibilities wholeheartedly. The isolation of pre-Pearl Harbor days was long forgotten. Nowhere was this new attitude better summed up than in Theodore Sorensen's speech for John F. Kennedy's inaugural address of 1961, which contained the words 'we shall pay any price, bear any burden'. Many saw it as a kind of global blank cheque. For America's fledgling intelligence agencies this was the springtime of hope. A Homeric clash of ideologies, fuelled by apparently limitless tax dollars, with an adamantine and resourceful enemy gave a fervour and conviction to the fight that only the noble and well-funded cause can bestow. Nowhere was this better exemplified than in the war in Vietnam.

Although Vietnam was essentially a French post-colonial problem, the British originally had a finger in the pie. Despite the rhetoric of de Gaulle and his Free French, France was incapable of immediately reasserting its authority over its pre-war colonial territories in the Far East when the Japanese surrendered in August 1945. A successful nationalist – but communist – resistance leader called Ho Chi Minh promptly proclaimed an Independent Democratic Republic of Vietnam in the name of the Vietminh (League for the Independence of Vietnam) on behalf of the Vietnamese people. In August and September 1945 the nearest Allied troops were British and not at all sympathetic to communist nationalist uprisings against the colonial power, for obvious reasons. So when General Douglas Gracey's 20th Indian Division reoccupied Saigon under the terms of the surrender document signed in Tokyo Bay, they promptly set about re-establishing the status quo antebellum.

Pragmatic as ever, and alive to the dangers of unrest on the streets, the British commanding general took the unusual step of rearming the Japanese soldiers, effectively swore in their officers as *Allied* deputies and sent the now-conquered conquerors back on to the streets of Hanoi to keep the law and order they had maintained so effectively for the previous three years, provisional new Vietnamese government or not. They were, once Vietnamese shock had abated at seeing the return of the Japanese, apparently very successful peacekeepers. Somewhat breathlessly, a hastily dispatched French colonial government team turned up late in September 1945 and stormed the headquarters of the Vietminh to reassert control of their colony. The British withdrew, leaving the French in charge of their reluctant Indochinese citizens.

Ironically, the USA spelled out its policy for Vietnam in 1948; which makes an interesting comparison with the reality of subsequent events:

> Our long-term objectives are… to see installed a self-governing nationalist state which will be friendly to the US… we have an immediate interest in maintaining in power a friendly French Government, to assist in the furtherance of our aims in Europe. This immediate and vital interest has in consequence taken precedence over active steps looking toward the realization of our objectives in Indochina.
>
> US Department of State, Policy Statement on Indochina,
> 27 September 1948.

It was too late, however. A savage war for Vietnamese independence quickly destabilized the new French regime, a war mainly led by the heroes of the anti-Japanese resistance (who had been well armed in 1944–45 by the British and Americans), the Vietminh, under their cunning and ruthless nationalist leader, Ho Chi Minh.

By 1954 it was all over. Despite their best efforts, the French were outgeneraled, outnumbered and outfought. The climax came in the north at Dien Bien Phu, 160 miles west of Hanoi, where the Vietminh under General Giap surrounded and trapped a large French garrison. Over a period of two months in the spring of 1954, 16,000 French troops were besieged and worn down by over 50,000 Vietnamese supported by massed batteries of artillery. The fall of the garrison on 8 May 1954 spelled final defeat for French power. They had seriously underestimated the determination, the skill and the combat power of the Vietminh Army, and the fall of Dien Bien Phu ensured the end of French colonial rule in Indochina.

Of the 8,000 Frenchmen who went into captivity, only 3,000 later returned to recount their ordeal to a nation that only wanted to forget the humiliation. The shadow of Dien Bien Phu and the memory of a well-trained and equipped Western army's humiliation by an Asian 'peasant army' was to haunt other generals in Vietnam in the years to come.

The Geneva Peace Settlement of 1954 gave Vietnam back to the Vietnamese but crucially split the land into two, with pro-communist North Vietnam north of the 17th parallel and anti-communist South Vietnam to the south. By 1956, Vietnam had polarized into two antagonistic nations: one a totalitarian communist state and the other a corrupt despotism. Within the southern half there were also seeds of future trouble. Not only did the communist north stoutly maintain Ho Chi Minh's claim to rule all Vietnam, but within the 900,000 refugees now in the South, many of them Catholics who had fled the communist purges in the Vietminh's workers' paradise, was contained a hard core of professional revolutionaries with instructions to destabilize the corrupt regime of President Diem. Thus was born the Vietcong, the military arm of the National Liberation Front of South Vietnam (NLF).

By 1961 this communist insurgency group had control of no less than 85 per cent of South Vietnam, mainly the countryside. Disaffection with Diem's imperious and corrupt rule ran high and a combination of communist, nationalist and religious opposition looked set to destabilize the whole country. There were 600 Vietcong attacks a month by the turn of the year. In the circumstances, Kennedy, the new American president, felt obliged to make a stand and show his support for such an avowedly anti-communist regime in a highly unstable region. Faced with the choice of supporting Laos – which was embroiled in its own anti-communist war – and the Republic of South Vietnam, Kennedy chose the second. It was the South East Asian domino that would be shored up at all costs by the USA as an example of America's willingness to 'support any friend, oppose any foe'.

To this day there is a continuing debate about the real factors that influenced Kennedy's final choice of domino. In addition to the ideological divide between north and south Indochina, there was a deep Vietnamese *religious* divide between Buddhism and Catholicism as well. After the communist victory over the French, many Catholics chose to relocate in the South. Diem, for all his dictatorial tendencies, was a practising Catholic and begged for Western support on that basis, among others. President Kennedy was a staunch Catholic whose family had milked the Catholic political constituency regularly over the years in pursuit of votes for the Kennedy clan. The influence of the Catholic Cardinal of Boston, Kennedy's home base, has never been clarified by students of the murky world of 1950s and 1960s New England politics, but no one disputes that there was *some* clerical influence. There remains strong scepticism among many American political observers that Kennedy's decision to support Diem was not entirely a disinterested one by America's first Catholic president.

Whatever the reason, it was to be a fateful decision. In December 1961, the first US combat units, with thirty-three heavy-lift helicopters, arrived in Vietnam, and in February 1962 the new United States Military Assistance Command, Vietnam (MACV) began operations. What was to be called 'America's long nightmare' had begun.

It was not helped by what was effectively an insurgency among Diem's own population in the South. The world was shocked by images of Buddhist monks burning themselves to death in protest. The corrupt Diem regime was scornful, even callous, in its treatment of events.

'If the Buddhists wish to have another barbecue, I'll gladly supply the gasoline and a match,' said Madame Nhu or 'the Dragon Lady', President Ngo Dinh Diem's unofficial first lady, commenting on the Buddhist monks who had set themselves on fire in the summer of 1963 to protest the rule of her brother-in-law.

America's involvement in Vietnam soon began to escalate. In 1965, the US 9th Marine Brigade splashed ashore at Da Nang, and in the spring of that year the US began a programme of overt offensive air operations against communist safe havens and installations in North Vietnam. To back up this military support, the USA pumped nearly a quarter of a billion dollars a year into the South over the next twelve months. The ground force commitment had swelled from 1,000 US troops in 1960 to 300,000 by 1966. America's military machine was fully committed to South East Asia.

Casualties mounted, too. In 1965, the USA had 1,484 men killed. Within one year, that number had increased to nearly 5,000. Suddenly, a faraway war was beginning to make an impact on homes and families across every state of the Union. More importantly, the war was taking on a new dimension. No longer was it just a battle for the hearts and minds of the South Vietnamese people: the war in Vietnam was now becoming a battle for the hearts and minds of the *American* people as well, who were being asked to support the

South Vietnamese not only with their tax dollars but also with the bodies of their treasured sons.

President Kennedy saw the dangers to America before his assassination very clearly, but Washington by then was too deeply committed:

> I don't think that unless a greater effort is made by the government to win popular [US domestic] support that the war can be won out there. In the final analysis, it is their war. The Vietnamese are the ones who have to win it or lose it. We can help them, we can give them equipment, we can send our men out there as advisers, but they have to win it, the people of Vietnam, against the communists.
>
> *JFK to TV reporter* Walter Cronkite *on 2 September 1963.*

Every aspect of the war in Vietnam became the subject of intense American press and television scrutiny, with the result that by 1966 the USA was effectively fighting on two fronts. It was conducting a savage daily battle with a ruthless and elusive enemy in South East Asia; at the same time it was trying to convince a sceptical public that propping up a corrupt and undemocratic foreign regime 'because of a quarrel in a faraway country between people of whom we know nothing' was in the interest of American families, voters and taxpayers. It was a challenging task, anti-communist crusade or not. For first Kennedy and then Johnson and their advisers it was a permanent source of worry: domestic issues always seemed to impinge on the conduct of an unpopular war.

By 1967 the Americans had effectively won. Their massive infusion of men, materiel and aid, allied to new tactics, better intelligence and reforms of the South Vietnamese administration and army had brought the Vietcong and their northern sponsors to the first stages of defeat. Moreover, despite an increasingly vocal anti-war movement in the USA, middle America still remained broadly supportive of President Johnson's prosecution of the war. General Westmoreland could write accurately, 'After only little more than a year of fighting sizeable numbers of American troops, communist losses were mounting dramatically, with nothing tangible to show for it.'

It was clear that the pacification efforts in the South were beginning to succeed, too. Security and increased economic well-being had brought a re-establishment of stable government. For example, by 1967 only twenty out of the 242 provincial districts in the South remained unpacified. The Vietcong logistics infrastructure, so carefully built up by the cadres and party faithful over ten long years, had been smashed. Moreover, it was not something that could be quickly replaced.

Nor could the morale and commitment of the North Vietnamese Army and their Vietcong allies, hammered out of their strongholds by a series of major US-Vietnamese sweep-and-destroy operations, be restored easily. One of the biggest, Operation Junction City in spring 1967, deployed over 26,000 US and Vietnamese troops, with massive air and fire support, and killed over 2,700 North Vietnamese Army (NVA) and Vietcong troops. The secret communist HQ in South Vietnam (the COSVN) was forced to flee for safety over the border into Cambodia. Both sides recognized Junction City and a number of accompanying smaller offensives quite properly as major US successes and serious defeats for the communists.

Captured documents support this view. Contemporary NVA texts record defections to the 'puppet' (i.e. the Army of the Republic of Vietnam, ARVN) regime to be rising and an increasing disillusion with the war by the hitherto committed communist fighters in the South. For example, the diary of an NVA soldier captured in 1967 talks of regular admonitions from his Party cadres (officers) 'not to defect to the puppet army' and records criticisms of his unit's 'weak ideology, poor sense of organization and poor execution of orders'. These and many similar documents of the time are not the record of a revolutionary force buoyed up by anticipation of final victory. On the contrary, they reek of disillusionment, appalling casualties, little food or ammunition, constant fear of US bombing, plummeting morale, failure and despair. The communists' operations were in ruins.

It was in this atmosphere of impending defeat that the Communist Party cadres in North Vietnam met in July 1967. The North Vietnamese leadership had been stunned by both the scale and success of the US intervention; more importantly, many of their Marxist analyses of the developing political-military situation had been shown to be so much rubbish. The ensuing debate over party strategy was lengthy, acrimonious and accusatory. The communists realized that their strategy to reunify the country was failing and that the combat power and commitment of their troops in the South was waning. However, they also realized that, despite the US and ARVN successes, there were serious potential weaknesses in the US position that could be exploited by a readjustment of the communists' priorities and resources.

The communist analysis identified a number of factors in the South that could be made use of. Two key areas were identified: the fault line between the American public's uncertain support for the war and the US government was seen as a potential weakness; and second, there were very real political difficulties inherent in the neo-colonialist US and South Vietnamese coalition. Both of these essentially political targets had, up to then, been relatively ignored by the North. On the military side it was recognized that uncoordinated military confrontation of US main force units was markedly unsuccessful and likely to remain so. However, reasoned the Northern strategists, limited 'spectaculars' against fixed logistics installations such as fuel and ammunition dumps and airbases were relatively easy to organize and did not risk heavy casualties. They would also make good television.

These were shrewd judgements. The seeds of the Tet offensive were sown. And Ho Chi Minh spelled out the continuing problem for America and North Vietnam's hidden strength: 'It may take three years, it may take five, it may take ten, but that will be the war of Indochina,' and 'Freedom for my people, independence for my country, this is all I want, all that I understand.'

The debate in Hanoi was also heavily influenced by other factors, not immediately obvious to Western observers at the time. (Unlike the more porous strategy debates of the democracies, Hanoi 'did not sell tickets to its inner party councils'.) Although no formal record exists of the secret policy and strategy conference held in Hanoi in July 1967, over the years it has been possible to piece together the main themes of the debate. For example, the US bombing campaign against the North was undoubtedly beginning to bite. Some 600,000 civilians had been mobilized to keep the country's infrastructure repaired and working, and another 145,000 troops were active in the air defence of North Vietnam. The bombing had caused serious economic disruption and hardship to the population. These were heavy drains on a small, poor and embattled country's resources.

In the circumstances, it would hardly be surprising if there had been no internal opposition to the war in the South among the North Vietnamese elite. By holding up to the mirror a curious article in the official magazine *Quan Doi Nhan Dan*, published on 22 July 1967, it is possible to see a reflection of the inner workings of the North Vietnamese communist leadership. The article (which is addressed to a North Vietnamese readership) explicitly criticizes 'officials... who fail to recognize the deadly and irreconcilable differences between the USA and North Vietnam', and appear 'to believe that Hanoi could make concessions for a negotiated settlement'.

The very existence, albeit by oblique identification, of a group of North Vietnamese Communist Party functionaries apparently *opposed* to the continuance of the war is a significant pointer to the heat and polarization of the secret Hanoi debate. When we recall that another genuine fear was that the USA might actually invade North Vietnam (General Giap, the victor of Dien Bien Phu, had made a speech earlier in 1967 alerting the party faithful to the need to defend the homeland against a US amphibious invasion), it is perfectly reasonable to believe that the North Vietnamese leadership was divided and fearful by mid-1967. There can be little doubt that the fateful Hanoi conference in July of that year was divided between doves and hawks, between those who wanted to seek an accommodation, albeit temporary, with the USA and those who wished to strike a spectacular blow in an attempt to re-energize the armed struggle to reunify Vietnam.

In the end, the hawks won. A magazine article by General Giap of September 1967 entitled 'The Big Victory, the Great Task' sets out in ringing tones what is almost a blueprint for the Tet Offensive of the following January. He identifies two themes in particular: 'the US unwillingness to face a protracted war' and 'US ruling circles would face... the increasing opposition of the US people.' The Americans were well aware of their weakness back home:

I think we have all underestimated the seriousness of this situation. Like giving cobalt treatment to a terminal cancer case. I think a long protracted war will disclose our weakness, not our strength.

Deputy Secretary of State George W. Ball in response to a question in July 1965 about whether the United States could win a war in the 'jungle rice-paddies' of Vietnam.

This encouraged the new North Vietnamese strategy. Giap also let slip some other interesting clues. He laid great stress on the courage and will to resist of the North Vietnamese people and their 'unshaken determination to endure as they advance towards the reunification of our beloved homeland'. This implies that at least some North Vietnamese morale was shaky and did, in fact, need bolstering. More ominously, he states that the necessary steps had already been taken to 'guard against the evil plotting of reactionaries and spies'. To connoisseurs of communist jargon this usually means only one thing: party members who have opposed the party line – and failed. More than 200 officials, including the head of the North Vietnamese intelligence service, were quietly arrested and disposed of by one means or another in the autumn of 1967. Opposition can be dangerous in a socialist people's paradise.

In Giap's view, the time had now come to reassert the basic aims of the whole long-term Vietminh strategy. What he proposed in September 1967 was nothing less than a spectacular *all-out offensive throughout South Vietnam* by every available NVA and Vietcong asset. This, he hoped, would accelerate the long hoped-for uprising of the South's oppressed masses. Giap genuinely believed that by mobilizing *every* communist resource – political, diplomatic and military – for a series of showpiece attacks in every town and city in the South, the Vietminh and the National Liberation Front of South Vietnam would provide the final revolutionary catalyst to bring the people out of their homes and throw off their yoke of capitalist oppression.

In military terms, given the conditions of the time in South Vietnam, Giap's politico-military analysis was little short of barmy. Sometimes, however, even a mistaken tactic can have unforeseen strategic and psychological results. Thus it was to prove with what became known as the Tet Offensive. In other respects Giap's analysis was remarkably perceptive. For example, he recognized a psychological flaw in the 'subjective and haughty' senior US officers. According to the North Vietnamese, senior US commanders were nothing more than military technicians, mere 'managers of violence' doing the bidding of their masters. They were conditioned only to think in very simple military terms. They were either winning or devising a new system to bring about battlefield advantage. Above all they were obsessed with numbers and 'the management of force'. They did not think like their enemies or even try to put themselves in an adversary's mind. In particular, their unwillingness to consider the idea of a sudden surprise attack from a retreating enemy was a very real flaw in their comprehension, reasoned Giap. For example, the American generals had failed to see the real political purpose behind the Battle of the Bulge in the Ardennes in 1944. Not only had the US commanders of the time been so swept up with their successes that they were oblivious to the possibility of a surprise attack, but they were also so politically blind to the real purpose of the war that they did not realize that an attack for essentially *political* motives was a distinct possibility.

Giap also correctly identified the precise reasons why the USA would find it impossible to increase troop levels in Vietnam in response to any sudden onslaught. The demands of worldwide US garrisons limited the number of divisions available; the whole of US strategic Cold War global policy was based on the doctrine of 'limited response'. Last, domestic and international political pressure would constrain any real attempt by the US military to go for the North Vietnamese jugular by, for example, the use of tactical nuclear weapons. Even so, the North Vietnamese never forgot that, with political will, the power of the full US military machine could have reduced North Vietnam to the Stone Age.

Giap also noted the growing US domestic unrest over the war. US senators agreed with him. Speaking in the Senate on 13 May 1970, Senator Frank Church said: 'This war has already stretched the generation gap so wide that it threatens to pull the country apart,' quoting in particular what Giap called the 'widespread struggle of the American Negroes', which with other US domestic constraints would restrict the range of American responses to his planned attack. Secure in his analysis of the problem, and with the total backing of his political masters, in September 1967 the hero of Dien Bien Phu began his final plan to win, at last, their historic war of national liberation.

The first requirement was to be secrecy. Here Giap ran head-on into the problem that was to bedevil all NVA planning for Tet. There were two key objectives of the North Vietnamese plan: the mobilization, simultaneously, of every available communist soldier and sympathizer in the South for a maximum effort; second, the need for absolute surprise to catch the South Vietnamese and their American allies completely off guard. To a degree these objectives were mutually exclusive. One required maximum publicity to get the message to all the party faithful; the other called for maximum secrecy so as to catch the enemy unawares. Publicity versus secrecy: it was an operational planner's conundrum.

Considerable thought went into a solution. Clearly, any deception plan would have to take into account the need for very public calls to arms to rouse the allegedly revolutionary masses in the South and the disheartened Vietcong hiding in the jungle. The final deception plan, like all the best deceptions, was a skilful blend of fact and fiction. It took account of what the USA and their allies expected and indeed wanted to see and combined it into a mix of contradictory signals that reinforced American prejudices.

The North Vietnamese also launched several initiatives to aid their deception schemes. For example, in October 1967 they let it be known that the VC and NLF would be observing a whole week's ceasefire from the beginning of the Tet Festival on 31 January 1968. The length of the truce surprised many observers, but as the NLF had for twenty years observed some kind of truce over the period of the Vietnamese New Year, this was both expected and welcomed.

US analysts assumed that the length of the truce was designed to allow the debilitated VC units in the South to be resupplied from North Vietnam without being harassed by US aerial bombing, which is precisely what had happened in previous years. In fact, a long truce over Tet *reinforced* the Americans' view that the NVA/VC were a well-beaten force. More than any other single measure, the week-long truce was designed to lull the USA into lowering its guard. It was also precisely the time period that would encourage the southern commanders of the ARVN to send their soldiers back to their families to get some decent home leave.

No other passive deception measure had anything like the same effect as this false truce; and after the Tet Offensive no other NVA ruse aroused such anger among the South Vietnamese population. It was as if the North had deliberately attacked at Christmas, New Year, Easter and the annual family visit to see Granny's grave all combined, after promising faithfully that it wanted a ceasefire. Tet is a sacred time and occupies a unique place in Vietnamese culture.

The USA was hoping, indeed *expecting*, to see some kind of peace-feelers as a reaction to the success of their bombing of the North and the National Liberation Front's military reverses in the South. The NVA command set out to ensure that every diplomatic channel would be used to indicate that they were hurting badly and wanted to talk terms. In September 1967, they decided on a deception operation intended both to offer the American authorities a tempting distress signal and at the same time to drive a wedge between the USA and their South Vietnamese allies along the neo-colonialist fault line they had identified as a potential weak link.

A VC agent called Ha, armed with suitably credible documents, contrived to be captured by the ARVN and obligingly told them that he had been sent to open a channel of negotiations with the Americans to discuss prisoners of war and political matters. When the US authorities were eventually informed, they opened discussions with Ha and tried to force some of his demands (such as the early release of convicted VC terrorists) on to the South Vietnamese regime, much to its anger. Distrust and dissension between the allies began to mount at a critical time, with the South Vietnamese deeply suspicious that the USA was plotting some kind of unilateral deal with the North behind their backs.

This deception was strongly reinforced by a later call on Radio Hanoi from the North Vietnamese Foreign Minister offering substantive talks if only the USA would stop bombing the North. This was taken as genuine confirmation that North Vietnam was beginning to respond to US pressure and its will to continue the war was weakening. Nothing could have been further from the truth.

These diplomatic and overt political gestures were part of what the North Vietnamese termed 'passive' deception, designed to conceal their real intentions. The other arm of the communist deception plan was what they called 'active' measures. This policy was designed deliberately to draw MACV's attention to a number of set-piece military attacks on key bases. The thinking was that if the NLF was going to be forced to trumpet a coming attack that would win the war, then it would be prudent to offer the USA just the sort of attack that the US military intelligence analysts would be looking for. This would not be a countrywide general uprising in the South but a major siege of an isolated and vulnerable US garrison: in fact, another Dien Bien Phu.

To ensure that the USA could not fail to spot the significance of the impending military attacks, Giap offered their principal enemy not one but *two* potential Dien Bien Phus. Both were near the North–South border and both were a long way from the true targets of the Tet Offensive, the main US logistics bases and populated areas. These diversionary attacks were specifically designed to draw American military attention away from the plans for Tet and to divert US reserves and firepower. They were also sufficiently 'noisy' to draw the attention of the whole of MACV and much of the world's press, even in the unlikely event that the US MACV J2 intelligence staff in Saigon had failed to collect good intelligence on the impending attacks in advance. If the USA was looking for military attacks on its troops, then Ho Chi Minh and General Giap were going to provide them.

The first onslaught was on a defended camp at Dak To, halfway up the country and out to the west near the Cambodian border. It started on 4 November 1967 and lasted until the end of the month. The attack cost the NVA over 6,000 casualties and was intended among other things, callous though it seems, partly as a live battle-training exercise for the NVA officers who were later to lead the Tet Offensive. From the US point of view it was an expensive communist defeat, but it achieved its primary aim: fixing Westmoreland and his staff's eyes firmly on communist set-piece attacks on isolated US garrisons at a crucial point during the real build-up to Tet. Was Dak To going to be the 'Great and Final Victory' that the communists kept talking about?

Dak To was merely the curtain-raiser. During December, final instructions went out to the province commanders of the communist forces in the South, including the following significant passage: 'In July 1967 a resolution for a general offensive and uprising was adopted... after a lengthy assessment of the current political and military situation... the general offensive will occur only once every 1,000 years... and will decide the fate of the war.' US intelligence was well aware of the coming storm from this and many other captured documents, all pointing to the same thing. Indeed, in early January 1968, MACV's Public Affairs Officer in Saigon actually issued a press release which amounted to the operation order for the Tet Offensive, based on a document captured by the US 101st Airborne Division in November 1967. The document included VC phrases like:

Use very strong military attacks in conjunction with the local people to take over towns and cities. Troops should flood the lowlands... and move towards liberating Saigon, seize power and rally enemy 'puppet' [i.e. South Vietnamese] units to our side.

It seems incomprehensible that, given this quality of intelligence, the USA could have been taken by surprise by Tet. Yet, with certain exceptions, Giap and Hanoi achieved complete *strategic* surprise. To understand how this came about we have to examine the organization and what a sociologist would call the 'belief structure' or culture of US intelligence on matters Vietnamese in late 1967.

The US intelligence machine did have one unusual advantage over many other intelligence organizations faced with similar problems. The US military had an almost limitless supply of knowledgeable, articulate, well-informed and highly co-operative 'country experts' on Vietnam: the South Vietnamese. Every document could be translated promptly; every prisoner interrogated without delay; and the linguistic nuances, the communist jargon and the regional prejudices of the country were completely transparent to US analysts – provided they consulted their allies. This was a remarkable trump card for any army fighting on foreign soil against an enemy with a difficult language and an alien culture.

Unfortunately, US military intelligence also had a number of inbuilt disadvantages working against them in Vietnam. These disadvantages would fatally distort both the US interpretation of the intelligence available on Tet and reaction to it. The principal disadvantage skewing American understanding was a particularly fixed perspective of history. As US policymakers and intelligence analysts (who should never enjoy too close a relationship – the political wishes of the policymakers invariably corrupt the objectivity of the intelligence officers who, being human, are usually only too anxious to please their masters) looked at the intelligence available on Tet, they sought historical parallels. In Vietnam, they did not have to look far. The spectre of the French defeat at Dien Bien Phu hovered over every Western analysis of North Vietnamese aims. Beyond Dien Bien Phu, communist strategy in Korea and even the Battle of the Bulge in 1944 were offered as analogies of the impending attack. In fact, the Chairman of the US Joint Chiefs of Staff gave a speech in Detroit in December 1967 stating that there might well soon be a last communist thrust comparable to the German attack in the Battle of the Bulge.

General Westmoreland, the MACV C-in-C, and his deputy, General Creighton Abrams, had actually served in the Ardennes in 1944. Dispassionately viewed, one might think that this analogy with von Rundstedt's last battle could have helped the senior US commanders in assessing the threat from a secretive North Vietnam they believed to be increasingly cornered and desperate. However, we are all prisoners of our own experience. Both Westmoreland and his senior advisers saw the analogy with the Battle of the Bulge as representing only the last *military* gasp of a fatally wounded adversary, and not as a general uprising for a specifically political goal.

From this image of a final military onslaught it is but a short step to conclude that the communists would resort to their tried and tested formula by trying to cut off a major chunk of the US forces, like Bastogne during the Ardennes Offensive, and eliminating them in a set-piece battle: just like Dien Bien Phu in 1954. The US analysts and their commanders genuinely believed that a desperate NVA would 'go for broke' in a *military* set piece designed to humiliate the USA and to increase domestic pressure back home to end the war. Although Dien Bien Phu was a tactical defeat for the French, history tends to forget that the rest of the French expeditionary force in Indochina remained largely undefeated, combat-ready and perfectly able to fulfil its mission, but Dien Bien Phu caused its recall by a war-weary metropolitan population. The Americans, in particular the CIA, had homed in on Dien Bien Phu from the moment they became involved in Vietnam. If, went the reasoning, an NVA attack to win the war was imminent *and* the communists were losing the war, they would go for a new Dien Bien Phu to eliminate the American people's support for Vietnam – it had to make sense.

An obsession with historical parallels was not the only weakness in the US position, however. The complex US-South Vietnamese command structure also increased their difficulties, in particular their ability to respond quickly. The grim fact from the C-in-C Westmoreland's point of view was that he was not solely in charge of the US effort in Vietnam. The Navy's Commander-in-Chief Pacific Fleet commanded all US strategic and maritime air power. The US Air Force was a separate service. The CIA ran its own operational programmes in-country, some of which (like the Phoenix covert operations and assassination programme) were definitely *not* for the conventional military. Ambassador Bunker in Saigon was in charge of all relations with South Vietnam. The South Vietnamese had their own military, administrative and regional organizations. Behind all this, the Johnson Democratic administration in Washington, sensitive – and rightly so – to every shift in Vietnam that could influence public opinion, was running an increasingly hands-on policy of micro-managing the war from 5,000 miles away.

The official at the centre of this centralizing policy was Robert McNamara, the ambitious and arrogant civilian who was Secretary of State for Defense and who believed passionately that the micro-management methods of the Harvard Business School were the only way to run a war. This soon reached an absurd level, with the president of the United States poring over tactical target maps of Vietnam and demanding detailed bomb damage assessments from his Air Force staff officers. Some of these were even transmitted to him in-flight aboard the presidential aircraft, Air Force One. In fact, LBJ is reputed to have said following one BDA review, 'Is that the best the Air Force can do? Blow up a few lousy shacks!'

By 1968, no real decisions were being delegated down the US military chain of command. Robert McNamara's way of dealing with the military was simple: those who disagreed with him he sacked if he could; and if he couldn't, he sidelined them and choked off their access to the president like some latter-day Renaissance cardinal. Under the Secretary of Defense's baleful influence, LBJ's lack of access to any military subordinate with a point of view that differed from Bob McNamara's would be a major factor in the debacle that was to follow.

Below this overcentralized National Command Authority was a mass of competing intelligence organizations that made any real central control of intelligence a C3 (Command, Control and Communications) nightmare. A list of some of the agencies involved gives a bewildering flavour of the Byzantine bureaucracy of intelligence collectors and analysts working on the Vietnam problem: Office of National Estimates, O/NE; Central Intelligence Agency,

CIA; Defense Intelligence Agency, DIA; National Security Agency, NSA; National Reconnaissance Office, NRO; Office of Naval Intelligence, ONI; Joint Intelligence (J2) Military Assistance Command, Vietnam, MACV; Combined Intelligence Center Vietnam, CICV; Combined Military Interrogation Center, CMIC; Combined Document Exploitation Center, CDEC; Combined Material Exploitation Center, CMEC. All these US agencies were paralleled to a degree by the Republic of Vietnam's *own* intelligence agencies and sources.

To further bedevil matters, most South Vietnamese officers working in the supposedly combined intelligence centres in Vietnam were not cleared for the most highly classified US material, such as NSA's 'NoForn' sigint. The need to know was applied so ruthlessly as to fragment the true intelligence picture. In their turn, the South Vietnamese intelligence officers (rather like the police officers of the Special Branch of the Royal Ulster Constabulary who were traditionally unwilling to pass on details of a prime IRA source to some 'foreign' British Army officer) were naturally reluctant to turn over their most sensitive humint to US intelligence officers, here today and gone tomorrow. The US one-year tour system for military personnel denied any real continuity or experience. To cap it all, the South Korean contingent, one of the toughest and most successful of the allied contingents, refused to turn over *any* intelligence from their patch unless specifically told to do so.

A dizzying amount of intelligence flooded through this labyrinth of Vietnam intelligence organizations. The Combined Document Exploitation Centre – which, given the language problem, was an ARVN fiefdom – was dealing with *half a million* pages of captured NLF and NVA material *every month*. About 10 per cent was of prime intelligence value, but every blood- or faeces-smeared page had to be handled and read. The workload was huge. The US problem was not that they lacked intelligence in Vietnam; they quite simply had too much.

To control and coordinate this vast effort would have taxed General Eisenhower's large and experienced joint intelligence staff in 1944. By late 1967, the US had appointed just *six* liaison officers to the South Vietnamese intelligence staff (RVN-J2). They promptly and unsurprisingly drowned in a flood of liaison requests and paperwork between the USA, MACV, all the US intelligence agencies in Vietnam and the Republic of Vietnam's own agencies supporting ARVN. The US had a very serious *intelligence* command, control and communications problem in Vietnam by December 1967. To put it bluntly, there was no real joint command and no one had the authority to ensure that everything was coordinated properly. This made a mockery of Robert McNamara's painstaking attempts to micro-manage 'his' war from Pennsylvania Avenue. The NVA and Vietcong were only too well aware of these command weaknesses, and as part of their planning for Tet they specifically targeted some Electronic Warfare (EW) jamming to blot out a number of key US radio links, but not AVRN's links. Command, control and communications of all types were to be a prime target for Tet.

To compound the problems of an obsession with the past and particularly with Dien Bien Phu, a muddled and divided command in Vietnam and too many uncoordinated intelligence agencies, the US authorities had a fatally flawed appreciation of NVA/VC strategy. By July 1967, the month of the secret Hanoi policy conference, US analysts had, they thought, identified the overall communist aims. Defeated in the South and on the defensive, hurting badly in North Vietnam under the US Rolling Thunder bombing campaign, surely the NVA could only strike effectively from border country, well away from the US build-up on the coast and populated areas. Only by threatening the whole of South Vietnam's 1,100 miles of mountainous and jungle-clad border, the theory went, could the communists hope to surprise and trap a sizeable US force, destroy it and with it destroy the American people's will to continue the war. Armed with this analysis, the US intelligence staffs began hunting for America's own possible Dien Bien Phu.

They did not have far to look. Even though the various US intelligence agencies in Vietnam were engaged in a bitter bureaucratic war of their own by the autumn of 1967, by late November and early December it was obvious to every informed observer that something unusual was going on. The intelligence indicators were changing. Truck movements along the Ho Chi Minh supply trail in Laos and Cambodia had increased from 500 in August to 6,300 in December 1967. Following the signing of a new arms deal with the Soviet Union, new weapons were appearing in the South. Signals traffic was increasing. Defectors were no longer coming in so readily. Captured documents talked of a great new offensive to win the war. Unusual troop movements and reinforcements were reported. The South Vietnamese confirmed that significant numbers of VCs in plain clothes were seeking false civilian documents and reconnoitring Saigon and US installations. Unusually, depleted Vietcong units were being brought up to strength by drafts of North Vietnamese Army volunteers for the first time. Puzzled US intelligence officers up-country in the Central Highlands were encountering newly uniformed, better-equipped enemy soldiers by the late autumn of 1967 as the build-up to Tet got under way.

If the key to intelligence interpretation is looking for the presence of the abnormal or the absence of the normal, and asking what it all means, then the US intelligence community had its indicators by the late autumn of 1967. But it could not agree on what it all meant; worse, it *would* not agree. Part of the problem was that the US intelligence agencies were deeply committed to various *policy* aspects of the Vietnam War. They were by no stretch of the imagination disinterested, objective observers. The US agencies all had a policy stake somewhere. The military (MACV) had an interest in proving that they were winning and that General Westmoreland's military policies were successful. Despite a long-standing, and as it turned out well-founded, pessimism about the whole Vietnam adventure, the CIA was hopelessly split in its assessments between its Field Office in Saigon and CIA Headquarters in Langley, Virginia. In their turn, the Joint Chiefs of Staff in Washington were paranoic about any increased estimates from MACV-J2 of NVA/VC strength as these could embarrass the Johnson administration and public opinion, and might lead to calls for increased troop levels in Vietnam. Political policies were distorting military objectivity.

The solution to such a problem is an independent national assessment staff, drawing on all available sources. Since the Second World War, the Americans had formed precisely such a staff: the Office of National Intelligence Estimates (O/NE), tasked with producing National Intelligence Estimates (NIE). The NIE process was specifically designed to avoid any more Pearl Harbors and to provide the highest quality objective assessments for the president and his advisers.

President Truman's original plan for US national intelligence in 1950 had been bold and powerful. A Director of Central Intelligence (DCI),

General Walter Bedell Smith, had been put to work. Bedell Smith had been Eisenhower's Chief of Staff in Europe and knew just how intelligence should work from his experience with the wartime Joint Intelligence Committee (JIC). The new DCI established the O/NE as an independent assessment group of the brightest and the best which would submit draft intelligence assessments to a committee of the heads of the national intelligence agencies under the chairmanship of the DCI.

Unfortunately, Bedell Smith was unable to prevent the intelligence agencies from disagreeing or setting up rival staffs. Under his own powerful chairmanship the system worked, but by 1968 the CIA had established its own separate Directorate of Intelligence (DDI) reporting daily to the White House, and the State Department had the Bureau of Intelligence and Research, equally prepared to challenge any NIE that did not fit the agenda of either CIA or State. In this climate, US National Intelligence Estimate 14–3/67 of autumn 1967 assessing the order of battle and enemy strength in Vietnam proved not to be a document which brought Washington consensus based on the fusion of all available sources, but merely an agenda for yet another vicious dispute between America's many competing intelligence agencies. Professor Parkinson would have understood only too clearly.

The battle lines were quickly drawn up. In the blue corner was the Vietnam military establishment led by MACV-J2; in the red corner was the CIA. Behind the protagonists, their backers hovered like nervous seconds, ever ready at a host of committee meetings with advice, support and the occasional political low blow. The issue was simple: just how many troops could the NVA/VC field against the USA and her allies? On the outcome of this bureaucratic battle would hang the honest assessment of the enemy forces available for any new communist offensive, and thus the proper US military response, with all its domestic political consequences.

MACV and its backer the Defense Intelligence Agency argued strenuously that Vietcong civilian supporters should *not* be included in any estimate of enemy strength. No one knew how many there were and anyway, you only had to go into any Vietnamese village and see that most of them were probably just harmless old men and children. The CIA on the other hand argued that to exclude anything between 120,000 and 150,000 assorted Vietcong auxiliaries capable of carrying a rifle or helping in the liberation struggle in the South was a lunatic attempt to gloss over the real size of the problem. This was not just some arcane matter of numbers. The answer would have very real practical military consequences. A simple analogy is whether the Germans should have included Britain's Home Guard in their total of potential enemy forces in 1940. Either way, it would have made a big difference to the Wehrmacht's assessment of the German troops required for an invasion.

The stakes in Vietnam were high, and the dispute bitter. At risk was the intensely sensitive political calculation of US troop-strength requirements in Vietnam, the barometer of MACV's success. The Joint Chiefs of Staff and MACV knew that *politically* they had just about reached their manpower limits by early 1968. If MACV's strategy really was winning the war in South Vietnam, as was claimed, what on earth would the American public make of a sudden leap in Vietcong strength? The issue went to the core of Johnson's presidency and domestic political agenda. In the words of the Chairman of the Joint Chiefs of Staff, in a private letter to Westmoreland:

I note that there is some feeling... about the relationship between 'statistical book keeping'... and future troop strengths... any attempts to 'weigh the dice' will only result in trouble for us all.

Thus was the issue spelled out clearly from the highest political-military level in Washington. Don't inflate the enemy numbers in any politically embarrassing attempt to get more US troops for Vietnam, went the message, otherwise Robert McNamara will fire you.

General Westmoreland and his MACV intelligence staff took the hint. When the Chairman of the Joint Chiefs of Staff warns someone not to cause 'trouble for us all', no politically astute commander in the field is going to ignore such advice. The real message was clear and unequivocal: don't tell the truth – this is *political*. Thus national policy, as spelled out by the Joint Chiefs of Staff, was going to dictate the military input to a key National Intelligence Estimate, not hard military facts. In the end, the Office of National Estimates did include 120,000 Vietnamese self-defence or auxiliary forces in their draft National Intelligence Estimate, and a furious row erupted. The military felt that the estimate contradicted their successful battle of attrition against the NVA/VC and threw doubt upon the extent of MACV's success in killing Vietcong.

The core of the issue was the infamous 'body count'. Not unlike General Haig on the Western Front in 1916–17, in Vietnam General Westmoreland had opted on the instructions of Robert McNamara for a brutal reckoning by numbers to wear down the enemy. Just as Haig plotted surviving German divisions and their combat worthiness, so Westmoreland plotted surviving and battleworthy NVA and VC. That genius of American management technique, quantification of the problem and cost efficiency, first applied in the Union's Springfield Armory in order to manufacture guns, was now a century later being applied to running a war. It was a strange and unsubtle way to achieve a military victory against an essentially political enemy, but new and unsubtle methods were ruling the thinking of Washington's military planners in the mid-1960s.

The problem with this method of measuring success lay with Robert McNamara, his methods and his placemen. One of those placemen was General Westmoreland, the Commander-in-Chief, Military Assistance Command in Vietnam. The appointment of 'Westy' was a direct product of McNamara's political influence on the conduct of the war. Westmoreland was a tall, handsome, well-connected South Carolinian, another product of the Southern elite that has traditionally chosen the United States Army as a career fit for a gentleman. It did not hurt that the powerful Chairman of the House Armed Services Committee, L. Mendel Rivers, was also a South Carolinian.

At the time, many of Westy's contemporaries believed he had reached his ceiling as a major general commanding the 101st Airborne Division in the early 1960s, and that he was intellectually and temperamentally unsuited to command at the highest level. He appeared to be better suited to the tactical level of battle where he could personally influence the activities of his troops – no one ever questioned Westy's undoubted courage and panache – than to the operational and strategic level of war. Quite simply, his peers felt that he lacked the necessary strategic vision to be an effective Commander-in-Chief. As such he was unlikely to challenge Robert McNamara's personal handling of 'his' war.

That suited the former Chief Executive of the Ford Motor Corporation just fine. No individual stands indicted for the failure of the American effort in Vietnam more than the US Secretary of Defense, Bob McNamara. He believed that he did not need generals other than to do his will and regarded traditional military experience as a positive handicap to the clear management thinking needed to exercise power efficiently in the modern world. Fresh from his victory over the military in toughing it out with Khrushchev as part of Kennedy's inner circle during the Cuban Missile Crisis, and from his business success in running an international automobile company, the politically astute McNamara now had only two clear goals: giving his political master, President Johnson, what he wanted, and forcing the military establishment to do things his way.

To achieve the first, McNamara unashamedly manipulated the Washington political system to ensure that he had total control of all military advice to the president. He played on LBJ's insecurities, which stemmed from a deep-seated feeling of insecurity as president because Johnson believed that his tenure in the White House was in some way illegitimate (LBJ had succeeded by default when John F. Kennedy was shot and killed). Johnson had a deeply rooted preference for avoiding confrontation and liked to do business without any controversy or open disagreements. Anyone who got in the way was 'fixed', bribed, muzzled, got his 'snout dunked in the pork barrel' or was 'gotten rid of'. It was the LBJ way of making things work around Washington.

Knowing this well, McNamara made sure that he laundered any dissent from the US military leadership over the conduct of the Vietnam War. He went to unusual lengths to ensure that the Joint Chiefs of Staff could not air their concerns about the way that the war was being fought either in private or in public. In particular, McNamara took special care to suppress any conflicting military advice that would have adverse political results, such as the US Marine Corps Commandant's advice behind closed doors that 'if the president wants to really *win* the war in Vietnam, then you'd better tell him it'll take half a million US troops and five years.' Fighting for the advancement of their single service budgets and personal power, the individual Chiefs of Staff were picked off one by one by McNamara using a combination of threats and political bribes, despite their constitutional responsibilities to report to Congress and not just to the C-in-C and his Secretary of Defense. Schooled in the rigorous school of democratic civilian control of the military, and mindful of the fate of General MacArthur in Korea, the Chiefs kept their mouths shut for far too long, until they themselves stood accused as accomplices in McNamara's and LBJ's half-baked Vietnam policies: but by then it was too late.

To achieve his second goal, that of bending the US military to do his bidding, McNamara applied the business methods that had served him well in civilian life and taken him to the top of the ladder in corporate America. On first coming to office as Secretary of Defense, he launched a blitz of civilian cost-effectiveness inspections at all levels of the US military machine, to the dismay of the more traditionally minded senior soldiers, sailors, airmen and marines. Dissenters were swiftly replaced and the cowed remainder went along with their new master's methods. Military waste and incompetence – of which there was much, as in any other operation run by a government – were identified with brutal efficiency by teams of bright young civilian MBAs, freshly hired from the major US business schools. Despite having never heard a shot fired in anger, they toured every major command treating experienced officers with a breathtaking arrogance and contempt for hard-won military experience.

Despite the wails of the military traditionalists, McNamara was in some respects absolutely right. It undoubtedly *was* rotten economics to have the aircraft carrier USS *Constellation* steaming off 'Yankee Station' at a cost of $30 million with the sole purpose of destroying North Vietnamese targets from the air, and then for her expensive aircraft and pilots to sprinkle free-falling iron bombs in the general area of the target. Better by far to make the national 'product investment strategy' worthwhile by using new, much more expensive precision-guided weapons that were *guaranteed* to strike their targets: suddenly the whole costly investment in the aircraft carrier could be justified. It was sound business economics. No taxpayer could argue with the logic of that.

McNamara and his circle do not appear to have thought the problem through one step further, however: whether bombing a scientifically chosen set of military targets is really the best strategy for winning a war against a resourceful and elusive guerrilla enemy whose goals are essentially political.

Numbers and statistics are only a small part of battle; much of warfare is inherently unquantifiable. Regrettably, McNamara proved to be ill-prepared for the subtle world of international policy and irregular warfare, and so he fell back on the things he really understood, like collecting the daily statistics of precisely how many VC had been killed in Vietnam. For Bob McNamara, if a lifetime in American business had taught him anything, 'the numbers' were everything. The 'body count' was his bottom line.

For McNamara's 'manager' in Vietnam, General Westmoreland, the key numbers were the 'crossover point', that magic moment when NVA/VC losses in South Vietnam measured by the body count would be greater than the NVA's ability to replace these losses. At this point MACV planners calculated that NVA/VC strength in-country would be in terminal decline. By mid-1967, according to MACV, with enemy casualties at 6,000 a month and replacements at only 3,500 a month, the crossover point had been reached, and so the pressure was off in terms of policy and troop levels. Yet here was the CIA with an extra 120,000 Vietcong troops challenging all MACV's carefully collected statistics in a National Intelligence Estimate that would only too quickly become public knowledge if 'leaky' Washington ran true to form.

An attempt at a compromise NIE and frantic visits to Saigon by DIA and CIA teams in September 1967 tried to sort out the discrepancy. According to the CIA's calculations, MACV's estimates of NVA/VC strength did not make sense. The bureaucratic fight was savage, with a MACV-J2 officer shouting across the table to the chief CIA analyst at one point, 'Adams, you're full of shit!' Even the CIA's Station Chief in Saigon was accused by his own superiors from Langley as 'having gone over to the military'.

The meeting broke up with an uneasy compromise which, like most bad compromises, neither party accepted. The result was that, as the indicators and warnings for the Tet Offensive piled up, ticking away at the heart of US national intelligence policy was a bitter political disagreement about just how many enemy could be deployed against General Westmoreland's command. The Office of National Intelligence Estimates, General Bedell Smith's careful creation to harmonize American intelligence at the national level, had been disabled twenty years on by feuding government agencies, anxious to prove that they alone were right.

Against this political chicanery and bureaucratic infighting, the NVA's careful plan to deceive the Americans in South Vietnam had only a limited impact. Although the NVA undoubtedly did succeed in poisoning the wells of accurate intelligence assessment, it can be argued that the NVA's complex deception schemes were to some degree incidental to the whole affair. In many ways the American intelligence community did not need deceiving: it was perfectly capable of deceiving itself, even without a careful enemy deception plan. In the words of some embittered US intelligence officers, 'the NVA would have done better *not* to have tried to attack the US Military Headquarters in Saigon on the night of Tet; success would only have *ended* the existing confusion within the ranks of the US Command in Vietnam.'

Whatever the power struggles in Washington, by early January 1968 in Vietnam it was blindingly obvious that something was up. North Vietnam's passive deception strategy was reopened at the highest political level by a New Year's proposal for bilateral talks (thus excluding South Vietnam, provided the USA stopped bombing the North). This set a new political agenda, and diverted attention from NVA/VC preparations elsewhere. In the South there was a flurry of small attacks on US installations and a clear movement of at least two NVA divisions towards Khe Sanh on the border between North and South Vietnam. US suspicions were further aroused when six NVA officers made an unsuccessful attempt to walk through the front gate of the Khe Sanh firebase dressed as US Marines. Alert US sentries shot the lot.

Khe Sanh was about as isolated a US garrison as there was in the whole of South Vietnam. Only 12 miles south of North Vietnam, 6 miles from Laos and 800 miles from Saigon, Khe Sanh sat firmly across one of the NVA's Ho Chi Minh supply trails draining into the northern corner of South Vietnam. It was garrisoned by two elite regiments of US Marines. The base was difficult to resupply and, being high in the mountains of the interior, frequently shrouded by fog. With its isolation, vulnerable airstrip and outposts, Khe Sanh had all the makings of another Dien Bien Phu. Most alarming of all, it was well within artillery range of guns firing from over the border in North Vietnam.

General Westmoreland let the ambassador in Saigon and Washington worry about political talks with North Vietnam and began a gradual build-up of operations designed to ensure that, should Khe Sanh indeed be the NVA's much heralded 'general onslaught to win the war', then the US Marines and their supporting forces would be ready. In Operation Niagara, thousands of the new Unattended Ground Sensors (UGS) were airdropped around the base to monitor North Vietnamese activity, and intelligence analysts at highly secret sigint bases in far-off Thailand were soon receiving conversations between puzzled NVA soldiers along the lines of 'What on earth is this metal spike, comrade?' and doubtless the equally soldierly response, 'Search me, comrade, but we're late getting to Khe Sanh.'

Operation Niagara around Khe Sanh was a huge intelligence success, and by mid-January 1968 it had identified 15,000 men of the NVA 325th and 304th Divisions definitely closing in on the US base. Patrols from the Marines began to clash with NVA regulars digging in on the surrounding hills as the communist noose tightened. General Westmoreland and his staff became even more convinced that Khe Sanh was the target of the long-promised decisive attack by the communists. That ever-reliable indicator of an enemy's intentions, signals intelligence, seemed to confirm this by reporting a growing volume of NVA military radio traffic building up around Khe Sanh. More puzzling, they reported a countrywide pattern of unusual VC activity and actually warned of impending attacks in the South. But it was too late; all eyes were fixed on the NVA's two divisions around Khe Sanh, not on the Vietcong trying to regroup and resupply themselves in the South.

Any last doubts were swept away on 20 January 1968 when a junior officer of the NVA defected to the Khe Sanh sentries and openly informed the Marines that two of the defenders' hill positions would be attacked that very evening, 'as a prelude to tomorrow's all-out attack on the US base'. The commander of the US Marines force, Colonel Lownds, acted swiftly. He needed to. The two hills were duly attacked and by dawn on 21 January 1968, two regiments of US Marines were trapped at Khe Sanh, and their South Vietnamese covering force had been forced to withdraw into the firebase perimeter. Khe Sanh was now cut off from the rest of Vietnam, besieged and under heavy attack. General Westmoreland, his staff officers and the US intelligence analysts had at last found their Dien Bien Phu.

It is difficult for us to overestimate the effect of the Khe Sanh attack on the US military psyche by New Year 1968. The whole cultural bias at the time was to expect a desperate military offensive by a trapped and beaten enemy, just like the Ardennes in 1944. The attack was *expected* to be on an isolated US garrison and designed to win a military victory targeted on public support for the war. America's micro-managed military machine immediately swung into action. Here was a crisis they could manage 'efficiently'. In the White House, President Johnson had a daily briefing on the conduct of the Khe Sanh siege on a specially constructed terrain model in the basement. Senior briefing officers were personally appointed by McNamara just to monitor the progress of the siege on a trench-by-trench basis. Nothing was to be left to chance; no statistic from the besieged garrison's command bunker was too insignificant to be overlooked in Washington's fixation with Khe Sanh's defence. Reinforcements and supplies were flown in to the garrison at great cost and with considerable bravery. No political or military effort was spared to ensure that the beleaguered American garrison would hold out. The alternative would be a military and public relations disaster not worthy of contemplation.

General Giap's principal active deception measure to mask his true offensive had worked brilliantly. Blinded by their own prejudices, the Americans had been inexorably drawn to the feint attack and not to the real onslaught, as surely as a charging bull is drawn to the matador's cape. It was a triumph for the North Vietnamese planners and a serious intelligence failure. General Westmoreland even issued a warning that 'attempts would be made elsewhere in South Vietnam to divert and disperse US strength away from the real attack… at Khe Sanh.' He was, unwittingly, referring to the main Tet Offensive, but all eyes were now focused on the diversionary attack on Khe Sanh.

Not everyone was fooled. The American and South Vietnamese intelligence collection effort was simply too big and too active to miss indicators of impending trouble elsewhere. Ironically, these indicators were now viewed by US commanders as *diversionary* measures intended to draw attention away from the 'real attack' on Khe Sanh and not the other way round. The NSA's signals intelligence effort in particular was concerned about the rising tide of messages in the South. In a special intelligence report issued exactly a week before Tet, they warned of a wave of coordinated attacks countrywide in Vietnam. In their turn, the AVRN's comprehensive humint coverage in the South picked up hundreds of indicators of planned VC attacks on military installations, and demonstrations. As a result, AVRN began a series of intelligence collection operations designed to find out exactly what was going on. In the coastal city of Qui Nhon on 28 January they struck gold.

On 28 and 29 January 1968, a police sweep captured a group of eleven Vietcong leaders and all their plans and preparations for the 'great liberation offensive' just three days away. In the bundles of captured documents and maps were included some audiotapes, intended to be broadcast once VC fighters had captured a number of radio stations. The startled South Vietnamese security police played the tapes. They were ringing exhortations to the populace 'to rise up and overthrow the puppet Ky government in South Vietnam now that the day of liberation is finally at hand', and to support the 'forces struggling for peace and national sovereignty who have seized the cities of Saigon, Hue and Da Nang'. Giap's view was of quiet triumph. The great deception had worked:

> Khe Sanh was not that important to us… it was the focus of attention in the United States because their prestige was at stake, but to us it was part of the greater battle that would begin after Tet. It was only a diversion, but one to be exploited if we could cause many casualties and win a big victory.
>
> *General Vo Nguyen Giap on the Battle of Khe Sanh*

So impressed were the AVRN authorities by their capture of the tapes, they played them over the telephone to American analysts in Saigon. Obviously the communists had not yet seized Hue and Saigon. Perhaps they were intending to? The MACV-J2 intelligence officers were interested and called for translations, but these would take time and would have to come by courier. The dinosaur-like nervous system of command and control between the US and the Vietnamese, and between the police and the military, had imposed another critical delay.

Twenty-four hours later, by the time the MACV-J2 analysts had received the transcripts and begun to assess the significance of the Qui Nonh audiotapes, a bigger threat was looming – or so they thought. With perfect timing, on the morning of 29 January 1968 (H-hour for Tet minus forty-eight hours) the US sensor station monitoring the Khe Sanh perimeter alerted MACV to a number of major NVA units closing in on the firebase. In fact, their report actually used the phrase, 'This looks like the "Big Push".' Even if it had not been before, the attention of the US commanders was now obsessively fixed on the Demilitarized Zone in the north and the threat to the beleaguered garrison. Any other intelligence indications of activity elsewhere were seen merely as attempts to divert US attention from the NVA's main battle effort. In all fairness, General Westmoreland and his staff were not blind to the forthcoming Tet Offensive; they just misunderstood its significance. To them it was simply a diversion.

On 29 January 1968, the Tet ceasefire took effect. Fortunately for the allies, neither the South nor the North Vietnamese gave it the weight that General Giap had intended. The North Vietnamese and their VC allies promptly broke the ceasefire by attacking prematurely in a number of towns throughout the south. This singular piece of military incompetence was caused mainly by poor NVA-VC communications. Thoroughly alerted, the South Vietnamese authorities curtailed the 50 per cent leave plans for their soldiers and issued warnings of probably widespread ceasefire violations by the NVA and VC. If not strategically, poor NVA/VC organization had seriously compromised Tet at the tactical level.

It did not matter. Even though a wave of communist attacks erupted prematurely in four provincial capitals at dawn on 30 January, the friction inherent in the complicated US-South Vietnamese command structure could not pass on the signals, analyse their significance and then warn thousands of allied units, civilian regional administrators and US billets throughout Vietnam in time. The senior intelligence officer in MACV and the principal architect and collator of the body count statistics, General Davidson, belatedly recognized the significance of events. Early on 30 January, he warned his C-in-C that 'major follow-up attacks could take place throughout Vietnam in the next 24–48 hours', and that the South Vietnamese Army was busy cancelling their own Tet ceasefire. General Westmoreland promptly alerted all major US commands to resume normal operations, and place 'troops on maximum alert... for the defence of HQs, logistic installations, airfields, population centres and billets'. With just twenty-four hours to go, the US military in Vietnam was beginning to gear up ponderously for trouble nationwide.

It was too late. In the words of Colonel James Wirtz's masterly study of the whole Tet intelligence problem, 'The [US] command structure was incapable of passing on the warning to all its units at such short notice.' Wirtz also points out that the communications network 'simply could not provide enough information to all the commanders in the field... in time'. General Giap had beaten General Westmoreland to the draw, despite the sophisticated US intelligence apparatus. If proof needs giving, Wirtz dryly recollects that:

> Two hundred Colonels, all assigned to the joint intelligence staff in the US military command in Vietnam, spent the evening of 30 January attending a [Tet] party in the Bachelor Officers' Quarters (BOQ) in Saigon.

No greater indictment of the failure of the intelligence community could be found. One of their number, the intelligence analyst Colonel James Meacham, next morning found himself manning a .50 calibre machine gun on the roof to defend the US Senior Officers Quarters, still blissfully unaware of the existence of any Tet Offensive. And he was a senior intelligence officer!

The Tet Offensive burst upon the US and MACV like a thunderbolt. Thirty-six out of forty-four provincial capitals were assaulted overnight on 31 May 1968 by a mixture of NVA and Vietcong units, as were five out of six 'autonomous cities', and fifty-eight of South Vietnam's 245 major towns. ARVN units and 'pacification hamlets' were particularly targeted. Major attacks took place in Saigon, where the US Embassy was attacked unsuccessfully under the eyes of US television cameras, Quang Tri, Nha Trang, Qui Nhon, Kontum, Ban Me Thuot, My Tho, Can Tho, Ben Tre and Hue. For a very short time the Vietcong actually managed to seize temporary control of ten provincial capitals.

The centre of Hue, the ancient capital in the North, was invaded despite a clear warning of attack issued by the ARVN Joint Intelligence Staff ten days previously and held by a mixture of VC and North Vietnamese regulars. The US and South Vietnamese closed in on the invaders and a fierce battle developed. As one US marine said, firing his M-16 at the advancing NVA,

'Those poor sad bastards have got us surrounded. Boy, are they gonna get themselves ******!' Trapped by an ARVN division and several battalions of US Marines, the communists sold their lives dearly. US television cameras faithfully recorded the stress of combat among the young Marines and flashed the message into every living room in the USA as their soldiers struggled with the life-and-death realities of a major battle, leaving an indelible impression that the US forces were *losing*. In fact, the reverse was true.

Unfortunately, the TV crews failed to flash the horrors of the besieged and doomed VC and their terrified South Vietnamese hostages trapped in Hue citadel with equal honesty. Such one-sided and inaccurate reporting by the US media was to alter the course of the war. The coverage was also to leave an ineradicable grievance in the US military mind against the lies, incompetence and self-seeking ambition of journalists in particular and the media in general. It remains to this day. In the words of one Vietnam veteran:

> We lost the [Vietnam] war at Tet, when those lying sons of bitches showed American boys fighting and dying in Saigon and Hue... Hell, what did they expect real combat looked like? A cat fight in the ladies room? But they never showed what was happening to the VC in the Citadel and what they were doing to those South Vietnamese civilians. They never explained just how we was whuppin' those NVA bastards' ass... I'll never, ever, trust the press again... They lied.

Encapsulated in that quotation was the American tragedy. For the Vietcong and the NVA, Tet was a total military disaster and a serious defeat. For the Americans and their allies, Tet was actually the successful repulse of a widespread surprise attack, with heavy enemy losses. But it was a public relations catastrophe.

In the first two weeks of the communist offensive, which petered out thereafter, the NVA/VC lost 33,000 killed, an estimated 60,000 wounded, 6,000 prisoners of war and failed to hold a single objective. The South Vietnamese Army in particular fought back both tenaciously and savagely. General Giap's *Khnoi Nghai* or 'general uprising of the oppressed masses in the South' failed to materialize. Not only that, the same ungrateful masses in the South proceeded to inform on the VC insurgents at every turn and, given the opportunity, took up arms to kill their 'liberators' or hand them over to ARVN who exacted rough military justice on their enemies. (The famous picture of Saigon Police Chief General Loan blowing out the brains of a VC prisoner captured in civilian clothes dates from Tet.)

From the perspective of Ho Chi Minh and the North Vietnamese Politburo, militarily Tet was a complete failure. Sometimes, however, perceptions of truth are more real than truth itself. Truth, for most people, is what can be seen on a television screen. 'The camera,' in the old cliché, 'cannot lie.' Of course it can. All images are selective. Documentaries are faked, actors paid to pretend to be real people, riots and demonstrations bought by TV teams with props and kerosene-soaked flags, and carefully selected shots represented as showing the whole scene. So it was with Tet. Damaged Vietnamese buildings were treated as if they were the ruins of Hiroshima; in the words of Charles MacDonald, 'Television cameras focusing on one badly damaged block in Vietnam could give the impression of an entire city in ruins.' The damage overall after Tet was light, but pictures of a burnt-out city block with a few bloodstained corpses, weeping refugees and nervous trigger-happy soldiers make hot copy.

The US and to a lesser extent the international press corps in Vietnam fell on the story with alacrity. A series of highly misleading television and press pictures were passed to the media audience with equally biased reports. Thus Saigon was alleged to be 'in ruins' – it was not. The communists had 'inflicted a bitter defeat on the US and South Vietnamese' – on the contrary, the US and ARVN forces had successfully repulsed the communists at the cost of only 2,800 ARVN and 1,100 US soldiers killed (less than 10 per cent of NVA/VC casualties). The press almost totally ignored the thousands of South Vietnamese refugees and victims of the communist offensive, and, to the undying shame of Western journalists in Vietnam, failed even to report the 5,000 South Vietnamese tortured and murdered by the VC during their brief occupation of Hue. To the press they did not matter. For the press in South Vietnam, only their copy and the career-enhancing story mattered. And the US press corps knew they had a story to tell.

It was a story of deceit, deceit on a massive scale by their government and by their armed forces. Had the Johnson administration and General

Westmoreland's command staff not been telling them for months that the war in Vietnam was as good as won? Was this not proof of the chicanery, deceit and lies of the smooth-talking, Martini-drinking public affairs briefing officers at Westmoreland's Saigon headquarters, known as the 'five o'clock follies', endlessly mouthing platitudes about pacification, progress and body counts? The press and thus by extension the American people had been systematically lied to. This was no victory. The communists had surprised the US Army and inflicted a shattering defeat upon America in South Vietnam. Anyone could see the truth. Even the great Walter Cronkite, TV anchorman and the voice of the suburbs, wailed plaintively, 'But I thought we were supposed to be winning.'

There was no conspiracy as such among the reporters. There was just their story as they saw it. Sceptical of official US claims, they individually and collectively came to the correct conclusion that the USA had been the victim of a successful surprise attack. Inexperienced in the confusion of war, they then incorrectly assumed that the American forces in Vietnam had suffered a serious reverse. Back home the editors uncritically accepted their correspondents' verdicts. Years later, one of the Saigon press corps, Peter Braestrup of the *Washington Post*, ruefully admitted how badly the press had misled the American public. In a TV documentary he confessed, 'Rarely had contemporary crisis journalism turned out, in retrospect, to have veered so widely from reality.' But by then it was ten years too late. Only in one aspect was the press verdict accurate. At Tet in January 1968, the US commanders *had* been taken by surprise. That much was true, and the blame for it lay in faulty intelligence, in particular poor intelligence assessments. Logically, it can be argued that it was the rotten intelligence assessments before Tet that lost the USA the Vietnam War.

The truth is that until Tet the USA had been winning. Tet was a massive military defeat for the North Vietnamese, as one who was there plainly saw:

We won the Tet Offensive. We decimated the Viet Cong. And our wonderful press made us losers. It was right at that point in time, I think, that the press fully turned on the war in Vietnam and started not necessarily generating news, but generating opinions. Because we decimated the Viet Cong during Tet. We decimated the North Vietnamese Army during Tet. Had we pressed the advantage the turnout would have been different. But when you are fighting a war based on politics, stuff happens.

Sergeant Allen Lynch, 1st Cavalry Division US Army,
Vietnam 1967–68

But by the time the reality of Tet had sunk in, the USA was only interested in getting out of Vietnam. The Tet Offensive was the decisive battle of the Vietnam War but not, ironically, for the reasons General Giap and his planning staff had sought. Tet marked, in Wirtz's phrase, 'the turning point between US escalation and US withdrawal from Vietnam'. The shock to American public opinion and to the US president, both conditioned by McNamara's bland assertions that the war he was 'managing' was well under control, was simply too great. Whatever Giap's dreadful losses at Tet, he had won the battle where it most counted – not in South Vietnam but in the hearts and minds of the American people. The great media guru Marshall McLuhan saw it clearly some years later with the benefit of lofty academic hindsight when he wrote, 'Television brought the brutality of war into the comfort of the living room. Vietnam was lost in the living rooms of America – not on the battlefields of Vietnam.' (*Montreal Gazette*, 16 May 1975)

No one was more surprised by all this than the North Vietnamese, who found the hysterical US reaction to Tet almost incomprehensible. Years later, one of the NVA's generals, Tran Do, admitted, 'In all honesty, we failed to achieve our objective, which was to start a general uprising in the South. As for making a propaganda impact in the USA, it had not been our principal intention – but it worked out as a very fortunate result for us.'

For the intelligence analyst the Tet Offensive is a brooding, sad tale of opportunities lost and bad assessments. With so much information available, just how could the US intelligence machine possibly have got it so wrong? This was no Pearl Harbor; the US military intelligence collection units did an amazing job, and MACV-J2 was awash with indicators of an impending attack, some of them accurate to the point of precision. The difficulty lay in the interpretation of the information.

Here the US system let them down. Intelligence is not just about collecting information in vast quantities. Drawer after drawer full of glossy 10x8 prints of communist units on the move, or technically brilliant intercepts and decoding of obscure radio transmitters lurking in some inaccessible jungle hideout, is not true intelligence. For information to become intelligence there is no substitute for sound and well-informed analysis. In the end, intelligence is just that: correct interpretation and analysis. The US military's intelligence system failed for a number of reasons: institutional, cultural and organizational. In their errors, however, US intelligence staffs were greatly helped by General Giap's deception plan to lure US commanders' attention to his diversionary attack and not to the main effort. There can be no equivocation about his final success. For the key US decision-makers, General Westmoreland and President Johnson, the diversion at Khe Sanh drew them like moths to a light.

Yet not all US analysis was wrong; therein lies part of the tragedy of Tet. For example, the CIA's Station Chief in Saigon, Joseph Hovey, produced a strikingly accurate all-source objective analysis of the Tet Offensive on 23 November 1967, two months before the attack. Unfettered by the institutional constraints of US government policy in Vietnam or the military's need to prove that MACV's strategy really was working, Hovey spelled out a clear interpretation of North Vietnam's combined military and political goals and just how they would plan to achieve them. He was spot on.

Nobody would listen. There were so many competing analyses of communist intentions doing the rounds in Washington that it was impossible to know which one was right, and there was no national organization to build a credible consensus. Hovey's accurate and highly relevant analysis was quickly disowned by his superiors at Langley. It did not accord with CIA Headquarters' view of events or the political wishes of the administration at that particular moment. For the bureaucrats in Washington, intelligence had become the view of the senior officer present; and well-informed analysis by those actually in the field was not welcome in the endless internecine war of the interagency committees. The methods of MacArthur and Willoughby hovered over all.

If analysis and interpretation let the US authorities down at Tet, then the final phase of the intelligence cycle – dissemination – assured their failure to react quickly. By the time they realized that a countrywide attack was imminent, it simply was too difficult to warn everyone in time. In some cases it did not matter, because alert local commanders and intelligence staffs realized that something was afoot and took action in their own patch on their own initiative. In other areas the attack came as a complete surprise. The result was that reactions to the Tet Offensive varied from place to place.

For example, the 173rd Airborne Brigade was refitting at Tuy Hoa, a provincial city on the coast south of Nha Trang, after several difficult months in combat up-country at Dak To. Thanks to a combination of good local intelligence and NVA miscalculation, this particular US light infantry brigade was alert and ready for Tet. In the words of one of the brigade's intelligence officers, Captain John Moon of the US Military Intelligence Corps:

The 173rd was ready for the Tet Offensive, although we didn't call it that until it was over. Our commanding general was a tough little Kansan called Leo H. Schweiter. He had been the intelligence officer of an American airborne division which dropped on D-Day. He had also been a special forces commander, so he knew just what intelligence could – and could not – do. He had an insatiable appetite for all the stuff we could provide. He ran his intel staff hard, and was always pushing us to know everything. He understood our business sometimes better than we did. Even though we were in a supposedly safe area he kept his guard up all the time. No sonofabitch was going to surprise his troops!

During the run up to Tet it was pretty clear to the brigade S2 (Intelligence) staff that something unusual was in the wind. Through the local ARVN we were aware that there were plenty of low-level indicators of some kind of activity; although, to be fair, we reckoned it was just in our tactical area. As a result, General Schweiter ordered the battalions to cut special landing zones [LZs] in the jungle so that the troops could be picked up and deployed quickly anywhere in our tactical area if there was any need. The local Vietnamese were on alert too, so we were all waiting for something to happen.

On the night of Tet the NVA took too much time to get into Tuy

Hoa as they got diverted by a small airfield and a radar site on their march route and the firefight started early. When the alert sounded, the brigade troopers were quickly airlifted in the dark into the battle area using the new LZs to block off all the approaches to Tuy Hoa and back into the forest. So the NVA found themselves with dawn breaking, short of their objective and cut off from the flanks and the rear as more and more US troops were airlifted in to surround them. To make things worse for the NVA, the Tuy Hoa airbase was only about five miles to the south.

It was a turkey shoot; the F-100 Super Sabres were barely tucking in their wheels before dropping their ordnance and getting straight back into the airfield circuit to land and rearm. God knows how many sorties the Air Force flew that day. There was so much shit going down into the North Vietnamese box that the local villagers just waded up to their necks into the warm water of the South China Sea to get out of the way. In the end only twenty-five NVA got into Tuy Hoa and the ARVN just mopped them up. The city itself was hardly damaged.

If Tet was meant to take over South Vietnam, then in Tuy Hoa it was a complete military failure and the attackers were massacred as well. The 173rd was good and ready and we reckoned we whupped 'em good that day.

The battle-hardened 173rd Infantry Brigade, which had been in Vietnam since 1965, was lucky to have such an experienced staff. Most other units of the allied forces in South Vietnam either found themselves responding to a sudden attack or, forewarned by some particular local event, 'stood to' in one alert state or another. The units round Qui Nhon, for example, went on red alert unilaterally on 29 January, following the capture of the two VC propaganda audiotapes.

The Tet ceasefire, its subsequent cancellation and the difficulty of reaching commanders going off for holiday leave compounded the problem of disseminating intelligence warnings. In the words of one US communications officer, 'Really we needed 36 to 48 hours to get a message down to everybody in MACV.' The US had less than eighteen hours to alert the whole of Military

Assistance Command, Vietnam. As a result, the majority of units were surprised by the attack when it came on the night of 31 January 1968.

To take one example, the US 1st Cavalry Division was sited around Quang Tri in the far north. To the surprise of Captain John Robbins, the youthful commander of the six guns of Alpha Battery, 2nd Airborne, his unit was relocated at short notice to LZ Ann, an isolated hill top about ten kilometres west of Quang Tri city on 28 January. The artillerymen dug in their 105 mm guns and chafed at being so far from the rest of civilization just before the Vietnamese New Year stand-down. It may have been that Captain Robbins's superiors in First Cavalry knew something, because on the night of the 31st, the bored gunners at LZ Ann were treated to what they thought was a spectacular fireworks display as the great Tet holiday festival got under way. In fact they were seeing NVA/VC 122 mm Soviet-supplied rockets streaking across the night sky to bombard Quang Tri city.

The next thing Robbins knew was a desperate call from his battalion headquarters in the middle of the town demanding that he get his guns into action as quickly as possible. To his request for a proper target and detailed fire order came the snarled response from the battalion fire team, who had never been on the receiving end of enemy fire before, 'Goddammit Captain, we're all sheltering under a table in the command post… just open fire on the sons of bitches.'

Obligingly, the guns on LZ Ann opened fire, aiming in the dark at the flashes of the rockets as they fired in the forest four miles away by a combination of eye and map, like Napoleonic gunners 200 years before. By dawn, Robbins ordered his men to cease fire, being down to ten rounds a gun, and a dense fog settling over the hilltop. It was nearly a week before Alpha Battery was relieved on LZ Ann: only then did it come home to the gunners just how big the attack had been, and that an NVA supply convoy of *elephants* carrying the rockets had been lumbering through the jungle immediately below LZ Ann on the night before Tet, both sides oblivious to the other's presence.

If the surprise of Tet to US commanders and troops in Vietnam was profound, in Washington it came as a total shock. President Johnson had not even had the advantage of General Davidson's last-minute intelligence briefing to his C-in-C on the morning of 30 January that trouble was brewing. In fact Westmoreland did not react over-much to his intelligence chief's warning, going home to bed as normal that night. Next morning, like so many of his officers and men in Saigon, he found himself embarrassingly trapped in his quarters by the communist attacks and so unable to get in to his command post until he was rescued by Military Police.

To the politicians and chattering classes of Washington, the Tet Offensive was 'an incredible shock, an unmitigated disaster'. The politicians felt deceived by their military advisers; the media felt cheated by the military and politicians alike. Had not McNamara and Westmoreland claimed victory and talked of US troop withdrawals in 1969? And yet here was the supposedly beaten VC inflicting a highly visible surprise attack and defeat on the USA and her allies throughout the whole of Vietnam. Tet was undoubtedly a local setback, but it was never the disaster the media subsequently portrayed, with breathless reporters (led by the doyen of journalistic responsibility, Walter Cronkite) and shocked and embarrassed military officers on television telling the story for all the world to see. The major casualty of Tet turned out to be the American people's faith in their president, their government and their army.

The ripples of the Tet Offensive spread far and wide long after the attack petered out over the next month or so. The usual bitter rows broke out between the intelligence agencies. The CIA pointed out that the Saigon estimates of the North Vietnamese and Vietcong casualties in Tet alone came to more than the official MACV estimates of total NVA/VC strength before the attack. Either the casualty figures were inflated or the CIA must have been right all along. They must have been deceived by the military in Saigon and McNamara's Defense Department. A new squabble erupted.

A disillusioned Robert McNamara resigned, unable to come to terms with the failure of his methods and his own responsibility for the war. His replacement, Clark Clifford, was ordered by Johnson to make a complete review of US strategy in Vietnam. To his astonishment, Clifford could not find a single senior officer who believed that the war could be won using the methods the USA was employing.

Washington never trusted MACV again. Anti-war demonstrations and protests increased. In March, President Johnson, worn out by his burdens, announced to a startled nation that he would not compete with Robert Kennedy and seek re-election for a second term of office. Much later, the world was to learn just how badly the protesters' gibes of 'Hey, hey, LBJ, how many kids did you kill today?' had struck home on a Texan politician who genuinely believed he was doing his best.

In April, General Westmoreland's relief as C-in-C MACV was announced. By December 1968, Richard Nixon was elected president, promising to bring the boys back home. Westmoreland was long gone, 'kicked upstairs' in the unkind judgement of his critics to become a pliant member of the Joint Chiefs of Staff, responsive to the politicians' whims as ever. Years later, however, Henry Kissinger gave the political truth away: 'Military men are just dumb, stupid animals to be used as pawns in foreign policy.'

The inevitable round of official inquiries was launched to identify the reasons for the surprise at Tet and a major shake-up of the intelligence structure was put in hand – too late. The whole course of American policy reversed. The US public wanted out, and an escape from the sticky clutches of the tar baby that was destroying presidents and reputations, and taking an ever-increasing toll of their sons. The American political belief in their cause and their will to win the war in Vietnam had gone. Despite Tet's military failure, General Giap's prize was eventually handed to the North Vietnamese by the Americans themselves.

On 14 April 1968, after a gallant defence and no fewer than 30,000 aircraft sorties in support of the firebase, the Khe Sanh garrison forced the battered NVA survivors to withdraw across the border, having inflicted at least 5,000 North Vietnamese casualties and probably many more. It was hailed with relief by America as a great victory: which it undoubtedly was.

Just two months later, on 23 June 1968, however, the USA abandoned the Khe Sanh firebase for ever. On 29 March 1973, the last American troops left South Vietnam, and only three years later, on 30 April 1975, the victorious North Vietnamese Army entered Saigon as rulers of a united Vietnam.

As an American military intelligence officer sadly observed, 'It all started to come unglued at Tet,' and in 1995 Robert McNamara finally acknowledged his error:

I believe we could and should have withdrawn from South Vietnam, either in late 1963 amid the turmoil following Diem's assassination, or in late 1964 or early 1965 in the face of increasing political and military weakness in South Vietnam. We misjudged the geopolitical intentions of our adversaries (in this case, North Vietnam and the Viet Cong...) and we exaggerated the dangers to the United States of their actions... We totally misjudged the political forces within Vietnam.

No one summed up the US failure that was Vietnam better than the unscrupulous, if clear-thinking, Henry Kissinger:

We fought a military war; our opponents fought a political one. We sought physical attrition; our opponents aimed for our psychological exhaustion. In the process we lost sight of one of the cardinal maxims of guerrilla war: *the guerrilla wins if he does not lose.* The conventional army loses if it does not win. The North Vietnamese used their armed forces the way a bullfighter uses his cape – to keep us lunging in areas of marginal political importance.

10

'PRIME MINISTER, THE WAR'S BEGUN ' – YOM KIPPUR, 1973

*'At [the airport], [General] Moshe Dayan was talking to me about
losing the Third Temple [Israel]. He was very hoarse, it was painful
to hear him. He was talking about a battle for nothing less than the
Land of Israel itself...'*

MAJOR GENERAL REHAVAM ZE'EVI, ISRAEL DEFENCE FORCES

If a defeat caused by a catastrophic failure of intelligence such as Pearl Harbor
can spur a nation into reforming its intelligence affairs, then paradoxically a
great victory assisted by brilliant intelligence can lead to complacency and
disaster. Thus it proved for the small state of Israel after its mauling at the
hands of the Arabs in October 1973.

On the Jewish Day of Atonement, Yom Kippur, 6 October 1973, the
Syrian and Egyptian armies fell on the extended borders of 'Greater Israel' and
inflicted grievous losses on the surprised and shocked Israeli Defence Forces
(IDF). After a bitter struggle lasting eighteen days, the invaders were flung
back with heavy loss and Israeli territory recaptured, but the damage was done.
The myth of Israeli invincibility and intelligence omniscience, so carefully
nurtured after the brilliant military successes of the Six-Day War of 1967,
had been shattered for ever. The gallant little state that always triumphed over
the odds despite struggling for its very existence surrounded by hostile Arab
neighbours emerged as just another country caught unawares by its adversaries
because of incompetent intelligence.

The roots of Arab-Israeli enmity went deep. In its most simple form the
dispute was over the land of Palestine, which Jewish settlers had begun taking
over piece by piece during the first half of the twentieth century. The Jewish
Diaspora had for nearly two millennia dreamed of a return to its Judean

homeland, which had been put to the sword by Titus in AD 70. The Roman legions put down the Jewish Rebellion of that year with all the efficient savagery peculiar to Imperial Rome in the Ancient World and scattered its population throughout the Mediterranean. 'Next year in Jerusalem!' was the historic toast of these dispersed Jews. By the end of the Second World War this had begun to look a possibility, as Zionism, the nineteenth-century movement to recreate the biblical homeland of the Jews, received powerful reinforcements from a war-shattered Europe.

The politics of guilt is rarely a sound recipe for even-handed reform. So it proved for the Jews of Europe. Horrified by the evidence of the Holocaust, and burdened with numerous displaced Jewish survivors, the victors of 1945 turned a blind eye to the new flood of Jewish refugees heading for Palestine to reinforce the half-million Jews who had bought and fought their way into Palestine during the 1920s and 1930s. Even the British, theoretically the UN power mandated to keep order in Palestine, made only half-hearted attempts to exert their authority over the intransigent and desperate Jewish refugees flooding into Palestine and their protective gangs of militant thugs before the 1939 war, terrorizing British and Arabs alike. In 1947, the British relinquished their responsibility for Palestine with obvious relief, leaving Arab and Jew to fight it out. After Auschwitz and Belsen, nobody by 1946 wanted to be seen to be standing in the way of a new Jewish homeland.

Even so, the state of Israel came into being like some latter-day Outremer, an interloper on the edge of a hostile Arab world. By the West it was seen as a haven and a solution to finding a historic home for the Jews. To the Arabs, on the other hand, Israel was seen as an artificial imposition that had acquired Arab – and particularly Palestinian – land by a mixture of bribes, blandishments, terrorism, theft and corruption. The Arab world felt no guilt for Hitler's treatment of the Jews: rather they pointed to Jewish colonists' treatment of their Arab neighbours and to the land battles of the 1930s. Thus was born a bitter enmity between new settlers and indigenous inhabitants.

On 14 May 1948, the State of Israel was formally declared. On 15 May 1948, the armed forces of Egypt, Syria and Transjordan, Lebanon and Iraq fell on the new nation simultaneously in an all-out bid to destroy it at birth by pushing the cuckoo in the Middle East nest, as they saw Israel, straight back into the Mediterranean Sea. They failed. With the courage of desperation and the moral fervour of their centuries-old crusade, the new Israelis flung back their Arab enemies at every point, despite being outnumbered many times over. Battered, defeated and licking their wounds, the Arab invaders retreated, astonished by the ferocity and fighting power of the Jewish state. Israel was born in bloodshed and straight away tempered in the fire of victory on the battlefield, although the Islamic world never accepted this state of affairs. Israel's very right to exist and the dispossession of the Palestinian people from their land became the irreconcilable poles of a dispute that has continued to this day.

Another war erupted in 1956, when the Israelis conspired with the French and British to attack Nasser's Egypt after he nationalized the Suez Canal. The result was the same as in 1948: Arab humiliation, Israeli triumph. The sore festered on. In 1967, surrounded by threatening Arab armies preparing to attack yet again, and desperately outnumbered, Israel struck first in one of the most dramatic pre-emptive strikes in the whole history of the bloody twentieth century. At dawn on 5 June 1967, the Israeli Air Force destroyed their Egyptian and Syrian counterparts on the ground, and then, with total air superiority, threw the Syrians off the Golan Heights on Israel's northern border, captured Jerusalem from the Jordanians in the east and seized the Gaza Strip and the whole of the Sinai Peninsula from a soundly beaten and fleeing Egyptian Army in the south. 'Greater Israel' was born.

By 1968, and for the first time since it came into being, Israel as a state could feel territorially secure behind defensible borders. In the north, the Golan Heights gave security and relieved the settlers on the *kibbutzim* from the need to raise their children under shellfire. In the east, the small but professionally competent Jordanian Army had been pushed out of the West Bank and was now penned across the River Jordan. And in the south, the Sinai Desert, once a 150-mile buffer zone between the Israeli and Egyptian front lines, had been replaced by a new border: the Suez Canal.

These extended frontiers may have given political and territorial security to Israel but, confronted by unwavering Arab hostility, they had also to be manned and protected like so many watchtowers ranged along on the battlements of Jericho's walls. This was a heavy burden in men and materiel for a small country. It also obscured the loss of the old buffer zone in the south. Before 1967, Egyptian forces had to traverse 150 miles of Sinai Desert to get at their Jewish opponents. Now all they had to do was cross 150 yards of Suez Canal. This was to prove a crucial difference in 1973.

The combatants of the Six-Day War were still hosing out the carbonized flesh from burnt-out tanks when fighting broke out again, albeit at the level of artillery duels and guerrilla attacks. As the Egyptians stoked the pressure, beginning six years of 'no peace, no war', Israel began to confront the realities and the cost of her new strategic position. In the month of July 1969 alone, the Israeli Defence Forces lost thirty-six killed and seventy-six wounded in action; and between January and July 1970, Israel sustained nearly 500 casualties. This rate of attrition could not be sustained for long, and so on 9 September 1969, the IDF set out to teach their Arab tormentors a sharp lesson.

In what became known as the 'ten-hour war', Israeli forces crossed the Suez Canal and, using captured Egyptian armoured vehicles manned by 150 Arabic-speaking soldiers, invaded Egypt on an extended punitive raid. This tiny force under its false colours spread mayhem in the Suez town area, causing 450 casualties, collecting vital intelligence and destroying three air defence radar stations. After ten hours, the Israeli commandos coolly re-embarked and, to add insult to injury, brought with them two of the latest Soviet T62 main battle tanks, captured in the confusion. To make the point, the Israelis crossed the southern end of the canal again later in 1969 and dismantled a brand-new Soviet P-12 radar system under the very noses of the Egyptians and their alarmed Soviet advisers.

Despite these demonstrative successes, Israel realized that some real defensive barrier was now needed. Lieutenant General Chaim Bar Lev, the Chief of Staff of the Israeli Army, gave his name to what was to become a line of fixed fortifications along the length of the Suez Canal. The Bar Lev Line eventually became a hundred-mile chain of sand-covered mutually supporting forts with deep shelters, minefields and weapon-firing pits, backed by a maze of trenches, covered roads, water-storage tanks and dug-in tanks and artillery. With the Bar Lev Line, Israel had exchanged the flexible defence of mobile armoured warfare for her own version of the Maginot Line. To further ensure that no one could sneak across the canal in rubber boats, selected forts also had underground oil and petrol systems with special pipes that could pump oil on to the canal and, set aflame, incinerate any would-be canal-crossers.

Israel needed the Bar Lev Line. The Egyptian war of attrition rumbled on for more than a year and a half before President Nasser accepted a ceasefire in July 1970. The Israeli population heaved a collective sigh of relief; no more would they have to live with daily newspapers marking the body count every morning with black funereal borders. Both sides took advantage of the lull. The Egyptians began to move forward the new air defence missiles and radars provided by their Soviet sponsors. Their aim was to provide a dense belt of anti-aircraft missiles over the whole length of the canal. In their turn the Israelis poured concrete – and cash – into building up the Bar Lev Line to new levels of solidity to keep the Egyptians at bay. One estimate for the expenditure on defence infrastructure for Sinai in 1971 is half a billion US dollars at 1970s prices.

In this the Israelis were helped enormously by money provided by Jewish donors overseas. In the aftermath of the 1967 war, and motivated by a mixture of pride, guilt and religious fervour, the Jewish Diaspora had trebled its contributions to the State of Israel. Money given by individuals and non-governmental bodies, many of them American, increased from about $400 million in 1967 to $1.2 billion after the Six-Day War. This income, together with generous US aid, enabled the living standards of the average Israeli family to increase faster than any other developed nation at the time, despite a defence budget that would have bankrupted another economy. Paradoxically, war was actually boosting Israel's national income. Israel needed this cash from overseas. Even with it she was forced to cut defence spending by $68 million in 1972.

Other events fuelled Israel's growing confidence, too. In the 'Black September' of 1970, King Hussein of Jordan's patience finally snapped and he ordered the regiments of his Arab Legion to evict the Palestinian guerrillas busily setting up a state within a state and conducting their own bloody squabbles inside the Hashemite kingdom. In the words of one observer, 'The well-trained Bedouin regulars slaughtered the [Palestinian] terrorists… they should not have tried to put up a fight against real, well-trained infantry.' Suddenly, with the flight of the Palestinian guerrillas to Syria and the Lebanon, for the first time since 1948, Israel's eastern border with Jordan was relatively tranquil.

On 28 September 1970 came even better news for Israel: President Nasser of Egypt died. At a stroke, the mouthpiece of Arab Socialism, Pan-Arab Nationalism and the Soviet Union's principal client in the Arab World was no more. His successor was Anwar Sadat, one of Nasser's original group of nationalist Egyptian officers. Apparently a devout Muslim, Sadat was more patient and thoughtful than the flamboyant and excitable Nasser. From the start he said quite openly that to achieve her goals, Egypt would have to fight. Despite this, Sadat was essentially a pragmatic politician who initially pursued a parallel policy of diplomacy in a search for a peaceful solution. Perhaps unwisely, he declared that '1971 will be the year of decision.'

Sadat's 'Year of Decision' started badly. Egyptian diplomatic initiatives were rejected or ignored, although in some respects they paralleled many aspects of Israeli thinking. Poor negotiating at the United Nations and hardening attitudes on both sides caused yet another mini-crisis, and in spring 1971 both sides began to reinforce the canal. Realizing that any attack by Egypt across the Suez Canal would now be met by a fully alerted and partially mobilized IDF, Sadat ordered the Egyptian Army not to fight. For his internal opponents – and probably to their Soviet backers – this was the last straw, and a coup against Sadat seemed imminent. The new president had funked his big battle in the Year of Decision, claimed his detractors. He would have to go.

The plotters, led by the pro-Soviet Ali Sabri, had miscalculated. Sadat may not have attacked the Israelis as they expected, but that was merely common prudence, not lack of resolution. He moved against the pro-Soviet faction in the Arab Socialist Union Central Committee on 25 April with a speed and ruthlessness that surprised many and his opponents most of all. Within a week, Ali Sabri and his fellow conspirators were safe under house arrest and any other opposition to the president of Egypt had prudently disappeared underground. The Soviet Union, which may well have encouraged the Ali Sabri plotters, pretended that nothing had happened, and Sadat, who needed Soviet arms and aid, pretended equally to be ignorant of any Soviet involvement. Both parties settled down to a new and harmonious – if slightly wary – relationship to discuss their mutual interest: the curtailment of US-Israeli influence in the region. To seal their new deal, Sadat signed a fifteen-year Treaty of Friendship and co-operation with the Soviet Union for arms and foreign aid.

For the rest of that year, Sadat's strategy drifted. He had to be content with vague Russian promises of aid, unreturned letters and calls, and being fobbed off as the Soviets vacillated. Moscow seemed not to be bothered, and Sadat's approaches to the Americans fell on equally deaf ears. Weeks turned into months as 1971 dragged on inconclusively. Even a long-postponed summit meeting in Moscow in February 1972 left Sadat with no real progress. Egyptian frustrations were starting to fester.

Sadat realized that time was running out. Jokes about the 'Year of Decision' and his leadership circulated among the wags in the cafés and souks. Like Nasser before him, he knew only too well that an Egyptian leader had to act if he wanted to survive. Every day that passed increased dissent in the Army and unrest on the streets. In fact we can trace Sadat's frustration and his thinking very clearly in an address to the leaders of serious student riots in Cairo on 25 January 1972, just before he flew to Moscow for his inconclusive meeting with Premier Brezhnev: '[The decision] to go to war against Israel has already been taken… this is no mere words; it is a fact.'

Again, the Soviets stalled. Arms supplies would be 'difficult'. Sadat emphasized the need for military action against the Israelis. The worried Soviets, with an eye on the growing policy of detente and superpower stand-offs, could not tolerate any resumption of fighting. By June 1972, Sadat had had enough of pointless meetings with the Soviets and diplomatic inactivity. He issued a questionnaire directly to the Soviet Premier, Brezhnev, bluntly warning that Egyptian-Soviet relations depended on the answers. Yet again the Soviets ignored the Egyptian president and talked of 'a general relaxation of tension in the region'.

Anwar Sadat decided to strike. The Soviets had built up a massive military presence in Egypt by summer 1972. The air defence of Cairo was covered by 200 Soviet fighters complete with Russian air and ground crews. The SAM umbrella over the canal was manned by an estimated 12,000 Soviet experts. In addition there were 5,000 other military advisers. 'The Soviets,' avowed one Egyptian officer, 'were everywhere.' But the Soviet presence was generally unwelcome. Their arrogance and contempt for the Egyptians infuriated a proud people who looked back to a golden age of the pharaohs when their civilization had led the world. Educated Egyptian officers found their Soviet counterparts ignorant and boorish. Worst of all in the Muslim world, they showed little respect for Islam.

On 8 July 1972, Sadat summoned the Soviet Ambassador and told him that all, repeat all, Soviet personnel must be out of Egypt within ten days. With the Soviet Ambassador, Vladimir Vinogradov, visibly stunned, Sadat left the meeting. Later he said, 'I felt that we all needed some kind of electric shock.' Sadat meant what he said. On 17 July, the Soviets began to pack their bags and leave. The expulsions strengthened Sadat's domestic standing enormously. The Army was glad to be rid of their patronizing advisers, and the mosques were openly delighted to see the back of a pack of godless heathens.

Once the euphoria and sense of liberation had worn off, however, Sadat's concerns grew again. His gesture had not solved Egypt's real problems. Hoped for peace-feelers from the USA and Israel failed to materialize. The Egyptian economy continued to be squeezed to near suffocation by the need to maintain the country as an armed camp, and social unrest, always a powerful attention-getter for Egyptian rulers, became an ever more serious threat. Sadat had to do something to break the logjam before it was too late. Sometime in late 1972, he made the fateful decision to attack Israel.

The first evidence of his resolution probably came at a closed meeting of the Arab Socialist Union Central Committee on 14 November 1972. From that moment, President Sadat's Egypt began planning to resume the long-running war with Israel by launching a full-scale surprise attack across the Suez Canal to seize limited chunks of occupied Sinai from the Israelis. The goals were mainly political. Israel would be given a short, sharp shock. The Arab and Islamic world would see Egypt in the forefront of the battle against the detested Jews. At home, Sadat's firmness and resolution would be applauded. It would reinforce his position as Egypt's leader in every way.

Having just evicted the Soviets, Sadat realized that he would still need allies. Egypt could not fight Israel on her own. Sadat needed three things for his enterprise: money, guns and a diversion. The money came from the oil-rich Arab states, especially Saudi Arabia, who welcomed Sadat as a conservative bastion against the potential excesses of radical leaders like the wild-eyed Colonel Qaddafi of Libya. The guns and other arms could be acquired from the long-suffering Soviet Union, but this time without massed legions of advisers; and finally the diversion would be provided by Syria, Egypt's partner in the humiliating defeat of 1967. In the last months of 1972, President Sadat of Egypt and President Assad of Syria began to build a secret military coalition to strike Israel by a surprise attack on two fronts simultaneously.

The Egyptian Army had not been idle since their humiliation in the Six-Day War. At the end of 1972, Sadat appointed General Ahmed Ismail Chief of Staff with strict instructions to prepare for war. Ismail was no socialist or political appointee. On the contrary, he was a highly competent and professional commander, and his impact was felt rapidly within Egyptian military planning circles. His particular expertise had been gained at the Soviet Staff College, which meant he knew how to plan an attack. Like the well-trained General Staff officer that he was, General Ismail put in hand a thorough appreciation of the situation, and he wisely insisted that the 'enemy forces' paragraph, the IDF, was to be made the subject of a completely separate appreciation.

From the point of view of the Egyptian General Staff planners, the Israel Defence Forces had five great advantages. The first four were: guaranteed arms supplies from the USA; a high preponderance of technological weapons systems; Western standards of training; and air superiority. The fifth and final Israeli advantage Egypt could do little about. Ismail was realistic enough to accept that a people who understood that their opponents could suffer many defeats but that Israel could not survive even one would fight to the bitter end. He made sure that any plan would be for limited objectives only. Israel was not going to be pushed back into the sea.

Nevertheless, Ismail reckoned that with good staff planning he could nullify the first four of Israel's advantages. More interestingly, he also identified what he believed to be a number of potential Israeli weaknesses. An enemy's weaknesses are always much more interesting than its strengths. The Egyptians pondered long and hard on the Israelis' failings, chief of which, they decided, was a potentially fatal overconfidence caused by a combination of arrogance and a superiority complex from constant victory.

It is an irony of history that both sides tend to draw different lessons from the same war. The victors invariably tell themselves that their success was entirely due to their brilliant generals, superb tactics, superior equipment and the matchless courage of their soldiers. The defeated tend to brood on their mistakes, note well their enemy's strengths, work out just how their conquerors actually won and resolve how best to ensure that it will be their turn to get it right next time.

Thus it proved after 1918 when the British quietly forgot their success at Amiens on 8 August 1918, when they combined tanks, aircraft, mobile artillery, good communications and a devastating surprise combined-arms attack to break through on a narrow front, in their desire to get back to 'real soldiering' in Aldershot after the war. The Germans, on the other hand, studied the lessons of what Ludendorff called 'the Black Day of the German Army' and by 1938 had come up with the tactics, doctrine and equipment for a sustained attack using the ideas pioneered by the British and Australians at Amiens twenty years before. The Germans called it *Blitzkrieg*.

Thus, reasoned Ismail, would it be for the ever-victorious Israelis, revelling in the hubris of their 1967 successes and declaring triumphantly that the Israeli armed forces were the best and most battle-hardened in the world. While this pride in Israeli martial superiority was well justified in view of events, it had begun to acquire more than a streak of arrogance by 1972. Unfortunately, it was also founded on a less attractive belief that the Jews were in some way *racially* superior to Arabs. Many earlier Zionists had viewed the Arabs as 'feudal, backward and pre-nationalistic'. This was a core belief of many pillars of Radical Socialist Zionism like Chaim Weizmann and Vladimir Jabotinsky and, despite the more tolerant views of liberal elements within Zionism, even David Ben-Gurion, the 'Father of the Jewish State', firmly believed in a permanently divided and backward Arab world. At a time when eugenics was accepted as hard science, such beliefs were widely held, and their echoes infected some Israeli thinking and still do to this day.

The Israelis had other, more concrete weaknesses. To their perennial problem of an inability to sustain a long war or heavy casualties was added a new dimension: long lines of communication. Traditionally Israel had always enjoyed the advantages of Napoleon's favourite strategy, the 'central position'. With short internal lines of communication and surrounded by enemies, Israel had always been able to concentrate forces rapidly in time and space to meet a threat from any direction. But now she was stretched. The gains of the Six-Day War meant that she could be pulled in one direction or another. Greater Israel had imposed a strategic problem: from the Golan Heights to the Suez Canal meant a 72-hour re-deployment for an armoured brigade, and possibly longer.

The Egyptian staff analysed every aspect of Israel's strengths and weaknesses before developing an operational concept for the coming battle. The plan capitalized on the seven main conclusions of the Egyptian intelligence appreciation:

1. Strike first by surprise to pre-empt the Israelis.

2. Use massive force on as wide a front as possible to disperse any attempt at a counter-attack.

3. Maintain an air defence umbrella over the ground forces at all times to keep the Israeli Air Force off the backs of the ground troops.

4. Force Israel to disperse resources between widely separated geographical combat areas.

5. Blunt any Israeli counter-attacks by emphasizing defensive weapons and fighting from defensive positions.

6. Force Israel to incur heavy casualties.

7. Ensure that Egyptian forces have the most up-to-date and technologically superior weaponry to match Israeli systems.

The last requirement, for technologically advanced weapons, sent the Egyptians speeding back to Moscow, demanding either the latest MiG-23 fighter-bombers or Scud surface-to-surface missiles from their long-suffering Soviet arms storemen. It took time, but by autumn 1973, Sadat's troops had the hi-tech weapons called for by 'The Plan' which had now acquired a name: Operation Badr.

Normally, the wide ranging and well-organized Israeli intelligence service would have picked up the first signals that something was brewing. With their superlative humint nets in the Arab world, the Israelis rarely failed to tap into some loquacious and well-informed source when the need arose. The Egyptian

General Staff operation planning officers would have been a particular target, at any time. On this occasion something went wrong. It may have been better Egyptian security, but, although Israeli intelligence was aware of Egyptian plans, they failed to react as before to a growing threat. In addition, the intelligence that was collected was distorted by a number of self-imposed and deliberate Israeli misconceptions. In Chaim Herzog's sardonic reference to the situation within the Israeli intelligence establishment of 1972–73, 'eyes they have but they see not'. It was a perceptive summary of the failure of Israel's much-vaunted intelligence system in the run-up to Yom Kippur.

The roots of the problem lay deep inside Israel's recent history and political organization. Israel is a small country and intensely politicized, partly because of her people's love of a good argument but, more important, also by a voting system of proportional representation. This made every Israeli Cabinet an uncomfortable alliance of differing views and differing agendas and increased the need for 'dual track' government. The result was a large and volatile Cabinet coalition which was essentially the public face of government (at one stage 30 per cent of the Knesset was in the Cabinet), and a much smaller kitchen cabinet that really ran the country. Golda Meir, the prime minister in 1973, certainly ran Israel precisely on those lines.

In 1973, the only organization that saw all collected information, processed and interpreted it and gave all-source evaluations and briefings to ministers was the Army, or more accurately AMAN, Military Intelligence. The Mossad, or Secret Intelligence Service, ran overseas operations; Shin Beth, the equivalent of Britain's MI5 or the Bundesrepublik's BfV, was limited to internal security, and the Foreign Ministry's Research and Evaluation Staff evaluated diplomatic traffic. All other intelligence – sigint, techint, order of battle, logistics intelligence, foreign liaison sources, targeting, overhead reconnaissance and foreign country assessments, even nuclear security (LAKAM) – was controlled by the military.

This unique situation had arisen because of Israel's growth as a warrior nation from the very start. Military Intelligence had always been dragged into the smoke-filled inner councils of Israeli prime ministers to say their piece – usually at two o'clock in the morning. In a nation in arms, every crisis was by definition a *military* crisis. Even when briefing the Cabinet, the Minister of

Defence always took not just the Chief of the Armed Forces but also the head of Military Intelligence. MI was the dominant national intelligence agency and its uniformed head was consulted directly as a matter of routine by every government and cabinet.

This is a dangerous position for any intelligence officer, however senior and however clever. Objective and often painful truths sometimes need to be uttered by fearless intelligence officers to their political masters without regard for the political consequences. Somewhere between 1967 and 1973 the rigid line between intelligence and policy in Israel was breached. Some commentators claim it never really existed. Military intelligence became national intelligence; and national intelligence became a matter of national *policy*. The line between military and ministerial responsibilities became blurred. This cosy arrangement invariably spells disaster somewhere along the line, as Tony Blair discovered in 2003. So it was to prove for Israeli intelligence.

The real problem lay in the membership of the inner policy-making group in Israel. With the passage of time, Golda Meir ignored the squabbling and contentious ranks of those outside her political magic circle and relied more and more on the favoured few. Israeli national security policy became an isolated and clandestine affair characterized by excessive secrecy, personal relationships, party loyalties and, most dangerous of all, a sense of self-righteousness. One stern Israeli critic of Meir's methods at the time, Professor Perlmutter, described it scathingly as 'a group interested primarily in its own fierce sense of exclusivity and collegiality'. This inner group was not going to disagree; its whole informal existence hinged on the belief that only its exclusive military and ministerial members really understood the finer points of Israel's national security needs. More sinister, the inner group believed that it was the *only* group really qualified to arbitrate on Israeli national security policy. To conceit was added conspiracy; to arrogance was added the moral rectitude of 'group think'. Any critic within the Group proclaiming a contrary view risked the ultimate rejection: exclusion from the Group and the secret inner sanctum of the nation's defence policy.

With this dangerous arrangement institutionalized at the heart of its national affairs, Israel began to evaluate the first indications of an Egyptian build-up during 1973. From the start, the whole process was bedevilled by political considerations imposed by Golda Meir's inner circle. The first of these was a classic example of 'group think' supported by politicians and military alike. The Arab armies and air forces had received such a thrashing in 1967, ran the thinking, that they would never dare to take on the Israelis again unless two conditions were fulfilled. In the first place, Egypt needed to be able to overcome Israeli air superiority before she would dare to attack, and for the second, only a joint Syrian and Egyptian attack could succeed. As neither condition was anywhere near to being fulfilled, reasoned the Israelis, then Israel was safe from any serious threat. Certainly the Arabs would try to attack again, but not now. They were just not strong enough. These political judgements became Israeli national policy, overriding any contrary views culled from intelligence; it was a classic example of confusing political aspirations with hard facts.

This was an astonishingly arrogant view of Israel's adversaries. The theory was even peddled as a serious policy of deterrence when combined with Israel's new extended borders. An Arab attack was now claimed to be so difficult that Greater Israel's overwhelming military strength and well-defended frontiers were in fact a real deterrent. By holding on to the 1967 gains, both territorial and psychological, Israel was doing nothing less than guaranteeing peace in the region. Israel's ownership of the conquered territories was a good thing. This was a bold claim, and that it was being made publicly by uniformed military intelligence officers to visiting delegations as a political policy should have worried dispassionate observers. Intelligence officers had crossed an invisible line and were now firmly cast in the role of 'policy advocates and not information assessors', in Edward Luttwak's phrase. Others warned of hubris and arrogance along with other factors working against Israeli military intelligence in the spring and summer of 1973.

In the aftermath of the Six-Day War and leading up to the Yom Kippur War, Israelis had absorbed a new mindset, the *conceptzia,* the conception. Many have described Israeli society as one characterized by bravado and even a sense of invincibility. Israeli citizens, the military and the government were absolutely convinced that Arab countries wouldn't dare to start another war against Israel, and that the devastation and humiliation from the Six-Day War were still too fresh. But perhaps this *conceptzia* blinded Israelis, suggests

Abraham Rabinovitch, author of the definitive book on the Yom Kippur War. He summarized it neatly: 'Israel had fallen victim to its own victory in 1967.'

Already burdened with the preconceptions of 'the Concept' and a falsely rooted idea of regional deterrence, the intelligence community now had to view developments through a number of other distorting prisms imposed on them as 'policy'. The first of these was the cost of mobilization. For example, in May 1973 the Israeli Chief of Staff, Lieutenant General David Elazar, ordered a partial mobilization, recognizing clearly a rising incidence of Egyptian attack indicators. The heightened regional tensions resulting from a PLO uprising in Lebanon and a civil war there that looked like spilling over into northern Israel. An attack failed to materialize; although the main Egyptian assault was initially planned for May, Sadat postponed it because of the trouble in Lebanon which he felt would detract from his great blow against Israeli prestige. This partial mobilization cost Israel $20 million, which the economy could ill afford. Thereafter at the back of every Israeli intelligence analyst's mind was an invisible brake on the answer to the question, 'Are these intelligence indicators serious enough to indicate war – and thus mobilization?' The flawed thinking behind the Concept and the high cost of any mobilization began to corrupt the honest intelligence answer, which should have been, 'Mobilization? That is a political judgement, Minister.'

Another factor that blunted intelligence assessments was the frequency of *Egyptian* mobilization. Since Sadat had taken over three years before, there had been at least three major Egyptian escalations of tension leading to call-ups and serious troop redeployments in Egypt, all spotted and monitored by the ever-vigilant collectors of Israel intelligence. In 1971, to calls from the Cairo press that war was inevitable, the Egyptians had mobilized, deployed their Army HQ into the desert, called up reservists and civilian vehicles, and marched tanks and floating bridges towards the Suez Canal. Nothing happened.

During the second major alert, in 1972, the interested Israelis watched the same thing unfold again, but this time without civilian mobilization or bridges moving to the canal. One difference was a sudden frenzy of building activity on the western bank of the canal as tank ramps, potential crossing points and ever higher Egyptian ramparts were constructed under the bemused gaze of the IDF conscripts manning their Bar Lev forts. Again, nothing happened.

There were two more major mobilizations in 1973: one in May, following the outbreak of fighting in Lebanon and to which Israel's General Elazar had reacted so strongly; and the final one in October 1973 for Yom Kippur.

The drumbeat of regular mobilization has an effect on intelligence observers. First it desensitizes them – 'Oh, it's just the Egyptians up to their old tricks again' – and, second, it conditions them to accept *abnormal* activity as a *normal* pattern of behaviour. Added to the constraining girdle of the Concept and a reluctance to be seen to cry wolf again and cause unnecessary expenditure, it is perhaps not surprising that the Israeli military intelligence system's reaction was decidedly muted when Sadat's fourth and final mobilization was identified in early October 1973. The Israelis had seen it all before; everyone knew that the Egyptians would not dare to attack Israel again until they had a decent air force and a full alliance with Syria. That was, after all, Israeli political-military policy – the Concept said so.

The Egyptians played on this in their deception plan for Operation Badr. They had three real secrets to conceal: their agreement with the Syrians for a simultaneous onslaught; their technical and other preparations for war; and finally the exact date and time of their attack. The last was in some ways easy to conceal because even the Egyptian commanders did not know. During 1973, Sadat kept changing his mind and postponing 'Y-Day'.

To conceal their political deal for a joint attack with Syria, the Egyptians and their northern ally resorted to a classic subterfuge that Machiavelli would have recognized. They lied. Even though the final broad arrangements were secretly agreed by the now 'federal' General Staffs of the armed forces of Egypt and Syria on 1 April, a senior Egyptian general was glumly playing up the problems by predicting on 22 April that there was still a long way to go before Egypt and Syria could co-operate properly militarily and that 'political and military problems [still] inhibit any joint action'. The misleading signals continued throughout the summer of 1973 as Egyptian diplomats flew all over the Middle East in a baffling series of 'initiatives' that smacked of growing desperation on the part of Anwar Sadat. In reality, Sadat was stitching together the broad Arab political support he would need on Y-Day. No initiative ever quite succeeded; nothing was ever definite. In one observer's phrase, 'It looked like the desperate calculations of a born gambler.'

The network of political deceit extended particularly to Israel's principal ally and guarantor, the USA. President Nixon had won the 1972 election by, among other things, openly wooing the Jewish vote. Wily Egyptian diplomats ensured that Secretary of State Rogers and his successor in summer 1973, Henry Kissinger, were sucked into the tangled web by stressing Egypt's need for negotiations to secure an equitable and peaceful settlement. It worked. Despite the alarm bells ringing in Washington, Henry Kissinger was eventually dismissive of the military threat. Indeed, in one meeting with Abba Eban, the Israeli Foreign Minister, just *two days* before the Yom Kippur War, both men airily assured each other that the general intelligence picture from both countries was reassuring, with little prospect of an early war.

Henry Kissinger, a man often accused of intellectual arrogance, should have been a little less smug. In the middle of 1973, as the secret Egyptian build-up began to gather pace, his own State Department's INR (Intelligence and Research Bureau) produced an internal analysis of the Middle East situation. Unusually, it was a predictive document. Intelligence agencies are frequently reluctant to commit themselves to predictions (although that is their prime task) for prediction can notoriously go wrong. No one wishes to lose bureaucratic credibility by 'being courageous', 'making unsubstantiated speculations', or, worst of all, *being wrong*. In the words of an anonymous British JIC analyst, 'We don't have a crystal ball, you know.' The INR in Washington was different. It had after all been proved right in the long-running internecine battle between US intelligence agencies that had accompanied the Vietnam War, on which it had been determinedly pessimistic.

So it was with the US-INR paper of June/July 1973 on the Middle East situation. Although the INR paper did not have the status of an NIE (National Intelligence Estimate), it drew broad support from the CIA, an old ally against the US military's Panglossian assessments on Vietnam. Both the CIA and the State Department's INR forecast a war in the Middle East by autumn 1973. (DIA, true to form, disagreed with CIA.) Henry Kissinger, a man who generally believed he knew better than his own intelligence specialists, not only ignored his own department's findings but also appears to have failed to alert his Israeli clients and allies to the misgivings now surfacing in Washington.

It was always going to be much harder for the Egyptians to hide their second secret, the technical and military preparations for war. Even if they had tried, they widely assumed that Israeli intelligence collectors would soon spot the growing military build-up. By late summer 1973, for example, the Syrian armed forces had imported from the Soviet Union over twice the amount of arms that they had imported in the whole of 1972. The Egyptians had brought in even more.

General Ismail's planning staff realized that the Israelis were bound to counter-attack any assault across the Suez Canal. This was established IDF doctrine and had almost always been successful in the past. These quick counter-attacks relied on two hammers to smash the Arab troops consolidating on a hard-won position: air superiority overhead and a scythe of tanks and armour on the ground.

The Egyptians took a leaf out of Rommel's book. For a year and a half in 1941 and 1942, the C-in-C of Panzer Korps Afrika had attacked by seizing ground and then holding it defensively, allowing waves of counter-attacking British tanks to beat themselves to death against a well-armed and concealed German anti-tank screen. Although Rommel's successes were strategic attacks, his desert tactics on the ground were essentially tactically *defensive*. To do this he had relied on technologically superior defensive weapons of the time: the superb 88 mm Panzer Abwehr Kanone (PAK) and its smaller brother, the 57 mm long-barrelled anti-tank gun, mounted on both tanks and in PAK artillery. The charging British tanks were just picked off in the open.

The Egyptian battle plan called for a reworking of Rommel's operational principles brought up to date. They planned limited attacks across the Suez Canal to seize ground and inflict a humiliating reverse on the Israelis. The political reverberations of this would then rumble around the world, which was all Sadat wanted: a political blow by a sharp military success. To do this the Egyptians needed a defensive umbrella of surface-to-air missiles (SAMs) over the Suez Canal and extending into the Sinai Desert, to cover their army as it crossed the canal. That would fend off the stooping hawks of the Israeli Air Force. On the ground the Israeli tanks could be relied upon to hurl themselves forward in furious counter-attacks against the Egyptian invaders.

To blunt their fury, the General Staff called for as many of the new Soviet anti-tank weapons as possible, especially the new generation of anti-tank guided missiles (ATGMs) known by its NATO identification as the Sagger. The small, suitcase-sized wire-guided weapons could be carried by two men and worked by one. With a range in flat desert of 1,500–2,000 metres, a man hiding behind a rock could, by the early 1970s, track and kill a moving tank over a mile distant. The Sagger, especially supplemented close in by the new rocket-propelled anti-tank grenades (RPG-7) from the Soviets, was a formidable weapon and represented a major shift in the constant tactical struggle between attacker and defender. Suddenly every infantryman, suitably equipped, could become a long-range tank destroyer.

These air defence and anti-tank weapons also had the beauty of being weapons for a *defensive* posture. Israeli analysts, who were tracking the flood of Soviet arms into Egypt and Syria in summer 1973, naturally drew the conclusion that the Arabs were only rearming to *defend* themselves, and not to attack Israel. The deception over arms procurement worked. Although intelligence analysts identified no fewer than 1,000 first-line SAM missiles of the secret Soviet SAM 6 system in Egypt and Syria, backed by dense belts of the SAM 3 and older SAM 2, they were not unduly concerned. So the Arabs were constructing the thickest air defence belt in the world on the Suez? Let them waste their money; Israel had no intention of attacking. Not every weapon system demanded by the Egyptians was defensive, however. Both Sadat and Nasser before him had pressed the Soviets for the latest MiG-23 swing-wing penetration bombers. The Soviet Union, mindful of the Americans' recent debacle in Vietnam, where a superpower had been sucked into virtually open-ended support for a major war by a client state, flatly refused.

Even with hindsight, it is difficult to appreciate the sheer scale of the Egyptian rearmament by 1973. The Egyptian Army was effectively re-equipped and retrained with the complete range of modern Soviet weapons from AK-47 rifles to (just prior to the outbreak of fighting in October 1973) Scud missiles. The Scuds, with a 180-mile radius of fire, could by no stretch of the imagination be described as defensive, but by then the die was cast and their presence was seen as a deterrent to counter any deep Israeli attacks on Egyptian population centres. The conclusion of the Israeli analysts was that the bulk of arms and technology shipped to the Arabs was for defence or, at worst, to deter an Israeli attack.

The third and final secret the Egyptians strove to hide was the date and time of their attack. If, in Chaim Herzog's words, they were to fall on the Israelis like a 'wolf on the fold' then they had an absolute need for total security if they were to surprise an unwary and unprepared adversary. The date of the attack was the subject of considerable debate within the coalition's secret planning cell. The final decision was taken surprisingly late, in August 1973, only two months before Y-Day. The so-called Federal High Command Planning Staff of Syrian and Egyptian commanders eventually decided on 6 October as the agreed date. The reasons were complex and a mixture of the practical and psychological.

The sixth of October would be a moonlit night and also one when the normally fast currents in the Suez Canal would be sufficiently slow to allow floating bridges to be safely built and anchored in midstream. The less tangible psychological reason had a particular significance for the Islamic world: 6 October that year was the tenth day of Ramadan and the anniversary of the Prophet Muhammad's victory at the Battle of Badr near Medina in AD 624. Badr established the Prophet Muhammad as both a political and religious leader. The symbolism was obvious. An intelligence purist would argue that this choice of code name was therefore an unnecessary risk and a potential breach of security.

In the Arab world, however, the power of gesture must sometimes outweigh the restrictive corset of security. 'Badr' proclaimed that the Egyptian and Syrian attack was more than just the continuation of hostilities in the Middle East; it was also a message as clear as any *muezzin's* call of the resurgence of Islamic might against the all-conquering Israelis. In fact it encapsulated almost precisely Sadat's goals for the attack, which were that it should be a spectacular military triumph, Islamic, limited and political, and for both domestic and international consumption. Badr it was to be.

Perhaps surprisingly, General Ismail's staff planners found the attack date relatively easy to conceal from prying Israeli intelligence. In this they were aided by the relatively short time (seven weeks) for the secret to leak out. Sadat's formidable internal security apparatus helped, but in the end the secret was kept by the best method of all – the planners did not tell anybody. The startled Syrian Defence Minister was only informed on 1 October: Y minus 5.

The Egyptians told a bare minimum of officers using the most ruthless need-to-know criteria. At one stage it was limited to just fourteen Egyptian and Syrian officers. Even that was felt by the Egyptians to be about ten people too many, given the talent of the Mossad (Israel's SIS) for finding senior Arab officers with access to classified information and encouraging them to reveal their innermost secrets by the traditional methods of the second oldest profession. The upshot was that the Egyptians made a considerable deception priority the deception of their *own* officer corps.

After the war, the baffled Israelis questioned their Egyptian prisoners of war closely about how much they had known before the attack. The answers startled the interrogators. Egyptian junior officers and men only learned of the attack on the morning of 6 October, and even then, many of them thought that it was just the start of another day's exercises. In one bizarre example, a staff colonel only realized war was imminent when he saw his commanding general take out a prayer mat and suddenly drop on his knees to face Mecca at the start of a hastily called meeting. In an even more extreme case, an Egyptian assault engineer platoon only realized it was not an exercise when they were told to uncrate their rubber boats and put them in the canal. 'So we won't be going back to barracks tonight then, sir?' one soldier is supposed to have enquired of Lieutenant Ibrahim of 16th Division as they began to paddle across the canal. In Chaim Herzog's words, 'The Egyptian planners had succeeded in misleading not only the Israeli Defence Forces and practically all the intelligence services in the West, but the bulk of the Egyptian Army as well!'

As September 1973 rolled on, the final preparations for war were made. This was the most dangerous time for the Egyptians. A concerted effort was made to keep up diplomatic pretences at the UN, as by now the Israeli intelligence collection boards would be filling with indicators of activity. They would note troops moving forward, reservists called up, bridge equipment on the move, ammunition outloaded, leave cancelled, new radio nets active and unusual aircraft maintenance. It would all add up to a pattern that spelled 'indicators of attack'.

Israeli intelligence had seen it all before, however. There had already been over twenty separate mobilizations of Egyptian reservists for training since the beginning of 1973. This was the third deferral of *demobilization* for Egyptian troops in 1973, although the Israeli analysts noted that the unfortunate conscripts had been told that it was only a temporary postponement – they would now be released on 8 October. The ploy was yet another example of the strategy of deception by repetition that worked so well to dull Israeli intelligence's reactions.

Everything else was normal. There was no call-up of civilian transport, no civil defence preparations, and even Sadat himself was banal and repetitive in his speech on Nasser Day, 26 September: 'I have not broached the subject of fighting because there has been enough talk. I only say that the liberation of the land… is the main task.' By the standards of Arab rhetoric this was routine stuff and hardly worth including in any critical intelligence analysis looking for the presence of the politically abnormal or the absence of the normal. However, it must be said that Israeli intelligence failed badly over Sadat's speech. A moment's thought should have suggested that picking up a lethal weapon while stating blandly that the user intends his neighbour no harm is suspicious under any circumstances.

The political and diplomatic round continued as normal, too. The repercussions from the shooting down of thirteen Syrian warplanes by the Israeli Air Force in an aerial battle following Syrian provocations in mid-September still rumbled on, but were slowly dying down. In the circumstances it seemed hardly surprising that Syria had mobilized some extra troops and was apparently hastily trying to fortify its southern border opposite the Golan Heights. This was clearly a defensive precaution following Israel's recent and aggressive aerial ambush. Besides, Radio Moscow seemed to confirm it by broadcasting to the Middle East that an *Israeli* attack was imminent and that Syria should 'prepare to defend itself'.

As September turned into October, the dam of security and deception began to leak. Uneasy Washington intelligence analysts in the State Department warned Kissinger that trouble was brewing, probably on or about 30 September. They reckoned without his ego. Apparently convinced of the inevitable success that would accompany *his* negotiations at the UN in November, Kissinger ignored his experts. The Director of the CIA complained later that even he despaired of getting an urgent appointment with the great man, so busy was Kissinger with own brand of personal shuttle diplomacy.

It is rare for there to be a hero in intelligence matters. Cerebral analysis and desk work far from the battlefield lack the glamour and appeal of those who risk their lives in battle. Perhaps that is why they are so rarely decorated. Physical courage that risks life in harm's way deserves its proper reward. However, a genuine Israeli hero now appeared. An officer with *moral* courage.

In the Sinai, a young Israeli intelligence officer in General Shmuel Gonen's Southern Command Intelligence Staff had been conscientiously 'ticking the boxes' as he filled in a standard 'indicators and warning collection plan'. He cared little for preconceived concepts or the national assessment. Lieutenant Benjamin Siman-Tov just methodically followed the intelligence cycle for the Egyptian order of battle in his office at Southern Command, and by 1 October 1973 he didn't like what he could see. Nearly all the attack indicators showed a build-up and many of the indicators were red, not green and 'confirmed safe'. Furthermore, too many indicators were still showing black, meaning 'unknown – no answer yet from the collection agency'. Accordingly, Siman-Tov drafted a short paper to his CO, Lieutenant Colonel Gedaliah, pointing out that the Egyptian combined arms exercise on the other side of the Suez Canal was, in his opinion, based on an objective analysis and interpretation of the available evidence, nothing less than a sophisticated deception plan to mask an imminent Egyptian attack.

There are few things more irritating than a clever subordinate. They make their presence felt like a stone in a shoe. In fact, one of the greatest tests of leadership is the ability to listen to inspired subordinates' views and judge their merits without resentment, jealousy or dismissing them when they do not agree with the management line. But restless subordinates undoubtedly pose a challenge for ambitious leaders and managers, especially politically aware officers or public service officials.

History doesn't record what Lieutenant Colonel Gedaliah, the Chief Intelligence Officer, Israeli Southern Command, said to his alert order of battle officer when he produced his memorandum. What it does record is what Gedaliah did with the 1 October paper and another follow-up paper which Siman-Tov submitted on 3 October. Gedaliah did something unforgivable which was to cost him dear: he deliberately suppressed the lieutenant's report. Normally even a contentious position paper, suitably marked with the disagreement of the branch chief, would have been circulated upwards for comment in the argumentative, free-wheeling atmosphere of the Israeli Army of 1948 to 1967. But the Army's new commander, General Elazar, wanted to tighten things up. He ruled that the Israeli Army was to become 'more like other armies'. He held conferences on discipline. He insisted on regular postings and a career structure for the officer corps. Elazar's reforms encouraged a lieutenant colonel to sit on a subordinate's intelligence report because he didn't agree with it. The Director of Military Intelligence, General Zeira, eventually did see the report in March 1974. By then it was six months too late for Siman-Tov, Gedaliah, Chief of Staff Elazar, DMI Zeira and indeed for Israel, although to his eternal credit General Zeira promoted the young man on the spot.

With yet another chance missed, the days turned to hours. By dawn on 5 October, both Egypt and Syria were on alert on Israel's frontiers. Egypt had 194 artillery batteries in the line and all five infantry divisions. Israeli officers in the Bar Lev Line warned that it looked as if an attack was imminent. GHQ demurred, but inside the inner councils of the Israeli military a bitter quarrel took place. On one side of the disagreement there was General Dayan, Minister of Defence, and General Tal, Chief Inspector of Armoured Forces, who both argued passionately for war and mobilization; on the other side, Chief of Staff Elazar (perhaps mindful of the unfortunate and expensive mobilization of May) and his Director of Military Intelligence, General Zeira, arguing equally forcibly that the Egyptians and Syrians were in fact mobilizing *because they were scared of Israel.* The irony is that Siman-Tov's paper may have tipped the scales in the hawks' favour, but the paper was safely tucked away from the decision-makers in Tel Aviv in the safe of the Chief Intelligence Officer, Southern Command.

The disagreement within Israel's senior military circles culminated in an unscheduled meeting of Golda Meir's National Security Committee on Wednesday 3 October (Y minus 3). As usual the crisis meeting was attended by the uniformed members: Dayan, Tal, Elazar, Zeira's deputy Sahev, and Zamir, the head of the Secret Service. The meeting examined all the evidence, and, despite Zamir's unease (he had a secret tip-off), concluded that the Arab build-up was *defensive,* as a reaction to the Schönau Incident.

It is impossible for us to understand the atmosphere in that last week before the Yom Kippur War without realizing just how much politicians' eyes were focused on an obscure terrorist attack on the Austrian border. On 28 September, two gunmen claiming to be Palestinian revolutionaries seized five Jewish emigrants and an Austrian customs official. Apart from the usual demands for an aeroplane to an Arab country, the incident sparked an agreement by the Austrian Chancellor, Bruno Kreisky, to close the transit centre for Soviet-Jewish emigrants at Schönau Castle. The Israelis were horrified. A major plank of their immigration policy had always been to encourage the Ashkenazi Jews of northern Europe over the oriental Sephardim. As the numbers of those displaced by the Holocaust faded in Europe, the Russian Jews were the only remaining source of Ashkenazim.

The Schönau Incident became a cause célèbre and Israeli political activity focused on it. Despite the problems at home, Mrs Meir made a major diversion on her return trip from the Council of Europe at Strasbourg on 1/2 October specifically to lobby the Austrian Chancellor (who was himself a Jew) to rescind his 'betrayal of Jewish interests' and to protest at his freeing of the Palestinian gunmen. Margaret Thatcher was not the first female premier to wield a handbag to good effect.

To the intelligence analyst the whole incident smacks of a *maskirovka* operation. The Soviet Army had for years had a doctrine of masking its intentions by every means possible. Western military staffs were invariably amazed at just how much effort was made by the Soviets to divert and deceive the enemy. No Russian staff planner would dare to submit an operational plan without a specific deception or *maskirovka* sub-plan. Western planners usually grumbled that it would be nice to have so many resources to divert, although interestingly the only other army that gave anything like the same weight to this doctrine was the Israeli Army.

The Syrians were linked more closely with the Soviet intelligence bureaucracy than any other Middle East country. The KGB and GRU maintained a strong presence in Damascus, and the Syrian secret services and their Palestinian clients were well infiltrated by 'socialist' idealists and informers. President Assad's Ba'ath Arab Socialist Party was the nearest thing to the Soviet system in the Middle East. The Schönau incident was a remarkably timely coincidence, if one believes in timely coincidences that just happen to divert Israeli attention immediately before a major Syrian attack. The gunmen claimed to be from an unknown group of Palestinians, but they were recruited from Saïka, the guerrilla group run by the Syrian Army and its secret services. There is no direct proof, but the conclusion must be that the Schönau incident was probably a deliberate Syrian deception to divert attention away from the coming attack.

It worked. Public indignation inside Israel at the release of the Palestinian terrorists ran high. Combined with the shooting down of the thirteen Syrian jets in September, the atmosphere of political crisis deepened. Would Israel retaliate for Schönau? No wonder the Syrians were reinforcing their border, concluded Mrs Meir and her kitchen cabinet on 3 October. Evidence of this version of events is that Golda Meir spoke for over two hours at the meeting – on Schönau.

By 4 October (Y minus 2), events began the final descent to war. Soviet families were evacuated from Syria and Egypt and further confirmation of the massive build-up on Israel's borders poured in. On Friday morning, 5 October (Y minus 1), the alarmed Israeli generals reported to Golda Meir, but following a meeting in Minister of Defence Dayan's office they advised her that the General Staff and Military Intelligence assessment was that the likelihood of war remained low. General Zeira, the head of Military Intelligence, emphasized several times that the Arab troop concentrations revealed by Israeli photo-reconnaissance flights could be for either attack *or* defence – which was true. However, as an insurance the meeting decided to place the Israeli Regular Army on the highest stage of peacetime warning: a 'C Alert'.

Golda Meir, on the advice of her generals and other advisers, declined **full** mobilization, citing this military advice, fear of bringing the economy to a halt and of course, ruining 'the *conceptzia*'. However, by Friday, 5 October 1973, the day before the war began, it became clear that Egypt would strike and the question then became whether Israel should make its own pre-emptive strike, as in 1967, or not. The army chief, General Elazar, suggested a pre-emptive strike, while the iconic military hero, Moshe Dayan, responded by arguing against action:

I believe we can complete the call-up tomorrow. It's not like in 1967.

The war will begin in the Suez and Golan Heights. It is important that they don't say we started it. Calling all the reserves to duty before one shot has been fired – they'll immediately say we are the aggressors.

Meir sided with Dayan, agreeing that a pre-emptive attack was very tempting, but unnecessary. The Israelis had missed their last chance.

The next step in the alert process would be the call-up of reservists for war. To ensure that this would be possible, Mrs Meir confirmed that reservist mobilization centres should remain open and manned during the Jewish Day of Atonement, Yom Kippur, on 6 October, despite the religious festival. Yom Kippur is the holy of holies of the Jewish calendar. (It is that rarest of religious holidays, a Jewish festival without food.) Instead it is a day of fasting and prayer, introspection and self-judgement when, collectively and repeatedly, Jews confess their sins and pray to be written into God's Book of Life.

It appears that one of the main reasons for the low-key Israeli response was the knowledge that their US mentors, who only ten days before were warning that hostilities looked imminent, had now reduced their threat assessment. In the US view, war was not imminent and the Arab moves were purely defensive. Kissinger had said as much to Abba Eban the day before.

There is in intelligence a well-defined syndrome known as 'circular intelligence' or the 'daisy chain'. What happens is that one agency reports an unconfirmed fact or assessment. This is subsequently picked up and repeated in a second agency's assessment as a straightforward report. The first agency then sees it in someone else's report and seizes on it as independent proof that their own information has now been confirmed by another source. In the jargon, B-6 information (B means a 'normally reliable source' and 6 means 'not confirmed information') suddenly becomes B-1 intelligence ('information from a normally reliable source now confirmed by other sources'). This is dangerous stuff and mechanisms exist inside the professional analytical intelligence process to stop it happening.

No such mechanism existed between Israel and Washington's intelligence exchange in 1973. The CIA and State Department had reduced their previously high assessment of the probability of war only because the *Israelis* had not been concerned by the Arab build-up. After all, if the Israelis – who had most to lose and had the best sources – were not alarmed then that was an important intelligence fact. The USA had downgraded its assessments accordingly.

When the Israelis saw that the USA was not worried by the build-up, they confirmed their earlier judgements. If Washington was unruffled, concluded Mrs Meir and her inner policy group on 5 October, then why should they be? It was a classic and vicious example of 'circular intelligence'. Each side was reporting the other as a reliable source. Everyone left the 5 October meetings uneasy and with a feeling that something was wrong. The combination of arrogance, flawed assumptions, suppressed information, circular intelligence reports and clever enemy deception had combined to lull Israeli intelligence and its political masters into a false sense of security. Against all the odds, General Ismail's deception plan had succeeded.

When the telephone rang before dawn on 6 October 1973, General Zeira 'just knew it was bad news'. It was. An unidentified source called him at home with absolute confirmation that Israel would be attacked that day on two fronts 'probably at 18.00 hours'. An alarmed Zeira immediately telephoned the head of the Israeli Army, General Elazar.

The telephone call was wrong in one important respect: the Arab attack *had* originally been planned for 18.00, but two days before the Egyptians and Syrians had compromised for practical reasons and agreed that the attack would now be brought forward to 14.00 local time. In fact, Israel's national command authorities now had less than seven hours to react to the telephone warning.

When Elazar got Zeira's call he immediately called his chief, Defence Minister Dayan. Dayan confirmed the warning: *he* claimed that he had just been phoned by a 'personal informant from abroad' to alert him, too. Some experts believe that this call may have come from a secret Jewish source of Dayan's in the US Defense Intelligence Agency. There are other, unconfirmed reports that a worried King Hussein had tried to stop the bloodshed. If true, the King took the secret with him to his grave. At the crisis meeting with the prime minister at 8 a.m., there were only two decisions to be made: first, how to pre-empt the now-obvious Arab build-up (Syrian units were reported redeploying into attack formation), and second, to order general mobilization.

The meeting decided to do neither. A pre-emptive air strike could not guarantee success against a well-dispersed Egyptian Air Force and risked jeopardizing Israel's principal asset, its own combat planes, against an unknown missile defence before the war had even started. On the question of mobilization, General Dayan, the hero of the 1956 and 1967 wars, dismissed General Elazar's demands for full mobilization with the airy assurance that Dayan's own measures – to call up a few senior commanders and tank reservists – would be sufficient. A furious Elazar was directed only to implement this partial mobilization. In fact Elazar disobeyed this order and was vindicated at 13.00 when a now thoroughly alarmed Israeli Cabinet ordered full mobilization. Dayan later took much of the blame for the debacle.

In the blizzard of recrimination and self-justification that surrounded the post-mortem after the war it is difficult to untangle the various claims and work out just who knew what and when, and who advocated which course of action. It did not matter. What we do know is that at 14.00 the door burst open on a Cabinet meeting in Golda Meir's office where the normal heated Israeli disagreement was in full voice, this time over whether the attack would begin at 18.00 that day or earlier. Her military secretary silenced the meeting by announcing baldly: 'Prime Minister, the war's begun.' The startled Cabinet recalled later that the distant wailing of an air raid siren broke the silence that followed.

The Yom Kippur War went exactly as Anwar Sadat had intended – at first. As planned, Egypt and Syria struck in unison at 14.00 and achieved both strategic and tactical surprise in the south and north. The first the Israelis knew about it on the Golan Heights was when a flight of Syrian jets suddenly appeared and started strafing their tanks while the dismounted crews were making lunch. The crews abandoned their meal and rushed for their vehicles. The survivors' next meal was two days later.

On the Suez Canal the lookouts in the Bar Lev Line gradually became aware that all the usual crowd of cheerful civilians and soldiers strolling around on the far bank had quietly disappeared. The next thing they knew was a devastating artillery barrage crashing down on the roof and, ominously, laying down a curtain of fire to cut off any retreat. Through the smoke and dust the startled defenders saw thousands of rubber boats crossing the canal packed full of Egyptian assault infantry.

The Bar Lev Line was only half-manned. In the gaps, the Egyptians now deployed their secret weapon: Magirus Deutz high-pressure water pumps. Blasting canal water at hundreds of pounds per square inch, the water jets cut through the Israelis' carefully constructed sand ramparts like so many laser knives. The horrified defenders saw their defences opened up with surgical skill and the very latest Soviet floating bridges swinging out across the canal to allow a flood of tanks, personnel carriers and guns to race into Sinai. The whole operation took less than three hours.

The Egyptians had their own surprises, too. Their specially trained sapper teams crossed the canal to plug the Israelis' 'floating fire' outlets under cover of smokescreens. Contemplating the rusty nozzles and plugged-up holes, they realized that they need not have bothered. The Israelis had long ago abandoned the concept. The current was too strong and dispersed the fire obstacle too quickly downstream.

The Egyptian attack across the canal shook the Israelis and demonstrated the soundness of Ismail's planning. By 8 October, Israel was in deep trouble.

Forty-six years after the 1973 Yom Kippur War, dramatic transcripts from the first chaotic days of the war, including plans for a massive attack on major cities in Arab countries, were declassified.

The documents show just how panicky the IDF High Command was and reveal details about plans for a bombing attack on Damascus that would change the rules of the game, revealing just how worried the IDF generals were.

In one section, the IDF Chief of Staff, General Elazar, tells General Ze'evi, 'I have two moves. The first is to destroy Syria. There will be an outcry from the world… but as a first step, let's break one.'

Ze'evi responded with a shrug: 'Whatever hurts.'

Most of what Elazar said next is still redacted, but a two-word phrase has been authorized for publication: '4 cities', a hint at the targets of the attack.

In the same meeting, General Tal suggests that Israel retreat from part of the Sinai Desert to concentrate its efforts on the northern front and on battles to check Syria.

'My operative proposal is to hold the Golan Heights steady with the ground forces and use the air force to help thwart [the Syrians]. Not desperate assistance, well-considered assistance in bad circumstances. In Egypt we need to fight wisely to hold them off,' he says.

One of the better-known quotes from the Yom Kippur War was uttered by then-Defense Minister Moshe Dayan, who voiced concern about the possible 'destruction of the Third Temple [meaning the state of Israel]'. The newly declassified transcripts show just how pessimistic Dayan was.

That same day, the generals spoke among themselves. 'At Sde Dov [the airport], Moshe was talking to me about losing the Third Temple. He was very hoarse; it was painful to hear him. He was talking about a battle for... the Land of Israel,' Ze'evi says.

Elazar replies that Dayan was in no way exaggerating: 'This, friends, this is truly a battle for the Land of Israel.'

The Israelis were right to be worried. The Egyptian Army occupied the whole east bank of the Suez Canal to a depth of about ten miles and awaited the inevitable counter-attack. Sure enough, the Israeli armour obliged. Tanks on the ground and aircraft overhead hurled themselves against the invaders to eject them from Sinai. Both ran into Egypt's new defensive weapons. The SAM air-defence umbrella hacked Israeli pilots from the sky. In the desert the Israeli tanks were stopped dead by the new anti-tank missile screen and suffered appalling casualties from 'little men with suitcases'. Some knocked-out M48 tanks were literally festooned with trailing wires from the dozens of missiles fired at them. Puzzled survivors of the Israeli tanks wondered just how the needle-sharp jets of the lightweight shaped-charge warheads had all been aimed at the most vulnerable parts of the US tanks where fuel and ammunition were stored. The answer was simple: the Egyptian techint staff had asked the US manufacturers for the sales handbooks, and then their soldiers had been trained to aim for the vital parts.

As Yousef Bar-On, a 1973 Intelligence Corps reservist found to his dismay:

My unit was guarding the West Bank and wired into the general army radio set-up... we were awed and struck by the clear sense of helplessness the tank crews were talking about facing Sagger anti-tank missiles in their hundreds. We had never heard of the Sagger. However, one afternoon I was searching through the old peacetime Israeli intelligence reports, manuals, etcetera, the junk that piles up in command posts. Among them I found an Intelligence report dated two years earlier and dedicated to the tech specs of the Soviet Sagger anti-tank missile! I literally rubbed my eyes and wondered why, if the missile had generated a report in an Israeli technical intelligence manual, our fighting forces had no idea of its existence. I still wonder about this... [5]

We now know just how desperate the Israelis and the IDF High Command were. According to the transcripts, Dayan also makes unprecedented proposals to meet the lack of manpower: 'We need to... look into the feasibility of enlisting Jews from all over the world – Americans, British, South Africans, anyone who wants to. And if any of them have [military] professions – pilots, tank drivers.'

Dayan has especially harsh criticism for the government and the prime minister, Golda Meir, and suggests alternatives that she had not approved. He told the generals:

The government has a different approach and a different spirit. I will have an obligation to you, to ourselves, to the army and to the people to say what I think needs to be done and we haven't done... When I told Golda [Meir] she was in shock, some of them [the government] don't understand the facts and the military interpretation of the situation.

However, while the battle raged for the Golan in the north, the weakness of the Egyptian plan became evident in the south. Having seized a limited objective but lacking depth inland in Sinai, and by now opting to defend the whole length of the Suez Canal, the Egyptians were in their turn vulnerable to a narrow surgical strike anywhere. The Israelis turned the tables. On 15 October, in one of the most daring and brilliantly conceived counterstrokes in Israel's military history, General Ariel Sharon, recalled to the colours by Dayan at the outbreak of war, sliced through the Egyptian southern defences at night and crossed the Suez Canal at the northern end of the Great Bitter

---

Lake near Deversoir. Once across, the plan was for Sharon's armour to fan out and blow a hole through Egypt's defensive SAM belt.

The plan succeeded beyond all expectations. Around 01.35 on 16 October, having fought their way through the administrative leaguers at the junction of the Egyptian 2nd and 3rd Armies in Sinai, the Israeli engineers cut through the barbed wire on the canal. By dawn the Israeli armour had a brigade three miles across the canal inside Egypt. Once across, their tanks dashed around with impunity, shooting up everything in sight and sowing chaos and confusion in the Egyptian rear. Running out of targets, two tank brigades then turned north and south respectively. By 21 October, Israeli paratroop infantry were fighting on the outskirts of Ismailia in the north on the road to Cairo, and in the south Israeli armour had reached the Red Sea at Suez, actually sinking two Egyptian torpedo boats by tank fire as they fled out to sea. The Israeli armies had cut the umbilical cord for the Egyptian 3rd Army in Sinai, now cut off from Egypt and trapped in the Sinai Desert without food, ammunition, water or hope. By 24 October, it was over. The USSR and the USA began to mobilize and go to nuclear alert to support their warring clients. To British alarm, the USA prepared to invade the Middle East. No one was willing to risk a nuclear war over the Arabs and Israelis battling it out – again; least of all by bombing Damascus or Cairo. The UN Security Council saved the Egyptians from further humiliation and Israel from more casualties and negotiated a ceasefire.

The intelligence lessons of Yom Kippur are very different from other wars. There can really be no excuse for the Israeli failure. Pearl Harbor was bad organization; Tet was internal feuding. Yom Kippur was none of these things. By a savage irony, the Israeli failure in 1973 can be traced directly to their triumphant and emphatic victory in 1967.

The first failure was the cardinal sin of any intelligence officer, organization or commander. The Israelis, flushed with success, discounted the Arabs' ability to learn from past mistakes. They discounted the Arabs' new weapon systems. Above all, they failed to take the revitalized Egyptian staff planning, Egyptian training and Egyptian bravery into account. It was the classic mistake, the fatal flaw: at every level Israel underestimated her enemy.

When the war was over, the Israelis captured vast amounts of Egyptian maps, code books and plans. (Fortunately for the Israelis, the IDF soldier can be relied on to turn in captured material, unlike his British counterpart who has a tendency to 'liberate' anything interesting from a pistol to a top-secret map as a souvenir either to show his mum back home or to sell to his mates in a pub in Aldershot.) To their horror, the Israelis discovered ample evidence that Egyptian intelligence was more than ready for the battle. Most shocking of all was the discovery of an Arab translation of Israel's pre-war and secret code map of Sinai, including the codes and nicknames for every location. As was usual in the stress of battle, Israeli radio operators had further compromised security by arguing in open speech. As a result, for the first week many of Israel's moves in Sinai had been an open book to the Russian-trained Egyptian sigint service.

Underestimating the enemy and overconfidence led directly to the second Israeli mistake: a curious inability to draw the right conclusions from a given set of facts. Thus the simultaneous build-ups in Syria and Egypt never appear to have been linked. The likelihood of an attack was just plain ignored. There seemed to be an absolute assumption that the Arabs could not attack until Israel's own political criteria for any Arab attack had been met. Sadly for Israel, Egypt in particular seemed not to have read Mrs Meir's kitchen cabinet agreed preconditions for war.

Israeli technical intelligence also contributed to the debacle. In 1973, Soviet ATGMs such as Sagger and SAMs such as the SAM 6 were seen as new and deadly battlefield threats – certainly by NATO who gave them their code names and passed Israel a lot of intelligence material under the counter through the US DIA. Confident of repeating her 1967 victories by boldly handled armour, Israel dismissed the new weapon systems as merely defensive. No proper evaluation of the Soviet missiles battlefield impact appears to have been done by Israeli operational research. Perhaps the Israelis thought that the simple peasant conscript Arab soldier would be unable to operate an anti-tank missile under fire for thirty seconds. Both on the ground in Sinai and in the air over the Golan, many Israelis were to die learning the real truth about the new weapons' capabilities and the capabilities of their adversaries. Israeli techint failed.

The final crucial mistake by Israeli intelligence was ossification. When Israel was young and 'everybody knew each other', genuine all-source debates took place among decision-makers with the intelligence experts chipping in their views. It worked. Somewhere along the line, Military Intelligence pulled all the strings into its hands and 'bureaucratized' intelligence. Hierarchies were established, chains of command imposed, unwelcome voices excluded and, most dangerous of all, heretical views suppressed. Even as late as 4 October, when Brigadier Joel Ben-Porat, Head of Intelligence Collection, expressed his concerns to his boss, an angry General Zeira snarled back at him: 'You just stick to collecting intelligence and let those with the responsibility do the assessing!' Military Intelligence had become powerful, highly political and sometimes inefficient.

As a result, the intelligence capabilities that had kept Israel informed and a step ahead were turned into just another intelligence bureaucracy. However, unlike its American and British counterparts, the Israeli Military Intelligence effectively had a national monopoly of all-source intelligence. No bureaucratic rival existed to challenge its assessments; and perhaps worst of all, its unrivalled access to even an official membership of national policy committees and the inner councils of state ate away at any pretence of political, let alone intelligence, objectivity.

In the ultimate test, Israeli Military Intelligence failed the nation in 1973. Despite having all the intelligence at its disposal, it was corroded from within by prejudice, politics, cronyism and just plain bad analysis. When we consider the sheer quality, expertise and range of Israeli intelligence resources, which had served the nation so well from the start, it is tempting on Yom Kippur to *reverse* Boulay de la Meurthe's scathing dictum: 'It is worse than a blunder, it is a crime.'

'NOTHING WE DON'T ALREADY KNOW' – THE FALKLAND ISLANDS, 1982

'Where the hell are the Falkland Islands?'

**BRITISH ARMY GENERAL TO HIS DEFENCE
INTELLIGENCE STAFF OFFICER, APRIL 1982**

There is a splendid story told in Whitehall about a retiring Foreign Office mandarin being interviewed on the steps at King Charles Street by the BBC in about 1950. The interviewer asks the self-satisfied official what has been his biggest problem in a distinguished career of over forty years.

Sir Humphrey replies promptly, 'The War Office.'

Surprised, the reporter asks why the War Office should be a problem for the FO.

'Because every Friday one of those damned fools from the War Office would come rushing into my office with a top secret file under his arm and tell us that there was a terrible crisis somewhere in the world. Then he'd demand to know what we chaps in the Foreign Office were going to do about it to stop a war breaking out. Terribly excitable people. My job was to calm 'em down and send 'em off to brief their Minister that the FO had the situation *completely* under control and not to worry about it. Then we could all get down to the country for the weekend.'

'Did it work, Sir Humphrey?'

'Invariably. Terribly excitable people, the War Office. We just calmed 'em down and sent 'em away happy; every week. And, do you know, we were proved right on almost every occasion.'

'*Almost* every occasion, Sir Humphrey? So you were wrong sometimes?'

'Very, very occasionally. In fact, in all my forty years in the FO we were only wrong twice.'

'And when was that, Sir Humphrey?'

'Er, as I recall… 1914 and 1939!'

This story, which tends to be greeted with a thin smile by any Foreign and Commonwealth Office (FCO) official, contains all the ingredients of the intelligence debacle that led two countries with a history of long and friendly ties to a major war in the South Atlantic in 1982.

The Falklands War came about through a combination of complacency, government misunderstanding and failure of national policy – on both sides. For the British the failure of policy over the Falklands was directly attributable to the deliberate ignoring of intelligence by Whitehall bureaucrats and their various political masters over the years. The Falklands War was not the result of just one or two mistakes, or poor organization, or even contempt for an inferior enemy; behind it there lay a long history of institutional arrogance and complacency.

The British have a reputation for hypocrisy among their neighbours. Well deserved or not, it is based not just on an ability to say one thing and do another (such as the frequent outbursts of public morality in the popular press) but also on a curiously dishonest ability to make a virtue out of necessity. Thus, an idea that is unacceptable can sometimes be rejected by the British as either not existing at all or as meaning something completely different which just happens to fit into the existing framework of policy at the time.

To take one example: in the 1960s, when NATO stood on the western side of the East German border, its likely enemy was the Soviet Union with 20,000 battle tanks in East Germany alone. At the time, everyone knew that the best defence against the tank was another tank. But tanks are expensive, and NATO had a serious numerical inferiority. The US and German armies agonized how to get more tanks to make good their tactical weakness. By a remarkable feat of mental gymnastics, the cost-cutting British acknowledged their own deficiency in armour but airily dismissed the tank problem by saying that it didn't really matter; their new anti-tank concept did not need that many tanks after all. Their tactical doctrine was specially designed to use fewer tanks, so no more were needed. Tanks were, according to the Brits, an unnecessary extravagance in an already overburdened defence budget. This piece of double-think fooled no one at the time, but it illustrates mental process that many foreign observers find at best self-deception and at worst pure hypocrisy.

There is a name for the phenomenon whereby people ignore something that does not fit their view of the world and pretend it does not exist, or will go away. Psychologists call it 'cognitive dissonance', an irritating piece of psychobabble that means nothing more than a child closing its ears and crying, 'I'm not listening, I'm not going to listen, it's not true!' Cognitive dissonance in a toddler's temper tantrum may be a source of amusement or irritation to the onlooker. In intelligence it can be lethal. Cognitive dissonance in the British civil service and government in 1982 was a major cause of the Falklands War. The British ignored the many intelligence warnings because they did not accord with what the British wanted to happen or with their Foreign Office's rather superior view of the world. British servicemen were to pay a heavy price for Whitehall's miscalculation.

The roots of the Falklands dispute lay quite simply in the ownership or sovereignty of the remote group of islands in the South Atlantic first recorded by a Dutch navigator in 1600. In 1690 a Captain James Strong named the sound between the two main islands after a British Admiralty Minister, Viscount Falkland, and sailed away from the little cluster of islands 400 miles to the north-east of the southern tip of South America.

To complicate matters, the first settler on the Falklands was a Frenchman, Louis-Antoine de Bougainville, in 1764; he built a fort, Port Louis, on the eastern island. The islands were first known as Iles Malouines, because they reminded the French of the islands off St Malo. A year later, in 1765, the British hove into sight again and, without knowing that the French were on *East* Falkland, landed on West Falkland Island, raised the flag, claimed the territories in the name of King George III and sailed away. They never realized the French were there.

A year later, the first British settlers arrived and were stunned to discover a thriving French settlement at Port Louis on East Falkland. At the time, France and Spain were allies, so as the area fell under Spanish global jurisdiction, the Iles Malouines were transferred to Spain in 1767 (becoming Islas Malvinas in the process) and Port Louis became Puerto Soledad. Within three years, the Spanish had evicted the British. A diplomatic wrangle ensued, conducted echoed by a British Royal Marine lieutenant of the time who wrote: 'I declare this to be the most detestable place I was ever at in all my life.'

Two hundred years later, in the early 1980s, another Royal Marine officer described the islanders, or Kelpers as they call themselves, as 'a mainly drunken, decadent, immoral and indolent collection of drop-outs... at all levels and with few exceptions'. This was a harsh but understandable judgement. By 1982 the islanders were a curious group, apathetic and relying on the generous teat of British tax money and the almost feudal suzerainty of the Falkland Islands Company for their economic survival. One Trade Union British Labour MP described them as 'company slaves'. This small, self-centred and fragile society had only one unifying attribute: the overwhelming majority wanted to remain under the British Crown. Under the United Nations' principles of self-determination this was a powerful brake on the British Foreign and Commonwealth Office's understandable policy of not allowing the views of 1,800 backward islanders to stand in the way of good diplomatic relations with 250 million South Americans. Unfortunately for the Foreign Office in Whitehall, it meant that the Kelpers had an effective veto on any FCO policy that did not suit their narrow interests.

In the overall scheme of withdrawal from Empire, the FCO had long looked on the Falklands as an irritating minor administrative problem. Argentina had equally long regarded the Malvinas as a matter of national honour and British sovereignty as a post-colonial affront. Most of the countries which made up the United Nations agreed with the Argentines.

The British were always ambivalent about their legal claim to the islands. For example, in October 1936, the chief of the Americas Department of the Foreign Office, John Troutbeck (in a similar position to that held by the current Governor of the Falklands/Malvinas), wrote: 'The difficulty of the position is that our seizure of the Falkland Islands in 1833 was so arbitrary a procedure as judged by the ideology of the present day it is therefore not easy to explain our possession without showing ourselves up as international bandits.'

The stumbling block for both sides was the stubborn refusal of the Falkland Islanders to acknowledge the geographical realities and their insistence on remaining British. Under Article 73 of the UN Charter, which guarantees with all the haste of seaborne eighteenth-century diplomacy. By 1790, agreement left the Spanish in sole charge under their colonial government in Buenos Aires, and a bronze plaque was all that remained to mark the British claim to West Falkland.

With the collapse of the Spanish Empire in Latin America, the islands became derelict and the haunt of local caudillos pirates. Eventually, in 1832, a US warship, the USS *Lexington*, cleared Puerto Soledad of its brigands and unilaterally declared it 'free of all government'. On whose authority this ringing declaration was made is an interesting point. Into the confusion sailed the Royal Navy with a well-armed battleship and in 1837 declared the islands to be part of the British Crown territories. Les Malouines were now the Falkland Islands. So they were to remain until 1 April 1982.

The Argentines subsequently claimed the islands, which they call Las Malvinas, when they threw off Spanish colonial rule in the early years of the nineteenth century; the British claimed the islands because they had occupied them continuously since 1837 and, much more importantly, because the tiny population of the islands were British citizens and stubbornly wished to remain so, as was their right.

However, the Argentine position was clear and the subject of several statements and UN reports (it is still Buenos Aires' policy):

> The present-day inhabitants of the Falklands/Malvinas do not constitute a separate people holder of the right of self-determination... They are of course entitled to human rights, both individually and collectively. Argentina has committed itself in its Constitution to respect the inhabitants' way of life. Quite simply, sixteen hundred and fifty British citizens do not have the right to decide a dispute between Argentina and the United Kingdom which involves more than 3 million square kilometres of land and sea, a surface bigger than continental Argentina and twice as big as the United Kingdom.

Anyone who has ever visited the Falkland Islands cannot fail to be surprised at their remoteness and bleakness. A Spanish priest said, in the 1760s, 'I tarry in this miserable desert, suffering everything for the love of God.' His view was the right of self-determination of peoples, they had rights and they were determined to exercise them. Looking at the dubious politics of the various regimes in Argentina since 1945, it is hard to fault their preference.

Matters came to a head in 1965, when the UN General Assembly passed an Argentine-inspired Resolution (2065) calling on Britain and Argentina to negotiate a settlement. Armed with the moral authority of a UN anti-colonial Resolution, Argentina proceeded to press her claim with vigour, forcing the world-weary British FCO to engage in UN-led negotiations on a subject they would have preferred quietly to go away. The two sides' aims were clear: in Simon Jenkins's words, 'The Argentines didn't really want a colony; they only wanted ownership.' And the British wanted neither the colony nor the ownership, but were stuck with the indignant islanders hanging round their neck like some ancient mariner's albatross and crying self-determination. For the FCO it was all very tiresome, the more so because they failed to mobilize any real political support for their policies.

The discussions dragged on for nearly seventeen years, and ended in a war. By one of those peculiar reversals of role, it was the British who were forever changing both negotiating position and negotiators through a succession of governments, while the Argentines, backed by a single team of long-standing experts with a clear political aim, kept up the pressure. So much so, that as yet another junior British Foreign Office Minister fumbled through his brief at his first meeting, one of the experienced Argentine negotiators is supposed to have murmured dryly in a stage whisper, '*and we are supposed to be the unstable regime!*'

While the Argentine negotiating position on the Falkland Islands remained consistent between 1966 and 1982, the same could not be said of Argentina itself. Internal Argentine politics had suffered a kind of delayed fascism. Up to the 1930s, Argentina had been very much part of Britain's commercial sphere of interest; the Buenos Aires railway network was but one part of Britain's export of the Industrial Revolution, and the North British Locomotive Company relied among others on regular orders from Argentina. The Argentine Navy was modelled on the British Royal Navy, although the Argentine Army was modelled on and influenced by the Prussian or German Army. During the early and middle years of the twentieth century, thousands of Italians, Germans and Spanish flocked to the Mediterranean climate and splendour of Buenos Aires and the glories of the Plate. They brought new ideas.

These new workers fuelled a late outpouring of nationalist and socialist sentiment, embodied in the person of General Juan Perón. Not for nothing did fleeing Nazis try to escape Germany in 1945 for what they saw as a safe haven in Argentina. Perón's dictatorship relied on what he called 'integral nationalism' to harness the industrial masses in support of what looked suspiciously like a one-party fascist state rooted in one-party national trade unionism, headed (naturally) by a strong and charismatic leader.

Perón's nationalist vision infected all aspects of Argentine thinking. From being a trivial international dispute, the Malvinas question was elevated to a national cause, taught in the schoolroom, uniting all classes and fundamental to Argentine national identity. Against this raw political fundamentalism on one side and the stubbornness of the Falkland Islanders on the other, the elegant sophistication of the Foreign and Commonwealth Office's Winchester and Balliol attitudes often appeared weak, indecisive and mendacious. Lingering relics of Empire were sometimes a patent embarrassment to the 'Rolls-Royce minds' of the FCO, anxious to be rid of the responsibilities of colonial administration and keen to get back to 'real' diplomacy.

For the British FCO is resolute upon not actually being responsible for anything. Making policy and expressing 'views on the situation' are the core ethos of Whitehall. In a supposedly non-political civil service where every high-flyer strives to become 'political' and at the very least 'brief the Minister', the Foreign Office has always represented the purest form of unaccountable bureaucracy. Not for nothing has the FCO taken such great care to ensure that other departments take responsibility for administration and actually *doing things*. That way, others take the budgets and the blame. The FCO deals in ideas and in policy. In the bitter words of a Ministry of Defence intelligence staff officer after a particularly slippery meeting with the Foreign Office in the 1980s, 'They're tarts – absolute bloody Whitehall tarts. They sit around that bloody committee table and pontificate, knowing they've got power and influence without any responsibility. Well, where I come from, that's a tart's privilege. We've got to make *real* decisions.

We've got to make the decision to spend public money, while they can sit back.' This view, while at times unfair, was not uncommon in Whitehall in the 1980s.

The FCO's well-bred distaste for rampant Argentine nationalism was justified in one respect: Argentina *was* inherently unstable. The instability led to a dangerous volatility in dealing with matters of national policy. In 1973, the ageing Perón returned to power ushering in a wave of crude nationalism. Immediately the carefully constructed artifices of the FCO's policy of quietly negotiating to sell off the Falklands to Argentina by a combination of subtlety, stealth and salami cuts was blown apart. Instead of being a low-key affair inaugurating a new communications agreement with Argentina, the first civilian flight between the Falklands and the mainland became instead a Perónist triumphal pageant with Argentine admirals in full rig posing proudly for the photographers as they heralded the first stage of the regaining of *nuestras Islas Malvinas*. The Falkland Islands Governor had to restrain the Kelpers and call out his token force of Royal Marines. The Postmaster reckoned it set back progress twenty years. Eventually the fuss died down, but the new umbilical cord with the mainland was always regarded with suspicion by the islanders, as a Trojan Horse and a potential threat to their independence. Relations cooled rapidly between Buenos Aires and Whitehall.

By 1976, Argentina had fallen apart internally with major civil unrest by left-wing guerrillas, the Montoneros, and a new hard-line military junta in government. The military strongmen of Argentina cracked down hard on dissent, and the basements of police stations and naval barracks began to fill with political agitators detained until further notice. The Mayor of Cordoba, unable to contain the civil unrest, begged the local army commander for help. Suddenly the army was on the streets, ostensibly in aid of the civil power but in reality taking over the responsibility for the so-called 'Dirty War' between left-wing revolutionaries and an establishment determined to resist political terrorism even if it meant turning a blind eye to legal niceties. US-built Ford Falcons prowled the big cities packed with grim-faced young men with short hair and guns under their coats looking for troublemakers. And as the helicopters took off full over the Bahia de la Plata and came back empty, the lists of *Los Desaparecidos* (The Disappeared) grew longer; and the wailing mothers outside the Casa Rosada in the Plaza de Mayo grew daily more numerous.

Faced with civil unrest and dictatorship in Argentina, the Falkland Islanders' intransigence grew. They were already angered by the 1976 Shackleton Report that depicted them as virtual bond serfs to the Falkland Islands Company. Now not only was the FCO trying to hand them over to Argentina by stealth, but the FCO was also about to sell British citizens into the clutches of a brutal military dictatorship armed with electrodes and rubber truncheons. It was, in political and PR terms, a trump card. In Simon Jenkins's vivid phrase, 'To Labour MPs as much as Tories, the idea of sacrificing the victims of capitalism to the torturers of Buenos Aires was unthinkable.' In London, the Falkland Islands lobby became ever more vocal and powerful.

As the dispute dragged on, it hotted up. In 1976, the Argentines quietly occupied South Thule, a desolate island in the South Atlantic. Not only did the FCO fail to react, it never even raised the issue in Parliament. The Argentines noted the British passivity as a discreet encouragement to proceed – with care. Only one note jarred the proceedings. In 1977, the prime minister, James Callaghan, spotted an FCO assessment at the bottom of his red box that the Argentines might be planning another escapade in their salami steps towards sovereignty. In a scene worthy of *Yes, Prime Minister*, he overrode his protesting officials and ordered a nuclear submarine to patrol off the Falklands as a deterrent to any Argentine adventurism. (Callaghan was an ex-naval man.) Although the aggrieved FCO later claimed that it was a pointless and expensive exercise, as the Argentines could not possibly have known that an SSN (nuclear hunter-killer submarine) was on station, the balance of evidence is that the Argentine Navy, which was growing ever more bellicose on the Falklands issue, *was* deterred in 1977. The crisis faded. Sending a gunboat – or a nuclear submarine – still worked with the Argentines.

By 1980 there was a new occupant in Downing Street: Margaret Thatcher. The new FCO Minister with responsibility for Latin America was Nicholas Ridley. He decided to 'sort the Falkland Islands problem out once and for all'. To the unease of the Falkland Islands lobbyists, he proposed a 'leaseback' deal, whereby the legal title to ownership of the islands would be transferred to Argentina, which would then lease back the islands to Britain for ninety-nine years. The settlers' way of life would be protected and guaranteed, Argentine pride over sovereignty would be satisfied and, the FCO fervently prayed, the problem would go away. It was an elegant and practical solution to a tricky problem.

It didn't work. Ridley reckoned without the Falkland Islands lobby. In 1980, Parliament rejected the proposals out of hand, giving Nicholas Ridley 'the worst day of his political life' in the process. Ridley left the baying House of Commons 'white-faced with shock'. The Falklands lobby had blocked the only solution in sight. The Islanders had won.

Argentina had one last try. In a tense session in 1981 in a private room at the UN in New York, the urbane Argentine Deputy Foreign Minister, Carlos Cavandoli, tried every blandishment to overcome the Falkland Islanders' doubts. In a scene likened by one observer dryly to 'Satan's Temptation of Christ', the polished Cavandoli confronted the real block to Argentine ambitions when he met a delegation of suspicious Falkland Islanders, silkily offering them every inducement available: special autonomous regional status, language, customs, money – anything. The Islanders refused, despite offers of schools, hospitals and roads.

One source in the Falklands in 1982 claimed that the Argentines were so desperate for any progress at the New York meeting that they had even offered 'a million dollars a family' for agreement to Argentine sovereignty. Allegedly this degenerated into a counter-demand by the islanders for 'a million dollars a *head*', and then amazingly, 'but only for *real* islanders', which was apparently defined by Kelper traditionalists as 'British citizens born on the Falklands'. (It must be stressed that this story comes from a single unconfirmed source, but, if true, shows that even sovereignty had its price. It also shows that Argentine patience must have been sorely tried.)

Argentine frustrations increased. By 1981, internally the battle against the left-wing rebels had been won, but it had been a messy victory with a bitter legacy of brutality, torture and military repression. Argentine politics were in turmoil, with unrest on the streets, hyper-inflation and mass unemployment. The military government was locked in a bitter international dispute with Argentina's neighbour, Chile, over the Beagle Channel round Cape Horn. In short, the ruling military junta of General Roberto Viola was beleaguered and in trouble at home and abroad. Only two shafts of light illuminated the political future: the new US administration's courting of the Argentine junta to build an anti-communist alliance in Latin America (which implied a degree of much-needed international recognition and respectability); and second, renewed hope that the Falklands issue might be resolved and deliver a national foreign policy triumph for the new junta, now led at the beginning of 1982 by Army General Leopoldo Fortunato Galtieri.

The Galtieri junta assumed supreme power in December 1981. Its three members were all military hard men, determined to sort out Argentina's problems and make a clean start. A 'Thatcherite' package of free market economic reforms ripped apart the failed Perónist structure of wages, taxes and jobs, and a new Foreign Minister, Nicanor Costa Méndez, came back to office with an equally tough brief on foreign affairs. Backed by Reagan's America, Argentina was now set to seize the initiative, assert herself in her international disputes and become the dominant regional power.

Galtieri's junta knew that they had to achieve results quickly. The economic reforms were painful and unless some kind of national success was assured, then the likelihood of major social unrest from the defiant unions and multi-party opposition was strong. A southern 'winter of discontent' was almost inevitable. With inflation running at over 140 per cent *a month*, life for the 28 million Argentinians was desperate during that southern summer from September 1981 to March 1982. The junta's policy initiatives at the time have a flavour of desperation and genuine urgency; something had to be done. For the Falklands, Galtieri's junta ordered a simple twin-track strategy: push hard diplomatically at the UN, but prepare to seize the islands by force should the British not agree a diplomatic solution.

The British, and particularly the Foreign and Commonwealth Office, gave the appearance early in 1982 of being caught like startled rabbits in the headlights as the junta sought a showdown. The first inkling of impatience came in the preparations for Costa Méndez's new round of talks at the UN. An article in the Argentine press in January 1982 claimed that, 'If the next round of negotiations with London fails, Buenos Aires will take over the islands by force this year.' When the Argentine delegation left for New York, they were mobbed by a crowd at the airport. The British FCO dismissed such behaviour as Latin exuberance. The two sides were beginning to misunderstand their respective positions.

The roots of the misunderstandings were clear: the British did not understand the internal pressures facing the Argentine junta, and the Argentines had completely misunderstood the British government's position for the previous ten years. The real British policy on the Falklands was to procrastinate. The Argentine Foreign Ministry could see that clearly. Although some diplomatic progress had been made, every time the FCO had begun to address the problem, the Falkland Islands lobby in the UK cut in, making the wishes of the islanders the sticking point, as the hapless Nicholas Ridley discovered. Even so, from the Argentine point of view, the British had given some very clear signals over the years, confirming that they were only talking for the sake of talking and really wanted to be free of their colonial burden.

These signals were never part of an integrated policy by successive British governments between 1965 and 1982; but the Argentines, who saw the Malvinas as their main foreign policy problem, believed they were. The Argentines believed that the British showed every sign of being willing to sell the pass and be rid of the Falklands. After all, the British had provided some unmistakable hints. In 1976, the Argentines had occupied South Thule in the South Sandwich Islands. The British had made only a mild protest. When a Falkland Islands communications agreement had been signed in the 1970s, the Argentine *military* had been encouraged to run LADE, the islands' airline link to the mainland, and the islands' fuel stocks were transported and managed by YPF, the Argentine national oil company. All of this had been accepted by the FCO as pragmatic political steps forward, and by the ever-suspicious islanders as giving them a better standard of living.

In 1981, two events occurred that confirmed the Argentine view. The Thatcher government announced that the ice patrol ship HMS *Endurance*, the Royal Navy's last presence in the South Atlantic, would be decommissioned the following year and would not be replaced. It is rumoured that a member of the Argentine Embassy actually telephoned the FCO and asked whether this represented a deliberate signal of a climbdown. An embarrassed FCO replied that it was nothing to do with them, it was a Ministry of Defence decision – which was true. At the time, the announcement was seen merely as part of the cost-cutting going on all round Whitehall, making the new Tory government deeply unpopular with those sections of society accustomed to the bottomless pockets of the state or of their fellow taxpayers, depending on which side of the political divide people sat. (It is one of the forgotten byways of history that by 1981, Margaret Thatcher was one of the most unpopular British prime ministers in history. By 1983 she was winning landslide elections.)

To the Argentine Naval Attaché in London, Admiral Allara, however, the withdrawal of a Royal Navy warship in the South Atlantic clearly meant that the British no longer felt any need to defend the Falklands. Taken with Defence Secretary John Nott's rundown of the Royal Navy in the 1981 Defence Review, here was a clear political signal to Allara and his two naval masters back in Argentina: Admiral Lombardo, the Commander-in-Chief of the Fleet, and the moody but passionate naval member of the junta, Admiral Anaya, who was already bent on recovering the Falklands. Anaya disliked the British intensely and considered that a naval victory to recover the Malvinas would be the crowning glory for the Argentine Navy and himself as he ended his career.

The second supposed signal from the British to the Argentines was a serious political miscalculation. In the 1981 British Nationality Bill, the Falkland Islanders suddenly lost their cherished right to full British citizenship. The Bill was designed by the British Home Office to keep out a flood of colonial immigration by offering full British citizenship to only so-called 'patrials' – a status where at least one grandparent had been born in Britain. The Kelpers of the Falkland Islands were therefore excluded by definition. History does not yet relate what the Foreign Secretary made of this particular new law when it was discussed in Cabinet, if it was discussed at all in the context of its implications for the Falklands and foreign policy: but it is fair to assume that the Home Office was not greatly concerned about the Falkland Islanders when it proposed the legislation.

To Argentina, however, this looked like a clear British signal that the islanders' permanent veto on progress was being deliberately and rather skilfully run by Mrs Thatcher and her Cabinet. What were in reality a series of random events and policy decisions were linked together by the Argentines to read like a coherent British policy, and it was a policy that clearly said 'disengagement'. The British were obviously slowly pulling back from the Falklands.

Although the FCO was blamed for the Falklands disaster, in all fairness it must be said that by the middle of 1981, Nicholas Ridley and his FCO team were beginning to be seriously concerned. They could not convince anyone in Whitehall to support their concerns, however, nor were they convinced that an Argentine invasion was a real possibility. An FCO protest about the decommissioning of HMS *Endurance* was met with a typically terse response from the MOD: 'OK – is the FCO budget going to pay for her? If not, take it up with the Minister.'

The FCO unease was reflected in a number of Whitehall initiatives. The MOD was asked to draw up a paper to examine possible responses to any Argentine moves against the Falklands; and the Cabinet's Joint Intelligence Committee (JIC) was asked to draw up a threat assessment. Neither option was considered urgent (the MOD took six months to produce the planning document) and the British Foreign Secretary squashed his FCO officials' request to take the matter to Cabinet in September 1981. 'Negotiations were the way ahead,' insisted Lord Carrington, a judgement that later was to cost him his job.

The Foreign Secretary had before him at that meeting the JIC paper of July 1981 which spelled out a clear intelligence warning, albeit in that peculiar brand of Whitehall-mandarin language known as 'JIC-speak', a careful and anodyne blend of ambiguities, pregnant with every alternative linguistic possibility. The JIC assessment laid out all the obvious escalatory steps the Argentines could follow, but concentrated on diplomatic and economic measures as the priority. Crucial to the JIC assessment was the assertion that provided Argentina considered the British government to be negotiating in good faith to transfer sovereignty at some point, the preferred path would be 'peaceful means'. However, like all good JIC assessments, the anonymous authors covered themselves by stating that 'if on the other hand' Argentina saw no hope of a peaceful transfer of the islands, then there would be 'a high risk of its resorting to more forcible measures against British interests...

In such circumstances, military action… or a full-scale invasion of the Falkland Islands could not be discounted.'

This was serious stuff, despite its careful ambiguities. Unfortunately no one seems to have taken any notice of it, least of all the Foreign Secretary at his meeting with Ridley and his Latin America Department in September 1981. The battered Ridley was then moved to the Treasury as part of the Cabinet reshuffle, leaving the FCO and its Latin America Department uneasily writing about their concerns to their ambassador in Buenos Aires. Ambassador Williams's reply was uncharacteristically undiplomatic, describing British policy as 'a general Micawberism'. He saw the dangers only too clearly: 'If ministers were really not serious about negotiating with Argentina it would be better to say so now and face the consequences,' he wrote in early October 1981. It seems hard to fault his judgement.

Lord Carrington's decision not to take the matter to Cabinet had stopped the affair dead. Despairing Foreign Office officials immediately pointed out the dangers of sitting on any intelligence that warns of military hostilities should a government refuse to negotiate, either seriously or at all. It was to no avail. Whitehall's obsession in 1981 was cost-cutting, not foreign adventures that were, frankly, unthinkable. It was inconceivable that the Argentines would ever use force. It could not happen; it was, in fact, cognitive dissonance.

If the British government did not take the Argentine junta seriously, it might have done had it paid more attention to the intelligence it was receiving. In all its travails between summer 1981 and the invasion in 1982, the junta was impelled by pressure and passions far removed from the calmer air of Whitehall. The junta was preparing to act. Later, the Franks Report (the British Privy Counsellor's report on the Falklands debacle after the war) dismissed any suggestion of complacency, claiming that 'the government not only did not, but could not, have had earlier warning… The invasion of the Falkland Islands could not have been foreseen.'

This is disingenuous nonsense. Although the Argentine decision to attack was taken only three days before it happened, on 29 March 1982, armies and navies do not mount major maritime operations at three days' notice. It takes much longer to mobilize and prepare an amphibious force. Franks was deliberately erecting a bureaucratic screen to obscure the difference between intelligence *intentions* and intelligence *capabilities*. The Argentine *order* to sail may well have been given with only three days to go, but putting together the capability, making the plan, assembling the ships, guns, stores, aeroplanes and men to invade the Falklands was the result of a decision made nearly four months before. It should have been spotted, but lacking good intelligence resources inside Argentina, the British were fatally blind to both Argentinian capabilities and intentions. Despite Franks's comforting assertion, the British should have been much more aware of what was going on: and Franks knew it.

The scheme to invade the Falklands was originally the brainchild of Admiral Anaya, the head of the Argentine Navy. At a private dinner on 9 December 1981, he had secretly offered the Navy's support to Galtieri in his coup against General Viola, in return for a promise that the Navy would be allowed to 'recover the Malvinas' in 1982. Galtieri agreed and went on to head the junta with Anaya as his naval member. Thus are cabinets assembled in military dictatorships.

The detailed plan was subsequently prepared in December 1981 by a small team in Admiral Lombardo's Fleet headquarters and briefed in great secrecy to the junta's senior military planning staff on 12 January 1982. It was not briefed to any civilian officials, even the Ministry of Foreign Affairs. Interestingly, when that indefatigable observer of the South Atlantic scene, Captain Nick Barker, Royal Navy of HMS *Endurance*, put in at the naval base at Ushuaia near the southern tip of Argentina on 25 January 1982 on a routine port call, he seems to have spotted that something was amiss immediately. He reported back that 'something was up with the [Argentine] Navy... very standoffish.' British intelligence in DI4 (Navy) failed to pick up on it.

Overseas intelligence is the province of three British agencies: the Secret Intelligence Service (SIS, often known as MI6), Government Communications Headquarters (GCHQ), the national signals intelligence agency, and the Defence Intelligence Staff (DIS). The last of these, DIS, is usually channelled through an embassy's resident defence service attachés, who, like any other accredited diplomats, have an information reporting responsibility as well as a representational function.

In the early 1980s, with the Cold War in full swing, Argentina came low on the list of Britain's intelligence collection priorities. The service attachés, particularly the Royal Navy's, were charged with wooing their Argentine counterparts, not collecting intelligence. Their main task was to encourage Argentina to buy British defence exports. As the Argentine Navy was equipped with Type 42 destroyers – the same type as the Royal Navy's HMS *Sheffield* and HMS *Coventry* – the promotion of defence sales, particularly Rolls-Royce marine gas turbines, figured much higher on the list of British service attachés' duties than intelligence collection, which risked upsetting both the host nation and the ambassador. The SIS was represented by a single officer who was 'declared' to the host government, and whose area of operations covered the whole of Latin America, not just Argentina. With GCHQ concentrating on electronic sigint, these three agencies were responsible for intelligence on Argentina.

In fact, there were just two key intelligence officers in place. The most prescient was the Army's Defence Attaché to Argentina, Colonel Stephen Love. Love, a gunner by background, was also an experienced intelligence staff officer, spoke Spanish and had a wide background working with international organizations. By sheer coincidence, he also knew the SIS Chief of Station, Mark Heathcote. Heathcote's father had commanded the Royal Artillery Regiment which Love had first joined as a young officer twenty years earlier.

Heathcote's job as SIS Chief of Station was humint, the cultivation of human sources, people with access to valuable classified information who could be induced or encouraged to divulge it. Secret sources, as every journalist or detective knows, are the most time-consuming and difficult to cultivate and recruit. Running agents is expensive in time and money and can be wearing on the nerves – for both parties. In 1981, Whitehall cost-cutting extended to SIS offices and operations. Agents cost money. The fictional James Bond never had to put up with the realities of working for a cost-conscious MI6 in the early 1980s.

Heathcote's problem was twofold. In the first place he was a 'declared' intelligence officer, in Argentina to co-operate with his Argentine hosts against the primary targets: the Soviet Union and the Eastern bloc. The Argentine junta was passionately anti-communist, if nothing else. Heathcote even had a formal Argentine liaison officer, Hector Valsecchi, seconded from Argentine

Naval Intelligence. So, with an official LO breathing down his neck, it was going to be extremely difficult for Heathcote to target the Argentine High Command, the obvious place to look for spies or sources with access to Argentina's secret plans. Secondly, Heathcote's job in Latin America took his attention far and wide in the Spanish-speaking countries. Heathcote's SIS brief may have included the junta as a target; but there is no record of his success, even if he had risked playing such a dangerous game.

The Defence Attaché's brief was even less likely to mine any rich vein of secret intelligence. If Love had engaged in any activity likely to bring discredit on the embassy (such as covert spying), Ambassador Williams would have run him out of Buenos Aires on the next flight. The more so since Williams, an international professional to his fingertips, realized only too well the potentially disastrous weakness of Britain's position and was determined not to do anything to make the position worse. (Williams was to pay dearly for his pragmatic approach later. After the war, diplomats who had taken the entirely sensible view that there was no point in taking a tough stance with Argentina unless Britain was prepared to back up its position with real force were quietly sidelined.) So the Defence Attaché was obliged to be discreet in his intelligence-gathering.

Defence attachés are invariably hampered by their slightly anomalous position as temporary diplomats among an embassy team of long-term professionals. Unless he is fully accepted in the hothouse intimacy of an embassy, usually as a commanding number three in the mission after the ambassador and head of chancery, as a genial and courteous socialite, or as an incisive expert on the host nation – or any combination of these three – a DA is unlikely to have a really comfortable tour among his FCO colleagues. If professional relationships break down between the DA and others on the embassy team, then the tensions often result in trouble. A good DA is careful never to overstep the mark with his FCO hosts. He is, after all, paid for by the FCO, not by the Ministry of Defence. As a long-term DA once dryly remarked, 'Never forget that the FCO only tolerate you… they never forget that they are the clever people even if they can't remember to wear matching socks. You must make them like you.'

So it proved for Colonel Love. However, he was able to put together a perceptive and accurate dossier on his hosts. As Argentina at the time was run by a military junta, the *political* implications of his brief were more profound than is usual for a DA. Love could express military-political views in a way that mere diplomats could not, and he enjoyed unusually good access to the military through the international freemasonry of soldiers. Love was also able to cull a wide range of open sources such as press, magazines, radio and TV together with trade magazines and journals. From this, during 1981 and early 1982, he began to see a consistent and alarming picture emerging. If London was being complacent, then Colonel Love was not. In early 1982 he visited the Falklands at his own expense, after much wrangling with his FCO paymasters, although the islands were theoretically not his responsibility.

Love's secret report of 2 March 1982 is a remarkable document, and a model of its kind. He spells out a clear warning of an increasingly hard line by the Argentine military and makes a clear connection between the need for General Galtieri's junta to make a bold gesture for domestic consumption and the use of force as a consequence of Anglo-Argentine negotiations breaking down. Colonel Love then goes on to make a sound military appreciation of the likely Argentine military courses of action: demonstrations of Argentine naval power in the islands as 'shots across the UK's bows', or a surprise *coup de main* or invasion to seize the islands by force. He concludes, perhaps with one eye on the superior 'politicals' in the Foreign Office back in London: 'I apologize… if I have worked with incomplete knowledge on territory which is theoretically outside my area of concern (and possibly arriving at conclusions contrary to official views to which I am not privy).' Colonel Love stands his ground, even on paper and in the eye of possible Foreign Office scorn: 'However, I am sure that as the diplomatic exchanges reach crunch point, we, the intelligence machine, should be clearing our minds… on what the military threat comprises… and the forces which pose this threat are definitely my concern.'

Colonel Love sent his memorandum to the Ministry of Defence (Defence Intelligence Staff), Defence Intelligence 4 (DI4, the department dealing with South America) and to Robin Fearn, the FCO official responsible for the Falklands. He also sent a copy to Rex Hunt, the Governor of the Falkland Islands. The FCO wearily wrote on their copy, 'I suspect that the Ambassador asked for this to be sent. It says nothing which we don't already know.' Another hand added, 'Yes, but it is useful nonetheless and has been copied to the MOD. My only concern is that this sort of unscheduled visit could be unhelpful.' The MOD's copy appears never to have circulated outside branch level in the MOD, although a minute about it was distributed. An angry Colonel Love had 'a furious row' with DIS when he got back after the war and discovered that his intelligence report had neither been circulated nor had his warnings been acted upon properly, in his view.

With the SIS concentrating on collaborating with the Argentines against communism in Latin America and the Defence Attaché reduced to filtering Argentine press reports, a lot depended on GCHQ's sigint to give warning of any planned aggression against the British. Britain's sigint depended at the time on a secret agreement with the USA to share responsibility for the worldwide sigint target. This 'UKUSA' agreement effectively carved up the world into collection areas. Southern and Latin America was primarily an American National Security Agency collection task.

Sigint requires at least four basic things: a suitable place from which to collect signals, a linguistically qualified intelligence staff to collate and interpret the information, clear political direction as to target priority, and last the ability to break other nations' codes. Britain's GCHQ had no real collecting posts in South America, a limited Spanish-speaking staff and a low priority for collecting Argentine transmissions. J and K divisions of GCHQ were of different sizes – J covered the Soviet bloc; the much smaller K covered the whole of the rest of the world. GCHQ's main station for all of Africa and South America was on Ascension Island, tucked away inside the Cable and Wireless establishment at Twin Boats up Ascension's volcano.

The only other sigint asset available to GCHQ was HMS *Endurance* which had been put up for disposal at the end of 1982. Its captain, Nick Barker, said that 'HMS *Endurance*'s real weapon was her sigint and electronic warfare listening suite.' The last capability required for sigint – an ability to break other nations' codes – is the most secret and protected area of all. Once an agency knows a code is broken it will simply change its systems, equipment or codes and the code-breakers have to start all over again. We do know that the British could read Argentine codes at the time. Ted Rowlands, a previous Labour Foreign Office Minister, said so in the House of Commons during the savage Saturday debate after the war broke out. He told Parliament that in his day as a minister (only two years before), 'Argentina, in terms of intelligence, was an open book.' We know from the resulting political row that this was a direct reference to British sigint access at the time.

The USA hoovered up transmissions from their station at Panama and almost certainly from its embassy in Buenos Aires. None of the sigint collected by any partner indicated any special intelligence directed against the Falklands. By March 1982, the sigint being broken – of which there was plenty, according to later reports – was consistent with a maritime build-up. This was not unusual. The sigint analysts and DI4 knew that the Argentine Navy was about to conduct its regular annual naval exercise with its Uruguayan neighbours, so the preparations were assessed as part of the normal pre-exercise activity.

With no humint sources in place, defence and naval attachés hampered by restrictions and protocol, and ambiguous sigint, the only other viable intelligence source able to check on Argentine capabilities was overhead and aerial reconnaissance. The British had no overflight capability in the South Atlantic. The Joint Air Reconnaissance Intelligence Centre (JARIC) at RAF Brampton depended on whatever crumbs fell from their rich American cousins' table. The US National Reconnaissance Office (NRO) had two strategic assets – reconnaissance satellites and SR-71 Blackbird overflights. If either US overhead source did yield anything significant in the first three months of 1982, it seems never to have been reported to JARIC, let alone to the MOD and the British intelligence community. In the circumstances that is hardly surprising. The KH11 satellites were targeted mainly at Soviet activities in the northern hemisphere and not on the South Atlantic.

With all its possible intelligence sources and agencies emasculated, diverted or non-existent, Britain was flying blind into the Falklands storm. The British had one last hope of redressing the intelligence vacuum: 'foreign liaison', the intelligence euphemism for other countries' information. With the British, that invariably means the USA. The Special Relationship was after all originally founded on an intelligence exchange between Roosevelt and Churchill, and has always been the real backbone of US-UK governmental relations.

Unfortunately, in the run-up to the Falklands War in 1982, the Anglo-American link became curiously non-committal. It appeared that the

Americans would not play ball, even with their closest ally. For America had its own agenda for Argentina. General Galtieri was to spearhead CIA Director Casey's anti-communist drive in Central America. The Americans needed a ready supply of cheap, ideologically committed, Spanish-speaking anti-communists, preferably experienced in dealing firmly with left-wing insurgents, to spearhead the CIA's drive against Sandinista Nicaragua. Casey even got $19 million allocated to the programme and almost certainly gave his approval to Galtieri's 22 December coup against his predecessor General Viola when Galtieri visited Washington in November 1981.

The upshot of the sweetheart deal between Galtieri and the CIA meant that the British were effectively sidelined. America had always been pointedly cool about Britain's claim to the Falklands: the hemispheric imperatives of the Monroe Doctrine had always placed the US in an ambivalent position over the issue. The end result was that even Britain's intelligence source of last resort, the USA, was not being completely forthcoming; at least until the real shooting war broke out.

Although the US Secretary of State, General Alexander Haig, swiftly grasped that the British saw the self-determination of the islanders as a make-or-break principle, he was quietly sceptical. In a closed session briefing to Congressmen, he said that while the principle was 'very laudable and supportable, they *[the British]* have created conditions on the Islands which make free choice by the population less than balanced'. He made a nasty joke about the islanders, which drew a laugh from his audience, but was particularly tasteless in the circumstances. (It was along the lines of, 'too few women, too many sheep'.) It is hard to believe he felt much sympathy for their plight. America, certainly at the start, was 'hands off'.

The national organization responsible for overseeing Britain's all-source intelligence assessments is the Joint Intelligence Committee or JIC. The JIC rose to pre-eminence during the Second World War. The pressure of life-and-death events between 1939 and 1945 brought an accuracy, focus and urgency to both the JIC's current and longer-term assessments, which were rightly highly regarded. Churchill insisted on real predictions based on hard evidence and rigorous analysis during wartime. After 1945, the perils and alarms of the Cold War kept the JIC's skills honed. The result was that the JIC became not only a trusted source of national strategic intelligence assessments but also the filter mechanism that brought all sources of intelligence around one table to smooth out the differences between the various agencies involved. It worked. The US Office of National Estimates could only envy the JIC's pre-eminence. The JIC's anonymous reports, devoid of departmental claims, did much to prevent the kind of interagency turf wars that have bedevilled US intelligence since 1960.

As always in Whitehall, however, a bloodless battle was being fought for control of influential resources that could impress ministers. A struggle had long been waged not just for the soul of the JIC's product but for control of the JIC itself. The FCO had managed to wrest control from the War Office in 1940. In the aftermath of Suez, a special new office inside the Cabinet Secretariat grew up to administer and direct the JIC on behalf of the Cabinet Office, not the FCO. However, the FCO still managed to control the JIC's deliberations to a marked degree by its permanent chairmanship of the committee. The FCO thus had two bites at influencing policy, not only as *primus inter pares* in the JIC's many regional subcommittees, the Current Intelligence Groups or CIGs, but also as the standing chairman of the final national assessment. It was an arrangement that suited the FCO's view of foreign affairs very well.

Despite the rising tide of both intelligence and political pressure between December 1981 and February 1982, the JIC did not make the Falklands question a major issue. Even the July 1981 Assessment (see page 297) was dismissed after the crisis by one informed source as little more than 'an annual review updated by changing the names of the junta'. There is no evidence that Galtieri's seizure of power in December 1981 was marked by any urgent new JIC assessment to take account of developments. The Latin America Current Intelligence Group (LACIG) met *eighteen* times between July 1981 and January 1982, but at no time does the Falklands crisis appear to have been on the agenda. Only when the final round of bilateral negotiations opened in New York in January 1982 did the FCO call for a new JIC assessment to act as a guidance document for the routine meeting of the Cabinet's Overseas and Defence Policy Committee scheduled for 16 March 1982. To compound their lack of intelligence, the British now added a lack of urgency.

No such bureaucratic inertia restrained the Argentines. After Admiral Anaya's naval staff had briefed the military planners on the secret Navy invasion plan on 12 and 13 January, all that remained was to see whether the military option for the dual-track Argentine strategy would be required. Would the bilateral negotiations at the UN in early 1982 bring about an acceptable result?

The Argentine-UK talks of January 1982 were a fiasco. The British proposed the usual lengthy round of future diplomatic meetings, and came away yet again congratulating themselves on having stalled as elegantly as ever and bought a few more months to wear down the objections of the intransigent islanders. In any case, the continuance in office of Galtieri's increasingly beleaguered junta was far from certain. The Argentines came away well aware that the British were stalling yet again and convinced that negotiations were leading nowhere. The talks ended with the issue of a by now familiar short and bland joint communiqué.

In Buenos Aires the junta was furious: they had wanted to stoke the fires of diplomatic pressure under the British, not issue platitudinous communiqués. Little did the British realize that their delaying tactics at the UN were the trigger for the other track of Argentine strategy: the decision to use force. To the horror of British diplomats, the Argentine government then issued its own unilateral communiqué the next day, on 2 March, stating baldly:

> At a meeting in New York… representatives considered an Argentine proposal [for] meetings to achieve recognition of Argentine Sovereignty over the Malvinas… to achieve substantial results… as time is short. Argentina has negotiated with Great Britain… with patience and good faith for 15 years. The new system constitutes an effective step for the early resolution of the dispute. However, should this not occur, Argentina reserves the right to terminate the working of this mechanism, and to choose freely the procedure which best accords with her interests.

An alarmed Foreign Office immediately demanded clarification of this unilateral declaration. Both the Argentine Foreign Minister, Nicanor Costa

Méndez and his UN negotiator, Enrique Ros, were reassuring; provided the talks went well, there was no problem. But it was too late. Whatever soothing assurances were given by the diplomats, the Argentine junta and in particular the Navy were now bent on the other option of the dual-track strategy. The fuse that led to the Falklands War had been lit.

What followed was pure farce, and a major distraction. To what extent it was a deliberate deception or test of British resolve has never been established. A team of patriotic Argentine scrap merchants suddenly landed on the frozen island of South Georgia, 800 miles to the east of the Falklands, on 19 March 1982 from an Argentine Navy auxiliary support ship, the *Buen Suceso*. The excited crew promptly ran up the Argentine flag, fired a volley of shots and sang the national anthem. Their leader, Señor Davidoff, declared that the 41-strong party was at South Georgia to fulfil an old contract to collect all the scrap from the old whaling ships at Leith Harbour, which was true, and offered the local British Antarctic Survey the aid of their doctor and medical staff if required. In Argentina, the C-in-C of the Argentine Fleet, Admiral Lombardo, was furious: this very public adventure in South Georgia risked the whole security of his Malvinas invasion plans; the British were bound to be alerted by this pantomime. Admiral Anaya soothed his fears. The British would do nothing.

The FCO was nonplussed. The Falklands problem had become the 'South Georgia crisis'. The usual exchange of diplomatic notes began, with the Argentine Foreign Ministry pleading complete ignorance. Then on 22 March came news that *Buen Suceso* and Sr Davidoff's scrap team had departed from South Georgia. Tension relaxed, only to rise sharply when HMS *Endurance* was suddenly diverted to South Georgia, when it transpired that ten Argentinians had stayed ashore after all, to remove them and take them to Port Stanley.

Colonel Love, who seems to have been the only person who was concerned by the growing crisis and who could see events from the perspective of Buenos Aires, the FCO and the armed forces of both Britain and Argentina, was by now thoroughly alarmed. On 24 March he sent a signal to the British Ministry of Defence reinforcing his earlier warnings. He specifically warned that HMS *Endurance* risked being intercepted (his colleague the Naval Attaché had warned him that Argentine ships were at sea) and any attempt to lift the remaining Argentines from South Georgia would be a provocation that could encourage a 'rescue mission' by the Argentine Navy.

Colonel Love was too late. By 25/26 March, three Argentine warships were heading for South Georgia, tasked with blocking HMS *Endurance*'s passage. Nick Barker wisely took to his heels and began playing hide and seek with the Argentine Navy in the watery wastes of the South Atlantic. Lord Carrington, now at last as seriously concerned as his attaché in Buenos Aires, alerted Mrs Thatcher and the Cabinet with belated understatement that 'a confrontation might need to be faced'.

GCHQ confirmed that two frigates were heading for Falklands waters, and the diesel-electric submarine *Santa Fe* had been ordered to land a special forces reconnaissance team on the Islands. There could only be one interpretation of such a set of orders. When tied in with clear intelligence indicators showing a clampdown of civilian access to Puerto Belgrano on the Argentine mainland, loading of a 900-strong marine amphibious force, a major naval task force at sea heading east, diversions from the annual joint Uruguayan naval exercises, sigint reports of discussions about how many Royal Marines were in Port Stanley (the garrison was being relieved) and unusual patterns of Air Force activity, then the indicators and warning board screamed 'invasion'.

Armed with this intelligence picture, the JIC's Latin America Current Intelligence Group met on the morning of 30 March under the chairmanship of the Foreign Office. Despite access to all this information, the LACIG calmly concluded that *an invasion was not imminent*. The build-up could be explained, it claimed, quoting the words of Ambassador Williams in Buenos Aires, because 'The Argentines intend no move in the dispute, but to let matters ride while they build up their strength in the area.' The ambassador's view was coloured by the denials from both Costa Méndez and Ros that there was any military pressure. Their line in response to the British Ambassador's increasingly searching questions was constant even at this late stage – that provided the British were negotiating in good faith, they faced no abrupt military action. It is conceivable that Costa Méndez and Ros knew no more, or at least not much more, because the junta distrusted politicians and had told Costa Méndez the bare minimum of military intentions in the name of security.

It seems incredible that the British National Intelligence Estimate could still be lulling themselves into such a false sense of security as late as 30 March 1982. With all the indicators available, they – or the FCO members who dominated the JIC process at the time – appear to have deliberately ignored the facts. The reasons appear to be based on Whitehall's – and particularly the FCO's – deeply held illusions of reality.

In the first place, the British had an absolute fear of provoking the Argentine military to violence. The alternative policy, of meeting the military threat head-on, would have meant turning the garrison down south into a 'Fortress Falklands', and that would have been expensive. In a Whitehall in 1981 deep in the throes of cutting defence expenditure (ironically, the Argentine Navy had been offered the new carrier HMS *Invincible* at a knock-down price in 1981 – by 1982 they probably wished that they had bought her while they had the chance), any policy advocating extra military spending 'out of area' equated to lunacy. Beyond a token garrison on the Falklands, the *only* policy open to Britain was a diplomatic settlement. There was simply no alternative.

Second, the Foreign Office had convinced itself that the Argentine unilateral communiqué of 2 March should be taken at face value. In the communiqué, the Argentines had given a deadline for negotiations of the end of 1982. Surely no sovereign government was going to do anything as silly and violent as perform a volte-face and invade the Falklands.

The third misapprehension in Whitehall was fear of crying wolf. In 1977 a nuclear submarine had been sent to the South Atlantic at great expense, and Argentina had done nothing. The MOD had claimed that it proved military force works as a deterrent, but the FCO and the rest of Whitehall regarded it as a costly and pointless exercise. The intelligence community was determined not to be seen to be overreacting.

Interestingly, these preoccupations were mirrored by the junta's own fears. Realizing Whitehall's strengths – nuclear submarines and a powerful international case should Argentina be seen to seize the islands by force – the junta knew that they had to move with a mixture of speed and restraint if the Argentine plan to grab the islands with minimum fuss was to succeed. Thus, when the junta realized that the British were alert to the Argentine fleet at sea (20–22 March), they moved quickly to pre-empt any real trouble before the British could react. The decision to invade was almost certainly taken at a meeting on Friday 26 March and was aimed at securing a bloodless victory. (Whether it was taken collectively or just by Admiral Anaya, anxious to rehabilitate his Navy, has never been established.) On Saturday 27 March, Costa Méndez announced the decision to a stunned meeting of senior Argentine Foreign Ministry diplomats, and by Sunday 28 March, the intelligence was piling up on the LACIG and other intelligence analysts' desks, awaiting their return to work in Whitehall the following day.

Despite a flurry of last-minute activity, briefings and warnings, on 2 April 1982 Argentine Marines landed at Mullet Creek on the south-east coast of East Falkland. Undetected, they collected their equipment and trekked across the boggy hills to Moody Brook outside Stanley, and at dawn they attacked the Royal Marines' sleeping huts and sheds, raking the buildings with automatic fire and closing in with phosphorus grenades. They need not have bothered. Thoroughly alerted, not least by jubilant Argentine radio proclamations that an invasion was afoot, the Royal Marines were by now well dug in in defensive locations around the Governor's residence. The battle for the Falklands was on.

By 08.30 that morning, it was over. Surrounded by over 900 men equipped with heavy weapons and with nowhere to retreat, Governor Hunt ordered his tiny force of Royal Marines, outnumbered ten to one, to surrender, but not before they had shot down a couple of Argentine Marines who had incautiously exposed themselves. In pictures that went round the world and sent a ripple of shock through the British armed services, proud Royal Marines were seen with their hands up, surrendering to Argentines. British officers later recalled that they had never seen such a wave of collective anger among serving soldiers as when they saw those pictures.

The Marines, angry and defeated, had only surrendered because the Governor had ordered it, and an unnamed Royal Marine was heard to warn his Argentine guard as he was marched away into captivity, 'Don't make yourself too comfy, mate – we'll be back.'

The victorious Argentines shipped the Marines out, together with a protesting Governor Hunt and any islander who wanted to leave.

This later turned out to be a mistake as it gave the irate Marines the chance to avenge their humiliation. Some of the first troops to reoccupy the Falklands after the British Task Force landed were members of 'Naval Party 8901', the original Royal Marine Falklands garrison, led by their commander, Major Mike Norman. Volunteers to a man, the British shipped the Marines straight back as Juliet Company of 42 Commando. Juliet Company went on to storm Mount Harriet with Colonel Nick Vaux's men in June 1982 as part of what is regarded professionally as the finest infantry night action since the Second World War.

The invasion was met by very contrasting reactions in Buenos Aires and London. In the Plaza de Mayo, triumphant Argentines bawled themselves hoarse singing their national anthem and waved flags. Forgotten were the shootings of demonstrators in that very square the month before. To General Galtieri, it looked as if the old dictator's ploy of using a foreign military adventure to direct attention from domestic ills and unify the populace had worked to perfection. Voice cracking with emotion, he told the crowd that his junta had only been 'expressing the popular will'. The crowd howled its approval.

London was shocked into silence. To make matters worse, the Cabinet lost touch, literally, with events. Suddenly there was no communication between London and the Falklands. For the whole of that 'Black Friday', opinion drifted rudderless and angry. Whitehall was in trauma, 'civil servants and politicians seemed to talk only in hushed tones as if contemplating some monstrous bereavement', in Max Hastings's phrase. One observer said that 'there were little groups muttering in corners. It was like the Roman Senate just before Julius Caesar was stabbed.'

Having presided over a debacle caused by, in her phrase, 'that hotbed of cold feet', the FCO, Margaret Thatcher now decided to fight. She had no choice. In the brooding atmosphere of recriminations and disaster that Friday, the debate in Parliament on Saturday would be crucial. British administrations had fallen for less; the ghosts of Eden and Chamberlain hovered in the wings. The Tory government of 1982, already desperately unpopular, looked trapped and wounded.

The only escape from humiliation came from the Royal Navy, who advised the prime minister that a task force was necessary and could sail within forty-eight hours with the objective to be: 'to bring about the withdrawal of Argentine forces from the Falkland Islands, and the re-establishment of British administration there, as quickly as possible'. Thatcher ordered the dispatch of the Task Force for the South Atlantic and went to face Parliament.

She stood her ground. Faced with a baying House of Commons, Thatcher acknowledged past failures and announced a decisive solution to restore British honour:

> The people of the Falkland Islands, like the people of the United Kingdom, are an island race. They are few in number but they have the right to live in peace, to choose their own way of life and to determine their own allegiance. Their way of life is British; their allegiance is to the Crown. It is the wish of the British people and the duty of Her Majesty's Government to do everything that we can to uphold that right. That will be our hope and our endeavour and, I believe, the resolve of every Member of this House.

Buoyed by Admiral Sir Henry Leach, the First Sea Lord, who had assured her (with an eye to saving the Royal Navy from the looming defence cuts, claimed the cynics) that it was possible for the Navy to win the islands back, and by her deputy, William Whitelaw, who told her that if she didn't stand and fight they could all be out of a job by Sunday, Thatcher ordered the dispatch of a large Naval Task Force to retake the Falkland Islands.

The announcement was met with jingoistic delight in Britain and astonishment by the rest of the world. Diplomatic sources muttered discreetly that if the Argentine junta had only known beforehand that the British would react so forcefully, they might never have tried to seize the Malvinas in the first place. But now it was too late for Argentina as well. There had been serious failures of intelligence on both sides. As one Argentine diplomat said after the event, 'We never dreamed that the British would send a Task Force. If we had, the sceptics in Buenos Aires would have had powerful evidence to counter the Navy's proposals to invade.'

The course of the Falklands War is well documented. As the British tried to cobble together a joint services Task Force with its stores and impedimenta to fight a lonely battle 8,000 miles away, frantic diplomats tried to find a solution. But the Argentines had no intention of leaving the islands now that they had got them back. The British tabloid press raged about the plight of the islanders, now suffering at the hands of 'a banana republic military dictatorship'.

In fact that was a gross slur on the Argentine occupation. The Argentine armed forces were the mildest of tyrants on the Falklands. Led by the well-liked, amiable and courteous Brigadier Mario Benjamin Menendez, who had worked on the islands, knew the islanders well and spoke good English, their brief reign was, in many ways, a kind of normality. In the words of one islander:

> I was never scared when the Argies were here. They kept themselves to themselves and were desperate not to upset us. You hardly ever saw them and they kept out of my way. The only time I was *really* frightened was when the British paras retook Stanley. They were like football hooligans with guns, shooting up things, looting and shouting, and I was even terrified they'd try to rape me... the Brits really were scary.[6]

In fact the Argentines' most obvious enforcement of their regime, apart from the wartime curfew and blackout, was the insistence that everyone now drive on the right. When an islander shouted tyranny, the mildly amused Argentines pointed out that it would be safer for everybody, including the islanders, as Stanley was now stuffed full of eighteen-year-old conscripts driving trucks who had only ever driven on the right. Ruefully, the islanders had to agree.

Even so, the incontrovertible fact was that the Argentines had seized sovereign territory by force of arms. Even the Americans recognized that. Although Jeane Kirkpatrick at the State Department (no lover of the English and a passionate IRA supporter) spelled out her view:

---

6   Personal debrief to the author, Port Stanley, July 1982

The Argentines, of course, have claimed for two hundred years that they own these islands. Now, if the Argentines own the islands, then moving troops into them is not armed aggression.

This did not please the White House. Although the president refused Haig's demand that Kirkpatrick should go, it is entirely plain that he did not share her views on this point. He knew armed aggression when he saw it, publicly and unequivocally describing the invasion in those terms himself, most notably on 30 April:

> We must remember that the aggression was on the part of Argentina in this dispute over the sovereignty of that little ice-cold bunch of land down there, and they finally just resorted to armed aggression, and there was bloodshed. And I think the principle that all of us must abide by is, armed aggression of that kind must not be allowed to succeed.

This notice of American support could hardly have been put more forcefully or helpfully by the president.

By the time the US-led diplomatic round at New York looked like coming up with a compromise, the Royal Navy was ready.

We now know that some help came from an unexpected source: Norway. According the Norwegian Broadcasting Corporation (NRK), the Norwegian Intelligence Service regularly intercepted Soviet satellite intelligence data, which was forwarded to the British. The British later admitted that:

> When the war broke out, we ourselves almost didn't have any intelligence information from this area. It was here we got help from the Norwegians, who gave us a stream of information about the Argentine warships' positions. The information came to us all the time and straight to our war headquarters at Northwood. The information was continuously updated and told us exactly where the Argentine ships were.

In a gradual escalation from maritime blockade to a full-scale air, land and sea war, the next two months saw warships sunk, burning aircraft tumbling from the sky and infantrymen with blackened faces grenading and bayoneting each other in trenches on dark mountains. The torpedoing and sinking of the Argentine cruiser *General Belgrano* caused an international stir but swept the seas clear for the Royal Navy. The attack submarine HMS *Conqueror*'s captain, Commander Chris Wreford-Brown RN, was unrepentant to the point of insouciance: 'The Royal Navy spent thirteen years preparing me for such an occasion. It would have been regarded as extremely dreary if I had fouled it up… '

To add to the Argentines' confusion, there were unadmitted British threats to Argentine cargoes in Spain and France and in 2002, Sir John Nott, Britain's Secretary of State for Defence during the conflict, admitted some shifty commercial activities by Britain's Secret Intelligence Service (MI6): 'I authorized our agents to pose as bona fide purchasers of equipment on the international market, ensuring that we outbid the Argentines, and other agents identified Exocet missiles in markets and rendered them inoperable.'

On 14 June 1982, it was all over; the Union Flag flew over Stanley and thousands of cold and tired Argentine soldiers and marines shambled out to Stanley airport to be shipped home, dejected and defeated. In many cases their officers had fled before the final British assault went in, to the bemusement of the Argentine conscripts and the utter contempt of their captors.

The cost was high. Over 1,000 men died and twice that number were wounded. Britain's blood and treasure were expended on a vast scale to retake the islands – ironically far more than the cost of keeping HMS *Endurance* or another couple of warships on station in the South Atlantic in 1981 to keep an eye on British interests. After the war it would have been unthinkable to give the islands to Argentina, so, by one of those curious paradoxes of history, the Falkland Islanders ended up by merely exchanging one invading army for another. By 1986, an expensive new military airbase had been constructed to protect them and a large, bored tri-service garrison added to the cost of Britain's overseas defence commitments. There would be no question now of ceding the islands to Argentina for a long, long time.

With hindsight, it is clear that it could all have been avoided. Each party to the dispute had misled the other. The difference between the Falklands crisis and many other international disputes is that neither party wanted to fight. A clear signal, or intelligence properly read, could well have altered the course of events.

There were two issues burning away at the core of the dispute. The British never really grasped just how strongly the Argentines – rightly or wrongly – felt about *nuestras Islas Malvinas*. One had only to pick over the pathetic corpses of the dead Argentinian soldiers after the battle and see the congratulatory letters written by anonymous schoolchildren back home 'to our brave soldiers in the Malvinas' to realize how deeply the claim to the islands was rooted in Argentine national life and culture. Every primary school pupil had gladly written to 'my elder "brother" in the islands'. The Argentine threat was always serious. British ambassadors and defence attachés realized it and reported it; but through the distorting prism of Whitehall's self-interest and cool reason, Latin fervour was reduced to noises far off, a kind of comic opera to be shelved and ignored.

This was a serious miscalculation. The more so, because if the Argentine threat was real, then the British were bluffing. Therein lay the second nucleus of the dispute. There was simply no way that Her Majesty's Government was going to defend the Falklands in 1979–81. It was unthinkable to Whitehall, preoccupied with cutting public expenditure after national near-bankruptcy had brought in the grey suits of the International Monetary Fund in 1978/9.

Mrs Thatcher put her finger on the problem in her speech to the House of Commons after the invasion: 'Several times in the past an invasion has been threatened. The only way of… preventing it would have been to keep a large fleet there… No government has been able to do that… the cost would have been enormous.' So, faced with a real threat, the British neither negotiated the problem away nor defended their position, until it was far too late. The British were not only bluffing but also they failed to make any effort to distinguish between Argentine sabre-rattling and the real thing should Argentina ever decide to call Britain's bluff.

The British were in a position not dissimilar to the Israelis before the 1973 Yom Kippur War. The Israelis had been led up the garden path by the Egyptians so many times that they decided at the highest levels to ignore the tactical military indicators of an impending attack to concentrate only on *politically* inspired strategic preconditions as absolute indicators of hostilities (such as an alliance between Egypt and Syria). Confronted by regular Argentine sabre-rattling, the British went one stage further. They did not even develop a coherent set of *any* indicators of real attack. They either ignored the problem, believing that an invasion could never happen, or, at best, allowed Foreign Office officials to dictate the intelligence indicators that suited the Foreign Office. (Gradual withdrawal of the Argentine air links and no move against the islands while the FCO was still engaged in bilateral talks were among them.) This was pure moonshine, not least because the Argentines were not reading the FCO's script with anything like the same care and diligence as junior Foreign Office ministers. It highlights the principal intelligence failure at the heart of the Falklands dispute: the FCO never tried to see the situation from the enemy's point of view. There appears to have been no effort to draw up an intelligence appreciation of the threat to the Falklands from an *Argentine perspective*.

Any such appreciation would have highlighted two crucial changes in the situation by 1982: the Argentines had lost faith in negotiations with Britain to regain sovereignty; and second, Buenos Aires believed Britain had clearly signalled her intention to disengage from the Falkland Islands. The islanders were no longer full British citizens, and the Royal Navy's guard ship was being scrapped without replacement. These were clear messages from the Argentine point of view. At this juncture, any normal government with a territorial claim might then have attempted to woo the islanders, invested money, begun a charm offensive and slowly smothered the suspicious and stubborn Kelpers with all the economic benefits that would flow from closer integration with the mainland of South America.

General Galtieri's junta was not a normal government, however, as the Foreign Office was only too fond of pointing out. No one needed to be an expert on Argentina to see that. The junta was a nationalist, authoritarian regime in desperate economic trouble at home and looking for some way to divert its discontented citizens from their domestic grievances. In the circumstances of 1982, the chance of such a group of politically desperate South American generals embarking on a long-term, politically sophisticated and expensive way of getting what they wanted was effectively zero. To think otherwise flies in the face of experience and logic.

Unlike many other critical intelligence judgements, this is not hindsight. It was as obvious then as it is now. The junta's defects were there for all to see, but the voice of reason appears not to have factored this common-sense judgement into any of the JIC or other British assessments made at the time, by diplomats, intelligence officers or, most damning of all, by those who claimed to be the real experts on foreign countries in general and Argentina in particular, and who effectively ran the various UK intelligence committees: the Foreign and Commonwealth Office.

The indictment gets worse. Even if the Foreign Office missed the significance of the junta's waning freedom of action before February 1982, they were given a warning served on a plate when Señor Davidoff and his team of muscular young men with short haircuts marched in step up the beach at South Georgia to begin their work as 'scrap merchants' in March 1982. If ever there was a litmus test of British resolve, this was it. The landing, which almost certainly had naval connivance and pre-planning, caught the Argentine national imagination. The British, on the other hand, first vacillated and then exacerbated the situation by sending in HMS *Endurance*, a guard ship woefully ill-equipped should force ever have to be used. No ultimatum was sent to General Galtieri, and British diplomats adopted an air of only mild indignation at the United Nations.

The reason was simple: there were no indications of an invasion of the *Falkland Islands*, as the British saw it, and the FCO was going to advise nothing that might make the Argentines even more bellicose or cost the British taxpayer money. It was the economics of appeasement. The only credible military deterrent would have been a regular submarine patrol lurking off the Falklands, the one threat to which the Argentines had no answer. Expensive though this would have been, it might have bought time for the politicians and avoided Britain's bluff being so humiliatingly called.

None of this explains the extraordinary passivity and inertia in Whitehall before March 1982. It really was an extraordinary collective psychological failure. The only rational explanation seems to be our old friend 'cognitive dissonance'. It could not be happening; it did not fit with Whitehall's world view or the FCO's increasingly wayward script. It was a kind of 'defensive avoidance' of an unpleasant reality. By the end, the British appeared to have no policy for the Falklands other than to hope and pray. In that situation the last thing an institution or an individual wants to hear is that something very nasty *is* going to happen. This may account, in part, for the failure to gather intelligence on Argentina and to ignore sound policy options to defend British interests if need be. Like some patient who suspects he might have terminal cancer, the last thing Whitehall appears to have wanted was an accurate diagnosis confirming its worst fears. This may explain the collective denial of an unpleasant reality in 1982. Once again, the British ability to see a set of facts and deny not just their meaning *but their very existence* played them false.

Self-deception based on poorly interpreted or ignored intelligence was not confined to the British, however. Argentina's capacity for self-deception was in some ways even worse. Despite crude journalistic attempts to portray the junta only as a group of unthinking nationalists, there is ample evidence that there was a calculated strategy behind their actions and a clear attempt to increase tension as part of a policy to put pressure on the British government and test its resolve. The junta may not, in fact, have had much choice, becoming in Richard Lebow's phrase 'prisoners of national passions they themselves had helped to arouse'. Once having embarked upon their course, however, they had no way to go but forward. Backing down would have meant near-certain political disaster. Last week's triumph in the Plaza de Mayo could easily revert to last month's anti-junta riots. Taking the Falklands back for Argentina meant national unity and more political legitimacy. Just like the British, General Galtieri and his colleagues had a vested interest in misunderstanding the other side's intentions. Galtieri admitted as much later: 'I'll tell you, that though an English [*sic*] reaction [like the Task Force] was a possibility, the Junta did not see it as at all probable. Personally I judged it hardly possible and totally improbable.'

Galtieri had good reason to believe as he did. Britain's real views were unknown to him but her actions spoke volumes: Britain wanted to be rid of the Falklands problem once and for all. *The Times*'s correspondent in Buenos Aires reported that Argentine officials believed that the British failure to respond to the Argentine provocations in March 1982 was a clear signal that they wanted no more to do with the problem. In this regard, British passivity and inaction encouraged the junta to invade.

The general was also encouraged in his course of action by universal professional opinion that the British could not retake the Falklands once they had been occupied. US admirals openly briefed correspondents that the British Task Force would be 'too weak, too small and too far from home to achieve its objective'. Above all, the received wisdom was that the Task Force lacked sufficient air power. If professional naval opinion was united in this view across the world, then Galtieri may be forgiven for thinking he could win.

After the war, there was confirmation of this particular viewpoint from an unlikely source. During the Cold War, Britain maintained a discreet and highly sensitive official liaison with the Soviet Army. In July 1982, a Soviet general quietly requested an exchange of intelligence on any subject of importance with his British counterparts. Slightly stunned, the UK military officer agreed and, after checking with an equally surprised MOD, a British officer asked the Russian a searching question on the top technical intelligence priority of the time. The Russian officer nodded, thought hard and then gave a brief but – as it was later confirmed – entirely honest answer about the secret capabilities of certain Soviet equipment. When he had finished, he turned to the British officer: 'Now, Tovarich, it is time for my question from MOD Moscow: how the hell did your Task Force *really* manage to retake the Falklands? Where do you secretly train your professional sergeants?'

General Galtieri's final intelligence miscalculation was a fascinating mirror image of his own position as a leader. Prudence suggests that an adversary faced with national humiliation and loss of office will do at least as much as you will. A proper analysis of their adversary would have told the junta that the odds were that the bellicose British in their pubs and bars would want to fight, even if the more delicate souls of their Foreign Office did not; and an elected leader who failed to reflect the popular mood and regain national honour would soon find herself out of a job and disgraced. The junta's misunderstanding of both the British character and its innate aggression was profound. Their intelligence services failed to brief them on either the British character or the implications for Britain's other colonial territories around the world – Gibraltar, Honduras and Belize among them – if an invasion of the Falklands went unchecked. There were, therefore, solid reasons, obvious to any Argentine intelligence 'Brit-watcher', why it was highly likely that Britain would meet force with force. The Argentine junta should have had this made clear to them. Mrs Thatcher was not the only leader let down badly by her intelligence services.

For the intelligence analyst there is something both frustrating and depressing about the Falklands War. There were ample indicators, but they were ignored. Everyone who was present in Whitehall at the time knew it was a war that should never have happened. Equally, there was genuine delight in the triumph of British arms. In particular, the Royal Navy had saved not just their reputation but their very existence. (Ironically, if Argentina had invaded a year later, the Task Force could never have been assembled. The ships would have been sold off.) Whatever the Franks Report said, however, the intelligence community knew the truth: Argentina was regarded as a backwater in the Cold War and had been ignored. Few intelligence officers specialized in Spanish or Rest of the World (ROW) targets. The Soviet Union was the main target.

The lessons of the Falklands War were many. Sailors learned that cheap plastic wiring in ships and cheap plastic trousers on men can be deadly as fire boils through a stricken ship. Intelligence officers learned that going to war with hastily photocopied pages taken from *Jane's Fighting Ships* and copies of private air-spotters' collections as the only current source of decent photographs of military aircraft taking off from obscure Argentine airfields is no substitute for up-to-date intelligence. The Defence Intelligence Staff learned that electronic warfare details of *allied* missiles – the pulse repetition frequencies (PRF) of the French Exocet anti-ship missile, for example – are every bit as vital as those of Soviet missiles, and often harder to obtain. Above all, Whitehall learned that Britain's National Intelligence Estimate cannot be entrusted to the ministry with the most interest in discounting intelligence that does not accord with its own policy advice to ministers. One of the first casualties of the war was the FCO's permanent chairmanship of the JIC. The Franks Report made sure that from 1983 on, the JIC became the responsibility of an Intelligence Co-ordinator working with an independent assessment staff; the FCO was now merely one of the members of the Current Intelligence Groups.

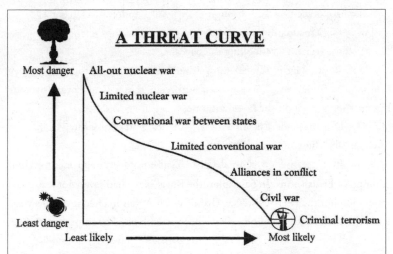

Fig. 3   The Threat Curve shows that the most dangerous threat (e.g., nuclear war) is usually the least likely. Terrorism is much more likely but poses fewer dangers to the state. The difficult judgment is usually halfway up the ladder – the Falklands War 1982 being the classic example. NATO's attack on Serbia and Kosovo in 1999 shows how easily limited military actions risk escalating into general war.

The most valuable lesson of all was the 'curve of probability' or Threat Curve (see fig. 3), a graph which suddenly began to appear on the walls of intelligence offices all over NATO in the mid-1980s. The graph demonstrated the relationship between the most dangerous and the most likely intelligence threats to even the most obdurate policymaker; and the Falklands War had occurred at the precise crossover point. Intelligence requirements were in future to be tailored to *probable risks* and not just the worst case. Attending the funerals of the dead British servicemen, Her Majesty's Government suddenly realized that there were other dangers in the world besides the Soviet Union. 'Out of area' conflicts quickly became a fashionable study at staff colleges all over the world.

The final word on the Falklands deserves to be given to the FCO, a much-maligned body of men and women among their euphoric colleagues in the British armed services after the war. As the Royal Marines and the Paras of the victory parade marched through the City of London in October 1982, an aspiring FCO mandarin leaned across to a member of the Defence Intelligence Staff on the balcony overlooking the pageant.

'You know, Harry, this all shows the results of letting some desperately unpopular tinpot autocrat use a crazy foreign military adventure to court popularity and get off the hook at home.'

The DIS man nodded knowingly, 'Charles, you're absolutely right. Yes, Galtieri and the junta really blew it.'

The FCO man snorted in disgust. 'Galtieri? Harry, I'm talking about Margaret Thatcher!'

12

'IF KUWAIT GREW CARROTS, WE WOULDN'T GIVE A DAMN' – THE GULF, 1991

'Iraqis will never forget that on 8 August 1990 Kuwait became part of Iraq legally, constitutionally and actually. It continued to do so until last night, when we were forced to withdraw'

SADDAM HUSSEIN

If the Gulf War was not an intelligence blunder, then it most certainly came as a rude surprise. As Saddam Hussein's Iraqi army poured into the tiny independent oil state of Kuwait at the head of the Persian Gulf on 2 August 1990, the reaction of journalists and intelligence officers around the world was the same: 'I don't believe it!' Once the shock had worn off, the second reaction of the Western intelligence community was equally universal: 'Mind you, with an army Iraq's size… '

What the invasion of Kuwait demonstrates perhaps more clearly than any other recent example of an intelligence failure is the clear distinction between *capabilities* and *intentions* in assessing intelligence. For if ever a nation had an obvious, ready-to-use military capability in 1990, it was Iraq. Iraq possessed an army with 5,000 tanks, 7,000 armoured infantry vehicles and 3,500 artillery pieces. There were up to a million Iraqi men under arms, *ten times* the size of the British Army. Iraq had more battlefield *helicopters* than the RAF and the British Army Air Corps had aircraft combined. It was an awesome military capability. The intelligence problem about Iraq in 1990 was really therefore quite straightforward. What would Saddam Hussein, a dictator with the fourth biggest army in the world, do next? The intelligence requirement was that most difficult, dangerous and ephemeral of all intelligence requirements: what were Saddam's intentions?

The task for the intelligence analysts and the country experts was to be able to put themselves into Saddam's mind. The only way this can be done is either by being able to see Saddam's secret orders or by recruiting an unimpeachable source as close to the Iraqi president as can be risked. It was a tall order, but it was essential.

Since Vietnam, the US intelligence community has led the world in collecting intelligence. The ability of the US national agencies, and their allies, to *collect* information is awesome. From satellites overhead to the Mark 1 eyeball on the ground, the US intelligence community collected everything it could on potential enemies, which until 1993 invariably meant the Soviet Union and the Communist Bloc. In the process they collated an intelligence database of encyclopedic proportions. In fact, the US Strategic Air Command's secret target list was even known as the 'BE': the 'Bombing Encyclopedia'.

The most influential and eagerly awaited publication of the late 1980s for the Western intelligence community was a document called *Soviet Military Power*, a glossy red handbook published every year by the US Department of Defense's Defense Intelligence Agency (DIA). For the intelligence expert, this document (which fell in classification over the years until eventually it became an unclassified book given free to journalists as part of Washington's public relations exercises) was an absolute feast of good things: pictures from space of new surface-to-surface missiles being rolled out of a secret hangar deep in the Siberian *taiga*; close-up snapshots of the latest Soviet tank leaving the factory; grainy photographs of some unknown attack helicopter turning over a distant airfield; even a pin-sharp long-lens shot of a sophisticated new – purpose unknown – radar antenna sticking out of the top of the fin on a Red Banner Fleet nuclear submarine which had never been seen before. It was all there, with charts, comparative tables and estimated performance figures. *Soviet Military Power* was an Order of Battle and Equipment (OOB&E) intelligence analyst's dream, and the genuine excitement at the arrival of the DIA travelling circus to brief the latest intelligence to NATO senior officers and their intelligence staffs should not be underestimated.

Whatever the value of *Soviet Military Power*, its arrival was not always met with unalloyed joy. Cynics, frequently from the signals intelligence community, would sometimes ask the question 'Do you have any new information on Soviet *intentions*?' of the visiting US briefer, who would then look hurt and mumble something about it not being his agency's responsibility, and anyway who could tell? The excited audience would then stare, irritated, at the questioner and the session would proceed, but the damage had been done, the bubble pricked. The truth is that *intentions* are always the real intelligence challenge. The invasion of Afghanistan in 1979, the near invasion of Poland in 1981, the collapse of communism in 1989–92 and the rape of Kuwait in 1990 all took the intelligence community completely by surprise, despite the vast sums of taxpayers' money spent on intelligence equipment and resources and the highly trained staff needed to operate them.

The problem of divining intentions is both a cultural and a practical one. The cultural problem is embedded deep in our modern psyche as a particular way of looking at the world. In order to be dealt with, a problem has to have three distinct phases. First, *identification* that there is a problem; second, once the problem has been identified, it has to be *measured*; and last, once we know the size of the problem, we must be able to identify the *solutions* needed to end it. The key to this materialist logic is the measurement of the problem: quantification. It pervades all our lives and has even extended into the humanities, where computers can now struggle to analyse the rhythms of Shakespeare. In Tom Wolfe's despairing cry, 'Goddammit! They've even started to put literature into a white coat!'

There is an important link here with the intelligence world. The modern world runs on scientific method – it can measure problems. It has to, in order to solve them. The *tangible* is given greater value than the *intangible*. A fact can be measured, proved, prodded, demonstrated. Intangibles are harder; by and large, they cannot be exhibited or put on an overhead vufoil at a management meeting.

Human nature being what it is, organizations and individuals tend to do that which is easiest and can be most clearly demonstrated. For example, the sales executive who mutters to his chairman that he *thinks* that blue cars will sell better than red cars next year had better be able to prove it if he wants to keep his job. Hunches count for little. If he can say, 'I've guessed right eighteen times in the last twenty years, boss; that's a 90 per cent track record,' then the hunch has been *quantified*; it is a *fact*. The chairman beams: these are 'good numbers'.

Thus it is in the world of intelligence. It is relatively easy to count tanks, ships and aircraft. The technical problems may be immense, the expense horrendous, but it can be done, given time, resources and technology. It is much harder to assess intentions. They cannot be measured. A politician or diplomat may say one thing at a cocktail party but change his mind next morning. Intentions rest on the shifting sands of the human psyche with all its inconsistencies and frailties. For example, the whole course of world history could have been altered if Adolf Hitler had answered 'Nein' in response to the question from his Chief of the General Staff 'Do we proceed, mein Führer?' on 31 August 1939. Intentions are to the intelligence world as 'fuzzy logic' is to mathematics.

Not only are intentions difficult to assess, requiring, as they do, access, risk and expense (and even then there is no guarantee that they will be cost-effective, as they are unquantifiable), but intentions also defy *measurement*. In Berlin at the height of the Cold War, some agencies tried to measure their intelligence officers' effectiveness by the number of low-level agents they recruited. So an agent handler running twenty agents, each making five reports a month from the East, whatever their quality, was more highly valued than an agent-handler with only one source, who never reported at all but had access to the East German government's intentions should a war ever seem likely. It is difficult to put a value on such a *potential* human intelligence source. In the circumstances, it is hardly surprising that hard-nosed intelligence agency managers and their budget-holders find intelligence capabilities much easier to deal with than intentions. Humint is not only difficult to measure; there are no guarantees of success either.

The second problem about humint is essentially a practical one: it is very hard to do successfully. To consider just one example, from the James Bond end of the intelligence spectrum, the Gordievsky case. Oleg Gordievsky was a career KGB officer who was recruited by the British SIS (MI6) and run as an agent in place for six years. The risks both to Gordievsky and to his handlers were horrific. At any time he could have been discovered and executed. The value of the information he had was incalculable and may even have helped to end the Cold War more quickly than might otherwise have happened. When Gordievsky came under suspicion, his KGB tails dogged his every step, and extracting him quite literally under the noses of his Soviet watchers ranks as one of the greatest 'exfiltration' secret operations ever.

At no time could the British be absolutely sure that Gordievsky was genuine and not a 'plant'. Only the passage of time has confirmed that he was, in fact, 100 per cent genuine and his intelligence equally good. As a humint operation, the Gordievsky case stands as a masterpiece of intelligence. But at what cost? How many similar operations were unsuccessful? Yet even if the Gordievsky case was only one of a hundred, the 1 per cent success rate turned out to be worth it in the end. The lesson is that humint is not only difficult to measure, but it is difficult to do. Confronted by a minister demanding 'Will it work?' the intelligence officer can only shrug and reply truthfully, 'We certainly hope so, minister.'

All intelligence bureaucracies – certainly the accountable ones – will instinctively veer towards the quantifiable and the easy, especially when results are hard to prove. Saddam Hussein and his invasion of Kuwait proved just how short-sighted this very understandable professional bias can be. Despite the most sophisticated intelligence systems in the world, the USA and her major allies were caught by surprise by the invasion. The real reason was that they lacked humint – agents in place to alert them to Saddam's intentions. If there had been an Iraqi Gordievsky sitting at Saddam Hussein's shoulder in the ruling Revolutionary Command Council, then the West might have been forewarned and Kuwait saved without the expense of the Gulf War. But there was no Iraqi Gordievsky, and no really good humint on Saddam's intentions.

Lack of intelligence was only half the problem in the Gulf in 1990. The other half of the equation was the personality and actions of Iraq's ruler, Saddam Hussein. From the start of the war between Iran and Iraq in the early 1980s, the West consistently underestimated the danger Saddam Hussein posed to the stability of the region. Attention centred on the new revolutionary regime in Iran, controlled since the overthrow of the Shah by a theocratic Shi'ite Islamic government headed by the fanatical Ayatollah Khomeini.

The new Iranian regime had engaged US foreign policy attentions from the start by invading the US Embassy in Tehran and taking its staff hostage. The disaster of Operation Eagle Claw, a bungled US rescue attempt that was aborted after a series of accidents, meant that President Carter's personal agony over Iran was only relieved by Ronald Reagan's election in 1980. President Reagan, in his turn, found Revolutionary Iran his major foreign policy preoccupation after the challenge of the Soviet Union. It was a preoccupation that led to the Iran-Contra scandal, via an obscure National Security Committee US Marine lieutenant colonel called Oliver North and secret arms shipments to right-wing Nicaraguan 'Contra' guerrillas as a means of freeing Iranian-controlled US hostages. It was all very messy and complicated and Iran remained intractably at the heart of the problem.

In this atmosphere of instability and Islamic fervour that threatened the conventions of international diplomacy, Iraq's decision to invade Revolutionary Iran in 1980 came as an unequivocal blessing to Western diplomats. The 'mad mullahs' and their 'revolutionary hordes' could beat themselves to death against Iraq's plentiful tanks and guns. With Iran locked in a bitter struggle with Iraq, stability of a kind returned for the next eight years as the two most powerful states in the region grappled themselves to exhaustion. In fact, Western analysts could view Iraq's war with Iran as being in the interests of the West and performing a service for the West's small oil-rich friends around the Persian Gulf. Saddam Hussein was doing the West a favour.

Saddam Hussein al-Takriti was an unlikely ally of the West. Born in Takrit in northern Iraq, he was raised in the hard world of the mountains and the mafia-like warlords and family clans that control them. Guns are as essential to a man in Takrit as a smallsword to an eighteenth-century gentleman, and it is alleged that Saddam had shot and killed his first man by the age of eleven. Saddam's subsequent rise through the ranks of Iraq's Arab Ba'ath Socialist Party owed more to ambition and force than to deep political convictions. Power meant more to Saddam than Arab unity, freedom and socialism. By 1970 he was vice president and by 1979 he had become president, taking over from the figurehead President Bakr in a bloodless transfer that recognized where power really lay in Iraq.

Saddam had no deep antagonism towards Iran. Indeed, in 1975 he had concluded a treaty personally with the Shah that removed many of the grievances between the two countries over the Shatt al-Arab estuary at the head of the Gulf. But Khomeini's revolution altered the status quo. Two events in particular stung Saddam into attacking Iran: an Iranian-inspired assassination attempt on his deputy, Tariq Aziz, in the heart of Baghdad; and second, Khomeini's unremitting call to Iraq's Shi'ite majority to rise up against the 'godless atheists' of the Ba'ath Socialist Party. Saddam dared not tolerate this direct challenge to his regime and struck back hard. In 1980 he invaded Iran with half the Iraqi Army in what was effectively a limited punitive expedition across the border against a confused and weakened neighbour.

One of the consistent themes of new revolutionary regimes is their reluctance to mind their own business. From Revolutionary France to Bolshevik Russia and Khomeini's Iran, the urge to spread the good news to nervous neighbours appears to be irresistible. An equally consistent theme is the angry neighbours' resentment and invariable reaction – to attack the source of trouble to stop it exporting its dangerous heresies. So it was with Saddam's first Gulf War in 1980. Although he stopped his forces five days into Iran and called for talks, the Iranians did not share his restraint. To cries of 'Allahu Akbar', the Islamic Revolutionary Guards of Khomeini's Iran hurled themselves upon the godless Iraqi invaders. Saddam's evil genie would not go back in the bottle.

By 1988, after an eight-year war that claimed over one and a half million casualties and saw the use of poison gas on a major scale for the first time since 1918, both sides signed a ceasefire of exhaustion. Saddam was now confronted by the task of reconstructing Iraq after a war longer than both of the century's world wars. Despite the general view that Iraq had won (Khomeini described the ceasefire as 'a poisoned chalice from which he reluctantly drank'), the euphoria of victory could not last. Although the gloom in Tehran was matched by dancing in the streets of Baghdad, the Iraqi economy was in ruins. Experts reckoned that it would cost $230 *billion* (at 1989 prices) and take fifteen to twenty years to rebuild Iraq to pre-1980 standard. The annual budget deficit was $10 billion and Iraq owed over $75 billion in foreign debt, much of it to Saudia Arabia and Kuwait. After his war, Saddam confronted an economic catastrophe.

The obvious priority was to wipe out the foreign debt and demobilize an army swollen by war. The 1980 class of eighteen-year-old conscripts were twenty-six when the war ended – if they had survived. Yet few of them were demobilized after the war because Iran initially refused to sign a peace treaty. All Saddam's attempts to salvage his position failed in the eighteen months after the first Gulf War. The flood of demobilized soldiers on to an already destabilized economy raised unemployment and further weakened Iraq's recovery. Iran stalled for time at the UN peace talks, forcing Iraq to keep a large army on alert which continued the drain on the nation's economic resources.

To make matters worse, Saddam's attempts to bully the other Arab states of the region into cancelling the Iraqi war debt fell on unsympathetic ears, despite his claims that Iraq had been fighting the Khomeini regime to protect all his Gulf neighbours from Shi'ite fundamentalism. Saddam's neighbours were having none of it and insisted on full repayment. He raised the stakes in early 1990, demanding not just cancellation of Iraq's debt to his oil-rich neighbours but also ready cash by means of an immediate injection of $30 billion. To these demands for aid, he also added a new, more menacing note: 'Let the Gulf regimes know that if they do not give this money, Iraq knows how to get it.'

These threats and demands were matched by a parallel drive by Iraq to cut back the overall production of oil in the Middle East. The point of this was to *increase* the world price of oil. The basic laws of supply and demand meant quite simply that if there was less oil available to Western buyers then the price of oil would go up; and if the price of oil increased, then Iraq, as a major producer-member of the Organization of Petroleum Exporting Countries (OPEC), stood to make a lot of money. Oil revenues were virtually Iraq's only source of income.

After the 1980–88 war, both Iraq and Iran had, as members of OPEC, demanded that their fellow members should reduce production in order to enable the two nations to recoup their war costs by selling more oil. The other OPEC members refused. Far worse, the United Arab Emirates (UAE) and Kuwait actually began to push the price of oil *down* by increasing their own production, thus choking off any hope of additional oil revenues to Iraq.

At the time, no intelligence analyst seems to have been able to identify just what a mortal threat this combination of dissatisfaction at home, bankruptcy abroad and non-co-operation from his neighbours posed to Saddam Hussein. Uneasy lies the head that wears the crown in the tense intrigues of Baghdad politics. He knew that his very survival as leader of Iraq was at stake unless he could deliver economic recovery after the war. In the circumstances, it seems hardly surprising that he began to take a tough line with, as he saw it, his tight-fisted and intransigent neighbours.

What is surprising is that the risks to regional stability were not taken more seriously at the time. After all, Iraq was a nation in arms at the end of the war with Iran. By 1990, Iraq was still a nation in arms, but now in dire economic straits with a burning sense of grievance and an increasingly paranoic dictator making the decisions. The situation posed a potentially explosive challenge to the ordered complacency of the area's rich oil-producing sheikhdoms. If the Gulf States were in any doubt about the seriousness of Iraqi intentions, the Arab summit in Baghdad in May 1990 should have made Saddam's position abundantly clear. He told his guests that 'for every single dollar off the price of a barrel of oil… Iraq loses a *billion* dollars a year'. He called for an OPEC adjustment to increase the price to $25 a barrel. When his plea failed to elicit a response, Saddam resorted to threats. In his view, the earlier decision by Kuwait and the United Arab Emirates to increase their own oil production and so drive down the price was a violation of quota agreements and in effect a declaration of economic war on Iraq. To ensure that there could be no possible misunderstanding, Saddam added that, 'War is fought with soldiers… but it is also done with economic means. Therefore we would ask our Arab brothers who do not wish to make war on Iraq – this is in fact a kind of war against Iraq. I believe our brothers are fully aware of our situation… but we have now reached the stage where we can no longer withstand this pressure.'

Now this was a serious *cri de coeur* from a dictator who was mindful of loss of face and his public image, and a clear warning about his views and his likely course of action. Although the statement was made behind closed doors, it soon leaked out to Western diplomats and Iraq-watchers. Saddam's concerns were being signalled very clearly to a wider audience, and no intelligence analysts could later honestly claim that they were unaware of Saddam's intentions should he not be given satisfaction.

The response of the Gulf States, especially the United Arab Emirates and Kuwait, to Saddam's admission of weakness and thinly veiled threat was effectively to ignore it; they neither declared a moratorium on Iraq's debts and gave Saddam more money, nor did they cut their own oil production. In defiance of the OPEC guidelines, they increased it. As a result, the price of oil actually fell further.

Saddam's anger and frustration showed. In June 1990, he denounced the UAE and Kuwait as members of 'a conspiracy against the region which serves Israel's interests'. The mention of Israel was significant and ominous. Saddam was running up a flag designed to unite his 'Arab brothers' against other Arabs. Just as 'patriotism is the last refuge of a scoundrel' in Dr Johnson's famous dictum, so any Arab call to rally against Israel is usually a prelude to bellicosity in one form or another, especially as Saddam had already shown considerable pragmatism by doing business with Israel during the war with Iran. At a time when he was in increasingly dire straits, Saddam was beginning to make warlike noises.

To add to his troubles, by the middle of 1990 Saddam was under serious pressure not just from his debts and regional difficulties, but also from a growing dispute with the West. Although Iraq had long enjoyed a special relationship with France – who, with the Soviet Union, had been a major supplier of arms – other Western nations had always been lukewarm supporters. Once the Gulf War was over, their support for the Iraqi regime faded with their need to contain Revolutionary Iran; Khomeini's debilitated regime posed little threat to anyone by 1989. Iraq's record as an oppressive dictatorship suddenly became much more of an issue, and the reality of Saddam's totalitarian regime was not an appetizing prospect to the more delicate democratic palates of the West.

Britain in particular had cause for complaint. An Iranian-born British citizen, a journalist called Farzad Bazoft, was arrested and executed for espionage in the spring of 1990. Bazoft, a journalist for a London weekly, had been caught sniffing around a secret Iraqi rocket development complex. Quite what his true purpose was, and whether he was indeed a secret agent for someone as the Iraqis claim, remains unclear to this day. With a contemptuous disregard for Bazoft's passport or background, Saddam ordered his execution as a signal to any other would-be spies or traitors in Iraq. As a gesture to cow internal opposition, Bazoft's execution may well have worked; as a message to international public opinion it was a public relations disaster.

Saddam's timing was particularly poor as the Western media were already alert to Iraq as a story. A ballistics expert called Dr Gerald Bull had been assassinated in mysterious circumstances by unknown killers in Brussels. As Bull was the world's leading expert on long-range artillery and was building a so-called 'supergun' for Iraq when he was killed, the case aroused intense interest, especially as the dirty tricks department of Israel's Secret Service, the Mossad, was blamed for his murder. At the same time, batches of high-quality machined steel tubes, almost certainly part of Iraq's new supergun, were impounded in the West.

To further attract the attention of Western investigative journalists, a mysterious consignment of electronic components alleged to be part of a nuclear initiation device was impounded at London Airport en route to Baghdad. Taken with the supergun affair it now looked as if Iraq was bent on rearming with new and deadly weapons which threatened the whole of the Middle East. As a result, by mid-1990 Iraq was fully in the Western media spotlight with a steady focus of damaging press stories on Iraq's poor record of human rights and attempts to rearm with weapons of mass destruction, and Saddam was not enjoying the criticism. Suddenly he was the 'man in the black hat' to the Western media, never noted at the best of times for sophistication in applying easy labels to complicated subjects. To Iranian enmity and the Gulf's contempt were now added Western hostility and personal criticism.

Israeli hostility could be taken for granted in Iraqi eyes. Ever since the successful Israeli precision bombing to neutralize Iraq's Osirak plutonium-producing reactor in 1981, Iraq had regarded Israel as little more than a temporarily quiescent enemy. It now appears that, to add to his troubles, Saddam had decided that Israel was conspiring to attack an enfeebled Iraq in the aftermath of the war with Iran. We now know that Saddam believed that any Israeli attack would end up with his own fall from power. We also know from Iraqi sources that the example of the Romanian dictator Nicolae Ceauşescu (who had recently been captured, tried and summarily executed with his wife) was at the forefront of Saddam's mind at this time.

Saddam's paranoia increased. Out of the blue, he began issuing threats against Israel accompanied by public denials that Iraq had developed nuclear weapons as the country 'already controlled a large chemical armoury'. 'But,' he added in a ringing denunciation of Israel, 'by God we will make fire eat half of Israel, should they dare attack Iraq.' Quite why Saddam thought Israel was planning to attack remains a mystery to this day. The most plausible theory is that Saddam was using the threat as a diversion from domestic problems for his own increasingly disgruntled citizens.

This fiery anti-Israeli rhetoric had two effects. Inevitably, it promptly won the backing of most of the Arab world, but it also scared the West, which began to view Saddam Hussein as an unstable warmonger. They were right, even though Saddam was not actively seeking a war. In fact he took great steps in 1990 to assure both Israel and the USA that his rhetoric was just that. 'Iraq does not want war,' he said. 'We have fought for eight long years and we know what war means.' To make sure the message had gone home, he repeated it to a visiting British diplomat.

By June 1990, the alarm bells should have been ringing very loudly among the intelligence analysts of the West with the responsibility for keeping an eye on Iraq. The evidence was clear: a well-armed and bankrupt Saddam Hussein was now making increasingly desperate threats to both his neighbours and to Israel. The threats to Israel had earned him considerable prestige in the wider Arab world, but little money. As a result, Saddam was like some new Nasser, but without the wherewithal to exercise his power to lead the Arabs. By any objective criteria the Iraqi leader was looking like a loose cannon in the Gulf region – unpredictable and dangerous. Saddam could not sustain his proud boasts and he was in trouble. The only question was what he would do next. How would he support his belligerent claims? What were his *intentions*?

The events that led to the invasion of Kuwait were clearly signposted. Iraq had long claimed ownership of her tiny southern neighbour. Since 1871, when the Ottoman Mufti, Abd Allah, had ruled Kuwait as a sub-province of Basra (Iraq's southernmost province), Baghdad had asserted her territorial rights over 'Iraq's seventeenth province'. Kuwait was rich in oil, one of the wealthiest sheikhdoms in the Gulf and almost defenceless, a tantalizing prospect to any robust heir to the Assyrian Empire. To a personality like Saddam Hussein, the temptation to solve his economic problems at a stroke must have been irresistible.

Not only did Iraq assert a claim to Kuwait, but she had tried to invade it before. In 1961, the failing government of the Iraqi leader, General Kassem, had mobilized for an invasion. Post-Imperial Britain, still with interests east of Suez, had moved to forestall the Iraqis by publicly landing marines and tanks to shore up the alarmed Kuwaiti regime. Other Arab states joined in. The show of strength worked. Deterred by the evidence of Britain's preparedness to use force, the Iraqis backed off.

For the intelligence analysts of Washington, London, Paris and Moscow, the picture about Kuwait could not have been clearer. Like some burglar intent on his next crime, Saddam Hussein had the motive, the opportunity and the means to invade Kuwait. Not only that, but his country had nearly done so before. Unless Saddam did something soon, he would be bankrupt at home and a laughing stock in the Arab world, just another self-important autocrat desperate to get his hands on his neighbour's money. Kuwait was the perfect victim for a spectacular international robbery. Saddam further helped the intelligence analysts in early summer 1990 by signalling his desperation in a string of personal attacks on Kuwait and the indifference of Kuwait's rulers, the al-Sabah family, to 'the imperialist Zionist plot poised like a dagger over Iraq's back'.

There is only so much humiliation that an Arab leader can endure, however. On 16 July 1990 came a clear sign that Saddam and his Revolutionary Command Council had had enough and were now embarking on a collision course with their uncooperative neighbours. Tariq Aziz, Iraq's Foreign Minister, accused Kuwait and the UAE of a hostile act against Iraq 'by implementing a deliberate plot to glut the oil market with a quantity of oil exceeding that permitted by OPEC'. Aziz claimed, rightly, that this had cost the Iraqi treasury $89 billion in lost revenue. Furthermore, he alleged an obvious *casus belli* by accusing Kuwait of having stolen Iraq's oil by extracting a disproportionate share of oil from the Rumaila field which straddled their common border.

At this stage, the Western intelligence community should have been thoroughly alarmed. The mystery is why they were not. Part of the problem for Western intelligence officers when evaluating the nuances of Arab intelligence is the language difficulty. Arab rhetoric bears little relationship to the clearer, more coolly worded signals pumped out from Western chanceries. In Arabic, the most blood-curdling threats are often merely linguistic expressions of various degrees of disapproval. With hyperbole a constant, it can be difficult to know precisely when an Arab threat is genuine, unless the listener is steeped in the culture. The problem for the analyst is not unlike that of the so-called Sovietologists, or Kremlin watchers, who alone could interpret the impenetrable 'party-speak' of Soviet utterances during the Cold War. For the Soviet Union, it was the language of Marxism that obscured reality and made divining truth difficult. For the Arab world, some other criterion or intelligence discriminator is equally required to separate the genuine threat from the ritual denunciation.

On this occasion, intelligence analysts failed to spot the shift in the spectrum. The intelligence alarms that should have indicated a serious danger of conflict on 16 July 1990, only seventeen days before the invasion of Kuwait, seem not to have been triggered. For some unexplained reason the evident signs of increasing Iraqi desperation were seen as just another turn of the diplomatic screw by the Iraqi leader.

They should not have been. On 15 and 16 July 1990, two divisions of the elite Iraqi Republican Guard moved south very publicly and took up battle positions in the desert twenty miles north of the Kuwaiti border. As a US NATO intelligence analyst who worked the problem non-stop from August 1990 until March 1991 later said, this was 'a bit of a hint' as to Saddam's intentions.

The very next day, Saddam himself raised the stakes still higher. Choosing the platform of a speech to the nation on the anniversary of the Ba'athist revolution, he issued a direct challenge to Kuwait and the UAE, citing Kuwait's theft of Iraqi oil, deliberate overproduction of oil as a hostile act, and, for the first time, border violations by Kuwait. This, he attested, amounted to a deliberate act of aggression. Finally, to add insult to injury, Saddam claimed that the perfidious Kuwaitis had conspired with Western and Zionist imperialists out to ruin the Arab cause. He demanded that the two 'rogue states' came to their senses immediately 'preferably by means of peace', but, should they choose not to, Saddam issued a clear warning, 'If words do not work to protect us, then we have no choice but by effective action to put things right.'

This sounds suspiciously like an ultimatum. It should have galvanized intelligence officers and policymakers to action, especially when combined with Iraq's economic plight, the movements of elite armoured divisions and Saddam's paranoia. The final key was Saddam's closing remarks, which made sure that there could be no possible misunderstanding by his listeners. He said that 'there was no time left for talking'; if Kuwait did not accede to Iraq's demands, 'it would face the consequences'.

America had, of course, spotted the troop movements. There is little in the Middle East, or anywhere else, that escapes the eagle eyes of the National Reconnaissance Office's (NRO) satellites. This, combined with the aggressive Iraqi statements, brought a clear and firm response from the Bush administration, warning Iraq that the USA would 'stand by its friends' in the region. This apparently prompt statement from the USA was not as robust as it sounded, however. It was undermined by men like Senator Daniel Moynihan, who said in a public confirmation meeting, 'You know, those Kuwaitis are really awful. They're just terrible people. I mean they are just... they didn't support us when we had the attack on the USS *Stark*. They're always going on and on saying things about their non-alignment. They're really awful.' (In May 1987, while patrolling off the coast of Saudi Arabia during the Iran-Iraq War, the US Navy frigate *Stark* had been struck by two Exocet missiles fired by an Iraqi jet. Thirty-seven USN personnel died, and the ship was badly damaged, although later repaired.)

Then, to make matters even worse, he added, 'I know how we can solve this problem. We should just divide Kuwait, give half to the Iraqis and half to the Saudis. That's what we should do. That's the way we'll solve it.'

This kind of public utterance by a senior senator muddied the waters still further: what did Washington *really* want?

This divided response made the Kuwaitis – not unnaturally – wary of Washington's real intentions. In fact, the US warnings were based on a miscalculation that Saddam did *not* mean what he had said, and Senator Moynihan did not reflect US policy; but its effect was to alarm the very people it was meant to help.

The US State Department and CIA were convinced that Saddam was bluffing and intended no action; and the by now thoroughly alarmed

Kuwaitis agreed, begging their American friends not to make any aggressive statements 'because they risked inflaming the situation'. Saddam was only using threats as a bargaining counter, claimed the Kuwaitis, and anyway (in a chilling reminder of so many intelligence blunders) they had been here before. Saddam Hussein had made similar threats in the past. There was 'no cause for alarm and the USA should refrain from making a difficult situation worse'. The Kuwaitis were wrong in one respect, however. Saddam had indeed made similar statements in the past, but then they had always been in Arab councils, behind closed doors. He had never before made threats like this in public. Given his precarious position as the self-proclaimed leader of the anti-Zionist Arabs, he now had much to lose should he fail to back his words with deeds, particularly at home.

America modified its own public statements to reflect Kuwait's concerns, but its internal actions show that not everyone in the US intelligence and policy-making community was convinced. By 24/25 July 1990, the US administration began to have serious doubts as to whether Saddam was merely 'sabre-rattling', as he assured a concerned President Mubarak of Egypt. US KC-135 tanker refuelling aircraft began to deploy to the Gulf and a major joint exercise was announced, much to the concern of the Kuwaitis. There were alarming reports in the Baghdad press about 'foreign troops intervening in the region'. For Kuwait, 'foreign troops' could mean two different things – US or Iraqi. They wanted *neither* and urged discretion upon Washington.

Looking back on the events of the last two weeks of July 1990, it is clear how the situation accelerated. Somewhere along the line, Saddam Hussein took the decision to begin the invasion process, but it is difficult to see precisely when. A good human source within the Revolutionary Command Council would have been useful at this point. Conspiracy theories about a long-standing Iraqi plan to seize Kuwait do not hold water. Iraq had always had a long-standing wish to get its hands on Kuwait and its oil, and an equally long-standing *capability* to do so – indeed, Iraq had a permanent military capability to take Kuwait. The intention to act was always the key to any action. That final decision cannot have been long in the making. What is clear is that Iraq was obviously sabre-rattling on 15/16 July. By 25 July, Saddam had decided to invade and the sabre was well out of the scabbard.

Two questions stand out for the intelligence analyst: could Iraq have been deterred; and second, what pushed Saddam Hussein from mere threats to risk-taking action? It is clear that the first intelligence indicators that trouble was really brewing occur in about May 1990, when Saddam began his verbal campaign against the UAE and Kuwait over the price of oil. Of course this is being clever after the event, and common sense tells us that no country risks a crisis on the strength of a few utterances by a boastful and bankrupt neighbour, even one ruled by a paranoiac dictator. Any reasonable assessment at the time would have given Saddam the benefit of the doubt, in the light of his predicament.

However, these preliminary indicators were subsequently reinforced by a steady drumbeat of aggressive statements and escalating demands. Somewhere between late May and July 1990, the isolated intelligence indicators turned from one or two alarms to dozens of threatening signals. A distinct pattern emerged on the indicators and warning boards of the Western intelligence agencies. Between May and July 1990, someone should have moved to deter Saddam from going too far.

The problem of deterring Saddam, even assuming that Western intelligence assessed an attack on Kuwait as a distinct probability, subsequently became mired in diplomatic ambiguity, with the USA trying to stand firm and yet at the same time weakening its tough stance by issuing curiously contradictory 'clarifications'. For example, when the US moved KC-135 tanker aircraft and ships to the Gulf on 21 July 'to lay down a marker for Saddam Hussein', in the words of the Pentagon, an aide to the Secretary to the Navy rushed to 'clarify the situation' by telling the press that the ships were *not* on alert. On 24 July, when the Pentagon stated that the 'US was committed to… supporting the self-defence of our friends in the Gulf', officials specifically refused to confirm whether the US would go to Kuwait's aid if Kuwait were attacked. This was news management gone mad. The spin doctors' 'clarifications' were damaging, not enhancing, the diplomatic signals.

This was confusing stuff. Was the US backing Kuwait in July 1990 or not? If, several years later, it is still not clear to us, then it was most certainly not clear to the Iraqis at the time. Several days after the Iraqi invasion, the *Washington Post* actually ran an inside-page story, 'Who gave the green light?' They recalled Senator Moynihan's remarks made on 25 July, during which he talked about dividing Kuwait between Iraq and Saudi Arabia. Even Washington was confused. 'Even though the CIA had changed their assessment, there were others who still said an invasion was ridiculous.'

They were confused. Was this the famous ambiguity inherent in US deterrence theory – the final uncertainty designed to make an aggressor pause and reconsider? Or was it mere window dressing, supporting the Kuwaitis with soft words but no deeds? What were President Bush's real intentions? On 25 July, a doubtless puzzled Saddam Hussein decided to find out. He suddenly sent for the US Ambassador to Baghdad at one hour's notice in order to discover just what the USA was up to. The ambassador, April Glaspie, had at last achieved the much sought-after diplomatic goal that had eluded her for the previous two years: a one-on-one meeting with the Iraqi dictator.

Every meeting has its chemistry and its psychology. Unpalatable as it may be to Western liberals, feminists or intellectuals, to send a female ambassador to an Arab country is always a calculated risk. In a culture where only men control power and events, and 'strong' men are much praised, female plenipotentiaries are always at a disadvantage unless they themselves can demonstrate that they are unusually powerful figures or are capable of wielding power forcefully. Political correctness may well humour the faculties of provincial universities, but does not necessarily play well with Arab potentates. One of the lessons diplomats learn or should learn very early in their careers is that they have to deal with the world as they find it, not as they might wish it to be. The practice of diplomacy saps both idealism and illusion among its more successful practitioners: not every nation shares the same moral values.

Ambassador Glaspie certainly appears not to have impressed Saddam Hussein with either her or her country's resolve to defend Kuwait.

What is clear is that at such short notice the ambassador had no time to seek guidance from Washington and had to represent America's interests within the guidelines of existing State Department policies which had been laid down weeks and months previously, and which may not have been entirely relevant in such a fast-developing crisis. On that hot afternoon in Baghdad, poor intelligence assessments, dated national policy, Iraqi desperation and professional diplomatic caution came together in a fatal combination. For it is universally acknowledged that 25 July was the USA's last real opportunity at the policy-making level to deter Saddam Hussein from invading Kuwait.

Saddam began the meeting with a typically lengthy diatribe against his Arab neighbours and the United States. In particular, he laid great emphasis on Iraq's economic plight, complaining about his specific grievances one by one in great detail. He accused the USA of 'supporting Kuwait's economic war against Iraq' and then, like many insecure bullies, he began to bluster: 'If you [the USA] use pressure and force against us, then, by God, we know how to respond. We can deploy pressure and force against America, too. We cannot come all the way to the United States, but individual Arabs can, and they may reach you.' Ambassador Glaspie understood that Saddam was threatening terrorism.

The ambassador kept her cool in the face of what must have seemed typical Arab hyperbole. Her difficulty lay in separating bluster from real threats and identifying any constructive signals that the incensed Iraqi leader might offer her as negotiating points. It was a tall order for her first real meeting with a strange, angry, unstable and cunning Arab dictator. But Glaspie had her State Department guidance. Her instructions were to defuse any crisis, not add fuel to the flames of Saddam's truculence.

Glaspie attempted to calm Hussein, pointing out that there was no US hostility to Iraq and certainly no conspiracy against Iraqi interests. She emphasized that she had 'direct instructions from the president to seek better relations with Iraq'. Had the president not personally obstructed Congress's attempts (based on Iraq's dismal human rights record) to impose economic sanctions against Iraq recently? She went on to spell out the US position by saying, 'President Bush is an intelligent man. He is not going to declare an economic war against Iraq.'

The meeting had by then developed a form and rhythm that were to have serious consequences. The brooding and forceful Iraqi president had listed his grievances and made threats about what he would do if he did not get his way. April Glaspie had soothed the sulky Arab, calmed him down and made reassuring noises that there was no real problem, they all wanted to be friends. Glaspie went further. Again acting on her dated instructions from Washington, she took the line that the US understood Saddam's economic plight over oil prices, even adding that there were many in American oil-producing states with an equal interest in oil prices at more than $25 a barrel who sympathized with his point of view. Saddam allowed himself to be mollified, but added that he was still determined not to let Kuwait continue cheating on its OPEC oil quota. The US Ambassador soothed him further, adding, 'My own estimate after twenty-five years of serving in your area is that your aims should receive strong support from your brother Arabs. The issue is not associated with America,' she said. 'The USA has no opinion on inter-Arab disputes such as your border dispute with Kuwait.' In fact, Secretary of State Baker had directed 'our official [i.e. US] spokesman to reiterate this stand'.

Ambassador Glaspie then delicately counter-attacked by asking for clarification of Iraq's intentions over Kuwait, albeit posing her question 'in a spirit of friendship, not confrontation'. Now it was Saddam's turn to reassure the US Ambassador and soothe *her* fears. He assured her that his preference was for a peaceful solution to the dispute: 'We will do nothing until we meet with the Kuwaitis. When we meet and we see that there is hope, then nothing will happen.' However, he kept his options open, adding, 'If we are unable to find a solution then it will be natural that Iraq will not accept death, even though wisdom is above all things.' Arab rhetoric or genuine threat? It was for the US Ambassador to judge for herself. She was at the meeting.

Saddam Hussein then left the room, leaving the presumably bemused US Ambassador alone for thirty minutes while he talked on the telephone to President Mubarak of Egypt who was trying to mediate in the crisis. When he returned he was smiling and relaxed, and anxious to wrap up the meeting, telling Glaspie that 'there was now no problem as Kuwait and Iraq would have full bilateral talks in Jeddah within the next week'.

Whether the US Ambassador did or did not wring a promise out of Saddam Hussein not to resort to force, as she claims, is immaterial. While any meeting or conversation taken out of context can be made to seem misleading, there can be little doubt that the tone and message of the meeting in Baghdad on 25 July are clear. The fact is that, having made a grumbling and threatening complaint, Saddam had been appeased. In Lawrence Freedman's elegantly simple phrase, from Saddam's point of view, 'The USA was still offering him the hand of friendship while urging him to be good.'

No US miscalculation before the Gulf War has received anything like the same scrutiny as Ambassador Glaspie's first and only substantive audience with the Iraqi dictator. Critics claim that she gave the green light to Saddam, implying at best (and specifically stating at worst) that the USA would stay aloof from any Iraqi action in the Gulf. Needless to say, this claim was later strongly denied by the US Ambassador herself. President Bush, several years later, questioned a State Department official about whether April Glaspie 'had gotten a bum rap'. The reply was, 'Yes, she did,' and he replied, 'Yes, I sort of thought so, too.'

April Glaspie left Baghdad the day before the invasion. Everyone was aware of her leave plans; she, as all ambassadors, had requested departmental permission to be absent from post. Glaspie had with her in Baghdad her mother who had lived with her for many, many years. And whom she was bringing to Europe for some medical attention; so there was a very valid reason for Glaspie to leave Baghdad:

> From the very beginning it was pretty clear that the goal was to scapegoat April Glaspie on the grounds that she had given Saddam a green light or a yellow light or what she had said to Saddam had been interpreted as a green light or a yellow light.
>
> There were a couple things that might have given rise to this view. Her cable of her meeting with Saddam reflected far more of what Saddam said to her than what she said to Saddam. Rightly so, in diplomacy.
>
> Even Iraqi minister Tariq Aziz said that Saddam was not looking for a green light, red light or yellow light; he didn't expect that from April Glaspie, and that that had not been the purpose of the meeting.
>
> But no one should hold Glaspie responsible for Saddam's invasion of Kuwait.
>
> *John Kelly, Assistant Secretary, Near Eastern Affairs Bureau, 1989–91*

Whatever the reason, if diplomacy is about sending clear and precise signals at a time of crisis, then diplomacy failed badly that afternoon. Not only was the road from Basra to Kuwait and its oil riches now declared open, but from Saddam Hussein's perspective it looked as if the president of the United

States, the only man who could close the gate, sympathized with him and was prepared to look the other way. However one considers the outcome of the meeting, it was an intelligence and diplomatic disaster. What perhaps makes it worse is that Ambassador Glaspie appears to have misread the mood and the consequences of the meeting. Confident that the crisis in US-Iraqi relations was now over, she cabled the State Department that '[Saddam's] emphasis that he wants a peaceful settlement is surely sincere'. While Saddam may have lied to her in some unrecorded way, the transcripts of the meeting do not support that view.

However, we now know that the unfortunate Glaspie had merely been parroting the agreed State Department and US line. Accounts of what was the seminal meeting of the Gulf War differ. There are two main sources for what occurred that day: the transcript of Ambassador Glaspie's testimony to the Senate Foreign Relations Committee in Washington on 20 March 1991, and Iraq's official version of the dialogue, which has never been disputed by the US State Department. The meeting appears, rightly or wrongly, to have given Saddam Hussein the impression that if he did move against Kuwait, then the USA would not intervene in any serious way. If so, it was a disastrous miscalculation by both parties.

'The US Congress forced the US Executive Branch to say that we have no legal obligation to come to the defense of Kuwait in the event of an invasion,' Ambassador Joseph Wilson, Deputy Chief of Mission, US Embassy Baghdad, 1988–91, later confirmed.

One final chance for peace remained: the joint Iraqi-Kuwaiti talks at Jeddah in Saudi Arabia scheduled for 31 July. Although the weight of evidence is that nothing short of a total capitulation by Kuwait at the meeting could have stopped the invasion, there was still a chance of dialogue. However, the Kuwaiti approach at the meeting was incautious to say the least. If the USA was not going to stand up to Iraq, then little Kuwait was. To the astonishment of Iraq's vice president, Izzat Ibrahim, the Kuwaiti delegation offered only a token sum of cash in aid ($9 billion) as a gesture of goodwill and agreed to consider writing off their portion of the Iraqi war debt, but only on condition that Iraq withdrew its territorial claims against Kuwait for all time. Ibrahim stormed out, back to Baghdad. The Kuwaiti delegation sat back to await the next round of what was clearly going to be a long and difficult session of Arab haggling.

Within twenty-four hours, it was all too late. Despite an urgent personal call on 31 July from King Hussein of Jordan to President Bush that the 'Iraqis are very angry and really do mean business', the time for talking had run out. Only a direct American threat from the US president could have stopped Saddam, but thanks to Ambassador Glaspie the Iraqi leader would have construed that as a *change* in the US position. Even at this late stage, Kuwait was still reluctant to ask for American help for fear of incurring Arab wrath. The US was equally reluctant to intervene and risk inflaming a tense situation with 100,000 Iraqi troops deployed on Kuwait's border. Events now overtook diplomatic calculations. By the end of 2 August 1990, Kuwait had been invaded and no longer existed as an independent nation.

The intelligence paper trail in those last few days is significant as an indicator of Saddam's true intentions. Sometime between Ambassador Glaspie's meeting with him on 25 July and the Jeddah talks on 31 July, the Iraqis began to reinforce their forces in the south. They sent ammunition and logistic convoys to their forward divisions and deployed from box leaguers of armour into attack formations. In Washington, intelligence analysts immediately picked up the change in status, probably from a combination of satellite reconnaissance and signals intelligence, and alerted the White House and State Department that Iraqi force levels and capabilities were now consistent with a genuine intention to attack. The force was now 'disproportionate to the task at hand if… it is really meant as a bluff', in the words of a DIA intelligence report of 30 July. The Pentagon and DIA continued that Saddam, in their opinion, 'intends to use this force'. This stands as a clear and timely intelligence warning, by any objective standards.

The rest of the US administration, however, trusting in Ambassador Glaspie's upbeat assessment, Saddam's soothing public utterances and a genuine belief that talks could still make progress, did nothing. A French source even claimed that Washington had an impeccable intelligence indicator of Iraqi intentions. The NSA allegedly had intercepted an Iraqi diplomatic assessment that listed America's track record of 'inactivity and passivity' in the face of strong actions in the past: Cyprus 1974, the Chinese in Tibet and the Soviet Union's invasion of Afghanistan in 1979 were apparently listed as examples where the USA stood back and did nothing. There could only be one reason for Iraq to be taking such a close interest in America's track record in the face of past provocation. If this French claim is true, it was yet another important intelligence indicator of Saddam's true intentions and thinking at the time.

It was all to no avail. In the early hours of 2 August 1990, two elite Iraqi Republican Guard units crossed the border to invade Kuwait. While the Soviet-supplied tanks of the Medina and Hammurabi Divisions raced southwards, a simultaneous *coup de main* operation seized the oil islands of Warbah and Bubiyan and special forces units attacked key points in Kuwait City. Saddam called for victory in unequivocal language: 'O Arabs, O Muslims, O believers in God wherever you are. This is your day to rise and spread quickly in order to defend Mecca, which is captive of the spears of the Americans and the Zionists.'

Within twenty-four hours the fighting was all over. Remarkably, the Kuwaitis took three hours after the fighting started before they finally called on the USA to help, and even then qualified their call for military aid with the plea that it be kept 'confidential, so as not to inflame the situation'.

Their plea was pointless. The situation was inflamed enough already with Kuwaitis being rounded up and shot and banks being ripped open and looted. Kuwait had become an occupied province of Iraq. One glimmer of hope for the future came, however, from a most unlikely humint source. The second in command of the Saudi Arabian Military Intelligence Agency dressed up as a wandering Bedouin and early in the occupation wandered inside Kuwait for three days noting Iraqi units before returning, undetected, to his relieved superiors to give them an up-to-date and accurate report of the deployments, equipment and morale of the Iraqi army of occupation. No amount of signals intelligence or satellite reconnaissance could give the kind of insights that this old-fashioned human intelligence reporting provided. Both have their place in the collation of good information.

Just as the Israelis had failed to spot impending trouble in 1973, and the British had ignored intelligence of the Argentine build-up before the Falklands War in 1982, so the United States had been lulled by its own diplomats and political establishment into pigeon-holing solid intelligence on Iraqi capabilities and intentions in 1990. Even so, the question about the intelligence mistakes of the Gulf War is not so much *how* the Bush administration missed all the indicators, but *why*. The failure was certainly not one of intelligence collection or collation – the USA has a vast establishment for that – but of analysis and interpretation. Yet again, it seems to prove that US policy overall, and perhaps foreign policy in particular, is frequently not centrally controlled but prey to a number of competing domestic influences. These forces may have a vested interest in not acknowledging the gravity of a crisis or, indeed, in admitting that there is a crisis at all. According to the *ABC* correspondent, John Cooley, speaking in 1991:

> Strong but essentially parochial commercial interests, such as continued grain sales to Iraq and economic and banking crises at home, helped the Bush administration, plus many Congressmen and others, to turn a blind eye to the nature and the obviously aggressive goals of Saddam Hussein.

Aided by Kuwait's terror of alienating the rest of the Arab world by openly asking for US assistance, that says it all.

It seems astonishing that the military success of the Gulf War, with at least 15,000 Iraqis killed and 30,000 wounded against fewer than 1,000 coalition casualties, can be regarded in some senses a failure. The success of the military and logistics forces on the ground, the accuracy of the new smart weapons shown nightly on TV by clinical and rather smug Air Force briefing officers, gives the impression of unrelieved success. In fact, not all the pictures of smart weapons were released to the public. There is endless footage of smart bombs focusing stubbornly on obscure patches of desert, and even one – rapidly suppressed – sequence where a TV camera in the nose of a smart bomb shows a bridge, with people on it, getting ever closer. The last frame is of a terrified Iraqi civilian's face as he suddenly looks up. Then the screen goes black. The military wisely chose not to show this particular technical achievement on primetime TV. NATO's subsequent bombing mistakes in Kosovo in the 1999 war serve only to emphasize the limitations of these supposedly smart missiles.

In the middle of all this military success and technological achievement, one area, sadly, failed in several respects despite the enormous sums of money invested in it: intelligence. Had the battlefield successes not obscured this failure, we would have heard much more about the shortcomings of US and allied intelligence both before and during the war. Long before the war, from the outbreak of the revolution in Iran in 1979, the West consistently underestimated the threat that Iraq under Saddam Hussein posed to Western interests and the Gulf region. Instead of being seen correctly as just one unstable factor in a highly unstable double-sided equation, Iraq was hailed as a valuable counter-balance to Iran's brand of Shi'ite fundamentalism. The US actually secretly supported Iraq with several intelligence and training programmes.

This was a serious failure of both policy and intelligence analysis, the more so because the friends of the West in the Gulf had warned over and over again that Saddam Hussein's particular blend of tyranny, military capabilities and restless ambition were as destabilizing as anything the mad mullahs of Tehran could dream up. For some unexplained reason this advice was consistently overlooked and Saddam represented to the policymakers of the West as a force for a more stable Middle East. The various Western intelligence agencies must bear a heavy responsibility for this Pollyanna-like misrepresentation and failure of analysis, particularly in the years from 1985 to 1989.

The judgement is all the more harsh because the intelligence agencies did not miss any of the intelligence available on Iraq before the Gulf War. On the contrary, they seem to have diligently collected it all. They just failed to understand the significance of what it really represented. As one CIA officer said ruefully afterwards, 'All we needed was one goddam agent on the RCC.' Good spies giving good human intelligence on dictators' fluid intentions can be difficult to achieve. It did not take a spy in the camp to discern just what sort of unstable tyrant Saddam Hussein was; there was a wealth of real evidence already available to Western observers.

The West had a long history of less than principled support for Saddam Hussein. In 1981, despite a determined Israeli sabotage attack on the Marseilles dock shipping the vital parts, the French completed the Osirak nuclear plant in Iraq. The Israelis promptly bombed the plutonium-producing facility to the undisguised fury of the French president, François Mitterrand, and the undisguised delight of the US Carter administration which had supplied the Israeli attackers with up-to-date targeting intelligence from their satellites.

Despite this initial setback, Western military support flowed to Saddam throughout the 1980s. The French alone did $2 billion worth of business each year and sold over $5.6 billion dollars' worth of arms to assist Saddam's forces in the first Gulf war. The French were rapidly joined by the ever-greedy US arms companies. America began pumping arms into Iraq after 1982: helicopters, marine engines for warships, ammunition and spare parts. American aid grew as the war with Iran dragged on. In 1984, Congress approved the 'tilt to Iraq' and the USA took Iraq off the official list of nations sponsoring terrorism. By the mid-1980s, America was even giving free trade credits to Baghdad of half a billion dollars simply for the Iraqis to buy 150,000 tons of American rice.

The USA was not alone. Britain jumped on the commercial bandwagon of profiting out of Saddam's need for support. Up to the very moment Iraq invaded Kuwait, Britain was supplying radars, communications equipment and even – astonishingly – a nuclear development package including such dangerous toys as plutonium and thorium for nuclear reactors, to go with the jet engines, artillery fire-control systems and new rocket-launcher artillery missiles from a Vickers company subsidiary. These goodies also included the supply of the potentially lethal chemicals thiodiglycol and thionyl chloride, whose only conceivable use was to make poison gases, and, to ram the point home, Iraq was also sold the antidote, Piptil, a nerve-gas suppressant, through a front company.

Not everyone in the intelligence community was easy about this lethal trade to supply a murderous dictator with weapons of mass destruction. In March 1992, Robin Robinson, a highly principled Quaker civil servant, resigned from the UK's Joint Intelligence Committee Secretariat, citing his concerns about the hypocrisy of the British government's arms trade with Iraq.

It made little difference. Trade with Iraq was big business.

In one of the murkier moves, in the late 1980s a US-Iraq Trade Forum was established by a retired American Ambassador, Marshall Wiley, representing the world of the big arms manufacturers, big business and government. Companies like Exxon, Mobil, Bell, Lockheed and General Motors were rapidly signed up, and even US aid seems to have been channelled to Iraq through this semi-official body. When $4 billion mysteriously disappeared from the Atlanta branch of the Forum's Italian bank, it came as no surprise to many that it was the US Treasury that intervened to block any public inquiry.

By late 1988, the Forum, with US government support, was openly hosting a major US high technology trade fair in Baghdad. In the words of Geoff Simons, the influential and well-informed writer on Iraq, 'By the late 1980s US-Iraq trade was worth billions of dollars with dozens of US companies involved. There can be no doubt that Saddam's strength was created largely by US business ambitions.'

The apogee of this unpublicized US support for the Iraqi regime and its murderous leader came on 12 April 1990, when a senior American delegation consisting of senators and government officials visited Iraq. It was accompanied by the US Ambassador to Iraq, April Glaspie. During the course of the delegation's meeting with Saddam in Mosul, it is alleged that Glaspie actually arranged a one-to-one telephone link with President George Bush so that the US president could personally endorse the delegation's trade proposals.

What these close and now embarrassing top-level trade links with Iraq explain is why Saddam felt in 1990 that the American government *was actually on his side*. Why, with all these intimate trading and other links, did the USA not see the threat sooner? Because, as Senator John F. Kerry later pointed out, there was another potent reason for America to be worried. In his own words:

I will be voting to give the President of the United States the authority to use force – if necessary – to disarm Saddam Hussein because I believe that a deadly arsenal of weapons of mass destruction in his hands is a real and grave threat to our security.

He reflected Washington's view on the eve of war:

We are confident that Saddam Hussein retains some stockpiles of chemical and biological weapons, and that he has since embarked on a crash course to build up his chemical and biological warfare capabilities. Intelligence reports indicate that he is seeking nuclear weapons.

Believing this, the West therefore could not ignore the Iraqi dictator. They had plenty of time to study Saddam. His origins, psychology, cruelty and the true nature of his regime were well understood by intelligence staffs specializing in the region from 1969 onwards, when Saddam was appointed vice president and given charge of Iraq's internal security apparatus.

The whole development of Saddam's regime and his personality was followed closely for the next two decades. The West should not have been surprised by anything Saddam did. Alarmed Americans sounded a warning long before the war.

Hillary Clinton made the potential threat clear:

In the four years since the inspectors left, intelligence reports show that Saddam Hussein has worked to rebuild his chemical and biological weapon stock, his missile delivery capability, and his nuclear programme. He has also given aid, comfort and sanctuary to terrorists, including al Qa'ida members… It is clear, however, that if left unchecked, Saddam Hussein will continue to increase his capacity to wage biological and chemical warfare, and will keep trying to develop nuclear weapons.

Others agreed.

In the words of one British intelligence officer, specializing in Arabia and the Gulf:

Saddam was a good old-fashioned Arab dictator. Everyone knew what he was and what he was capable of. He was devious, untrustworthy, greedy, ambitious and scared shitless of being topped in yet another Iraqi coup, just like so many of his predecessors. He came out of the Iran war broke, paranoic and desperate. He was also terrified of plots – after all, his own people did have about three goes at assassinating him in the seven months before he invaded Kuwait. To think that a psychotic dictator with 5,000 tanks is going to sit back alongside a defenceless neighbour, that just happens to be one of the richest countries in the world, while they stick two fingers up and tell him to push off because he's not getting any of their money, is just plain stupid. Especially when the US Ambassador says that it doesn't matter if he robs the bank. Anyone who's studied the region for any length of time could have taken bets on him trying his luck. It was a simple intelligence matter of capabilities and intentions, and knowing your man. In the circumstances, what else was Saddam Hussein to do?

The poor intelligence assessments in the run-up to the Gulf War are only one part of the indictment. Even after the invasion and the subsequent outbreak of war in January 1991, there were serious failures of intelligence both in Operation Desert Shield and Desert Storm.

To begin with, no one seemed able to determine the exact size of the Iraqi armed forces. General Schwarzkopf went to war on 16 January 1991 believing that there were 600,000 Iraqis under arms. Later the true figure was revealed to be 250,000 at the most. The problem of numbers was compounded by poor assessment of the Iraqi units' combat effectiveness. The received wisdom at the time was that the Republican Guard in particular were well equipped, battle-hardened and loyal, dedicated and well trained. Some intelligence analysts, seeking an easy analogy, even described them as 'Saddam's Waffen-SS', equipped with the most potent Soviet hardware.

This misreading of Iraqi competence came as a result of misreading the Iraqi victory in the long and costly war with Iran from 1980 to 1988. The truth was that the Iraqis won the first Gulf War by default. Instead of realizing that Iraq had not so much *won* as Iran *lost* (because of military incompetence, poor leadership at the higher levels and unacceptable casualties), the intelligence assessments gave undue weight to Iraqi combat experience, equipment and professional competence. These delusions of Iraqi capabilities spilled over into the Gulf War assessments of 1990–91.

This overestimation of combat competence on the ground extended far more seriously into the balance in the air, where numbers and capabilities are usually subject to intense professional scrutiny. It is not just the size of a nation's equipment that counts; it is also important to know whether a nation knows how to use that equipment properly. Nowhere is this more important than in technical areas such as air power.

Both Iraq and Iran possessed large quantities of sophisticated US and Soviet weapon systems. (The Shah had even bought top-of-the-range US F-14 fighters in the 1970s.) But neither side used them well. The Iranians could not maintain their US equipment, and the Iraqis, having thus obtained air superiority by default, proved themselves incapable of pressing home coordinated aerial attacks on the Iranian ground forces either as long-range interdiction or as close air support. Although air intelligence officers briefed these professional weaknesses regularly between 1981 and 1988, few high-level intelligence estimates before the Gulf War highlighted these serious Iraqi deficiencies; they all harped on about Iraq's numbers (which were impressive) and little on performance. The end result was that even the capabilities intelligence, it seemed, was reduced to mere bean-counting, and flawed and inaccurate bean-counting at that. It was, in the words of one seasoned intelligence observer, 'not OOB [order of battle] Intelligence's best performance'.

The result was that Washington genuinely believed and clung to a common belief that Saddam Hussein was a very well-armed tyrant and a threat to the peace and stability of the region. He had ignored the mandate of the United Nations and was building weapons of mass destruction and the means of delivering them. All this was partially true but for the WMDs, which were a pipedream for Saddam rooted in a small CW capability. Al Gore even stated, 'We know that he has stored secret supplies of biological and chemical weapons throughout his country.'

This wasn't entirely true, but Washington believed it was. Partial intelligence can easily mislead even the most experienced analyst.

The progress of the '100-hour war' after the allied ground attack on 24 February 1991 raised even more questions about modern Western intelligence. The course of the battles is well documented. Less well exposed are the failures of the US and Western intelligence agencies during the fighting to support the battle commanders on the ground. It seems to be an ironic paradox that the more effort and resources that were pumped into CENTCOM, General Schwarzkopf's HQ in Saudi Arabia, the less intelligence seemed to reach the fighting units in the field. Nimble minds may construe this as a triumph of operational security, but to the angry commander of a battalion of fifty tanks advancing into the smoke, fear and danger of an armoured battle with an Iraqi Republican Guard division, this view gives little comfort. Frustrated senior officers in British infantry units said after the war to incoming intelligence officers, in an eerie echo of the Falklands nine years before, 'Where were you?' The truth is that the flow of intelligence to senior operational commanders at division level *and above* had never been greater. The problem was the old one of dissemination; yet again it proved extremely difficult to get intelligence disseminated *downwards*.

The reasons were twofold.

The first is the classic problem that much intelligence is so secret because of the way it has been collected (sigint, overhead imagery, electronic warfare, etc.) that it cannot be passed down without risk of compromising the source. 'Protect the source' is the clarion call of the really secret world. In the US system it becomes 'Special Compartmentalized' material and can only be released to specially cleared personnel. The fear is that the enemy will find out just how much you *do* know.

One compromise of your ability to read an enemy's codes, and he will change them. Then you can't. Some secrets really do have to be kept. It is a serious problem and the genuine efforts of intelligence officers to release sensitive information 'out of channels', supported by 'collateral' press reports or any other credible source should not be underestimated. If the intelligence could only have come from one secret source, however, then the risk of disclosure, compromise and waste of taxpayers' money to buy expensive intelligence technology is just too great. Ultra in the Second World War is the classic example. In 1941–42, whole Atlantic convoys were hazarded to protect the Ultra secret from Karl Dönitz's U-boats. It is better to have one convoy cut to ribbons than to lose the ability to protect every future convoy.

To take just two modern examples: if Saddam's entourage knew that at precisely 13.04 Baghdad time a US spy satellite was overhead for precisely twenty-seven minutes, then all military activity would freeze or go into the hangar for the next half-hour. If Saddam's Revolutionary Guard had suspected that every conversation between Baghdad and the divisional commanders in Kuwait was being intercepted, broken and transcribed by the American NSA at Fort Meade, Maryland, then all radio communications (apart from deception transmissions designed to feed misleading intelligence to the attentive allied listeners) would have switched overnight. As the highly security-conscious Iraqis used landline telephones, the second problem never seems to have arisen.

The second reason for the poor intelligence flow during the Gulf War was relatively new, but had begun to be a serious problem in Vietnam. There was simply *too much* intelligence. The system was flooded. One satellite pass overhead (and the US had up to six Keyhole satellites available, together with high-resolution radar that can see through clouds) or a photo-reconnaissance aircraft sortie meant literally thousands – truckloads – of pictures. These had to be looked at, analysed, interpreted and briefed to decision-makers in good time.

Suddenly technology had brought the kind of secret intelligence that was only available in 1944 to Churchill and Eisenhower into a form where every battalion commander could use it if he had access through a device called the Secondary Imaging Dissemination System or SIDS. SIDS was nothing more than a high-resolution, optical transmission device rather like an incredibly sharp fax machine. At least twelve went to the Gulf, but only four worked properly. However, SIDS meant that every combat unit could theoretically get access to the latest intelligence. And they knew it. So, not unreasonably, they wanted it.

With hundreds of ground and air force commanders screaming for pictures of their targets every day, the dissemination system for pushing out target intelligence collapsed. In the words of an intelligence officer at CENTCOM, giving testimony to the US Congressional Committee after the war:

Intel data could be passed in real time... but because of the lack of common imagery data dissemination systems, the component [single service] commanders, as well as the forward deployed units, could not always gain timely access to imagery intelligence.

In plain English, the IO was saying that the US Army, Navy and Air Force systems turned out to be technically incompatible and could not pass intelligence in time. To make things worse, once the battle was joined, the system collapsed completely under its own weight of information. The US 82nd Airborne Division, set out on the west to guard the open desert flank, claimed to have received better intelligence in the end from the French screening division on its left using traditional chinagraph and paper methods than from its own HQ US XVIII Corps. The old problem of getting very secret, compartmentalized intelligence into the hands of those who really needed to use it had proved to be too difficult in the heat of action, despite all the good intentions and the best technology in the world.

Another intelligence area of less than shining triumph during the war was the 'Great Scud Hunt', where allied intelligence tried desperately to locate the Iraqis' limited stock of Scud surface-to-surface missiles. The Iraqi leader deliberately targeted his missiles against Israel, in a frantic attempt to bring the Israelis into the war and so split the Arabs off from the allied coalition. It did not work, but the track record of allied intelligence in locating the mobile missiles in order to destroy them was dismal. As one derisive British special forces officer said later, 'We might as well have been hunting the Snark for all the intelligence we got on Scuds.'

The final major intelligence failure during the war itself was the Bomb Damage Assessment (BDA) row which erupted midway through the air campaign in January and February 1991. BDA is difficult at the best of times, but air targeting depends on accurate assessment of results to measure success. The problem is that a knocked-out T72 tank dug into a defensive position behind a pile of sand still looks from the air exactly like a combat-ready T72 dug in behind a pile of sand even after it had been holed, unless its turret has been blown off or it is a smoking heap.

Quite early in the campaign it became apparent from sigint and other sources that allied air force claims for tank kills were exaggerated. This is quite normal. Aircrew always exaggerate. They enjoy being shot at no more than other men, so tend not to hang around the battlefield and its flak a moment longer than is necessary to carry out their mission. And, in all fairness, a truck can easily look like a tank from an aircraft attacking at low level at 400 knots. The inevitable intelligence policy of confirmation from other sources caused considerable friction with aircrews, who considered CENTCOM's estimates to be much too conservative. The air forces (argued the air forces) had spent a fortune in time and expensive weapons – they *must* have achieved better results. NATO's later efforts in 1999 against Serb armour in Kosovo were to be depressingly similar: air power has serious limitations.

Into this inter-service dispute now came the pessimists of the CIA and DIA in Washington. They claimed that, far from being too conservative, the BDA results reported by CENTCOM were themselves exaggerated and should be reduced. An infuriated Schwarzkopf told the experts from Washington to 'sort it out' with his harassed intelligence staff, and grumbled later that 'he'd still be sitting on his ass after the war if he'd relied on the [intelligence] agencies to agree that the Iraqi military had been weakened sufficiently for the ground war to begin on 24 February 1991.' As a matter of record, the final confirmed attrition rates at the start of the ground forces' attack on 24 February are interesting. At that point the Iraqis had lost only 40 per cent of their tanks, 30 per cent of their armoured personnel carriers and about 42 per cent of their artillery to the strategic air campaign. This was a far cry from the extravagant claims of some aviators that up to 80 per cent of the Iraqi equipment had been destroyed, and that, 'If the war had been just left to the air forces, they could have done the job on their own.'

The BDA row festered on throughout the war and afterwards, poisoning relations between the Gulf and Washington, the ground forces and the air forces and proving that, for all the 'gee-whiz' technology, intelligence still couldn't be relied on to get it right when it really mattered. For the US armed forces, at least, the ghosts of Vietnam reared their heads again. In the words of the senior US Marine officer in the Gulf, Lieutenant General Walter Boomer: 'I remember being in Vietnam for two tours, and not getting a single piece of useful intelligence, not once. It has gotten better, but we still can't get down to the company level what they need to do the job.'

The coalition forces succeeded in the Gulf, but the contribution of intelligence during the battles was sometimes far from the definition of 'accurate information passed in a timely fashion to decision-makers to enable them to make correct decisions'.

'Progress means deterioration' is not just the cry of technophobes. Anyone who has ever wished for the voice of an honest-to-God telephone receptionist instead of a pre-recorded message saying 'press #1 if you know the extension you require' will understand how many commanders in the Gulf felt about the complicated technology sold to them by slick intelligence salesmen from the US defence contractors.

When the military's new techno-intelligence system was running in real time – and when it actually worked – information would be passed directly to the operational commanders on the ground. Thus the J-STARS aircraft, which took radar images of enemy troops moving across the desert from a safe distance, were able to patch their radar pictures directly to the operational fire-control cells in the coalition divisions below, enabling the gunners to select and engage targets at will, without any reference to intelligence. 'Intelligence' had become, in naval terms, 'action (or operational) targeting information'. It worked.

When the intelligence came from super-sensitive or secret sources, however, such as high-resolution satellites using millimetric wavelength synthetic-aperture radar or from secret intercepts of high-level radio transmissions, then it had to be protected. The full intelligence cycle not just of collection but of collation, interpretation and dissemination had to be carried out in conditions of absolute security and only disseminated to those with a strict need to know.

In 1960, that would have meant a few overhead photographs or a single red-hot piece of signals intelligence. By 1990, however, it meant over 20,000 images from a single satellite pass, with aircraft bombed-up on the runway, 'turning and burning', impatient for the photographs of their targets. Intelligence on the battlefield was no longer the sphere of a few highly trained and expert specialists. Intelligence had become a growth industry with a distribution problem for its product only rivalled by that other battle winner, logistics. During the Gulf War, the information revolution had transformed military intelligence and the military staff systems struggled hard to keep up, not always successfully. The information age had arrived.

Away from the blast furnace of the battlefield, older, calmer lessons remained. If battlefield and operational intelligence was less than perfect during the Gulf War, then it was plain old-fashioned diplomatic miscalculation and bungled national intelligence that got the West into the war in the first place. There was no failure of technology or intelligence staff support systems before the Gulf War. There was a serious failure of human intelligence. The target was human too, of course: Saddam Hussein, the 'onlie begetter' of the Gulf War. The whole war and the crisis that preceded it are to be found in his psyche, insecurity and his actions. Add to his personal problems a desperate need for oil and easy money, and much is explained.

The Gulf crisis was, in fact, a good old-fashioned mistake: an intelligence blunder of classic dimensions. Yet, using the information available at the time, it is now clear that a great deal was known about Saddam, and not just by retired intelligence officers or academics specializing in Iraqi affairs. Nor were the intelligence failures limited to the Western intelligence agencies and Saddam's blundering. Saddam's fellow Arabs made the same mistakes as well. Prince Khaled bin Sultan, the senior Saudi General and Joint Forces Commander in the Gulf, later acknowledged that even the Saudi Arabian Intelligence Service – which tried to keep a very close eye on Saddam indeed – got it wrong, too. After the war, the Prince admitted ruefully that, despite a very clear Arab understanding of Saddam's temperament, character and regime, they too had misread the Iraqi leader's intentions. It was 'a failure of human intelligence'. Saddam, said the Prince, 'had bluffed us'. The aim of intelligence is to see through an aggressor's bluffs.

In a curious echo of the British and the Argentines over the Falklands nine years before, serious intelligence miscalculations and mistakes happened on *both* sides before the Gulf War. Iraq's intelligence system misled its leaders just as badly as did those in the West. It was obvious that the Iraqi dictator had little understanding of international affairs. His Revolutionary Command Council, as sycophantic a support group as any dictator could wish for, was unlikely to tell him the truth and risk being put up against a wall and shot, even if they had a separate view of events. It was the task of his intelligence services to tell him the unvarnished truth. In a despotism like Iraq it is a brave man who tells the great leader what he does not want to hear.

Badly informed throughout, Saddam blundered into the *political* mistake of thinking that he could get away with his aggression without retaliation – partly encouraged by the US – and the *military* mistake of believing that his armed forces could win any war. He was wrong on both counts and was lucky to escape unscathed. Even so, Saddam survived the Gulf War, to the surprise of many observers. To the astonishment of Westerners who have still not grasped what makes the Arab world tick, once Saddam saw that he could survive and that coalition forces were not bent on attacking or deposing him personally, he claimed a great victory against the Americans and their imperialist allies.

Had not his heroic Republican Guards stopped the USA and their lackeys dead on the Basra road, denying them the advance on Baghdad? 'It must be true,' he trumpeted, 'for I am here and where are Bush and Thatcher? Gone!'

The victor of the Gulf War bestrode Iraq in the 1990s like some vengeful Colossus, putting down rebellion and tightening his grip on power. He erected victory memorials to his army's 'defeat of colonialism'. Like his predecessor, Nebuchadnezzar, he even had bricks with his name cast in the clay to commemorate his heroic triumph for all time in new buildings that would immortalize his reign. Saddam never entirely deluded himself, however. He learned from his defeat, seeking to repair the damage to his regime and to build up his weapons capability to ensure that he would not be defeated again. In the words of a former head of Iraqi Military Intelligence, 'Saddam's theory is war. He cannot survive without war.'

Next time, Saddam determined, he would have weapons of mass destruction, especially chemical and biological weapons, to enforce his will. Once the UNSCOM weapon inspection teams were kicked out of Iraq in the late 1990s, there was little to impede his weapon development programme. The key to the instability in the Gulf remained, as before 1990, in the paranoia and instability of the dictator's character and the prospect of easy oil and money.

The Gulf War was the first test of President George Bush's New World Order and it succeeded. The coalition's vigorous response, with Moscow and the European Union supporting the new *Pax Americana* based on armed enforcement, established a global precedent. In terms of lives – but not Iraqi lives – the war was relatively cheap. The coalition lost only 223 killed and 697 wounded. Ironically, many of the allied casualties were caused by trigger-happy young American pilots, bringing the old German D-Day joke up to date: 'When the USAF comes over, *even the Allies* duck… ' Thirteen years later the Americans and their allies had to do it all over again.

The Gulf War also made clear that aggression against a neighbour is an international issue in itself and can be punished, should the nations concerned wish to do so over an important issue like oil. The US and Western economic interest was, in the words of the secret US national policy guidance document, 'for a secure guaranteed flow of cheap oil from tame oil-producing states who could be manipulated at will'. Lawrence Korb, an Assistant US Secretary of Defense, spelled it out in 1990: '*If Kuwait grew carrots, we wouldn't give a damn.*'

The war had a hidden cost to America. The United States government was proud that, although perhaps 100,000 Iraqis had died in the Gulf War of 1991, there were only forty-eight American battle casualties. What it has concealed from the public is that 206,000 veterans of that war subsequently filed claims with the Veterans' Administration (VA) for injuries and illnesses. In the years since that war, 9,000 veterans have died, and 160,000 claims for disability have been recognized by the VA. The war left a bitter harvest for the victor as well.

The Kuwaiti war also leaves us with a deep lesson. In order to influence the future we have to understand the present. The present will always reflect human nature, where greed and the thirst for land or power, the battle for resources – oil, water or minerals – and the unremitting lust for conquest still lie deep in the psyche of the powerful. These catalysts for conflict remain unchanging in all ages and all societies, and will remain. Only by knowledge of the present and the past can we control the future. Intelligence is our warning mechanism against future Saddams.

Not just their capabilities: their intentions too.

THE GLOBALIZATION OF TERROR

'Terrorism has become the systematic weapon of a war that knows no borders and seldom has a face'

JACQUES CHIRAC

Intentions are everything to the terrorist.

It doesn't take any great capability or special weapons to be a successful terrorist. Terrorism is relatively easy to do provided the determination is there, although its consequences can be immense. A single knife or just one gun in the hands of a fanatic can change history. When Gavrilo Prinçip shot and killed the Austrian Crown Duke at Sarajevo in 1914, he lit a powder trail that led to the detonation and collapse of the whole European edifice. At the time his act was merely the latest in a long and depressing catalogue of Balkan and Anarchist atrocities, for terrorism is as old as warfare itself.

In the first-century Palestine of Jesus Christ, Jewish religious zealots called *'sicarii'* terrorized the Roman garrison by plunging curved stabbing knives into the backs of unsuspecting Roman legionaries and their families in the narrow alleys of Jerusalem. These proto-typical ancestors of the Stern Gang and Irgun were conducting their own version of a Holy War in a bid to force the occupying superpower out, prevent them polluting the Holy Places of the Temple and Judaism, and establish a strict religious regime based on the Jewish Law.

Thousands were caught and crucified by the governing superpower, roped up on T-shaped stakes as a warning to passers-by, with the Governor of Judea's sentence pinned above their heads as an example of Roman justice. After three days in the blazing sun, the guards smashed any survivors' legs, forcing their weight to hang helplessly down on to their shattered bones while the victims slowly died in dreadful agony. Historically, terrorists could expect little mercy if arrested; unusually, at least the Romans gave them a show trial before crucifying the ones they caught.

Despite the risks, however, for the weak, the dispossessed and the just plain ruthless, sometimes the stiletto in the back can be just as efficient as the steamroller head-on – and has the great advantage of being easier to do. The Western idea that all warfare is waged primarily through decisive head-to-head battles is a serious mistake. While brief and bloody pitched battles may have been a rapid, cost-effective solution to the manpower problems of fighting during the harvest for the ancient Greeks, there is no particular reason why they should have become the Napoleonic-style model for the 'Western way of war'. Because battles are by no means the only way for men to fight. The pinprick warfare of terrorism has a long and bloody history as old as warfare itself.

The notion, therefore, that terrorism is some kind of a new phenomenon is quite simply wrong, and the idea that somehow terrorism is not a 'legitimate' or rational weapon for 'furthering policy by violent means' (the Clausewitzian definition of war) is both naive and self-serving. From ancient Rome to Pol Pot, terror has been used to terrify not just individuals but whole populations. The truth is, like it or not, that terrorism is just another part of mankind's brutal spectrum for resolving disputes.

Terrorism's high profile nowadays owes its notoriety to the modern conjunction of an unholy trinity. First, a tradition of successful political violence since the end of the Second World War; secondly, the spread and sophistication of modern media to communicate the images of terror; and lastly, the potential of new technology and weapons, offering hitherto undreamed-of ways to kill, maim and terrify. For men – and women – with 'a cause', a grievance so important as to be worth slaughtering others for, terrorism nowadays offers a lip-smacking opportunity to implement and publicize their aims at very little cost to themselves.

Terrorism is nothing more than the calculated use of violence to achieve a political goal by killing and maiming in order to terrify and intimidate as many people as possible. In this it is little different from war itself: the 'continuation of politics by violent means'. The expert views of some practitioners of State terrorism are instructive: 'Kill one – terrify ten thousand!' said Stalin. And

Lenin, who had clearly pondered at length on the subject of State terror, mused that 'the purpose of terror is, quite simply, to terrify.'

In his memoirs, Field Marshal Montgomery saw very clearly the purpose and the inevitable logic of terrorism. Recalling his experiences in the Irish Republican Army's struggle to evict their English rulers in 1921, he wrote:

> In many ways this war [against Irish terrorists] was far worse than the Great War... It developed into a murder campaign in which, in the end, the soldiers became very skilful and more than held their own.

Like most professional soldiers, Montgomery harboured a deep dislike of terrorism and its practitioners. He saw a clear distinction between the way of the warrior and the murderer. Many normal people share the same feeling of unease and worry over the difference between killing in battle and murder. The difference is the grievance. Most soldiers are not deeply aggrieved and victims with 'a cause'. Terrorists are men – and women – with a deep and burning grievance.

It soon becomes clear when studying terrorism that it is a very complicated social subject. Only by exploring the underlying processes ranging from individual to social issues can we begin to understand the terrorist's mind and motivation. We can begin to understand the complex and different motives of diverse terrorist groups only by recognizing the differences. Evidence tends to show that some individuals are more inclined to adopt violent means because of psychological traits or of a particular personal history, while other motives can be found in social identity and political decisions to foster the growth of terrorism. Terrorism is complex.

What drives *most* terrorists (psychopathic killers become terrorists for sick reasons of their own) is 'The Cause', some deep grievance that can make reasonable human beings abandon their normal sense of values, transcends their natural human impulses and extinguishes all sense of proportion or mercy by imbuing the terrorist with a higher calling for their actions. 'The Cause' can make men and women fanatics; and fanatics with a cause and a gun can be very dangerous indeed. Their 'Cause' absolves them from their actions, however dreadful. It can turn even nice old grey-haired grandmothers into hate-filled fanatics with a suspended sense of Catholic values, as BBC reporter Fergal Keane realized, listening with growing unease to his Irish grandparents gleefully recounting their tales of the IRA and 'the Troubles' of the 1920s.

For Lenin and his fellow Bolsheviks, their grievance was against the authoritarian repression of Czarist Russia and their Marxist dream of a better Russia – governed by them, naturally. With other terrorists, the grievance that inspires and drives 'The Cause' varies, but always there is the deep-seated *grievance*, some sense of burning injustice that overrides morality and the laws of normal society. For the Palestinians it is Israel; for the IRA it is the British in the six counties of Ulster; for the pro-lifers it is abortion clinics. Carried to extremes, such logic can even encourage the militants of the Animal Liberation Front to believe that it is actually morally right to murder human beings in order to be kind to animals.

With logic like this to guide their actions, it follows that terrorists are not like normal people. For whatever reason their normal belief system has been distorted or bypassed. Normal people like you and I therefore have great difficulty understanding the terrorist mind. No one knows this better than those on the receiving end of terrorism, from ETA in Spain's Basque country to the PIRA in Northern Ireland.

The Northern Irish politician Ken Maginnis, now Lord Maginnis of Drumglass, was targeted by the IRA and survived no fewer than eleven murder attempts in his role as both Loyalist politician and commander of a company of the Ulster Defence Regiment during 'the Troubles'. He knows better than most about the motivation and tactics of terrorists. His judgement of the terrorist campaign from 1969 to 1998 is well-informed and scathing.

Of course we all knew about the old IRA ever since we were wee kids. Living on a farm halfway between Loch Neagh and Aughnacloy [in County Tyrone], everyone knew about the bad guys still roaming south of the border. It all went sour in 1968 when civil rights marches in Belfast and Londonderry degenerated into internecine riots. I remember the British Army coming in to stop the violence and being greeted at first as peacemakers. Then the bad guys of the Provisional IRA turned up, Marxists at heart, waving stolen rifles and determined by 1970 to impose a political solution on the rest of us.

They started a terrorist campaign by shooting soldiers and policemen and intimidating the Nationalists and Catholic community. Despite its aggressive efforts to disarm Republican paramilitaries by searching Nationalist – which meant Catholic – homes, the army was quickly painted by the IRA as the real enemy and the 'Provos' became the sainted defenders of Sinn Féin's nationalist cause.

In the countryside that turned into guerrilla warfare with bombings, ambushes and political murder: all designed to frighten us into a united Ireland. The army retaliated, of course, and things got very ugly. Overall, I think it was sometimes almost a civil war, certainly in the countryside. I myself was a prime target of eleven attempts to kill me, from raw youths nervously firing a revolver and then running away, to clever bombs under my car. I never stopped looking for danger for nearly twenty years. The terrorists seemed to be either impressionable youths or, much more dangerous, fanatics to their cause who cared nothing for ordinary people. To this hard core of killers, killing for the cause was the only thing that mattered. They had been brainwashed into believing that any murder was a step towards a united Ireland. These terrorists were obsessed; I think it took over their lives.

By 1995 it was clear that the PIRA were unlikely to succeed in their Long War campaign. They were riddled with informers: our intelligence had penetrated them at every level, knew exactly who they were and they were a beaten force. So I welcomed the return of peace to Ulster with the Good Friday Agreement of 1998, albeit at a heavy price: some 3,600 people were killed and more than 30,000 more were wounded during my time.

But, to be honest, many of the hard terrorists just turned to crime and blackmail. They were fanatics living outside the law by their own perverted standards, and still are in many cases. The old ideas have never really gone away for some and, let's be honest, never will for at least another generation. Terrorism and murder became a way of life and defined their whole existence… '

Most grievances in the majority of societies are resolved by a graduated range of responses and dialogue. For example, the local residents don't like the plans for a new nuclear waste processing plant being planned in the neighbourhood. 'Not in my backyard!' goes up the cry; residents' associations are formed; public meetings are held; and soon appeals to government at both local and national level kick in. Protesters are organized by activists and leaders, frequently self-selecting from the most vociferous or just plain bloody-minded. But they have a just case; and *they are right*. The grievance is further mobilized by marches, banners, publicity on television, minor acts of damage or attacks on any policemen unlucky enough to get in the way. Thus the threshold of legality is effortlessly passed, once 'direct action' becomes part of the protest against the grievance.

Should the issue still not be resolved to the protesters' satisfaction (even when they are in a clear minority, as with the IRA), or should there be no mechanism for protest against perceived injustice – as, for example, in the Israeli-Palestinian dispute – then the protesters with their grievance and their 'Cause' face a hard choice. Deeply alienated from society for whatever reason, they can either give up or continue the fight by 'non-parliamentary means'. Historically the disaffected resort to terrorism when they believe all other avenues have failed, or they see no other way forward. Direct action then swiftly becomes a targeted attack against an individual; if the grievance still festers, then a general attack on the 'enemy group' and its supporters is the obvious next step. The spectrum of disaffection and protest has now become terrorism (see figure overleaf).

This pattern of disaffection can be clearly traced in terror's bloody progress over the last 150 years. The Russian Radicals, the Anarchists, the IRA, the Israeli terrorist Stern Gang and Irgun, the anti-Colonialist movements like the Mau Mau, the Red Brigades, the anti-Vietnam protests, 'Shining Path', the Montañeros, the Palestinians, the Animal Liberation Front or the Anti-Abortion League and the Islamic extremists; the list of the embittered, or the fanatics with a grievance for which to kill is long. Although every group is slightly different, the recipe always contains the same basic ingredients: there is a deeply held grievance; resentment at the inability to win their case by legal means or total alienation from a political system that offers no redress; and finally, a resort to very public violence to coerce the 'enemy' to change its policy.

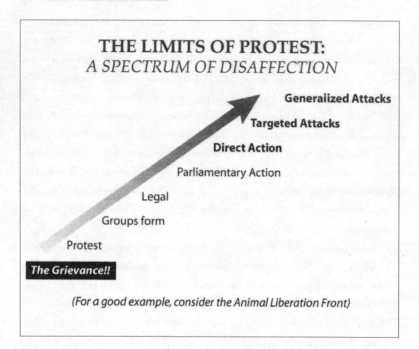

THE LIMITS OF PROTEST:
A SPECTRUM OF DISAFFECTION

Generalized Attacks

Targeted Attacks

Direct Action

Parliamentary Action

Legal

Groups form

Protest

The Grievance!!

(For a good example, consider the Animal Liberation Front)

One major change over the past 150 years, however, has been the loss of restraint and the killing of the innocent. The attitude towards the terrorists' audience, the public, has hardened. For example, on several occasions in the nineteenth century, the Russian Radicals aborted assassination attacks on the Czar at the last moment out of concern for innocent bystanders, women and children. Nowadays their more ruthless successors deliberately target and kill innocent third parties in an effort to get the attention of their real audience – not the public but the government; the Omagh bombing in Northern Ireland stands as the classic example.

Worse still, the Islamic Fundamentalists of al Qa'ida appear to have no intention of even attempting to try and modify their enemies' policy or to 'win their case'. For them the *audience* is the target and the almost nihilistic attack on the World Trade Center (WTC) seems merely a demonstration of their hatred and contempt for the West, rather than any attempt to coerce governments into change. Al Qa'ida's grievance admits of no redress and has uneasy parallels with some anarchist violence.

The heart of the problem revolves around 'the grievance' and what can actually spark it off. General Sir James Glover (who enjoyed considerable success commanding the British Security Forces against the Provisional IRA in the 1970s) had thought deeply about terrorism and the sources of disaffection. He believed potential grievances abounded at all times and in all societies and felt that a skilful politician should be able to spot grievances early and defuse them before they became the triggers for social unrest and terrorism. He called these triggers 'the catalysts for conflict'. These are, like terrorism, as old as mankind itself. Some examples of these grievances and catalysts for conflict are:

- Autonomy – ETA and the Basques
- Class – Lenin and the Kulaks
- Control – Kashmir
- Culture – Al Qa'ida and the West
- Drugs – Colombia and the cartels
- Envy – Industrial unrest
- Fear and suspicion – Hindu and Muslim, India
- Food supplies – the depopulation war on Easter Island
- Freedom – East Timor
- Greed – the Conquistadores
- Hegemony – Chechnya
- Ideology – Pol Pot and Cambodia
- Land – European settlers and the Native Americans
- Language – Walloons and Flemings, Belgium
- Natural resources – Sierra Leone's diamonds/Japan's invasion of Manchuria
- Oil – Kuwait 1991/Spratly Islands
- People – Mao Tse Tung and China
- Politics – the Red Brigades
- Poverty – Tutsis and Hutus, Rwanda
- Power – Hitler and Czechoslovakia
- Precious metals and stones – South Africa, 1890–1903
- Religion – the Crusades and the Reformation
- Revenge – Oklahoma City bombing

- Self-determination – the American Civil War
- Survival – the Warsaw Ghetto uprising
- Water – the headwaters of the Jordan

All the factors have led to strife and bloodshed throughout human history. This list is surprisingly long but by no means exhaustive. It is hard, for example, to see just how the Baader-Meinhof Gang or the Red Brigade terrorist groups fit into such a spectrum other than as old-fashioned outlaws, troublemakers or criminal psychopaths.[7] But all these catalysts for conflict, if not addressed, can trigger some deep grievance and spark the terrorist to act.

With such a grievance and their 'righteous' cause, the profile of the average terrorist is surprisingly easy to discern. They believe in and have 'A Cause'. They are right and we are wrong so, by definition, they are better people than the rest of us: being members of a Righteous Cause, 'The Struggle' against an unworthy enemy now defines their whole identity and existence and so 'The Group' soon becomes their 'family'. The Group exists for and believes in some hope-filled future, where victory for the Cause is assured and always just around the corner. For the committed terrorist, all it will take are a few more atrocities and a few more killings to bend the rest of humanity to see just why they should do what the terrorists want them to do. The mind of the committed terrorist is, in fact, little different clinically to that of that of a self-assured psychopath. Normal reality, let alone normal *morality*, is suspended.

Perhaps the most dangerous aspect of all is the terrorist's inability to turn back, to change his or her mind. Because the struggle is their very reason for living, and the group and the Cause gradually become everything to them. Sweet reason or other voices are excluded. Their whole life and being are now defined by the Cause and by their involvement in what is quite literally a criminal conspiracy.[8] With such a mindset, it soon follows, therefore, that anyone not with them, even moderates in their own camp, eventually become

---

7 Andreas Baader, the German terrorist, is alleged to have brought one particularly indecisive and disputatious meeting of his gang to an end by seizing his gun and shouting, 'For God's sake stop arguing! Let's just go and kill a policeman!'

8 Some groups (e.g. the Mau Mau in Kenya) even followed the Mafia's example and insisted that any new member of the organization must commit a major criminal act before being accepted. That way all are then irrevocably involved or implicated and there is no turning back.

potential traitors and enemies. To those within the little bubble of criminal conspirators, everyone eventually *outside* their circle becomes a potential betrayer either of them or the Cause. Murder and conspiracy, paranoia and infighting follow as inevitably as night follows day, and the struggle spreads to warring factions within the community of terrorists. Terrorism, like revolution, tends to devour its children. Islamic terrorism has followed this classic pattern almost to the letter.

No greater dispute reared its head in the last half of the twentieth century than the Arab-Israeli dispute.

Whatever the rights and wrongs of the case, the fact is that by 1968 the majority of the Palestinian people and their Arab friends realized that, after the Israeli Defence Force's stunning victories in 1968, there was no possibility of ejecting the Israelis from the land of Israel by main force. Dispossessed, sullen, brooding in their filthy, overcrowded camps in Gaza and the West Bank, the Palestinians looked for another way of bringing their cause to an uninterested world's attention. In a series of daring coups, televised live around the world, the militants of the Palestine Liberation Organization (PLO) hijacked airliners and blew them up on prime-time TV. An astonished world looked on amazed and strong insurance brokers wept into their champagne over lost profits.

In 1972, eleven Israeli athletes were kidnapped and gunned down at the Munich Olympic Games, along with five of their captors. This time the world recoiled in horror; but the 'armed propaganda' of the PLO was stunningly successful. Suddenly the world was very interested indeed in the Palestinians' problems. Within two years, Yasser Arafat, the PLO's leader, was addressing the United Nations General Assembly in New York, pleading his cause at the world's highest political forum. Terrorism worked.

Where the PLO led so spectacularly, others swiftly followed. In 1969, Northern Ireland (the six counties of Ulster that had voted to stay in union with Britain) came under an unremitting terror campaign from the ever-evolving Irish Republican Army (IRA). Like a rash, terrorism spread across the globe. From the Irish to the Basques, from the Baader-Meinhof gangs to the Red Brigades, 'terrorism' became the cutting edge of groups with a grievance. It reached a zenith – or nadir – in an attack on the Tokyo subway in 1995 by a tiny group of religious fanatics, who attracted global publicity by killing 12 innocent travellers with the nerve gas sarin. They had found and copied the formula off the Internet. Technology, publicity, death and terror had united in support of a bunch of Japanese religious crackpots whose only motive was the mind-numbing logic that 'hating the evil of the world, we sought to destroy that evil'.

In this escalation of terrorist atrocities, one dispute remained as a constant catalyst for conflict: the Arab-Israeli struggle, rumbling along at its various intensities. And, as its echoes spread, the conflict began to reverberate ever more loudly. From a dispute over the land of Palestine in 1948, by the end of the century the Arab-Israeli conflict had escalated into a full-blown clash of cultures. The bitter regional quarrels between colonial settlers and the dispossessed mutated into a wider ideological crusade, this time of fanatical Islamic terrorists waging their own version of Jihad against the global commercial and political influence of the West. The stage was set for catastrophe.

Islam has a long tradition of political violence and terrorism. Indeed, many Muslims genuinely believe that violence is legitimate in defence of their faith because the Koran says so; or at least if the local imam says it does.

An explosive fourth factor had now been added to terrorism's unholy trinity of success, the oxygen of publicity and efficient modern technology. From Algeria to Afghanistan, Islamic militants now had the blessing of Holy Writ.

Islamic militants were also encouraged to strike at the West by the ease with which they could exploit Western liberal democracies' vulnerabilities. Open borders, lengthy legal procedures, a culture of free speech, free association and free movement were a positive invitation to attack for determined terrorists. To further the terrorists' cause even more, moral ambiguity reigned. Pleas from Britain for American citizens to stop funding Irish terrorism fell on deaf ears as the NORAID collecting tins rattled in Boston bars among the Irish diaspora, cheerfully supporting 'their Freedom Fighters' of the Provisional IRA. London filled up with so many Islamic dissidents from the Middle East plotting revolution back home that some suburbs were jokingly referred to as 'Londonistan'.

Nervous governments even sought accommodation with these dangerous guests in return for immunity from the contagion of terror elsewhere. Many governments found it easier to turn a blind eye to killers and organizers of terror in their midst provided they kept their noses clean.

Fanatical Islam took note of these Western weaknesses and feeble responses that amounted to little more than appeasement. Even when governments struck back hard against killers and terrorists, as did the Spanish and British anti-terrorist forces in the Basque country, Northern Ireland, London and Gibraltar, droves of well-paid lawyers and journalists strove to prove that their very own protector, the State, had in fact been acting outside the law. From such a pusillanimous response, Islamic terrorism took much comfort and planned accordingly: for Islam had a serious grievance against the West.

The fundamental roots of Islamic hostility to the West lie deep. A hundred years after the Prophet's death in AD 632, his Muslim warriors had conquered most of the Middle East, western Asia, the North African littoral and Spain. Over the next 500 years, Islam developed an advanced scientific and literary culture previously unknown in history. Astronomy, botany, geography, mathematics, medicine, music, poetry and metallurgy all flourished at a time when most Europeans lived in disease, despair and darkness. By 1095, Islam's dynamic cultural and military expansion towards Constantinople and into Palestine triggered thousands of credulous and ignorant Christians to set out on their long trek to evict the heathen from the Holy Land. The First Crusade had begun.

The seven crusades that followed established a pattern of historic enmity between Christian and Muslim. No sooner had the West established its short-lived Crusader kingdoms in Palestine than the Muslim leader Salah-ad-Din (Saladin) recaptured Jerusalem in 1187. Over the next two centuries, surviving crusaders came home to import the wonders and learning of Islam into Western Europe.

The historic result was that although the Crusades may have been ineffective, their legacy was an explosive renaissance of knowledge and enlightenment in the West. By the beginning of the twentieth century, Western expansion had the crumbling Ottoman Empire and Islam in retreat on every front – colonial, economic, cultural, scientific and, most dangerous of all, religious.

Where force of arms had failed nine centuries before, Western commerce and colonialism now colonized, exploited and reigned triumphant over the lands of Allah. For the true believer contemplating Islam's glorious past, it was a deeply humiliating prospect.

The post-colonial leaders of the emerging Arab world now provided another bone of contention for the faithful who had hoped that with the end of colonialism true Islamic values would rule.

A tide of nationalism swept aside any ideas of a true Islamic state as the new Arab leaders consolidated their hold; and they were as authoritarian and corrupt in every way as any of the pre-colonial Ottoman regimes. The new nationalist leaders' pleas for modernity and the London School of Economics' enlightened belief in 'progress' fell on the imams' deaf ears. For true believers, Paradise was not some Western-style secular state. The true way was the Community of the Faithful, *Umma*, based on an Islamic ideal and the revealed word of God. The ancient concept of a single 'Kingdom of God' (*Dar el Islam* – the land of Islam) had already been fragmented by the different nationalist priorities of states from Algeria to Pakistan. Now the Islamic world's new leaders were openly ignoring the *Ulemas* and centuries of religious teaching and heritage.

Although they paid lip service to the mosque, the new Arab nationalist leaders were essentially secular leaders. Other than for cosmetic reasons, they tended to ignore the age-old Islamic teachings of the clerics or *Ulema*, to follow an unashamedly modernist and secular agenda.

For rulers like Nasser of Egypt, Assad of Syria and the reinstalled Shah in Iran, their radical Muslim clerics represented nothing but trouble. They resolved the clash between nationalism and 'Islamism' by ruthless repression. In Syria, outspoken Muslim opponents of the regime quietly disappeared into Damascus's version of the Lubyanka. In Egypt, the Muslim Brotherhood was suppressed, and in 1966 Sayyid Qutb, its great theoretical voice, was hanged. In Shi'ite Iran, opponents of the Shah's regime – who referred to the Shi'a imams contemptuously as 'his black crows' – fled to avoid prison. Chief among these Iranian exiles was an obscure Shi'ite Ayatollah, or 'Leader of the Imams', Khomeini. A clear fault line was emerging between the Mosque and the State, even in the Islamic world.

To the burning grievance against the West for centuries of colonialism and humiliation was now added yet another cause for resentment: domestic oppression. From Rabat to Rawalpindi, Islam now trod carefully under the watchful eye of the State and its secret policemen and informers, alert for any signs of discontent. The exploding populations of the bazaars of Algiers, Baghdad, Cairo, Damascus and Islamabad bred in a world of disease, poverty and powerlessness where dictators ruled. Inequalities were everywhere. For many of the young people there seemed no way out of the hopelessness of existence. But from the Mosque came reassurance for the faithful: hope was at hand from Islam and the establishment of God's kingdom on earth.

For the Mosque had not been idle while it had appeared to be quiescent. The imams may have been forced to bow their heads meekly to the State and the secular men of power, but they had preached sedition whenever they could. For whatever their differences of class, nationalism, culture or language, every true believer across the Muslim world was now being told that there was one simple solution to all their problems of oppression and public corruption by their new rulers.

They only had to set up a single state with Sharia law and the sacred texts of the Koran to bring about God's kingdom on earth, with freedom and justice for all. In simple, clear, modern language the radical Muslim clerics proclaimed a gospel of hope in the 1960s and 1970s and fired up a new generation of post-colonial Muslim youth imbued with a single burning slogan: 'The Koran is our constitution'. From an oppressed present the Mosque brooded on its hopes for the future.

Events on the wider world stage eventually brought the extremists and fanatics the very opportunity for which they had been waiting, and also the God-given enemy against which all Islam could unite – Israel. Ironically it was the victory of the arch-enemy itself that indirectly triggered Islam's great rallying cry and call to arms.

In 1973, President Sadat of Egypt struck across the Suez Canal to attack Israel. Despite bitter fighting on the Golan and in Sinai, once again the Israelis pushed their attackers back. But the Yom Kippur War triggered a series of events that were to alter the balance of power in Islam's favour.

With the Suez Canal blocked, economic chaos reigned. The price of oil suddenly rocketed from around $12 a barrel in 1971 to around $24 a barrel in the late 1970s. Sadat's Operation Badr had revealed a powerful new Arab weapon – oil. The Organization of the Petroleum Exporting Countries' (OPEC) restrictions on petroleum exports turned the screw still further. Money poured into the coffers of the oil states and the 1970s oil crisis brought Western economies to the brink of disaster. The Islamic world had rediscovered real global power – thanks to oil.

The result was that by the 1980s, Saudi Arabia became the epicentre of both OPEC and the Islamic world. With their new-found petro-dollar wealth, the Saudis and their rich Gulf State allies were able to fund a massive expansion of the faith, bankrolling thousands of mosques worldwide and making donations to Islamic charities on a global scale through a network of Saudi-controlled banks.

As well as pumping out money, the Saudis held another vital trump card in the Islamic world. They were also able to capitalize on their stewardship of the sacred places of Islam. The high-living but cautious Saudi rulers had always realized that their Wahhabite doctrine of asceticism and strict Islamic observance was essential for the guardians of Mecca. They had to be *seen* to behave as strict Muslims for the regime to survive. By 1986, when King Saud formally took the title of 'Custodian of the Holy Places', this combination of great wealth and public piety allowed the Saudis to become the focus of the hopes of the Islamic world.

But not all Muslims are Sunni. Shi'ite Iran was beginning to stir. Shi'ites, who make up about 15 per cent of the Islamic world, believe that the true path for Islam are the teachings of the Prophet's cousin Ali, murdered in AD 661 by Islamic rivals in the struggle for the succession and the soul of Islam. The imam traditionally exercises greater influence in Shi'a Islam, both over the faithful and, ideally, over society.

By the mid-1970s, despite the best efforts of his secret police, the Shah's regime in Iran was confronting a tide of agitation and discontent. The Peacock Throne faced two growing threats. The first was a group of young militant intellectuals heavily influenced by Marxist ideas and the other revolutionary moments of the 1960s. Despairing of finding a democratic voice in the tightly controlled autocracy of the Shah's Iran, the students plotted in their universities and colleges, hoping to mobilize the workers and peasants to red revolution.

The second threat was an elderly cleric brooding in exile across the border in Iraq in the sacred Shi'ite city of Najaf. His name was Ayatollah Khomeini.

Khomeini's contribution to Islamic thought rests principally on his 'Islamic Government under the Guidance of the Law'. While never exactly a best-seller in Western bookstores, Khomeini's collection of sermons advocated an Islamic revolution leading to the '*Dar el Islam*', ruled by godly men and following strict Sharia law. Such a state would, of course, need to be guided by a wise supreme counsellor to whom all could turn for clarification over tricky points of the Law and the real will of Allah. (Khomeini felt that this was a role to which he could perhaps make some modest contribution.) This combination of angry young middle-class students seeking to overthrow the Shah's regime, and the revealed Shi'ite word of Allah, proved an explosive mixture.

With falling oil revenues, unemployment, extra taxes and student unrest on the streets, by 1977 the Shah's regime was in serious trouble. As SAVAK, his secret police, cracked down, agitation increased. From abroad, Khomeini stepped up his sermons, blasting bloodcurdling anathemas on the luckless Shah and appealing to the 'disinherited' of Iran to rise up against the godless dictator and his corrupt regime and seize power in the name of Allah, the compassionate and the merciful. The exiled Ayatollah became the symbol around which enemies of the Shah could rally. To cries of '*Allahu Akbar!*' the poor, the workers, the middle class, the students and finally the Armed Forces — even, astonishingly, the communists — united by despair of the Shah and hopes for a better future, pledged allegiance to Allah and loyalty to Khomeini. In February 1979, the Shah abdicated and fled to Egypt to die in exile. Khomeini returned in triumph to adoring crowds in Tehran.

The brooding figure of a malevolent old ayatollah with dictatorial powers now ruled Iran and the Shi'a Muslim world. Khomeini's word was law. With a ruthless single-mindedness at odds with his claims to other-worldly spirituality, Khomeini swiftly set about putting his own draconian version of the rule of Allah the compassionate and merciful into action. The hangman and the firing squad found no shortage of work as a vengeful Khomeini took revenge on his opponents and let the Mosque settle old scores under the pretext of cleaning out the stables. Political opponents and members of the old regime were butchered or fled at the same time as thieves lost their hands, homosexuals were executed and sophisticated Tehran women were forced out of Yves Saint Laurent and Dior back into the *chador* and *burka*. Alcohol was poured into the drains and everywhere symbols of Western capitalism and decadence were torn down or defaced. Politics in Iran became synonymous with the Mosque: and the Mosque was synonymous with the Ayatollah's medieval view of God's kingdom on earth.

Within the year, Iran was officially declared an 'Islamic' republic, with Khomeini unsurprisingly enthroned as 'Supreme Guide of Allah' and all secular opposition crushed or sidelined. Even dissenting clerics were imprisoned or worse. In a final explosive gesture of defiance and demonstration of Khomeini's internal power, the American Embassy in Tehran was stormed and occupied in November 1979 by militant students of Khomeini's 'Party of the Iranian Revolution' (PIR). The new Islamic regime sent out shock waves both to the West and throughout the Muslim world.

Khomeini was stopped in his tracks by an unlikely adversary. Saddam Hussein, the 'Godless Ba'athist of Baghdad', ruled over a predominantly 75 per cent Shi'ite Iraq. Mindful of the adage that when your neighbour's house is on fire it is wise to take precautions, in 1980 he invaded Iran to seize the vital oil-exporting installations in the Shatt al-Arab. Saddam may also have calculated that Khomeini's fanaticism needed to be stopped from sending too many revolutionary sparks on to Iraq's somewhat incendiary Shi'ite roof.

Faced with a mortal threat to his revolution, Khomeini one last time turned to Iran's vast army of poor, young, urban, working-class men and peasants. These were the foot soldiers and simple faithful who had swept him to power. Like the alienated Iranian middle class, they were now beginning to question the real benefits of Khomeini's emphasis on Islamist ideals at the expense of tangible prosperity and progress. After a year of clerical privilege and the absence of material benefits they were also becoming restive. Khomeini sent out a rallying call to divert them to their new holy task – invoking the Shi'ite concept of martyrdom in defence of the Faith.

Hundreds of thousands of young Iranians volunteered to fight the Iraqis and, in a welter of bloodletting not seen since 1914–18, they were hurled against the invader. The volunteers (*Bassidji*) died like flies in frontal attacks against Saddam's army but stopped the advance.[9] Khomeini trumpeted their sacrifice, claiming that they had been 'martyred for Allah' against the 'Godless Ba'athist of Baghdad'. Iranian blood, martyrdom and sacrifice again became the symbols of militant Islam.

The mantle of Islamic leadership now passed from the cautious but generous Saudis to the fiery and revolutionary Iranians. The new message to the faithful was clear: 'Rise up against your impious and corrupt leaders, take up arms against the foes of God, and Jihad and martyrdom will win the day.' In images of blood and religious fervour, Khomeini's Iran exported its Islamic revolution to the rest of the Islamic world.

Among the teeming millions of this Arab and Islamic world, where 50 per cent of the population is under thirty and extremely poor, the Iranian call to arms struck home. Nowhere did it have a greater impact than in Lebanon, Palestine, Gaza and the West Bank, where disaffected young Arabs, long without hope and searching for a means of hitting back at Israel, rallied to the fundamentalist cause. For the first time the 'call of Allah' became synonymous with opposition to Israel. Opposition to Israel and religion were now fused as one cause and with explosive consequences. Anyone who supported Israel was now declared to be a legitimate target for the faithful.

Hizbollah, the popular movement backed by Iran, invoked the call of martyrdom and carried out a series of spectacular suicide bombings against Western targets. In one bombing in Beirut, 258 US Marines died and the Western powers rapidly withdrew from Lebanon, leaving it to the locals to sort out their own arguments. The mullahs and imams proclaimed the victory: martyrdom and terror could even frighten off the mighty USA. Suddenly Khomeini's Islamic revolution was inspiring passions and uniting Arabs far beyond Iran's borders.

In the end, like many old men in a hurry, Khomeini overreached himself. He had long coveted the ownership and control of the Holy Places of Islam for his Shi'a faithful. After an abortive 'spontaneous uprising' at the 1987

---

9 The Iran–Iraq War (1980–88) lasted twice as long as the First World War and probably killed more than a million men.

Hajj in Mecca, an appalled Muslim world surveyed the 400 dead pilgrims and unequivocally blamed the baleful old man of the Persian mountains. Exhaustion on the battlefield and a renewed offensive in the long-running war with Iraq in 1988 finally forced Khomeini to 'drink the poisoned chalice' and sign a peace treaty with Saddam Hussein to ensure the survival of his own regime. But his legacy of terror, martyrdom and jihad lived on. Meanwhile the fanatics and the militants looked for new causes.

Nowhere was there a better cause for radical Islam than in Afghanistan. In 1979 – the same year as Khomeini's revolution and the storming of the US Embassy in Tehran – the Soviet Union invaded the country of confused, backward and warring tribes that made up one of the world's most primitive states.

The invasion, on Boxing Day 1979, took NATO and the rest of the world completely by surprise. Astonished and worried intelligence officers were recalled from leave as planeload after planeload of Soviet special forces landed at Kabul to seize power. President Amin was murdered in his palace and a Soviet-style communist regime seemed assured. But as the weeks progressed, a combination of Afghan nationalism and Islamic fervour united the mujahideen fighters from the tribes against the godless Marxists from the north. The Soviets found themselves embroiled in a war of national resistance against a determined and courageous enemy. Moreover, it was an increasingly well-armed enemy. The mujahideen seemed to have endless supplies of good machine guns, specialist advisers and dangerously effective anti-helicopter missiles. Pakistan – backed by the CIA – was arming the Afghan resistance, in particular an Islamic group known as *Hezb-e-Islam*. America, 'the great Satan', was actually arming Islamic fundamentalists. One of America's clients was an obscure Saudi resistance organizer, called Osama bin Laden.

Bin Laden was born in 1957, the son of a rich Yemeni contractor who had made a fortune from restoring Saudi Arabia's 'Holy Places'. Osama's mother had occupied a lowly place in his father's house, being referred to as the 'slave bride' by the senior wives, and the young boy, his mother's only child, had wandered the family mansion, alone and friendless. From such childish psychological scars, great consequences can befall.

Bin Laden's early career appears to have followed the standard pattern of rich young Saudis: university in Lebanon, wild drinking sprees with loose women and his friends, and cruising Jeddah in a canary yellow Mercedes 450SL. The playboy's days of gladness ended abruptly in 1977 when he made his Hajj to Mecca. Suddenly, Osama bin Laden became a born-again Muslim. Like many a fanatical convert before, his burning desire to atone for past misdeeds now went looking for some pious outlet to express his new-found zeal.

By the time of the Soviet invasion, bin Laden was in his early twenties, devout, clever, ambitious and rich. He rapidly fell under the spell of a Palestinian, Abdullah Azzam. Azzam, as well as being a fiery preacher of Islam, was busy in the 1980s organizing a supply of dedicated Muslim volunteers to fight in Afghanistan. Bin Laden now had his cause and his teacher. Osama learned his skills in Azzam's 'Office of Service', recruiting, training and moving the volunteers to a network of camps and bases in Pakistan and Afghanistan. Bin Laden proved to be a good pupil and a skilful organizer, and the 'Office of Service' eventually pumped over 30,000 volunteer Islamic fighters from all over the world into Afghanistan, backed by a ready supply of Saudi Arabian government aid, Pakistani logistics, CIA intelligence and American Stinger missiles.

When the Soviets finally quit Afghanistan in 1989, the battle-hardened veterans of 'The Office' dispersed back to their home countries. These 'Afghan-Arab' fighters took with them a radicalized, armed view of Islam and a track record of success and victory fighting Islam's foes. From this network of veterans and Azzam's 'Office' sprang the idea of *al Qa'ida*, 'the cell', a looser international grouping of like-minded Islamic warriors and men of action, all bound by their mutual great calling and all determined to carry on their life's work – fighting for the name of Allah. As Azzam and Khomeini had made clear, Jihad and martyrdom in Afghanistan were just the beginning of the fight to establish God's kingdom on earth.

Flushed with success, Bin Laden returned to his native Saudi Arabia and soon ran into trouble. By 1991, the desert kingdom was packed with foreign troops, mostly American, busy preparing for and then fighting 'Desert Storm', the first Iraq War. To the devout bin Laden, raised in the Wahhabi tradition of strict puritanical observance of the Koran and the law, these impure foreigners so close to the Holy Places were a source of corruption and pollution in every way. He said so openly, and offered his own wealth and organization as a defensive bulwark to the House of Saud. Rejecting this poisoned cup, the Saudi regime found bin Laden and his followers too great a challenge and took steps to force him out. By 1991, a resentful Osama found himself exiled in the Sudan behind a Khartoum office whose brass plate openly displayed the name of his business: 'al Qa'ida'.

Al Qa'ida's business remained as it had been when bin Laden worked for Azzam's 'Office' in Afghanistan: raising funds, recruiting and training suitable volunteers, moving men and money round the world and creating an international organization dedicated to fighting the foes of Islam. But by 1992, the year America invaded Somalia, the foes of Islam were no longer the 'Godless Marxists' of the Soviet Union. They had long gone. The new foe was the United States of America and the 'arch-oppressors' of the Palestinian people – the state of Israel.

Al Qa'ida openly joined the warlords and clans fighting against American troops in Somalia, and by 1996, when bin Laden issued a fatwa against the US and was then forced to flee from East Africa to Afghanistan, the organization had become a clearly identified terrorist threat. Afghanistan provided the perfect haven for bin Laden and his followers. The fanatical Taliban regime of young students, fired with missionary zeal in their madrasas or religious schools, brought a brand of puritanical Islamic asceticism that echoed bin Laden's own Wahhabi views. Here in Afghanistan he could live a godly, quiet and sober life, plotting global murder and mayhem. In 1998, the year al Qa'ida began suicide bombings against American embassies in Africa, he issued a rallying call to the faithful, proclaiming his 'World Islamic Front for Jihad against Jews and Crusaders' (WIFJ), an organization whose title is also helpfully its mission statement. With al Qa'ida and bin Laden at its heart, the WIFJ spelled out bin Laden's aims: free the Holy Places of Arabia from foreign influence, drive the Jews out of Palestine and kill anyone who dares to obstruct Allah's warriors or aid their enemies.

Muslim terrorism was on the march around the world – with a cause and a burning desire for vengeance.

14

THE BIGGEST BLUNDER? – THE ATTACK ON THE WORLD TRADE CENTER

'Across the Government, there were failures of imagination, policy, capabilities and management'

THE 9/11 COMMISSION (NATIONAL COMMISSION ON TERRORIST ATTACKS UPON THE UNITED STATES), FINAL REPORT, 22 JULY 2004

At a stroke, Israel, the USA, the West and any Muslim who disagreed with al Qa'ida's view of the world were brought into Arab terrorists' gunsights as legitimate targets for Osama bin Laden and his followers. The battle lines for global terror and the horrors of '9/11' were now openly drawn up by the 1990s. On the one side stood the fanatical warriors of Allah, united by a common cause, an historic grievance against the West, with access to millions of disaffected supporters, unlimited funds and a worldwide network of sympathetic organizations. On the other stood the Great Satan and its allies, with its network of military bases, global capitalism and local collaborators, standing as an affront to Islam and its values while offering a feast of soft targets.

The planning for the WTC attacks on the World Trade Center (WTC) in New York and the Pentagon near Washington DC had started five years earlier. On 26 February 1993, a half-ton truck bomb put together by an Arab called 'Youssef' detonated under the World Trade Center in New York, killing six and injuring 1,000. Youssef escaped.[10] The bombing, timed to correspond with the anniversary of the ejection of Saddam Hussein's armies from Kuwait two years before, had all the hallmarks of the carefully planned terrorist attack and was almost certainly controlled by Iraqi agents based in the USA.

---

10 Youssef was later arrested for planning to hijack twelve US airliners simultaneously over the Pacific.

Youssef's massive bomb blasted down through six levels, but Yamasaki's innovative architecture and the thousands of workers in the building survived the explosion. However, the WTC's vulnerabilities were openly exposed and explored in the extensive media coverage after the attack, especially its propensity to progressive collapse if hit higher up. The 1993 attack proved that the WTC was a tempting target and, moreover, it also showed how the twin towers, symbol of America, capitalism and the rule of the Godless could be brought down.

The mysterious 'Youssef' had drawn up a blueprint for disaster.

By 2000 the CIA knew all about al Qa'ida. After the attack on the USS *Cole* off Yemen in June 2000, which killed seventeen American sailors, the world's intelligence agencies also knew that they were facing a well-coordinated, clever and fanatical organization that was prepared to deliver suicide bombs by unconventional means (the *Cole* had been blown open by a suicide boat coming alongside). They also had incontrovertible evidence that they were up against an enemy that was perfectly capable of planning and executing decisive attacks against well-defended Western targets.

The Koran strictly forbids suicide. *Intehar*, or killing oneself, is specifically against the law. However, martyrdom, *shahid*, and acts of self-martyrdom – *intishad* – for the cause of Allah are not only accepted but praiseworthy. Not every Muslim imam agrees; even Sheikh Fadlallah of Hizbollah has condemned the practice of suicide bombings. However, bin Laden's mentor in Afghanistan, the Palestinian Abdullah Azzam, had laid great stress on the glories to be obtained by martyrdom, even writing: 'Glory does not build its lofty edifice except with skulls,' and elsewhere: 'Those who think that they can change reality without blood sacrifice... do not understand our religion.' The concept of martyrdom is in fact deeply entrenched in Islamic tradition, especially the Shi'ite sect.

Hizbollah was the first modern Islamic group to make a policy of suicide bombers, or martyrs. Between 1982 and 1996 they waged a successful campaign against the Israelis, emulating the suicide bombers of the Tamil Tigers in Sri Lanka who, in turn, modelled themselves on the Japanese Kamikaze pilots of 1945. Inside Palestine, suicide attacks are portrayed as heroic acts and families gain both honour and hard cash from their children's sacrifices. Polls show that two-thirds of Palestinians support suicide bombing as a tactic. It is regarded as both cost effective in terms of getting Israelis to pay attention (suicide bombers account for only 1 per cent of attacks on Israeli targets, but cause 44 per cent of Israeli casualties, according to Hamas) and also a good way of getting publicity for the Palestinian cause.

Fanatical young Muslims, many well educated and with at least 10 per cent young women in their ranks, volunteered to carry the fight to the Israeli camp. Although hard for the Western mind to understand, an instantaneous death, while smiting down the enemies of God, is for many Muslims a guaranteed passport to Paradise – and they believe it. By their sacrificial act they also establish their true identity for all time; not as some worthless, half-educated, unemployed youth, but as a religious warrior with a glorious new identity and a name that will live on for ever. For impressionable young people imbued with and schooled in religious fanaticism since birth, this is an enticing prospect, however incomprehensible it may seem to Western eyes. The martyr's last days are carefully controlled by the hard-eyed godfathers of terror to nurture and reinforce this idea. Like some human sacrifice of the Aztecs, the 'living martyr's' final glorious week is marked by feasting, one last – or even first – taste of earthly pleasures, adulation and admiration from all around and writing or videoing final emotional messages from the afterlife. Once trapped in this web of public commitment there is no going back for the suicide bomber. He – or she – is committed, and the waiting audience expectant.

Al Qa'ida's suicide bombers followed a similar pattern to Hizbollah and Hamas, but with less frenzy and an altogether cooler determination to strike bigger targets than just small knots of hapless young IDF conscripts waiting at a bus stop. After the USS *Cole*, Osama bin Laden was after much bigger fish, a global audience and, thanks to 1993, he even knew the right target. The World Trade Center beckoned.

In June 2002, members of the US Congress heard a detailed report on the most public, if not the worst (that doleful distinction falls to Pearl Harbor) intelligence blunder in American history.

In a closed-door, top-secret session with the Directors of the NSA, CIA and FBI, both the Chairman and Deputy Chairman of the Senate Intelligence Committee heard an extraordinary tale of intelligence lapses and mistakes in the months before al Qa'ida's attack on the twin towers. In their findings, the inquiry concluded that there had been no single piece of evidence, no 'smoking gun' to indicate that al Qa'ida was planning to use civil airliners as bombs and fly them into prestige US buildings on 11 September 2001. This chimed with the conventional wisdom that the terrorist kamikaze attacks on the WTC and the Pentagon with airliners were so extraordinary that they could just not have been predicted. Nothing could be further from the truth for, contrary to ideas that 'the attack could not have been foreseen', the Congressional Report went on in the fine print to say that key intelligence which could have thwarted al Qa'ida's plot had been only too available. Sadly it had been ignored, mishandled or just not distributed by the US intelligence agencies. The attack on the World Trade Center and the Pentagon was in fact a monumental intelligence blunder.

While it was true that there was no one single piece of 100 per cent clear and accurate intelligence giving the exact date, time and location of the aircraft attacks on 11 September 2001, it is clear from the secret testimony at the Congressional Inquiry that the old, familiar problems of the American intelligence agencies had reasserted themselves once again.

Astonished American intelligence committee members heard that there had in fact been an abundance of intelligence available to the US intelligence community before the so-called '9/11' bombings. Literally dozens of clear indicators emerged of an impending al Qa'ida terrorist attack by aircraft against prestige buildings inside continental USA.

The intelligence committee heard a litany as familiar as the story of Pearl Harbor. Information that should have been communicated between intelligence and law enforcement agencies was not passed on; the significance of some intelligence reports was neither understood nor pursued; and key information that *had* been gathered was not even analysed or its significance assessed. From the post-attack analysis, the truth emerged of one of the greatest intelligence failures in American history. While the US – and other – intelligence organizations never identified the exact time and place of the impending WTC attack in September

2001, the US Congressional Inquiry revealed that their intelligence agencies had, however, amassed a great deal of detail about al Qa'ida's capabilities and intentions well before the WTC bombings.

Al Qa'ida's plot went back a long way. As early as December 1994 an Air France flight to Algiers was hijacked by Algerian GIA[11] terrorists who planned to crash the aircraft into the Eiffel Tower. French special forces took out the hijackers on the ground, but the warning both of terrorist capability and intention was there for all to see. In February 1995, the US Congress's Special Task Force on Terrorism and Unconventional Warfare actually published a warning that al Qa'ida was planning a terrorist attack on lower Manhattan using hijacked civilian airliners as flying bombs. The US intelligence agencies all received copies of the report which were duly filed away. More was to follow.

In January of that year, as part of the precautionary security for Pope John Paul's visit, the Philippine police had burst into a Manila apartment shared by three known Islamic militants. Among the items they seized was a computer belonging to one Abdul Murad, a known terrorist suspect, containing specific details of an al Qa'ida plan to hijack eleven airliners and either blow them up simultaneously or to fly them directly into prestige US buildings as suicide bombs. The plot was codenamed 'Operation Bojinka', a Serbo-Croat term for a big bang.

This strange story was confirmed later in 1995 when Pakistan handed Murad over to the US as a wanted terrorist. Under questioning, Murad turned out to be none other than the accomplice of 'Youssef', the mysterious 1993 WTC bomber. Murad boasted openly to American Federal agents about an al Qa'ida plan to dive-bomb airliners against US buildings. Rafael Garcia, the IT expert who had unbuttoned the captured computer for the Philippine National Bureau of Investigation, later revealed that when he downloaded the target list, the names of the White House, the Pentagon, CIA Headquarters and the World Trade Center appeared. He passed the information to the FBI.

The FBI interrogated Murad and he confessed to being a trainee suicide pilot with orders to learn how to fly civilian airliners for attacks on US targets.

---

11 GIA: from French Groupe Islamique Armé, 'Armed Islamic Group', an Algerian Islamic extremist group.

Armed with the names of his accomplices, the US authorities rapidly closed in on the 1993 WTC bombers and yet again the Pakistani police were helpful: 'Youssef', al Qa'ida's master bomber and their hero of the first World Trade Center bombing, was arrested while hiding in Islamabad and extradited to the USA. In 1996, the Great Satan tried, convicted and sentenced him to a lifetime in an American prison. The date of the first WTC bomber's US conviction and sentence was 11 September.

With Youssef and Murad safely out of the way, Project Bojinka was filed away by the CIA, NSA and FBI. The FBI congratulated itself on yet another successful anti-terrorist conviction. There was no attempt to issue new intelligence collection priorities from the Counterterrorism Center (CTC) set up by the CIA in 1986,[12] and there is no record of any special watch being kept on young Muslims suddenly wanting to learn to fly civilian airliners. For the FBI, the US's domestic security arm, the case was closed.

The FBI did, however, take the threat seriously enough to issue special air alert warnings during the 1996 Atlanta Olympic Games. In particular, they warned local law enforcement and security agencies to watch out for straying crop-dusting flights and demanded stronger than usual anti-hijack measures, 'to make sure that no one hijacked a small aircraft and flew it into one of the [Olympic Games] venues'. This awareness of the changing threat is confirmed by the Federal Aviation Authority's (FAA) 1999 and 2000 annual reports, both of which specifically highlighted bin Laden and al Qa'ida as 'posing a specific threat to the security of US airliners'. The idea of an airborne attack was at least embedded somewhere in the collective US security consciousness.

Between June 1998 and September 2001, no fewer than seventeen separate reports linked bin Laden and al Qa'ida with an attack on the USA, many indicating that an aircraft would be used.[13] Reports were received from Israel, Germany, the UK and Pakistan. This information failed to stimulate any reaction or revised threat assessment, despite a secret briefing by the Director of Central Intelligence, George Tenet, to his senior staff in the summer

---

12 In classic Washington style, the FBI promptly established their own version of a national anti-terrorist cell, the RFU.

13 See the US Congressional Report on the events leading up to 9/11, US Government Printing Office, June 2002.

of 1998 at which he declared, apropos of al Qa'ida, 'We are now at war.' Unfortunately he doesn't appear to have lobbied to change the national intelligence collection priorities to reflect this historic judgement; nor did the head of the CIA allocate any extra resources to counter al Qa'ida.

During the spring and summer of 2001 there was a 'significant increase' in reports of al Qa'ida activity indicating a strike against the US, and possibly a prestige target within America itself. Even more damning evidence began to accumulate in both CIA and FBI files, reporting that the terrorists were still contemplating using airliners as flying bombs. The National Security Agency (NSA), which is responsible for intercepting electronic communications, had not been idle either. Their Echelon intercept system (which hoovers up all communications and then checks them against key words such as 'terrorism', 'bomb', 'targets', 'al Qa'ida', 'spying', etc.) was clearly reading al Qa'ida's communications. Following the bombing of US embassies in Africa in 1996, al Qa'ida had become a priority target, and after the events of 9/11 the NSA admitted that they had 'intercepted multiple phone conversations from al Qa'ida operatives'. For example, early in 1999 NSA intercepted the name of one Nawaf al Hazmi as a likely al Qa'ida hijacker. The information was filed but apparently not passed on. More key telephone calls were intercepted, including calls from Abu Zubaydah, al Qa'ida's Chief Operational Planner and even Osama bin Laden himself. During the course of the Congressional Inquiry in 2002, embarrassed NSA Director Michael Hayden admitted that his agency had decoded no fewer than thirty-three warnings of an al Qa'ida attack between May and July 2001 – but had failed to pass them on for action.

In its turn, the CIA had little reason to crow at NSA's discomfiture. Although its Director, George Tenet, had been 'literally pounding on desks and warning of trouble' in the summer of 2001 and issuing apocalyptic warnings of war to his assistant directors, it transpired that he hadn't actually done much about his own warning.

A lack of suitable field officers meant that the CIA relied almost entirely on foreign agents and informers for its human intelligence on al Qa'ida. There were few – if any – American spies working inside Islamic terror groups. In the words of one unnamed CIA source after 9/11, 'The agency no longer risked mainstream US field officers in what were known as "diarrhoea" postings.'

As a result, a stream of uncoordinated reports in several languages, and of varying quality, poured into the CIA HQ at Langley, where understaffed and overworked analysts struggled to make sense of them. The truth was that there was a desperate shortage of Arabic-speaking analysts in the CIA's Counterterrorism Center. Most of the existing manpower there was heavily tasked to the existing national intelligence priorities: the continuing operations against the 'no fly zone' in Saddam Hussein's Iraq, al Qa'ida movements worldwide, WMD proliferation, Afghanistan, events in the Middle East and tracking the numerous militant Islamic groups popping up all over the world. To make matters worse, being an analyst at CIA HQ was considered a low-status assignment compared with the prestige postings to 'Operations', and most officers posted there were moved on after only three years. The result was, in the words of one critic:

> ... most [of the CTC analysts] lacked any real ability... to put the events they were seeing into any kind of true historical context... It was all short term tactical stuff... to save lives... It was a failure of comprehension as much as anything else.

It transpired that, between 1994 and September 2001, the CTC collated no fewer than twelve specific reports warning that terrorists were scheming to hijack an airliner and fly it into a prestige target. Several of the reports actually named bin Laden and al Qa'ida. One of these reports came from a 'walk-in' to the FBI's New Jersey office, where a stunned FBI agent was told that al Qa'ida were planning to hijack a plane and fly it into a building. Despite polygraph checks that proved the informant was telling the truth, nothing was done to alert other agencies. The idea was inconceivable; more like something out of a Tom Clancy novel than real life.

Despite all these clues as to al Qa'ida's intentions, the intelligence analysts of CTC and the other agencies made no effort to update and amend its collection plan to include indicators that al Qa'ida might be planning to use aeroplanes as bombs. No new Critical Intelligence Requirements (CIRs) were issued or called for. The US intelligence community remained fragmented and divided, complacently going about business as usual.

The truth is that the Counterterrorism Center was often not informed or involved in much of the intelligence reporting from the FBI or NSA, appearing to act merely as a Congressional fig leaf to cover the lack of serious awareness of the threat. CTC attempts to task the National Reconnaissance's satellites were sometimes overruled to keep them locked on to other more important non-terrorist targets. Even attempts to track Osama bin Laden's funds and banking network were aborted for lack of manpower and financial expertise, despite the CIA's notoriously close links with Wall Street and 'big money'. This was later to prove a deadly weakness in the final days before the attack.

As 2001 wore on, yet more indicators of trouble loomed over the horizon. Even for the most overworked intelligence analysts, some of the indicators were very clear indeed.

Early in 2001, the CIA's Malaysian Station had detected two known senior al Qa'ida terrorists, Khalid al Mihdhar and Nawaf al Hazmi, meeting at an apartment in Malaysia and then travelling on to America. The importance of this meeting was not lost on the CIA as 'Khallad', the al Qa'ida terrorist behind the bombing of the USS *Cole*, was present and in the chair. It was the same man. Al Hazmi was also well known to the NSA in Fort Meade, Maryland. Their signals intelligence operators had intercepted a message in 1999 proving that al Hazmi was an al Qa'ida terrorist and that he was plotting to hijack American airliners. They had, however, apparently not told the CIA or FBI.

In their turn, having watched this extraordinary gathering of terrorists at an al Qa'ida planning meeting in Malaysia, CIA HQ at Langley now failed to notify the FBI to put the two terrorist suspects on the watch lists for entry into the US. The result was that the FBI and the US Immigration Service looked on with only routine curiosity as both these would-be hijackers and known al Qa'ida terrorists flew openly into the USA. They subsequently made close contacts with an identified al Qa'ida paymaster, Omar al-Bayoumi, in Los Angeles, and later with a third hijacker, Hani Hanjour. A complete terrorist support team swung into action under the FBI's very nose as two known Islamic terrorists were helpfully provided with an apartment, clothes, cars, driving licences and all the administrative paraphernalia needed to settle in a strange new country by a hitherto unidentified al Qa'ida US logistics network.

All those involved were careful to shave off their beards, 'go Western' and be seen drinking in clubs and bars. The FBI filed routine reports. After all, wasn't this the normal pattern for these 'Ay-rabs' loose in the fleshpots of the USA for the first time?

Neither the CIA nor the FBI linked the significance of the group's activities in the West to al Qa'ida's intentions. A frustrated FBI agent said later that if the CIA had ever told him that al Mihdhar and al Hazmi were known terrorist players and were travelling to California to meet other al Qa'ida suspects, it would have made a 'huge difference'. (The FBI later admitted that no fewer than fourteen known terrorist suspects had been identified making contact with the al Qa'ida men roaming the west coast, but that the reports 'had not been followed up'.) The Federal Aviation Authority later complained bitterly that if al Mihdhar and al Hazmi had been placed on the governmental watch lists, then the two hijackers would never have been allowed to board Flight 77 on the morning of 11 September before it took off on its final flight into the Pentagon.

To add insult to injury, it later turned out that the FBI could have found out a great deal more about al Qa'ida's western cell if they had wanted to. For when all the pieces were later put together, it emerged that during this period both of the al Qa'ida terrorists had also met a key FBI undercover source in San Diego, California. The individual in question was an unnamed FBI Muslim informant *whose primary mission was to report on Islamic terrorism in the US*. This source was never tasked by the FBI to report on his two new Islamic acquaintances, and so appears to have kept his distance and made no attempt to gain the two al Qa'ida men's confidence. The result was that the FBI missed the chance to task a uniquely placed informant to collect intelligence on the al Qa'ida hijackers' plans.

Other warnings crowded in during the summer of 2001. In July 2001, the FBI field office in Phoenix, Arizona, sent an urgent message to the counter-terrorist offices at FBI headquarters and the New York office, specifically alerting them that al Qa'ida agents were now active in the US. It also warned that according to the flight school owners, the two Arabs 'were showing an inordinate amount of interest in learning to fly' but 'weren't taking much interest in take-offs and landings'. The Phoenix FBI's e-mail, that later became famous at the Congressional Inquiry as the 'electronic communication', then requested four specific actions:

- An immediate check on the background of all foreign students at flying schools in the US
- A check on the visas of foreign students learning to fly in the US
- The establishment of routine liaison reporting with all flying schools to keep watch and report on suspicious activity in future
- An urgent meeting with the CIA and other interested parties to discuss the significance of these intelligence reports

The 'electronic communication' was sent to the FBI's RFU, the NY Field Office (which had a lead responsibility on terrorism within the US), the FBI Terrorist Squad and the FBI's dedicated Osama bin Laden Squad. No one did anything. FBI HQ ignored the intelligence and took no action. They were, after all, as FBI lawyers pointed out on several occasions, 'a law enforcement organization, not an intelligence collection agency'. This was 'no Federal crime'.

Worse was to come. On 16 August 2001, the Minneapolis FBI was tipped off by a local flying school that a suspicious Arab had joined a flying training course in Minnesota and was 'interested in flying large commercial airliners'. Immediately suspecting preparations for a hijack, local FBI agents detained the Arab, Zacarias Moussaoui, who had entered the USA on 23 January 2001 on a ninety-day visa. That visa expired on 22 May, so when Moussaoui enrolled for a flying course on 11 August, he was quite clearly an illegal resident in the US.

The local FBI duly searched him and found that he had shin guards, padded gloves and a knife in his possession. When asked why he needed these, Moussaoui lamely said that he needed them 'for protection'. When asked 'what protection?' he had replied, 'because a believer must be prepared to fight to defend the faith'. The Minneapolis FBI arrested him and carried out their standard checks. They discovered from his instructors and classmates that although Moussaoui had claimed he was of French origin, he spoke little or no French. They also discovered that although he said he was going to be an airline pilot after the course, he too wasn't interested in take-offs or landings but only in flying the Boeing airliner simulator.

Suspecting that they had definitely bagged a would-be hijacker, the local FBI now alerted FBI HQ and requested a court order to search Moussaoui's rooms and place him under surveillance, using the Foreign Intelligence Surveillance Act (FISA). However, the FBI's Washington lawyers refused to apply for a court order against the suspect, citing legal technicalities with the FISA and again emphasizing 'law enforcement, not intelligence' was the FBI's prime task.

Worse still, they totally ignored the intelligence value of the information. No attempt was made to collate or connect it with the activities of al Mihdhar or al Hazmi, despite a warning from the French authorities that Moussaoui was a well-known suspected terrorist and wanted by them. In vain the Minneapolis FBI office pleaded that Moussaoui had a suspicious collection of civil airliner operating manuals in his possession and a letter from one Yazid Sufaat. Was there any trace on Yazid Sufaat? HQ FBI in DC loftily ignored this fuss out in the boonies while their headquarters lawyers debated long over the constitutional and legal niceties of the FIS Act.

The FBI might have reacted a lot more strongly if they had realized that 'Yazid Sufaat' was in fact a well-known al Qa'ida paymaster and the owner of the al Qa'ida apartment in Malaysia. This was the apartment in which al Mihdhar, al Hazmi and 'Khallad' the *Cole* bomber had held their January 2001 meeting watched over by the CIA; *but the CIA had never informed the FBI*. In the world's only intelligence superpower, with the best computer links on the planet, no one, not even the CIA's own analysts at their Counterterrorism Center, was bothering to collate the information and to make the intelligence connections. The CIA and FBI might as well have been operating on separate planets.

As the summer of 2001 wore on, the CIA also gradually became aware of the importance of an al Qa'ida cell based in Hamburg. The BfV (German domestic Security Service, the Office for the Protection of the Constitution) informed the CIA that one of the Hamburg cell's members, a Mohamed Atta, had now moved to the USA. (Later, after the 9/11 attacks, it emerged that at least three of the presumed hijacker pilots had lived together as part of the radical Islamic cell in Hamburg in the 1990s and had probably been recruited by al Qa'ida while there. In all fairness this was hindsight. The CIA had not known this fact before 11 September.)

What the CIA *had* known, however, was that Mohamed Atta was a well-known al Qa'ida terrorist suspect with a track record of smuggling explosives in Germany, and was wanted for a terrorist bombing in Israel. Yet, despite his blatant and known terrorist connections, Atta was allowed to enter and roam free in the US, *even in violation of his expired entry visa*, a fact that raises deep suspicions of incompetence at best, or something much more sinister at worst.

The puzzle as to what the CIA *really* did know about the al Qa'ida plotters before the WTC attack grows even more baffling when some of the other details are put under the microscope.

If their claims are to be believed, neither the CIA nor the FBI were at any time aware that what was effectively a complete training programme for a cadre of would-be al Qa'ida pilots was being held at Huffman Aviation's Flying School in Venice, Florida. Quite how this managed to go unnoticed is a bit of a mystery, because at the time a CIA front company called Air Caribe was also operating out of the very same hangar at Venice airport as Huffman's Flying School. However, despite this, it appears that Mohamed Atta and his Arab friends' flying lessons somehow managed to go completely unnoticed and unreported by the Feds. This highly curious coincidence must inevitably raise some suspicions of just how much the CIA really did know before 9/11. Was the CIA trying to infiltrate and 'double' the US-based al Qa'ida cell, in the hope of using it against Osama bin Laden's organization in the future?

The CIA was also well aware that the real mastermind behind al Qa'ida and Osama bin Laden was one Khalid Sheikh Mohammed (KSM). Khalid Sheikh Mohammed's nickname within al Qa'ida was 'al Mukhtar', 'the Brain', and he had a long record of terrorist involvement and planning with Osama bin Laden. He was well known to the CIA as the mastermind behind the Philippines Bojinka plot of 1995 and had even been indicted by the US authorities in 1996 as a wanted terrorist. KSM was one of the most wanted terrorists in the world.

In spring 2001, several foreign intelligence services warned the US that KSM was not only positively identified as the key planner for al Qa'ida but that he was also actively organizing a major strike against a prestige US target. Instead of issuing revised warnings to the FBI and NSA and drawing up a new collection plan to meet this emerging threat, the CIA analysts and the CTC continued doggedly on through the summer, even failing to appreciate the significance of KSM ordering extra terrorist agents into the US during June 2001.

From late July onwards, the indicators of an impending terrorist attack against the US began to flow thick and fast. These intelligence indicators were quite clear at the time and not just with the benefit of the 'retroscope' of 20/20 hindsight either. By 8 September 2001, US Intelligence knew that:

1. The White House National Coordinator for Counter-Terrorism, Richard Clarke, had issued a warning of impending terrorist attack to all agencies.

2. The NSA had collected clear intelligence from Echelon that the White House, Pentagon and WTC were being targeted by al Qa'ida.

3. The FBI knew that al Qa'ida terrorists were at large and active in the US.

4. The CIA was well aware that high-level dedicated Islamic terrorists were planning another atrocity and had moved to the USA.

5. The FBI and the CIA knew that suspected terrorists were learning to fly in the US and were interested in flying airliners.

6. There was plentiful intelligence that al Qa'ida had been planning for years (Operation Bojinka) to attack US targets using civilian airliners as flying bombs.

7. Israeli Intelligence liaison in Washington had warned the US of 'imminent attacks against highly visible US targets'.

8. The Russian government had warned the US 'in the strongest possible terms' that the USA was 'at imminent risk from an Islamic strike by terrorist aeroplanes against civilian buildings' and that 'twenty-five suicide pilots have been trained for this task'.

9. The French Secret Service (DST) had warned that 'very specific information indicates an imminent terrorist strike against the USA with the order coming from within Afghanistan'.

10. Egyptian President Mubarak had formally warned the White House at the end of August that his intelligence services were expecting an attack on America 'in the near future'.

11. Al Qa'ida's internal traffic was warning of 'impending Hiroshima against the great Satan of America'.

12. The Philippine government had warned CIA liaison that 11 September was a likely anniversary for some kind of retaliation for the imprisonment of 'Youssef'.

13. To add insult to injury, in late June 2001, Osama bin Laden had openly boasted in the Arab press: '*within the next two months*, an attack against the great Satan that will shake the world.' (Even allowing for Arab rhetoric, this must be considered to be a bit of a clue as to terrorist intentions.)

All these intelligence indicators that al Qa'ida's long-cherished Plan Bojinka was now up and running were in the hands of US intelligence officers by 7 September 2001. This was the day when the US issued a general alert that 'American citizens may be a target of a terrorist threat from extreme groups with links to Osama bin Laden's al Qa'ida organization.' There was no indication of any specific areas at risk, no mention of the well-advertised threat to lower Manhattan, and the FAA were not briefed on the real threat from kamikaze hijacked airliners.

Two final clues that something really big was cooking came in the week before 11 September. NSA allegedly picked up a telephone conversation between bin Laden and his mother on 8 or 9 September, in which the Saudi terrorist leader said, 'In two days you are going to hear big, big news and then you're not going to hear from me for a while.'[14] This piece of sigint from within one of the most secretive organizations in the US government cannot be corroborated; but if true, this was a crucial piece of evidence that something big really was going on involving al Qa'ida, particularly when combined with all the other pieces of intelligence.

The second clue that was a clear indicator that something was afoot came from that well-known source of good intelligence, the New York Stock Exchange.

Every experienced intelligence officer knows that the real weakness of 'OPSEC', operational security, always lies in the administration. For example, the maps that are issued before an attack are a complete giveaway as to where you are going to attack. Even money, however, can betray operations.

---

14 See NBC news report, 4 October 2001.

Thus in Northern Ireland, the IRA soon learned to look out for the 'extra duty claims' from British Intelligence operators working undercover. Even for the most dangerous clandestine work, MOD civil servants at HQ Northern Ireland insisted on detailed 'claims' and pored suspiciously over government forms for money spent. Their jobs were to make sure that an Intelligence Corps corporal working at great risk under cover on the economy was not defrauding the taxpayer of the price of a pint of beer, let alone the cost of a civilian hire car. Every penny spent needed the appropriate MOD 'claim form' with the operator's date, place and time. IRA spies in the Vehicle Registration Department and the Northern Ireland Claims Office rapidly discovered this Achilles heel of Whitehall finance, and used it to find out about the Army's secret operations to try and murder the undercover soldiers.

Operation Bojinka was no exception to this golden rule. In the last week before the attack, some very odd financial transactions swept the US stock markets. If anything gave away that something was imminent, the flurry of last-minute share dealing by those in the know pointed to some imminent major event that would shake the financial markets to their core.

A 'put option' is basically a bet on the future price of a share. For very little outlay, the investor signs up to an option to buy up a number of shares. He enters into a contract, guaranteeing to pay for these shares at some point in the future at an agreed fixed price. This 'fixed price' is usually below the market price on the day of the contract. He is basically taking a chance on buying more cheaply.

If, when the option date arrives, this fixed buying price is well below the original value of the shares, the investor has bought expensive shares at a very cheap price. If he gets it wrong and the price of the shares has gone *up* then he is lumbered with a very big bill. Essentially, the investor is gambling that the share price in the future will go down. Options, for those without strong nerves or a crystal ball, are little more than bets on the future.

In the days just before the WTC attack, something remarkable took place. In Chicago, over 4,500 United Airlines 'put options' were signed off on 10 September. Normally there would only be a few dozen. In New York there was a positive run *against* the share price of United Airlines and American Airlines – the companies whose planes were used to attack the Twin Towers

– in the three days before 11 September. Someone was staking a lot of money on the chance that the share price of the big US airlines would plunge. This was insider trading on a mammoth scale.

Morgan Stanley – who sadly traded from the WTC building itself – reported 'put options' suddenly leaping from twenty-seven contracts per day on 5 September to over *2,100* in the last three days before the attack on the WTC. Whoever made just these trading deals alone was guaranteed to make well over a million dollars when they closed their option. Merrill Lynch reported a *1,200* per cent jump in 'put options' on American and United Airlines. It appears that al Qa'ida was actually planning to 'make a killing' in more ways than one. In Europe, alarmed investors like the French insurance giant AXA blew the whistle for the regulatory authorities to step in and investigate what was going on. But it was too late.

The seismic shock waves of the attack when it came are too well known to need detailed re-examination. In a series of devastating attacks watched live on television by a stunned and shocked world, on 11 September 2001 al Qa'ida's Operation Bojinka swung into action. In a carefully planned and executed operation, four heavily laden US airliners with 261 passengers and crew on board were hijacked simultaneously on the US eastern seaboard. Two airliners plunged into the twin towers of the World Trade Center in Manhattan bringing them crashing to the ground. One plunged into the Pentagon in Washington DC and one crashed upside down in a field in Pennsylvania following a struggle between brave passengers and their hijackers. Everyone on board the airliners, including the 19 hijackers, was killed. One hundred and twenty-four died in the Pentagon and 2,792 workers and visitors from sixty-two countries died at the World Trade Center, including 418 New York firemen and policemen. Total casualties were 3,030. It was terrorism's most spectacular and grievous blow against the West.

American reaction on the day was uncoordinated and feeble. According to the Final Report to Congress, shootdown authorization was not communicated to the NORAD air-defence sector until 28 minutes *after* United 93 had crashed in Pennsylvania. Planes were scrambled, but ineffectively, as they did not know where to go or what targets they were to intercept. And, once the shootdown order was given, it was not communicated to the pilots. In short, while leaders in Washington believed that the fighters circling above them had been instructed to 'take out' hostile aircraft, the only orders actually conveyed to the pilots were to 'ID type and tail'.

There is some evidence that the apocalyptic images of 11 September shocked even bin Laden and his followers. When the Taliban were later ejected from Jalalabad as part of the US's carefully measured retaliation, an al Qa'ida videotape was discovered, on which bin Laden admits that even he had been surprised at the effectiveness of the WTC attack.

As the recriminations flew thick and fast after the attack, there was little argument that the attacks had been a monumental intelligence blunder. For a variety of reasons, the US intelligence community, despite the establishment of a dedicated Counterterrorism Center in 1986 specifically intended to monitor this sort of activity, completely failed to piece together the jigsaw so painstakingly collected by its three key national intelligence agencies. The NSA heard what the terrorists were up to; the CIA learned what the terrorists were up to; and the FBI saw the terrorists training and meeting in the US. No one bothered to connect the three. Despite the CTC's alleged charter, no single US agency was maintaining an indicators and warning board for the emerging terrorist threat, let alone coordinating the US national effort against terrorism. By the first week of September 2001, the US intelligence agencies had failed to appreciate the intelligence reports that they had in their hands, indicating that some kind of major terrorist aircraft-borne attack against a prestige target in the US was being contemplated, even if they didn't know all the details. Yet again, no one was putting the jigsaw together.

The truth was that the US intelligence community was neither organized nor equipped to meet a terrorist attack on the US before September 2001. Worse still, lack of communication, insularity and competition between the agencies, plus an inability to be flexible and adapt to new threats, meant that US intelligence, despite all the money lavished upon it, was unable to carry out one of its prime functions: to warn the president and the people of threats to the nation. There was no counter-terrorist plan, no counter-terrorist strategy, no counter-terrorist warning system. In the command bunker at Cheyenne Mountain, the USAAF's impressive automated indicators and warning radar display could track space junk over the Pole, let alone incoming nuclear missiles.

But, inside the USA, determined killers were running around planning an equally deadly strike and there was no comparable system of early warning.

Even the extra funding voted by Congress to beef up the US's counter-terrorist efforts during the late 1990s had been misapplied or wasted. Although the counter-terrorist budget had leapt from $5 billion in 1996 to nearly $11 billion in 2000, there was still no national database, the agencies' computers were not compatible and there was a grievous lack of analysts and therefore *analysis* of the threat. In particular, the level of Arabic-speakers was lamentable; only 30 per cent of some key Arabic- and Pashto-speaking posts were actually manned. When pilloried later at the Congressional Inquiry, the CTC's Director angrily flung the criticisms back in his accusers' faces, agreeing that he could indeed have done something if he had only had three things right before 9/11: 'the right people, the right budget and the right operational support with political approval'. The committee wisely backed off.

It was not just resources. The American effort was also hampered by legal considerations. While NSA could intercept al Qa'ida transmissions from Kabul and Quetta, it was theoretically prevented by law from monitoring transmissions inside the USA without specific legal authority. The CIA didn't talk to the FBI, the FBI were prohibited by law from collecting intelligence on American citizens, no matter how dangerous, and the whole counter-terrorist system was completely fragmented. The US didn't even have a national focus to which everyone had to report, let alone a national counter-terrorist strategy. In such circumstances it comes as no surprise that the president was never even offered a National Intelligence Estimate (NIE) spelling out the terrorist threat. After all the money, all the lessons of the past and all the work of dedicated men and women, American intelligence was still, sixty years after Pearl Harbor, in an uncoordinated mess.

In the welter of recriminations, claim and counter-claim in the days immediately after the attacks, it was clear that al Qa'ida was the only real suspect. America's response to the outrage surprised no one except those who had anticipated a blind knee-jerk spasm of rage. President George W. Bush declared open war on global terrorism. In a series of carefully calculated measures, the US then moved later in 2001 against al Qa'ida and its sanctuary base among the Taliban regime in Afghanistan. The American president followed this with a ringing denunciation of an 'axis of evil' naming North Korea, Iraq, al Qa'ida and Iran. (The last one was a dangerous choice, as yet again it alienated Iran's Shi'ite leadership and moderates. After Iran's discreet help in ousting the Taliban from Afghanistan, this was not only ungenerous but unwise.)

American policy was not to be swayed from its tough new policies, however. In the spring of 2003, the United States and its closest allies moved decisively into the Middle East, invading Iraq, ousting its dictator Saddam Hussein and, coincidentally, providing al Qa'ida and its Islamic fanatics with a 'target-enriched environment'. US policy had come full circle, confronting the Islamic world and the Middle East head-on and providing al Qa'ida with US soldiers and plump Western civilian aid organizations on their doorstep as fresh targets for terrorism.

The US was now involved in a new world war. From bombs in Bali to Baghdad, from French tankers off Yemen and attacks on Christians at worship in Pakistan; from explosive shoes in airliners over the Atlantic to stabbing police officers in leafy British suburbs, the sons of Allah locked themselves into a titanic worldwide struggle with the Western forces of law and order. In its blind hatred of the US, Israel and all it stands for, al Qa'ida has transformed itself into a global movement of autonomous local fanatics. Just as the World Trade Organization has transformed global capitalism, so then has Osama bin Laden and his Islamic fundamental followers globalized terrorism.

The War on Terror now began to close in on Afghanistan.

AFGHANISTAN – GETTING THE AIM WRONG

'As for the United States' future in Afghanistan, it will be fire and hell and total defeat, God willing, as it was for their predecessors – the Soviets and, before them, the British'

MOHAMMED OMAR

After the World Trade Center attacks, America went seeking revenge. Osama bin Laden became not just the 'most wanted' to the FBI but the 'most wanted man on the planet'. As the Americans closed in, hot for vengeance, Osama's options to evade justice shrank. However much gleeful Muslims celebrated over the destruction of the WTC, self-preservation made offering a bolthole for the al Qa'ida terrorists a dangerous occupation. As Osama's options for safety dried up, he and his followers eventually found themselves bottled up in Afghanistan.

Afghanistan was a final sanctuary for Islamist terrorists on the run. The mountainous north-east corner of the subcontinent was never really centrally controlled and housed a nest of Muslim fanatics and medieval warlords. The impenetrable jumble of the mountainous labyrinth of caves at Tora Bora could hide whole armies of frustrated searchers. Even the Americans could do little to winkle out this nest of terrorists, short of invading Afghanistan.

Osama bin Laden at last felt secure in his rocky sanctuary.

Any intelligence officer worth his salt has groaned on about being handed a cheerful note from the boss, saying, 'Let me have a three-page brief on "whither Afghanistan?" for tomorrow's meeting.' His counter should have been brief and to the point: 'Don't go there, Boss. It's a bad idea… '

The best response is to wave a copy of the last hundred or so intelligence briefs on Afghanistan over the past two centuries. All carry the same message, obvious to any student of national security, conflict or international affairs. For centuries the message has remained the same: 'Afghanistan is the graveyard of empires.'

Afghanistan has no real place in Western geostrategy. Thousands of Western soldiers have lost their lives and their sanity in Afghanistan since 1840. The various invaders and their partners owe it to history to examine why they lost, in the hope that they'll never repeat those mistakes.

Alexander the Great came and went; even the great Genghis Khan backed away from the rugged mountains and fierce warrior tribes.

The reasons are simple and unchanged. Afghanistan is a geostrategic trap for any invader and always has been. The huge landlocked country is a physical barrier to the Indian subcontinent, guarded by high mountain passes and worse, a primitive war-like population. The country's highest point is Noshaq, an intimidating 24,500 feet above sea level. Frozen in winter and scorching hot in summer: this is not good campaigning country.

The British, worried about Russia and the Czars moving into the North-West Frontier in the nineteenth century, lit the warning beacons of defeat in 1844. The region became a never-ending source of trouble.

The 'Great Game' was played out for a hundred years between the British, nervous as a long-tailed cat in a room full of rocking chairs about their precious Raj, and Czarist Russia, who never really got past Persia.

The reason was not just the fierce terrain. The second factor was the Afghan population. This was an amalgam of constantly warring, vengeful, bloody-minded warrior tribes. The Pashtuns are the largest ethnic group, comprising 39 per cent, followed by Tajiks, comprising 37 per cent of the country's population, and the Hazaras and Uzbeks largely make up the rest. They have a long history of rivalry, murder and double-dealing.

A primitive Sunni Islam is the only unifying factor that dominates the wild men of the hills. That and vendetta, which in the hands of Afghans can last for hundreds of years.

'The wound of the sword/gun will heal, but not that of the tongue,' is a common saying among the tribes where duplicity and oath-breaking are much admired as evidence of cunning. Afghans are universally distrusted in the subcontinent: 'Beware the kiss of the Afghan – it hides an adder's bite.'

The rout and destruction of the invading British, vainly trying to pacify the region in the 1840s, set the tone. In 1843, the British army chaplain, G.R. Gleig, wrote a memoir of the disastrous First Anglo-Afghan War, describing it as:

> … a war begun for no wise purpose, carried on with a strange mixture of rashness and timidity, brought to a close after suffering and disaster, without much glory attached either to the government which directed, or the great body of troops which waged it. Not one benefit, political or military, was acquired with this war. Our eventual evacuation of the country resembled the retreat of an army defeated.

With the British pushed back to lick their wounds, the tribesmen returned to their traditional pursuits of vendetta, robbery, double-crossing their neighbours and a surprisingly well-armed anarchy: because the nineteenth century brought two important innovations to the medieval warriors of the Hindu Kush.

The first was the modern bolt-action rifle, which enabled a tribesman to shoot his enemy from the comfort of his own home across the valley 1,000 yards away. The second, and less welcome, was the persistent British punitive expeditions to root out the wild men of the hills and secure the North-West Frontier.

When the British launched short-lived punitive expeditions, the Afghans learnt, over many decades of fighting, that they were no match for the well-organized British in set-piece battles. Instead, they relied on classic guerrilla tactics, withdrawing to their hills when confronted by a superior force, and then launching highly effective ambushes from their rugged mountain fastnesses.

The British in their turn developed a healthy respect for their tribal enemies and their vengeful women, summed up by Kipling's famous verse:

> When you're wounded and left on Afghanistan's plains,
> And the women come out to cut up what remains,
> Jest roll to your rifle and blow out your brains
> An' go to your Gawd like a soldier.

The North-West Frontier reverted to a kind of grumbling appendix of the subcontinent, ruled by reluctant puppet kings trying to bind the warring clans together, far to the north of the growing prosperity of British India.

Until 1946, a figurehead, King Zahir, ruled. He began an experiment allowing greater political freedom, but quickly reversed the policy when it got out of control. He was replaced in 1953 by Mohammed Daoud Khan, a Pashtun nationalist who sought the creation of a 'Pashtunistan' state.

King Zahir had sought a policy of maintaining national independence while pursuing gradual modernization, creating nationalist feeling to fill the vacuum, now that the troublesome British had gone. Into this vacuum came a new generation of politicians all too eager to meddle.

This leads us inevitably to von Clausewitz's hoary dictum: 'War is but a continuation of politics by other means'; because the lure of political meddling in Afghanistan by invaders never went away.

However, Afghanistan remained neutral and non-aligned with either power bloc in the Cold War. In 1973, Daoud Khan, the King's cousin, launched a bloodless coup and became the first president of Afghanistan, setting up the Marxist People's Democratic Party of Afghanistan (PDPA). This led to a civil war by 1979, between the Islamic guerrilla mujahideen and Taliban against the regime in Kabul.

Wary of a semi-Marxist regime not controlled by Moscow, and distrusting of Amin's government, the Soviet Army invaded the country in December 1979, heading for Kabul and 'liquidating' Amin just three days later. The Kremlin was in charge now.

Afghanistan's war had gone public and international.

The Russians learned very quickly the conundrum that is Afghanistan: what is our aim? From that simple Clausewitzian question came Afghan's problem, starting from Russia's heavy-handed intervention. 'Minister; what exactly are you/we trying to achieve?'

The Russians could police the valleys but the rough hill country was a dangerous lure to any attempts at pacification. The Soviets got bogged down as casualties mounted.

The key question for the Kremlin's politicians remained: what is our aim and strategy?

Two failings immediately stand out: the Soviets underestimated the strength and tenacity of the mujahideen; and there was no clear political aim from the Kremlin, other than to support and control a vaguely Marxist ally to the south. The Afghan War became a stalemate, 100,000 Soviet troops controlled the cities, larger towns and major garrisons, leaving the anti-communist mujahideen to control the countryside. Soviet troops tried to crush the insurgency by various tactics, but the guerrillas generally achieved a military dominance with highly accurate SAMs such as Stinger and Blowpipe to take out the hitherto dominant Russian attack helicopters. By 1988, the defeated Soviets had gone, leaving 60,000 dead, retreating across the Hairatan Bridge and leaving the Afghans to fight it out.

Afghanistan reverted to a nest of Islamic terrorism, out of control and locked in an endless civil war, with the Taliban movement (the follow on to the mujahideen) controlling 80 per cent of the territory.

Then in 2001 the event happened that changed the world. The airliner attacks on the World Trade Center in New York astounded most US citizens and shocked the world.

'It can't happen here!' was the horrified cry of middle America. America was inviolate, surely? The attitude of the people was best encapsulated by a dishevelled, disbelieving lawyer fleeing the WTC. 'I just missed an important contract meeting. Someone is gonna get their ass sued… '

Unfortunately for the sad lawyer (and despite plenty of intelligence warnings), WTC lawyers and lawsuits were no counter to a terrorist atrocity. As Cicero long ago observed, 'In war the laws are dumb… ' Suddenly, just like everyone else, America was a target. Wall Street lawyers or not, Middle America was enraged. As a result, and in a popular demand for revenge after the 11 September attacks, US President George W. Bush demanded that the Taliban hand over Osama bin Laden and expel al Qa'ida. The Taliban refused to extradite him and treated American demands to shut down terrorist bases and expel suspected terrorists with contempt. Hot for revenge, an invasion of Afghanistan was planned. It was firmly grounded in the theory of *'jus ad bellum'*. The US had been attacked by al Qa'ida. The remnants of al Qa'ida was based out of Afghanistan and had been encouraged by the Taliban. The US had just cause to respond, as it had been directly attacked on US soil. The UN agreed: the response was proportional, and it was a last resort, as the US cannot negotiate with terrorists. President Bush launched Operation Enduring Freedom on 7 October 2001, with the United Kingdom and its allies.

The United States and its close allies invaded Afghanistan and toppled the Taliban government. The invasion's aims were simple and clear: to dismantle al Qa'ida, which had executed the WTC attacks, and to deny it a safe base of operations in Afghanistan by removing the Taliban government from power. The British offered support for military action from the start. The invasion came on top of the fighting between the Taliban and the Northern Alliance groups, resulting in the Taliban controlling 80 per cent of the country by 2002. Unfortunately, the invasion was only the start of the first phase of the twenty-year-long war in Afghanistan and marked the beginning of the American 'War on Terror'.

The US and its allies swiftly drove the Taliban from power by 2002 and built military bases near major cities across the country. Al Qa'ida and Taliban members fled to neighbouring Pakistan or retreated to rural or remote regions such as the mountain fastness of Tora Bora. The invasion's original aims, to dismantle al Qa'ida, which had executed the 11 September attacks, and to deny terrorists a safe base of operations in Afghanistan by removing the Taliban government from power, had succeeded.

That was the easy bit: the real challenge was, 'What next?' Where the Afghanistan War started to run off the rails was with a lack of clearly defined political objectives. By 2004, the Allies had found themselves in the position of the Soviets before them. Thus began the disastrous 'mission creep' as Washington worked out what to do next.

The US decided to 'rebuild' Afghanistan. When NATO and the International Security Assistance Force (ISAF) assumed control of the mission in 2002–03, they began pursuing increasingly unrealistic goals. During those years, the mission grew geographically to include all of Afghanistan, while troop strength spiked from fewer than 10,000 to more than 100,000. A nationwide network of Provincial Reconstruction Teams was established to foster local governance and economic growth, and social goals were expanded to include democracy, women's rights, education, ethnic diversity and inclusion, and anti-corruption. All balm to liberal Western ears but a direct clash with Afghan culture.

Hundreds of billions of dollars were spent in an effort to strengthen Afghan institutions, pay teachers' salaries, and build schools, medical clinics, military headquarters, troop barracks, roads and bridges – part of the nearly endless list of projects and programmes siphoned off to US corporations, designed to improve Afghan quality of life. But, ultimately, these resources were expended and in many cases wasted in a place that did not matter to vital US and allied interests, in support of a government that was inept, venal and corrupt.

At various points, the US strategy grew to:

- Eliminate al Qa'ida and destroy the Taliban
- Deny all terrorist groups a safe haven in Afghanistan
- Build Afghan security forces so they could deny terrorists a safe haven
- Build new infrastructure such as roads, dams and bridges
- Ensure women's liberation
- Help the new civilian government to become politically legitimate and able to win the trust of Afghans

From this mishmash of competing priorities, the US government struggled to develop and implement a single coherent strategy for what it hoped NATO would achieve. The division of responsibilities among agencies did not always take into account each agency's strengths and weaknesses. For example, the US Department of State was supposed to lead reconstruction efforts, but it lacked the expertise and resources to take the lead and own the strategy in Afghanistan. In contrast, the DOD had the necessary resources and expertise to manage strategies, but not for large-scale reconstruction missions with significant economic and governance components. This meant no single agency had the necessary experience, expertise and resources to develop and manage the strategy to rebuild Afghanistan.

While initially tied to the destruction of al Qa'ida, the strategy grew from including the defeat of the Taliban, an insurgent group now deeply entrenched in Afghan communities, then expanded again to include corrupt Afghan officials. Meanwhile, deteriorating security compelled the combat mission to grow even further. US officials believed the solution to insecurity was pouring ever more resources into Afghan institutions – but the absence of progress after the surge of civilian and military assistance between 2009 and 2011 made it clear that the fundamental problems were unlikely to be addressed just by pumping in more dollars. The US government was simply not equipped to undertake something that ambitious in such an uncompromising environment, no matter the budget.

Washington spent twenty years trying to rebuild Afghanistan, its security forces, civilian government institutions, economy and civil society. The Department of Defense (DOD) spent *$850 billion* on war fighting, during which 2,500 American troops and 1,150 allied troops were killed and 20,000 US troops wounded. At least 66,000 Afghan troops died. More than 48,000 Afghan civilians were killed, and at least 75,000 injured – probably an underestimate. These extraordinary costs reflected the strategic muddle the Americans had allowed themselves to be sucked into through changing aims and no clear strategic aim and as priorities changed.

Some Americans were worried from the start. 'We were devoid of a fundamental understanding of Afghanistan. We didn't know what we were doing,' Lieutenant General Douglas Lute of the NSC pointed out.

The ghost of Clausewitz hangs over the whole tragedy. Rarely has the adage, 'War is nothing but a continuation of politics with the admixture of other means' been so clearly demonstrated.

At this stage a purist might argue that this is not an intelligence problem; but it is. Because the critical questions intelligence had to answer in Afghanistan were always as muddled as the ever-evolving mixture of strategies that spawned them. Only by accepting Clausewitz's point can we unravel the demands and failures of intelligence. A brief selection of key intelligence demands can easily be identified from just the early phases of the war:

- Find bin Laden and al Qa'ida
- Identify terrorist bases
- Find safe villages
- Hunt out the Taliban
- Identify any likely attacks on allied villages and strong points

The truth is that having semi-occupied Afghanistan, the latest invaders didn't know what to do next, except flail away at their elusive rural enemy – just like the Russians – while trying at the same time to build a new nation from the historic rubble of the past. The absence of violence was a critical precondition for everything US officials tried to do in Afghanistan; yet the US effort to rebuild the country took place while it was being torn apart and while corrupt Afghan elites helped themselves to welcome stacks of US greenbacks.

And as the Congressional Committee of 2015 concluded:

The [Taliban – Mujahideen] activities range from opium trafficking, extortion and kidnapping that fuels the insurgency, to high-profile attacks in populated areas and improvised explosive attacks along road networks that both typically result in high Afghan civilian casualties. Rural areas of Afghanistan and the Afghanistan-Pakistan border regions remain a sanctuary for these various groups, and the remote and rugged terrain of these areas only adds to security challenges they pose.

Washington's knee-jerk reaction was, as ever, to throw more dollars at the various problems and tasks. The surprised and grateful Afghan elite, corrupt as usual, realized they could take these rich suckers for as much as they wanted. Congress sadly observed:

The deteriorating security compelled the mission to grow even further in scope. US officials believed the solution to insecurity was pouring ever more resources into Afghan institutions – but the absence of progress after the surge of civilian and military assistance between 2009 and 2011 made it clear that the fundamental problems were unlikely to be addressed by changing resource levels.

One US aid official lamented, 'We turned the spigot on and watched the money disappear into a hundred phoney projects like water on to dry ground.'

They were not helped by the rush to fill well-paid jobs by unqualified American contractors. There were very few genuine experts with knowledge

of Afghanistan. As one US contactor said, 'I knew hell about Afghanistan…
I got this job because I had a PhD and a pulse.'

This detachment from the people went deep in Kabul. There were thousands
of Americans working at the US embassies in Kabul and Islamabad, but
many admitted to little contact with the world outside their safe compounds.
Discouraged from venturing outside the closed US world of the compound,
many threw themselves into other vital national priorities, such as organizing
a cat society, hosting themed dinners and perfecting their tennis backhand.

In the middle of all this mixture of incompetence, greed, corruption and
the hunt for a dangerous enemy, 'intelligence' in all its forms floundered to
meet conflicting demands. To identify the problems, what better way than
to look at the intelligence cycle as it evolved over the twenty-year campaign?

Douglas London served in the CIA's Clandestine Service for more than
thirty-four years, mostly in the Middle East, South and Central Asia and
Africa, including Chief of Station and as the CIA's Counterterrorism Chief
for South and South West Asia. He pointed out early the lack of a clear
unifying aim:

- 'First, the Alliance fought in a strategically irrelevant place against
  the wrong enemy.
- Second, although driven by good intentions, allies expanded *the
  scale and scope of the mission well beyond the strategic level of interest.*
- Third, NATO sought to build security forces that were badly out of
  step with Afghan culture and technological capacity.
- Finally, the allies fooled themselves and their publics about the
  conditions on the ground.
- At each fundamental stage of the intelligence cycle – collection,
  analysis and dissemination – errors occur. When wrong intelligence
  data or assessments factor into major national security decisions,
  you've got a no-kidding intelligence failure.'

Collection

Collection was never going to be easy. There were three main sources: agents
and humint; surveillance ISTAR assets such as satellites and drones; and
electronic warfare as sigint. Each had their strengths and weaknesses.

America went, naturally, for technical solutions for collection: they could afford it. 'Diarrhoea postings' have never been popular in the CIA and the way to preferment was back in the clean corridors of Langley, not begging in some dusty, dirty 'rag top' market. Washington put its faith into sophisticated RPVs, drones and satellites combing the ground looking for the enemy.

ISTAR was the great US success. 'Insatiable' is how the United States Army's demand for unmanned aerial vehicles (UAVs) was described. The advantages of ISTAR (intelligence, surveillance, target acquisition and reconnaissance) saved manpower, and subsequently lives, by keeping troops out of the line of fire. United States Secretary of Defense Robert Gates was among those behind the growing use of UAVs in Afghanistan by the US and UK Army.

In 2007, a remarkable example of ISTARS in action brings the point home. Operation SEASONS was only one of several similar incursions into Zharey District in the summer of 2007 by a Canadian-led battle group. ISTAR identified a massive build-up of Taliban fighters near Kandahar. ISTARS directed the well-drilled and efficient Canadians into place; and ISTARS directed fire on to a force of several hundred enemy fighters, splitting them up and killing several hundred.

US Air Force A-10 Thunderbolt ground attack aircraft then swept the field with low-level strafing runs firing 30 mm multi cannon. Thanks to ISTARS the Taliban massing at Howz-e Madad were identified, engaged and destroyed. It was a textbook example of joint air/ground coordination only made possible by the various ISTARS airborne platforms.

The British, hampered by the usual Whitehall penury, were forced to turn to old-fashioned agents on the ground. Pretending to be a local was always a challenge but, in all fairness, the British, with their experience of hunting down the IRA in Northern Ireland, were surprisingly successful at some street-level surveillance. Talking to the locals and knowing their patch, brave individuals risked their lives to report from the ground. Humint, erratic as ever, was surprisingly successful – but only up to a point.

Analysis and Interpretation

Analytic errors were legion in Afghanistan, especially in the early days. Military intelligence officers with little knowledge of Afghan culture and society failed to analyse available information effectively and, through ignorance, made serious mistakes. One of the most famous was a report one night from an aerial observer that a column of cars with young men firing out of the windows had been spotted. The information was duly tracked and verified. The analyst on duty said that it was obviously a night-time raid by the Taliban. An armed helicopter strafed the convoy and wiped it out.

A cold dawn revealed the bodies of an Afghan wedding party, off to celebrate in traditional Afghan manner.

Such mistakes by half-trained, ignorant military analysts were hard to forgive – or forget. As a member of London's RUSI pointed out, 'They would have been better served by recruiting nerdy university academics who knew Afghanistan…'

Analysts might also err by presenting biased assessments, losing their objectivity as they told policymakers what they thought policymakers wanted to hear and corrupting the analytic process.

Dissemination

Intelligence officers often made correct, objective and timely assessments but communicated them ineffectively. If an important judgement isn't presented clearly to the principal, the intelligence process falls short. Afghanistan with its multi-layer cake of competing international agencies was a Gordian knot.

Worse; there were numerous examples of the intelligence officer thinking that the message has been delivered clearly enough, but the policymaker claims not to have seen it that way. The Afghans – to whom knowledge was power to be kept and used for advantage – frequently failed to pass on vital information. Henry Kissinger, national security adviser for two presidents, reportedly told his intelligence officers – who, he acknowledged, had briefed him correctly on what proved to be a timely intelligence warning – by weaselling out later, 'You warned me, but you didn't convince me.' From Washington to Kabul, no one was ever on top of all the multi-source intelligence available, least of all politicians with an agenda.

And in Afghanistan the personal desires of ambitious military commanders to push their mission all too often muzzled critical assessments saying unwelcome things they didn't want to hear. Analysts and intelligence officers worry about their jobs and pensions like everybody else.

In this case, context really matters. If the judgement was clear and effectively delivered, that's a policymaker problem – even if that policymaker claims the intelligence officer should have pressed the case harder.

As a result, reports from the field were often overly optimistic and late or watered down as they climbed the chain of command. Civilian leaders inside Washington's Beltway in particular also deserve much of the blame, as many political appointees at the Departments of State and Defense were more concerned about protecting the sitting president's chances of re-election (and their cushy jobs) than they were about telling the truth about the lack of progress in Afghanistan.

In the end, the chickens came home to roost. According to former Vice Chief of Staff of the Army, General Jack Keane, 'After the Vietnam War, we purged ourselves of everything that had to do with irregular warfare or insurgency, because it had to do with how we lost that war. In hindsight, that was a bad decision.'

Tragically, declining to prepare after Vietnam did not prevent the wars in Iraq and Afghanistan; instead, it ensured they would become quagmires.

For example, while it's certainly convenient to depict the shock and miscalculation US officials claim over Afghanistan's final tragic, rapid fall to the Taliban as an intelligence failure, the reality is far worse. It's a convenient deflection of government responsibility for decisions taken owing to political and ideological considerations, and provides a scapegoat for a policy decision that has no persuasive defence. The record shows that, from a multitude of sources, intelligence staffs warned their political masters of the impending tragedy.

Well-intentioned political leaders across the Alliance (and around the world) believed that Afghanistan could be turned into something more. Ignoring the British and Russian experiences, Western leaders sought to turn Afghanistan from what had traditionally been a corrupt tribal state with no history of centralized power into a nice new democracy governed from Kabul, with equal rights all round, and well-stocked supermarkets for all. The ignorance of and refusal to build on Afghan strengths was marked.

These attitudes went deep. The Afghan warriors of generations past, who defeated both the British and the Soviets, were known for their physical and mental toughness, mastery of stealth and bravery under fire. But the United States took these vaunted mountain fighters and forced them into its own hometown mould, ignoring their inherent strengths and weaknesses.

Afghan troops should have been primarily mobile, light infantry fighters living among the people and relying on minimal logistics. The Afghan Army was saddled with the trappings of a Western military. Instead of walking and using donkeys to carry their gear, they used trucks that tied them to the roads and flew in helicopters that were too expensive and complex to maintain.

Afghan troops should have lived in the local communities they were defending – but instead the United States and NATO allies built entire bases, where they lived in expensive barracks and ate in mess halls.

When it was time to patrol or carry out other combat operations, these troops deployed from their bases into the countryside, just like the foreign forces. Unlike the Taliban (and the mujahideen that preceded them), the Afghan infantry that the United States and NATO trained and equipped were hesitant to engage in close combat – unless an allied aircraft appeared overhead for close support.

One notable exception were the Afghan commandos, who performed brilliantly and bravely. These troops, modelled after allied special forces, understood the Afghan military tradition because they fought in small teams in hit-and-run actions. But their numbers were too small, and they were hamstrung by the military bureaucracy that surrounded the Afghan and US Army.

Over the course of the war, corrupt Afghan generals eroded the combat power of their troops by plundering their wages, food and ammunition and even selling their soldiers' rifles. As US and NATO forces withdrew, it became clear that Afghan Army trucks and helicopters couldn't even budge without the support of tens of thousands of well-paid US civilian contractors.

As the war drifted to its muddled close, poorly led and abandoned by their leaders, local troops surrendered to the battle-hardened and motivated Taliban fighters – who harnessed their own cultural-military traditions and remained unconstrained by the burden of a foreign-imposed bureaucracy.

There is an old axiom that 'war is too important to leave to the generals.' In Afghanistan many NATO generals were too close to the conflict to think objectively about the war. They'd spent a large portion of their professional lives leading troops in battles across Helmand, Kandahar and Khost provinces. For them, the war was personal; they'd lost men and women on the battlefield and would be damned if the Alliance was simply going to walk away, negating those sacrifices.

There were some brave souls and organizations that had it right all along. For their part, the CIA and the Defense Intelligence Agency had been clear ten years before the collapse that counterinsurgency operations were unlikely to succeed.

Special Inspector General for Afghanistan Reconstruction John Sopko bravely reported failure after failure when it came to reconstruction and the development of the Afghan security forces. Likewise, the free press accurately reported from the field, in one article after another, that the Afghan government and security forces were inept, riddled with corruption and doomed to failure.

Skye Christensen led a team of 250 professionals implementing reforms and stabilization efforts, working closely with the national and regional governments on transitional security and governance arrangements, financing and socio-economic development planning:

I am not an expert on foreign affairs, but will share with you my experiences as an Afghanistan/Pakistan Hand (AFPAK Hand) member working in Afghanistan to train, advise and assist the new government's national defense institutions on how to properly plan, program, budget and execute funding in support of military and policing operations.

I found myself caught in the midst of what seemed to be our endless attempt at bad parenting. Some reasons people chose to do things the way they did, I still can't understand. You can point out countless clichés, but it all boiled down to a systemic trend of sending in poorly trained military advisers and ego-driven leaders at all levels. Compounding this fact was that many corrupt Afghan leaders had no desire to change or embrace advances in their system until they could figure out a way to effectively manipulate it, especially if the advances didn't serve their personal interest, greed, or some prefer calling it, 'self-preservation'.

What appears to have been a catastrophic intelligence failure in Afghanistan is a sobering reminder that it was much more. Diplomatic presence in challenging places isn't working well enough. Our Western diplomatic and intelligence teams appear to have misunderstood their role and their responsibilities.

How did a 4,000-strong embassy misjudge something as fundamental as the stability of the host government? The truth is that US and Western embassies and consulates in challenging locations today function as gated communities, sealed off by an overbearing security apparatus that prevents them from doing diplomacy or intelligence effectively.

Such risk-averse thinking makes it probable that diplomats were badly out of touch with the country in which they were working. That was a function of the rules and structures, and deep-bred fear of lawyers and litigation that strangled Alliance diplomats from doing diplomacy and our spies from spying.

Doing good diplomacy, collecting intelligence and exerting influence is not possible if teams are cut off from the outside world.

The US consulate in Peshawar had little reference to the internecine politics of the North-West Frontier and its war-like neighbour. Security rules meant they scarcely leave the fortified compound. Not able to meet people outside, diplomats tried to lure thirsty Pashtuns into the compound with offers of bourbon and beer at the famed consulate bar…

The isolation of diplomats was further exacerbated by the practice of rotating diplomats out of stations before they could gain any understanding of the context. Many were in the country for less than a year, a period far too short to develop good relationships or even a decent understanding of the situation. Since most diplomats are freshly arrived, they are vulnerable to manipulation by various local 'experts' and gatekeepers who make a profession of brokering information and access.

As one of the few Americans working in the real world outside the consulate, I was regularly asked to brief US Government counterparts on what was going on 'out there'. The allure of first-hand information meant that these meetings were often so oversubscribed that it was difficult to get a seat in one of the embassy's large meeting halls.

An Assistant Secretary General for Operations at NATO has been equally frank: in a remarkable echo of many of his colleagues' views he recalled:

> I was responsible for writing the Alliance's lessons of Afghanistan in late 2021. While the full document remains classified, the key lessons themselves are not. In fact, they're obvious to any student of national security, conflict or international affairs.
> - First, the Alliance fought in a strategically irrelevant place against the wrong enemy.
> - Second, although driven by good intentions, allies expanded the scale and scope of the mission well beyond the strategic level of interest.
> - Third, NATO sought to build security forces that were badly out of step with Afghan culture and technological capacity.
> - Finally, the allies fooled themselves and their publics about the conditions on the ground.

It will be obvious to the reader that what is striking about this now-familiar litany of errors is *they basically are all the same.* When a number of highly qualified and knowledgeable commentators (the Assistant Secretary General of NATO, a senior member of the US National Security Committee, the CIA's local Head of Counter-Terrorism, the Head of Reconstruction and various reports to the US Congress) all express the same misgivings and, independently, make exactly the same points, it poses the question: why was this expert advice ignored at the time? The UK intelligence community had been aware of the potential for cultural bias and underestimating the Afghans for decades, and warned the US and ISAF of the need for more academic, cultural and socio-aware input. The Afghan souk is not like Main Street, USA. In the case of Afghanistan, these endemic problems led to failures at all four stages of the traditional intelligence cycle – agreeing critical elements of information; collection, assessment and lastly, dissemination. However, the main blame attaches to the politicians or advisors in Washington who misused and abused intelligence to justify their purely political decisions.

By 2021 it was all over. The Taliban closed in on Kabul so rapidly that the US had to stage the largest-ever evacuation of non-combatants from the Hamid Karzai Airport. This was a final humiliation to cap off twenty years of operations in Afghanistan. America cut and ran, defeated just as in the final days of South Vietnam. The US had a moral and ethical duty to their trusting allies left behind, and it failed to fulfil its promise, as thousands were left behind to confront a Taliban government that would sign their death warrants.

This woeful catalogue of error leads but to one conclusion. The fault of the Afghanistan campaign can be distilled into a failure to direct the first and most basic principle of conflict: 'the selection and maintenance of the aim'. All Afghans' problems stem from that; and that was a *political* not an intelligence failure. The 'War on Terror' had no strategic aim.

Sir Simon Fraser of Chatham House, an experienced diplomat, summed it up in magisterial, measured style:

> The outcome in Afghanistan should not have been a surprise, even if the way it finally happened was a shock. For foreign policy in general, and foreign military interventions in particular, it is essential to be clear about goals and the capacity to deliver. In Afghanistan, the US and its allies fell short on both these counts.

The initial intervention was legitimate and justified as an act of self-defence following an international terror outrage. But it was always likely the goalposts would shift. Dislodging al Qa'ida morphed into removing the Taliban, then suppressing drug-related poppy production, occupying regions, protecting and supporting women and girls, building institutions, dams and bridges and training armed forces. All laudable *but open-ended commitments*.

The lesson is familiar. Intervention is not always to be avoided, but it must be clear about where it will lead. This was mission creep on a scale the US and NATO allies could not hope to resource adequately in a huge, rugged country, rife with armed factions and corruption, and in a sensitive, contested part of the world. And with an ever-changing mission 'intelligence' cannot handle all the permutations demanded by its political masters at once: order; counter order; disorder…

Afghanistan remains a revelation of the West's weaknesses and lack of focus. Bad politics, and underestimating the task to be done, not intelligence failure, was the guilty party.

THE RUSSIAN INVASION OF UKRAINE, 2022

'President Putin has chosen a path of bloodshed and destruction by launching this unprovoked attack on Ukraine… this is a catastrophe for our continent'

BORIS JOHNSON

One of the problems of history is that we don't realize we are living it. Today's events are tomorrow's memories and next year's history; but they are happening now, all round us.

What is true for historical events – that is, today's 'big news' – is our failure to acknowledge them as we live through them. Memory and history blur into one. For example, an old man of eighty remembers the Falklands War. Or the paddy fields of Vietnam. He was there. He experienced them. It is a vivid – sometimes too vivid – memory. But to his grandchildren it is ancient history, on a par with teacher's tales of Greece and Rome. Memory and history have become mixed and are viewed differently…

Armed with this insight it is clear that, even unfinished, the Russian invasion of Ukraine is a historic event and one that will linger as long as memory permits. And yet it is clear that we are daily living through history, just like our grandfathers. It therefore demands that we examine just what is going on in this full-blown war (at the time this book went to press) going on around us *now*. Ukraine already provides a rich harvest of lessons for the craft of intelligence. We do not have to look far for bungling, underestimation of the enemy and sheer bad interpretation, generously provided by the Kremlin's ill-judged land grab for what Russians see rightly or wrongly as part of the 'Rodina', historic Mother Russia.

Using our knowledge of how intelligence is supposed to work, we can see the Ukraine war as a litany of intelligence mistakes: an accumulation of errors that show every sign of becoming a long and wearing struggle.

With the war at its first anniversary, diplomatic observers believe there is little likelihood for political settlement or a cessation of hostilities. Russia is unlikely on current form to seek a political settlement or ceasefire. The evidence is quite the opposite. Unless Moscow believes it has made enough territorial gains to present a victorious narrative to domestic audiences, the war will continue, much to the satisfaction of the big Western arms manufacturers and their shareholders, busy arming the Ukrainians. For Ukraine proves yet again truly, 'now thrive the armourers'. And their shareholders.

It is time to examine, using our old friend the intelligence cycle, just how Russia – and Ukraine – came to be trapped in this bloody impasse. Who gave the order for war? And why? What direction was given by the leadership?

Analysts are still speculating on the balance between advisers providing misleading information to Putin or the Russian leadership thrusting unrealistic objectives on to the Russian military. But clearly someone made a plan and someone decided on the actions to be taken.

All roads lead to Russia's dictator in all but name, Vladimir Putin, president of Russia.

We can backtrack what appears to have happened by unravelling events and facts. During 2021, Russia began to concentrate large forces around Ukraine, along a front of about 4,000 kilometres, from Belarus to Crimea and the Black Sea. On 24 February 2022, Putin launched what appears to have been a swift attack along the border, aiming to:

- Seize key points such as a corridor to the Crimea
- Control the religious heartland of the Russian Orthodox Church in Kyiv
- Topple the Zelenskyy Ukrainian government
- Occupy the friendly and pro-Russian Donbas
- Gain air superiority
- Drive the Armed Forces of Ukraine (ZSU, anglicized to AFU) into a retreat west of the River Dnieper
- Take out the AFU command and control centres in a decapitation operation

Russia seems to have had no plans to wage a lengthy all-out war of conquest in Ukraine. There were insufficient numbers of troops, and their fragmented and uncoordinated actions, weak logistical support and other indicators point to the original order having been for a land grab, not a long war.

This appears to be confirmed by the release of captured Russian documents purporting to detail Moscow's real plans for Ukraine after the initial invasion. If true, the UK's Royal United Services Institute for Defence and Security Studies (RUSI) leaked document of 2022 was a genuine showstopper. The oldest defence and security think tank in the world revealed details of Moscow's pre-invasion plan for Ukraine. According to the captured Russian document, apparently signed off by Vladimir Putin, even deputy heads of branches within the Russian military were unaware of the plan to invade and occupy Ukraine until days before the invasion began, and tactical military units didn't receive orders until hours before.

However, in autumn 2022 the captured document gave us a very different view of Putin's war. Key points were:

- Russia had planned to take over Ukraine over ten days and annex it.
- The documents also revealed that Russia planned to capture Ukraine's power stations (especially nuclear), airfields, water supplies, central bank and parliament – and that Russian special services were tasked with killing the Ukrainian leadership.
- They appeared to assume Ukrainian government officials would 'either flee or be captured as a result of the speed of the invasion'.
- Ukraine's intelligence community also believed Russia planned to use Belarusian airborne units to capture the Rivne and Khmelnytsky nuclear power plants.
- The invasion plan reportedly detailed plots to capture Ukraine's nuclear power plants in order to shelter Russian troops, gain control over the country's energy system, and potentially blackmail European countries with the risk of radiation pollution.
- Russia planned to start the invasion with a 'massive missile and airstrike campaign' against Ukrainian military targets, RUSI said.

- It added that Moscow would not target critical infrastructure such as power stations and railways because these were key to its plans to occupy the country.
- Getting rid of Ukrainian officials was a priority target. The Russian counterintelligence regime had compiled lists of some Ukrainians, divided into four categories:
  - Those who should be killed
  - Those in need of suppression and intimidation
  - Those considered neutral who should be encouraged to collaborate
  - Those prepared to collaborate
- Russian officials planned to register the population through door-to-door sweeps and screening camps.
- Russia also reportedly planned the coerced co-operation of regional governors and local authorities, and the FSB (State Security) had been tasked with capturing local officials.
- Over time, it planned to bring teachers and other officials from Russia to start the 're-education of Ukrainians'.

From this we can infer the *direction* given by Putin and his planning group and their initial intelligence demands of their staff. These all seem to have misfired; in some cases, quite badly.

By far the biggest failure was to underestimate their enemy. In this misjudgement they join the smug British colonials before the debacle of Malaya and Singapore. Because the Armed Forces of Ukraine (AFU) didn't fold up meekly, and neither surrendered en masse nor were quickly defeated. On the contrary, the Ukrainians fought back tenaciously and, with a sudden supply of sophisticated Western hi-tech weapons and missiles, wreaked havoc on the invaders. The attack stalled. Even Kyiv, a key strategic and propaganda objective, fought its would-be besiegers off and forced them to withdraw. Russian intelligence had let its masters down.

It is interesting to speculate on exactly what was the Kremlin's intelligence collection plan for the invasion. Of two things we can be certain: first, Ukraine was riddled with Russian agents; second, the plan would have relied disproportionately on humint. Russia has a long and successful tradition of spies and human intelligence. The Glavnoye Razvedyvatelnoye Upravlenie ('chief intelligence directorate' or GRU) military intelligence directorate would have been the agency responsible. The GRU prioritizes agents, not technology.

The upshot of this means that American military intelligence chiefs concluded that President Putin can no longer achieve the goal with which he began the invasion of Ukraine. His intelligence was way off the mark.

Putin ordered the invasion of Ukraine in February 2022 and dubbed it as a 'special military operation'. The Western analysts agree that it was at some unstated, deep level really aimed at overthrowing the West-backed Ukrainian government led by President Zelenskyy and setting up a puppet government in Kyiv, sympathetic to Moscow. This seems to be confirmed by the RUSI document. However, Russia's setbacks and stretched resources in Ukraine show its forces have completely failed to achieve that goal. This has been the verdict of the US Defence Intelligence Agency (DIA) and the Western intelligence establishment. Realizing this, it is worth examining what else the Kremlin got wrong.

For a start, underestimating the enemy is the greatest blunder of all. 'Know your enemy' is as old as Sun Tzu. This failure of intelligence by the Russians underpins the whole invasion and resulted later in the wholesale sackings of intelligence staff in Moscow. The roots of this underestimation was the core belief that Kyiv's forces would not be able to stand and fight the might of the Russian army, allied to the misconception that many Ukrainians were really sympathetic towards Russia and still hankered for the 'good old days'. The GRU were confident that Ukraine was stuffed full of fifth columnists and fellow travellers, all amenable to being used as reliable human agents of influence, if not open spying. Moscow and the GRU were badly mistaken.

What this means is that Putin is going to have to issue some new and relevant intelligence requirements to his minions. But first he has to decide what he wants and what is achievable. DIA chief Lieutenant General Scott Berrier spoke for all in autumn 2022 when he said that it was obvious that Russia's master plan had failed to achieve its objectives:

'We're coming to a point right now where I think Putin is going to have to revise what his objectives are for this operation. It's pretty clear right now that he's not going to be able to do what he initially intended to do.'

Before constructing what Moscow needs to do next, it is prudent to examine what Moscow got wrong or failed to do for the initial invasion.

First, the original **collection plan** was obviously flawed, as it failed to provide warnings of problems. Assuming that Putin intends to fight on, greater emphasis needs to be given to cold-bloodedly analysing the AFU's strengths and weakness, in particular its morale and competence as well as its weapons stocks, their capability and vulnerability.

We can assume that the **collation** of intelligence was thorough and, unless skewed *à la* Stalin by malign human behaviour, was perfectly competent in today's computer age. It is the *interpretation* phase that is of most interest. What did the Russian analysts make of the facts collected and presented? Were they swayed by their master's wishes? It certainly appears that way. The greatest mistake seems to have been over the human factors present on the Ukrainian side.

No one expected the AFU to fight back and resist the Russian invaders with a ferocity which shattered the Russian battle groups and surprised Western observers. Morale was high among the defenders just as it slumped among the hapless, poorly trained Russian conscripts, many of whom didn't realize they had invaded a foreign country. And Ukraine, far from welcoming the Russians, reacted angrily, becoming overnight a nation united by war. In this the AFU was helped by new Western weapons that sliced apart the long, vulnerable lines of Russian armoured vehicles and destroyed priceless supply trucks on an alarming scale.

'The Russians planned for an occupation, not necessarily an invasion, and that has set them back,' was the CIA assessment, backed by the DIA's chief speaking in autumn 2022:

'Putin's coming to a decision point. What that decision will be we don't know. But that will largely drive how long this conflict lasts.'

Putin needs to keep up the offensive to survive. Evidence of a long war is plain for all to see. The intelligence indicators are clear and unambiguous. According to Britain's Ministry of Defence (MOD), Moscow has been forced to 'relocate supply nodes' further south and east due to Ukrainian strikes. Russia's withdrawal from the west bank of the River Dnieper has presented Ukraine with 'opportunities to strike additional Russian logistics nodes and lines of communication'.

The MOD added: 'This threat has highly likely prompted Russian logisticians to relocate supply nodes, including rail transfer points, further south and east.' Russian logistics units will need to conduct extra labour-intensive loading and unloading from rail to road transport. Road moves will subsequently still be vulnerable to Ukrainian artillery as they move on to supply Russian forward defensive positions.

Russia's shortage of munitions (exacerbated by these logistics challenges) is only one of the main factors currently limiting Russia's potential to restart effective, large-scale offensive ground operations. To emphasize the point, Russian arms production is moving to war production targets and limited conscription of likely soldiers has intensified. These moves are not those of a country looking for a peaceful solution. The truth is that Putin would be unlikely to survive a major defeat in Ukraine. He needs to keep going and harness his undoubted popularity among many Russians. The cult of the 'Vozhd', or strong man ruler, is deeply engrained in the Russian psyche. And herein lies the danger of a setback of a defeat for Putin in Ukraine.

The unpalatable problem is that a Russian defeat could spell serious difficulty for the West as well. Putin's dilemma poses real problems – and not just for Russia. Putin may appear to be an irreplaceable leader, but his hold on power depends on his success – or failure – in Ukraine. There is much social discontent below the surface of Russia today. The Chekists of the past could put down discord and dissent with practised ease, especially among Russia's elites or *nomenklatura*. But in the wake of any defeat in Ukraine, the turbulent situation on the streets, any trigger – a minor mutiny in a demoralized battle group, an outburst of protests in a recession-hit region, or a technical accident in a poorly serviced oilfield – could generate a sudden but uncontainable political crisis in Moscow. Russian public support for 'Putin's War' is weakening. So Putin's genuine intelligence woes now encompass keeping an even more watchful eye on his social and domestic problems. The GRU and State Security can handle that and allow him to start collecting hard intelligence on Ukraine for an inevitable offensive with fresh troops, and new weapons; but only with the realization that failure is not an option.

The future looks gloomy, assuming Putin wishes to stay in power. His options look limited as we go to press, and unfortunately 2023 can offer little but more of the same, according to long-time Kremlinologist Ted Galen Carpenter, Senior Fellow at the CATO Institute. The Washington think tank highlights four main options for the future.

Option 1: Moscow could launch a new offensive focused on the Black Sea port of Odessa, Ukraine's last outlet on the Black Sea. Its capture would make Ukraine a landlocked country. Such a move would choke off Ukraine's economic lifeline, as well as being a major psychological blow to Ukraine. There is, therefore, a high probability that Odessa could become Moscow's principal target, aiming to link up with a sympathetic Moldova to the west. Ukrainian forces in the south would be very hard-pressed to repel any major Russian attack and cutting off Ukraine's link to the sea would be a game-changer for Ukraine and the war.

Option 2: It could be a giant strategic 'pincer movement', sending troops from southern Ukraine while simultaneously launching a fresh offensive from Russia into Ukraine's north-east. The goal would be to cut off the large numbers of Ukrainian troops in the centre. Such a strategy would be reminiscent of the Soviet Union's wider strategic offensives on the Eastern Front after 1942 that trapped an entire German army in Stalingrad and destroyed Army Group Centre in 1944. However, the logistics of supporting such a manoeuvre over a wide territory would be a major challenge, particularly since logistics have been revealed as a serious weakness of the Russian military.

Option 3: Putin could order a full *national mobilization*. So far, Russia has fought the war in Ukraine with only limited forces. That decision appears to have been based on the initial interpretation of faulty intelligence, based on a belief that that Kyiv's military would collapse, pro-Russians in the east would rally to Russia's cause, and Ukrainian president Volodymyr Zelenskyy's government would be forced to sue for peace. None of this happened. In addition, the Kremlin failed to factor in the strength of NATO's support to Kyiv with large quantities of high-tech weapons.

Putin may now decide to correct his initial blunder and go for broke. The grinding war has already taken a great toll on Ukraine's military personnel. Since Russia's population is nearly three times as large as Ukraine's, it is unlikely that Kyiv could survive any long war of attrition. Full mobilization, a long, grinding offensive and total war would give Moscow an insurmountable advantage.

Option 4: This is the riskiest and most dangerous option, even though Putin has openly mentioned it on several occasions. Russia, in a desperate bid to resolve matters quickly and decisively, could theoretically use selective low yield tactical nuclear weapons against a limited number of key military targets. Such a managed strike with even a few weapons would wipe out large portions of Kyiv's military and cause effective resistance to disperse for safety. However, crossing the nuclear threshold is fraught politically and would be an extremely dangerous move, which Putin understands very well. Nevertheless, if he concludes that the only alternative is accepting a humiliating, NATO-imposed settlement that would threaten his hold on power (and his personal survival), it would be foolish to assume that he would never take the risk *in extremis*. Trapped, frightened rats often turn and bite.

These four options are by no means the only guaranteed outcomes for Putin and the Kremlin's dilemma. They are, at the start of 2023, the most obvious. They do, however, spell out the stark Russian choices for Putin's future imperfect.

Intelligence can do no more…

'HOW DO WE DEAL WITH FANATICISM ARMED WITH POWER?' – WILL IT EVER GET ANY BETTER?

'The applications of artificial intelligence are likely to impact critical facets of our economy and society over the coming decade. We are in what many credible experts view as the most promising era in technology innovation and value creation for the foreseeable future.'

GAURAY TEWARI, *FORBES* MAGAZINE

Afghanistan was but the pointer to a future imperfect. In thirty years, terrorism has grown from cowardly Irish gunmen, sneaking up to shoot unsuspecting policemen in the back amid the dreary spires of Belfast, Omagh and Armagh, into a worldwide organization of suicidal, like-minded fanatics armed with endless supplies of money, guns, mobile phones, the Internet and a burning grievance. The organization can call on a seemingly limitless worldwide pool of supporters prepared to give their lives for 'the Cause' and access to weapons that have hitherto been the monopoly of nation states.

Should there be any doubt as to their future plans, the chilling words of Hussein Massaur, one of the early leaders of Hizbollah, 'the Party of God', spell out the intentions of Islamic terrorists clearly enough: 'We are not fighting to wring some concession from our enemy: we are fighting to wipe out our enemy.'

The truth is that the USA still cannot coordinate its intelligence agencies properly in a crisis, however much information it collects. It cannot manage its assets. Like medieval barons, the big American intelligence agencies feud between themselves for power and influence at the Presidential Court.

This quotation from the first edition of *Military Intelligence Blunders* was written in 1999, two years before the horrific events of 9/11. It went to the heart of the question: 'Will it ever get any better?' The dismal catalogue of chances missed, information ignored and failure to tell others what you know that preceded al Qa'ida's deadly strike would seem to indicate that little has changed in the way the US system deals with intelligence since Pearl Harbor eight decades ago.

The problems facing the intelligence world in the twenty-first century have changed, however. The big bureaucracies and agencies may not have moved much, but the ground on which they play has changed shape. The Russian invasion of Ukraine demonstrates that old-fashioned war has not gone away. Three particular new factors are changing the face of intelligence for the future: technology, globalization and the 'politicization of intelligence'.

Technology has advanced so quickly, even in the last decade, that it is hard to remember that only twenty years ago, fax machines were almost universal. Nowadays the Internet and the scanner make fax machines seem decidedly old-fashioned. While it is easy to get infatuated with technology for novelty's sake, the fact is that the accelerating pace of change means that new technologies are revolutionizing both the tasks of intelligence and the way in which it delivers its intelligence product to the user. For example, the explosion of Internet and text communication from computers and mobile phones – undreamed of only ten years ago – means that intelligence agencies like the American NSA and Britain's GCHQ now face massive challenges if they are to do their job – snooping on millions of other people's private conversations on behalf of the State.

The world of the all-intrusive spook has changed. Methods for querying and mining 'Big Data' are fundamentally different from yesterday's statistical analysis on limited targets. Today's Big Data is often noisy, dynamic, confusing, inter-related and untrustworthy. Nevertheless, even noisy Big Data can be more valuable than concentrating on single intelligence targets, because general statistics obtained from frequent patterns and wider analysis tend to overpower individual searches and often disclose more reliable hidden patterns and knowledge.

Where technology sets the open challenge, however, technology offers solutions. The US-UK Echelon computerized signals interception organization harnesses modern computer technology to try and unravel the very difficulties technology has created. The system doesn't try to listen to transmissions; it just records everything it hears. Sophisticated computer programs then scan the material, looking for key words of interest to intelligence: 'spies', 'bombs', 'terrorist', 'al Qa'ida', 'Kalashnikov', 'Hamas', 'nuclear', etc. Only the communications containing these key words are examined, first by a second and then by a third even more detailed electronic scan, to uncover further key words – perhaps 'industrial espionage', 'yellow cake', 'red mercury' and 'nuclear bomb'. Then, if enough computer 'matches' have been made, and only then, the signal in question is selected for examination on a computer screen by an intelligence officer. Technology is being rapidly incorporated into the whole business of future intelligence handling.

Wealthy countries are today investing heavily in artificial intelligence (AI) as the way ahead for faster real-time intelligence. AI is essentially computers that can 'learn' from their mistakes. The US Department of Defense has for years *recognized the value of AI* – both on and off the battlefield – and has subsequently invested billions in its R&D. US projects such as Linchpin have become the key collaboration between the US Program Executive Office for Intelligence, Electronic Warfare and Sensors, the Army Research Lab and Army Futures Command's AI integration hub. The plan is to use new technology to help vehicles navigate, predict when maintenance is required, to assist identification and classification of targets, and to aid analysts sifting through tides of incoming information. The aim is to create a single controlling hub to harness the 'infrastructure and environment' needed to deliver AI capabilities for use across the intelligence, cyber and electronic warfare spaces. AI will revolutionize the way intelligence is integrated and handled, and change the way individual targets are identified and located on land, sea and air.

The fact is that technology can do the job more and more in the future. It does, however, offer us a new challenge: how will we manage all this information? Today we are awash in a flood of data. In a wide range of application areas, data is being collected on an unprecedented scale. Decisions that previously were based on guesswork, or on painstakingly constructed theoretical models, can now be made based on the data itself. Big Data analysis now drives nearly every aspect of our modern society, including mobile services, retail, manufacturing, financial services, as well as intelligence.

Technology has therefore not solved the problems of mass intelligence collection. However, it does offer, further along in the intelligence cycle, solutions for the overworked collator and even solves some of the biggest problems of dissemination. For the collator, modern information technology means that amounts of material undreamed of by his predecessors can be stored – and, more importantly, *retrieved* – in conditions of great security. For the analysts, 'electronic brain' AI programs can remember information, compare old facts and highlight any changes. Above all, it turns old-fashioned intelligence into targeting intelligence. For the 'targeteer', computer programs can disseminate and display real-time, live-target intelligence in the cockpit of the attacking bomber as it flies in to unload its ordnance, turning 'intelligence' straight into 'targets'.

The 'globalization' of intelligence on the other hand is a much more complicated affair. What this means is that the demands for nations to share their intelligence has spread much more widely than ever in the past. Where once a nation guarded its secrets closely, nowadays its allies, collaborators and international partners expect to share in the information available. The international intelligence alliance known as the Five Eyes is a good example, offering as it does the resources of the USA, UK, Australia, Canada and New Zealand. Coalition partners cannot be expected to fight and risk their soldiers' lives without knowing all there is to be known about the enemy. Precious intelligence and vital information will have to be shared far more in the future. That raises new problems of security.

The problem is that sharing secrets is anathema to most intelligence organizations. The big agencies' monopoly of power or influence, their budgets, their whole *raison d'être*, rests upon keeping their secret pearls safely locked up and only showing them discreetly to well-known, regular customers behind closed doors. Now, suddenly, it seems the whole world wants access to secrets that are too sensitive to be shown even to the people who actually paid for them, the taxpayer, let alone some loose-mouthed foreigner. Questions of source protection, need to know and operational security loom large.

While intelligence officers may flinch like nervous gazelles round the waterhole at the scent of a dangerous threat to their monopoly of secret information, they cannot flee from the much wider demand for intelligence. In a globalized world where joint international ventures with foreign partners are now the military as well as the commercial norm, intelligence is increasingly going to have to be shared whether 'intelligence' likes it or not. Operations with the UN, coalition partners, foreign governments and even non-governmental organizations (NGOs) like the Red Cross and UNHCR, demand that vital information is passed on. But it has not always been so.

Traditionally, even in NATO, intelligence sharing was one of the most difficult and contentious areas for the Alliance over the past half-century. Fortunately, the sophisticated and carefully managed NATO procedures and systems that evolved for fusing intelligence from a variety of secret and delicate national sources can now be applied to providing equally effective all-source intelligence for organizations like the United Nations on operations.

With the NGOs it is a completely different matter. Not so long ago, big international NGOs like the Red Cross and the UNHCR would have absolutely nothing to do with 'intelligence' whatsoever. Traditionally, international aid agencies have hung strings of garlic round their necks, crossed their fingers to ward off the evil eye and erected castle walls around their HQs; *anything* to keep the evil and dangerous vampire of 'intelligence' out. NGOs would do anything to avoid being contaminated by 'intelligence' for fear of compromising their virtue, and woe betide the hapless intelligence officer caught trying to target UN agencies, or worse, trying to sneak in and use an NGO as a cover for his devious trade. Shrieks of outrage – often synthetic – would echo down the diplomatic corridors and another overenthusiastic intelligence officer would be dismissed from his job as a token sacrifice.

All that has now changed. Globalization has involved us all in matters that were once limited by geography. Now the worldwide risks of weapons of mass destruction (WMD) proliferation, international drugs trading, the mass movement of asylum seekers, conflict prevention and the need for international co-operation means that even NGOs are very much part of the joint efforts to deal with these common problems. International agencies and NGOs now recognize that in order to do their job properly, and indeed for their own protection, they need to have at least the same information as both the country in which they are operating and any national forces co-operating with them. If the NGOs are not given access to the best available intelligence, they are effectively operating blindfold. NGOs now expect to share in the intelligence debate.

All this intelligence sharing raises huge problems over the security, and indeed the ethics, of covert intelligence. In an international world of co-operation, should we still be devoting so much attention to spying and secret espionage? Against this concern, however, the question arises in the modern information age: 'Just how much information really is secret and classified?'

For the truth is that unclassified open-source information is now by far the biggest single source of intelligence. This is not to say that there is no longer any need for secrets. On the contrary, there will always be secrets; but the media now provides the greatest volume of *information*. For the NGO, and for those charged with providing intelligence to the NGOs, this flood of open-source material is an absolute blessing. Satellite photographs that not so long ago were the hottest secret America held can nowadays be openly bought on the Internet from private satellite companies. The better-organized NGOs now even have a line entry for 'aerial photographs' as part of their pre-deployment budgets. Most of the NGOs' information/intelligence requirements can now be provided without having to resort to subterfuge, deniability or complicated 'sanitization' procedures. In a world that has globalized commerce and, thanks to Osama bin Laden and al Qa'ida, has also globalized terrorism, technology and demand are slowly globalizing 'intelligence'.

The third big change for intelligence is its 'politicization'. Domestic politics and the 'government's view' has, certainly in Britain, begun to erode intelligence's long reputation for impartiality and objectivity. Ever since the Joint Intelligence Committee (JIC) was formed in 1936, British national intelligence assessment has been provided by an impartial committee consisting of the heads of the agencies (SIS, MI5, GCHQ, the Defence Intelligence Staff, plus the Foreign and Commonwealth Office and the Treasury) sitting under a neutral chairman to review all the available intelligence and report to ministers and decision-makers. The aim of such an exalted gathering was to make the best intelligence assessment possible from all sources and pass it on to customers with a need to know. Although the system was uniquely British – the USA, France and Russia had different systems – it was widely held by many to be a national model for hammering out the best agreed intelligence for decision-makers.

The system had both its critics and its failures. For many Americans, used to Washington's robust, competitive, dialectic process of argument and rival agency positions, the JIC's product often appears bland, consensual and, in the words of one British cabinet minister 'just plain boring'. A combination of British understatement and the natural caution of the successful bureaucrat often results in JIC intelligence assessments seeming more 'Lowest Common Denominator' rather than 'Highest Common Factor'. Critics also pointed to the JIC's failures: for example, its weak, and just plain *wrong*, assessment over the Argentine decision to invade the Falkland Islands in 1982, in spite of all the evidence to the contrary, and its failure to predict the collapse of communism and the Soviet Union. One feature of the JIC that particularly infuriated its American readers was the JIC's wishy-washy habit of drafting its assessments in bland, anodyne language that admits of any possibility... 'on the other hand... '. US policymakers can quickly spot the 'CYA syndrome', much preferring their assessments to be spelled out in simple, clear language without ambiguity or equivocation, right or wrong. All that changed with the election of Britain's 'New Labour' government in 1997. Prime Minister Blair's administration had succeeded in opposition by skilful management of the media. Marshall McLuhan's puzzling assertion from the 1960s that 'the medium is the message' was taken to heart by a new administration determined to control communication of its image and presentation. Critics soon began to point out that this obsession with all aspects of the government's public face would one day have serious consequences for civil service objectivity. They were right.

The appointment of a Labour Party activist, the journalist Alastair Campbell, as the prime minister's spokesman at Downing Street, had repercussions throughout Whitehall. Infuriated by what he saw as weak and indecisive civil servants speaking for the government, Campbell demanded and was given power to direct career civil servants. By 2001, every press spokesman in every ministry in Whitehall was either appointed or approved by the Downing Street 'spin machine' and took their orders from Campbell and his team. News management was centralized and controlled only to present the message the government wanted to get across and nothing else. Somewhere along the road in Whitehall, truth became another victim of politics and 'good management'.

Matters soon came to a head over intelligence. This was predictable, because the JIC process was designed to be totally impartial and objective, tasked to present neutral intelligence assessments to its customers, leaving Whitehall decision-makers to use the material in the national interest. The trouble was that the last thing that Prime Minister Blair's No. 10 news-management teams wanted was impartiality and objectivity in its public utterances. What they wanted were facts presented and spun only in a way that buttressed whatever government policy required. The spin doctors were essentially government propagandists and unconscious disciples of Dr Goebbels. The logic was that the public would have to believe what the government of the day wanted them to believe and to hell with objective facts.

Up to the period before the second Iraq War of spring 2003, 'intelligence' had managed to avoid conflict with the propagandists of Britain's New Labour. Most intelligence assessments were highly classified and therefore of little use for presenting governmental messages to the wider public. Apart from the odd spat over Prime Minister Blair's bombing of the former Yugoslavia's tanks in the Kosovo War of 1999, the Whitehall intelligence establishment grumbled about 'nonsense in the newspapers' but went quietly about its work. But all that changed in the summer of 2002.

One of the aftershocks of the bombing of the World Trade Center was US President George W. Bush's determination to prosecute what he called the 'war on terror'. By the middle of 2002, the Taliban's nest of fundamentalist fanatics that had been Afghanistan had been smoked out, leaving the Taliban and Osama bin Laden hurriedly skipping over Afghanistan's rocky passes to escape the avenging Americans and hide in the hills.

President George W. Bush now turned his attention to a piece of unfinished business left over from 1991 and his father's term in the White House – Saddam Hussein's dictatorial and oppressive regime. In April and August of 2002, the decisions were taken to prepare for an invasion of Iraq.

Prime Minister Blair swiftly tied the United Kingdom to the US decision. If he wanted to maintain the exclusive intelligence and nuclear links that made for the real 'special relationship' with the US, the UK premier, like all his predecessors, had little choice.

The news that the UK was going to back the US in an aggressive invasion of another sovereign nation's territory was not greeted with universal acclaim in Britain. Many Britons expressed serious reservations, both about the legality of any attack on Iraq and also about the reason behind it. Distinguished former generals, politicians and political commentators and, crucially, the BBC, all queried the purpose of any war. Socialist luminaries called for peace at any cost. What threat did Saddam Hussein really pose to the UK?

While Prime Minister Blair tried (unsuccessfully) to rally support and allies from a sceptical European Union, diplomats attempted to win support for the war at the United Nations. In vain, British and American diplomats pleaded that Saddam Hussein was flouting UN Security Council resolutions and that the UN arms control inspectors searching for Iraq's WMDs were being balked and deceived at every turn by the wily Saddam. Britain and America's Security Council colleagues firmly voted '*Non!*' to any attempt to use a UN resolution as a legal fig leaf for attacking Iraq. This mattered little to the hawkish US administration that had determined to invade Iraq and change the regime whatever the outcome.

For Prime Minister Blair and his government, however, the UN's refusal to condone, let alone support, the planned attack on Iraq was a disaster. A sceptical British public did not believe in yet another war. They saw no reason to commit British troops to another unnecessary foreign adventure without a clear threat to British interests. Worse still, the prime minister's own party was deeply hostile to any aggressive war against Iraq. It ran counter to all the traditional instincts of the old Labour Party, rooted in concepts of socialism, the brotherhood of man, pacifism and, above all, profoundly anti-American, especially to a Republican administration they saw as only just legal.

Without the UN's blessing, the British public felt strongly that their government had no mandate for war, so Tony Blair turned to his spin doctors and news managers to manufacture one.

In August 2002, the JIC had been tasked to report on Baghdad's WMDs.

Ever since the gassing of the Kurds in 1988, it was a matter of public record that Saddam Hussein had a chemical capability and possessed an armoury of lethal gases; he had also openly dabbled in nuclear technology. It was no secret that since the Israelis' destruction of the Osirak nuclear plant in 1981, he had long nursed the desire to build a nuclear warhead. Furthermore, he was known to be interested in developing a bacteriological warfare capability. These programmes were the very WMDs that the UNSCOM inspectors were finding so hard to uncover. The Iraqis claimed – and many experts in the West agreed – that the reason the weapons inspectors could not find the WMDs was because they no longer existed.

The JIC took all the reports prepared by a special all-source intelligence team working for the Defence Intelligence Staff in August 2002 and issued a classified assessment at the beginning of September. It reviewed Baghdad's WMD capability and pointed out that such a capability was not new but always had the potential to become a threat at some point in the future.

Desperate for a *casus belli*, the Blair government latched on to this *potential threat* and decided to publish an amended version of the JIC assessment as a piece of government propaganda. The JIC raised its collective eyebrows but did as it was ordered by its political masters, producing a sanitized, unclassified 'draft dossier' for the prime minister. Intelligence was now to be used to convince a sceptical public opinion that there really was a threat to Britain from Iraq, true or not.

Up to this point, 'intelligence' had been used perfectly legitimately, if unusually, by its controllers, the elected politicians. What happened next was explosive and amounted to nothing less than the distortion of truth and the politicization of intelligence.

Within the fevered and embattled atmosphere of No. 10 trying to make a case for war, the prime minister's spin doctors decided that the JIC's draft dossier just wasn't convincing enough for their propaganda purposes and demanded that it be changed in order to sell government policy. The JIC, under its ambitious chairman John Scarlett, acceded, even allowing the prime minister's personal propagandist to chair a JIC meeting to discuss and amend the national intelligence assessment to make it suit government policy. No. 10's party appointees were now 'presenting' their own version of national intelligence assessments for distribution to the British public, the media and to Parliament, stressing the 'imminent threat' from Saddam's WMD. It worked.

There was a second 'dossier' in February 2003, reinforcing the alleged WMD threat, this time openly produced by the government media spin doctors in No. 10. Despite the fact that this was quickly proved to be merely a pastiche of old facts and extracts from a ten-year-old PhD thesis discovered on the Internet, the die was cast in March 2003 and Britain went to war, invading Iraq alongside the USA, 'to remove Saddam's WMDs'.

The second Iraq War was never popular in the UK. Many harboured deep doubts about its morality and aims, but the alleged WMD threat had tipped the balance – just. Preventing nuclear proliferation was felt by many Britons to be a legitimate cause for war, although not everyone agreed. Many influential commentators remained deeply sceptical, claiming that Britain had been duped into going to war on a false prospectus. In particular, the BBC's news coverage of the war reflected these very real public doubts, to No. 10's fury.

The allegation therefore made three months after the war by a BBC reporter that the prime minister's chief press spokesman had 'sexed up' the so-called 'dodgy dossier' to better sell the case for war to a dubious public, came as no surprise to many. What did come as a surprise was the reaction from No. 10. A furious row broke out between Downing Street and the BBC. Like a brush fire, the conflagration spread with bitter allegations of duplicity, bad faith, deceit and lies from both sides. The unfortunate senior British inspector of Iraq's WMDs was publicly named as the source of the BBC's story. He was then promptly interrogated by the Security Services at the government's request, threatened with the police or worse, forced to confess in public before what looked suspiciously like a rigged parliamentary committee and hounded at his home by the press. Desperate, terrified of losing his career and his status, frightened and alone, MOD scientist Dr David Kelly allegedly committed suicide by cutting his wrist on a lonely hillside.

The political fallout for the government was immediate and dramatic. Victory in Iraq suddenly turned to ashes. A grey-faced and visibly shocked prime minister was asked in public by a journalist, 'Have you got blood on your hands, Prime Minister?' The subsequent inquiry set up to investigate the circumstances surrounding Dr Kelly's death was, in truth, seen by many as nothing less than an inquiry into the claim that the British people and Parliament had been conned into going to war against Iraq by an exaggerated and distorted intelligence assessment of the true threat from Saddam Hussein's Iraq. Moreover, it was claimed, the most senior British intelligence officers had behaved like political puppets and connived in an assessment they knew to be exaggerated. Intelligence had been falsified and used for political purposes. It was not British intelligence, or the JIC's, finest hour.

While this politicization of intelligence represented a dangerous and disturbing trend for the UK, it is not unusual in other countries. American intelligence has often been influenced by political priorities, for example: J. Edgar Hoover's deliberate 'hands off the Mafia'; Kissinger's duplicitous assessments on Cambodia, China and Vietnam; the White House intelligence advisers deliberately ignoring China's blatant and aggressive intelligence attack to steal US secrets. All these American intelligence assessments reflected the political bias of the administration in power at the time.

But even in the United States, intelligence is being politicized in new ways. In 2003, for the second Gulf War, the Department of Defense, egged on by a hawkish White House Chief of Staff, Defense Secretary and a vice president determined to get their own way, actually set up its own 'private' intelligence collection and assessment department inside the Pentagon. This secret Office of Special Projects was specifically designed to challenge the intelligence assessments of the CIA and the State Department where they were found to be too weak or not politically in tune with the administration's real wishes. This is dangerous stuff, and only a whisker away from Stalin and his intelligence henchman Golikov accepting only intelligence they agreed with in the paranoiac and incompetent Kremlin of spring 1941. Intelligence is categorically never the view of the senior officer present; intelligence is truth – or it should be.

With quantum leaps in technology, a global village linked by ever-expanding communications, and increasing diktats over what 'intelligence' is politically acceptable, the intelligence officer of the twenty-first century faces some tough challenges. He, or she, will have to cope with a rapidly evolving environment and against vicious new enemies. Questions of legality (is it ethical to use torture against captured al Qa'ida terrorists to save thousands of civilian lives? What is the latest international court ruling?); questions of technology (it will soon be possible, using C4 and cyberspace to disable an enemy without firing a shot by hacking into and disabling all his computer systems); and questions of the relationship between intelligence agencies and the government of the day will loom large.

But the great tasks of intelligence will remain. Information will still need to be collected. If the State is at risk – from whatever area – then some kind of defence is part of the contract between the governed and their government. Information will still need to be collated and analysed for its significance, and analysed information will still have to be disseminated as intelligence to users with a need to know in sufficient time for decision-makers to take action.

Although covert collection will probably diminish as a percentage of the overall intelligence 'take', it will still be needed. Where there are secret intentions that threaten, they will need to be unmasked. Perhaps multi-national groupings and multi-lateral action will mean that more intelligence has to be shared; but the State will still need to protect its citizens' secrets. Even international law may begin to intrude on national sovereignty, but intelligence will not wither away.

As long as there are nation states that compete and as long as those states harbour secrets, intelligence will remain a permanent fixture of foreign affairs, diplomacy and the relationship between states. Nations will always need to spy on each other. Intelligence will still be needed in the twenty-first century because human nature and human reactions will not change.

For instance, fear seems to be a consistent thread in intelligence mistakes, as Stalin demonstrated before Barbarossa. Bungling incompetence, however, is much more pervasive and will continue to rate higher than mere fear of a potential enemy; Pearl Harbor and Malaya were positive triumphs of institutional bungling. Add to this a contempt for the Japanese and both events become monuments to the folly of underestimating your enemy as well. Even the dreadful events of 9/11 contain an element of underestimating al Qa'ida – 'they couldn't possibly do that... could they?' This – underestimating your enemy – is the most common theme, as Ukraine has proved, and will undoubtedly remain a problem for future intelligence officers and their political masters. It is probably the most grievous intelligence blunder of all.

Persistent underestimation of the enemy may be the common factor that lies deep at the heart of all intelligence bungling, because from underestimation of an enemy comes the misreading of an enemy's intentions. There are no shortages of examples of that; it is a common thread. In the Falklands, in the Gulf, at Yom Kippur, the WTC attacks, the enemy intentions were hopelessly misinterpreted because it was felt that the enemy would not do the very thing for which he had prepared over many years, and for which he had built up a substantial and obvious capability. All the indications are that this trend will get worse, not better, in the future.

The results of this blend of inefficiency, internal feuding and underestimation of potential enemies have one consistent result, as steady as a drumbeat: the big intelligence organizations can always be relied on for one thing – to get it wrong. It is a frightening consistency. In 1991, after the Gulf War, Daniel Moynihan rounded on the American intelligence establishment in the *New York Times*: 'For a quarter of a century the CIA has been repeatedly wrong about every major political and economic question entrusted to its analysts.' And he was right.

The CIA is not alone in this, we can be sure. There was no rush of British intelligence agencies in 1978 warning that the Shah was soon going to be toppled in Iran, or that the Russians were going to invade Afghanistan in 1979. Nor was there a clamour from the big agencies warning the politicians that Saddam Hussein was about to do something foolish in Kuwait either. Despite good, clear indications – including a public threat warning from Osama bin Laden himself – the American intelligence machine still failed to alert the nation to the threat of 9/11. Despite the money lavished on them, the intelligence agencies have frequently failed to do the job they are paid for until it is far too late.

Since then things do not seem to be improving. The truth is that all the big intelligence agencies are basically more interested in their own bureaucratic survival than in dealing with the real needs of national security. The modern intelligence community tends to be obsessed more with clever *collecting* than with working out what all the information actually means. It is, after all, the correct interpretation and the dissemination of intelligence that is more important. Even then the big agencies, like the canny bureaucrats they are, know that they have to keep their paymasters sweet and will always tend to tell their political masters what they want to hear. That is not objective intelligence and it is a dangerous development.

Because, at the end of the day, only one question stands out: what is intelligence for? Clearly it is to enable responsible people to make informed decisions. The way intelligence now does this has changed in today's information age. The old difficulty of collecting the secrets has now become the challenge of *finding* the secrets among the mass of information pouring like a torrent past our nose. The difficulty is spotting the key facts we need and fishing them out as the flood pours by. In the jargon, the intelligence experts now have to be able to 'identify and retrieve the essential information quickly and in a usable form for the decision-makers'.

As the twenty-first century unwinds, the truth really will be out there – if only we know *who* has got it when we want it. The key intelligence players of the future will not be the collectors but the interpreters, managers and above all the *disseminators* of accurate intelligence. For example, it will be no good if the US National Reconnaissance Office has exact satellite pictures, in real time, of a terrorist gang transporting a small nuclear bomb if the NRO cannot – or will not – pass this vital secret information on to a user to *do* something about it.

The problem is becoming one of *dissemination*, because unused intelligence, however expensively and cleverly collected, is *useless intelligence*. Stalin's intelligence officers, if they were still alive, would doubtless be nodding their heads and agreeing fervently with this. So might the analysts of America's Counterterrorism Center, reviewing the disastrous events of 9/11.

Does any of this revolution in information really change anything in intelligence at the top? The answer is still probably not. For whatever pearls of information can be put before any nation's leaders or policymakers, as long as there are human beings in the system, then the system is vulnerable to the vanities and frailties of humanity: another Mountbatten or MacArthur, too ambitious and concerned with his own personal advancement to worry about collecting proper intelligence; another complacent set of civil servants thinking 'it can't happen to me' like the British in Malaya; or diplomats who could not distinguish good old-fashioned lying and deception to sort out capabilities from intentions, like those duped by Saddam Hussein in the Gulf.

Human nature will not change, nor will the relationships between bureaucrats and their masters.

The problem is not helped by the fact that in democracies, leaders tend not to dictate exactly what intelligence they expect to receive. Elected politicians have to rely on their intelligence experts – the non-elected 'advisers' in the civil service or the military – who are secure in the knowledge that no one is going to deselect *them*. The handling and distribution of intelligence is, after all, the province of experts. The problem is that it is the experts who keep getting it wrong, frequently leaving the politicians to take the blame; mainly because they will always try to please their masters.

The intelligence problem will get worse, if anything. Intelligence blunders will become very expensive mistakes in the future. The world in the twenty-first century will need to keep a very close eye on who really does have nuclear weapons or other nasty instruments of mass destruction tucked away in their production facility, or even in their garage out the back; for we are entering an age where the power to wage war is passing from the hands of even renegade governments back to individuals and groups. Terrorists, drug-traffickers and fanatics from extremist groups of all kinds will soon have access to weapons with unbelievable killing power, as proved by the sarin attack in the Tokyo subway.

To make this even more difficult, technology digitization and AI know few boundaries today and electronic communications devices and security toys that were once the monopoly of governments can now be bought freely by any terrorist group with the money. The real terror has always been that of 'the fanatic with a weapon'; now the weapon in the hands of the terrorist, whether he be a lone killer with a grievance, a terrorist group or a nation's leader bent on war, is likely to be something that could easily kill as many people as a Second World War bombing raid. Science's perverted achievement has been to make weapons of mass destruction available to the fanatic and the terrorist. It is a frightening prospect.

In such a world, governments will need to keep a very close eye on these developments for their own survival, let alone the taxpayers who pay governments to ensure their own security. To do this, governments will still need intelligence – properly organized, properly resourced and properly managed. They will need to listen dispassionately to the evidence and intelligence brought before them by their expensive staffs of experts and make sure that their system is as bungle-free as possible. Above all, they will need to see that their intelligence system can get to the centre of a potential enemy's brain to try and find out what he – or she – intends to do next. Because at the end of the day the purpose of intelligence is still to avoid nasty surprises – no more and no less.

In fact, despite change, technology, the information revolution and 'post modernism', the real intelligence problem has not changed very much at all. The modern intelligence requirement goes to the very heart of the old, historic intelligence conundrum. The most expensive intelligence collection toys can tell you what an enemy has got and where it is; but it still needs a good old-fashioned spy or a spying device to tell you what an enemy is going to *do*. It is our old friend, capabilities versus intentions, that cannot be 'technologized' away by expensive mechanical trickery. We still need that oldest of weapons: a trustworthy spy in the enemy camp to tell us what devilry is being planned for us.

With such a historic intelligence requirement, perhaps it is best to leave the final word to Sun Tzu, a Chinese general writing about 510 BC, over a hundred years before Athens and Sparta.

In his book *The Art of War* (*Ping-Fu*), he looked carefully at the problems of intelligence and espionage. Sun Tzu was a shrewd and perceptive observer, not just of the military but also of their relationship with politicians and mandarins in the civil service of his day. He wrote: 'A hundred ounces of silver spent for intelligence may save ten thousand ounces spent on war.' It is an aphorism that has stood the test of time. But Sun Tzu also wrote probably the most profound insight into intelligence ever, and one that should hang on the wall of every president, prime minister, civil servant and military commander:

> If you know the enemy and know yourself, you need not fear a thousand battles. If you know yourself and not the enemy, for every victory you will suffer a defeat. But if you know neither yourself nor the enemy, then you are a fool and will meet defeat in every battle.

That still seems to be the best advice ever written for avoiding disastrous intelligence blunders.

ACKNOWLEDGEMENTS

A book like this does not get written on its own. In putting all this together I have been aided enormously by a number of commentators, such as the librarian of the Royal United Services Institute in Whitehall. Professor Chris Bellamy, of Cranfield University, at the Defence Academy of the UK and author of *Absolute War*, helped unbutton many of the mysteries of Barbarossa. The staff of the Conflict Studies Centre at the Royal Military Academy Sandhurst were also invaluable allies over Barbarossa and the Byzantine details of Stalin's court, while Peter Shepherd's revelations over his meeting with a drunken Japanese who revealed the secrets of Pearl Harbor have since been recognized by his own book on the subject. For details of Vietnam, I owe a considerable debt to my many American friends and colleagues over the years, including several anonymous ex-CIA and DIA members. On Vietnam, Colonel John Moon and Colonel John Robbins of the United States Army made many perceptive comments on my drafts of American events, and also helped with their previously unpublished memories of Tet. Captain Frank Okata, USN, contributed on the doings of the US Navy at Midway, as did Yousef Bar-On for Israel and the 1973 war.

On the Falklands campaign and the Gulf War, I should declare a personal interest, having been intimately involved in both conflicts. However, the best recollections of the Falklands intelligence organization and operations 'down south' have invariably come from the long-suffering and patient Colonel David Burrill and our many comrades in arms.

Many others in the intelligence world of several nationalities have helped me, both on and off the record, including South Koreans and Brigadier

Brian Parritt, who fought and was wounded in Korea. Several anonymous Afghanistan veterans have been invaluable; and on terrorism, Lord Maginnis of Drumglass recorded his time as a member of the Ulster Defence Regiment with a well-informed and dry wit as an IRA target.

Any errors and omissions, however, are my own, as are the opinions expressed; especially on the outcome of the Ukrainian war. They represent the broad overview of forty years working with, and thinking about, 'military intelligence'. Having said that, this is most certainly not a theoretical text about international affairs, but a book that is meant to be read and enjoyed by the general reader, journalist and the intelligence professional alike; I genuinely hope all gain something from my labours.

JOHN HUGHES-WILSON
North Cyprus, 2023

SOURCES AND FURTHER READING

There are literally thousands of published works on the subjects covered in this book and a positive embarrassment of riches when it comes to records and sources, both primary and secondary. *Military Intelligence Blunders* draws primarily on the following sources, plus the numerous unsung individuals who, for one reason or another, have preferred to remain anonymous.

Preface
Suvorov, Viktor, *Osnova Shpionazha – Kratkii Kurs (The Principles of Espionage)*, Russian edition, Moscow, Dobraya Kniga, 2016

Chapter 1 On Intelligence
Chandler, David, *The Campaigns of Napoleon*, Weidenfeld & Nicolson, 1967
Herman, Michael, *Intelligence Power in Peace and War*, Frank Cass, 2001
JIS (NE), intelligence briefs (various), 1974–75
Marshall-Cornwall, General Sir James, personal interview with the author, Ashford, Kent, 1976
Polmar, Norman and Allen, Thomas B., *The Spy Book: The Encyclopaedia of Espionage*, London, Greenhill, 1997
SACEUR's briefing, Exercise WINTEX, NATO, 1979
School of Service Intelligence, *Intelligence Training* (Restricted), Ashford, Kent, 1974 et seq.
Shulsky, Abram, *Silent Warfare*, Brassey's USA, 1991
Urquhart, Brian, personal interview with the author, UNFICYP, Cyprus, 1975

Chapter 2 D-Day 1944
Bennett, Ralph, *Ultra in the West*, London, Hutchinson, 1979
— *Behind the Battle*, London, Pimlico, 1994
Brown, Anthony Cave, *Bodyguard of Lies*, New York, Harper & Row, 1975
Cruickshank, Charles, *Deception in WWII*, Oxford, OUP, 1979
Harwell, Jack, *The Intelligence & Deception of the D-Day Landings*, Batsford, 1979
Hastings, Max, *Overlord*, London, Pan Books, 1985
Haswell, Jock, *British Military Intelligence*, London, Weidenfeld & Nicolson, 1973
Hinsley, F. H. (ed.), *British Intelligence in the Second World War*, 6 vols, London, HMSO, 1979–93
Howard, Sir Michael, *Strategic Deception in the Second World War*, London, HMSO, 1990, and, Pimlico, 1992
Kahn, David, *The Codebreakers*, London, Weidenfeld & Nicolson, 1968
Masterman, Sir John, *The Double Cross System*, Yale University Press, 1972
National Archives, The (TNA; formerly PRO), CAB 80/63, COS (42) 180(0), 21 June 1942
— JIC (43) 385(0), 25 September 1943.
— CAB 80/77, COS (43) 779(0) Final, 23 January 1944
Perrault, Gilles, *The Secrets of D-Day*, English edition, London, Arthur Barker, 1965
Skillen, Hugh, *Enigma and its Achilles Heel*, c/o The Military Intelligence

Museum, Chicksands, Bedfordshire (by appointment only: https://www.
militaryintelligencemuseum.org/)
Tute, Warren, Costello, John and Hughes, Terry, *D-Day*, London, Sidgwick & Jackson,
1974
Winterbotham, F.W., *The Ultra Secret*, London, Weidenfeld & Nicolson, 1974

Chapter 3 Barbarossa, 1941
Andrew, Christopher and Gordievsky, Oleg, *KGB: The Inside Story*, London, Hodder &
Stoughton, 1990
Bialer, Seweryn, *Stalin and his Generals*, reprint edition, Boulder, CO, 1994
Bullock, Alan, *Hitler and Stalin*, London, HarperCollins, 1991
Carrell, Paul, *Der RusslandKrieg*, Ullstein Verlag Frankfurt, 1964
Deacon, Richard, *A History of the Russian Secret Service*, London, Grafton, 1987
Erickson, John, *The Road to Stalingrad: Stalin's War with Germany*, London, Weidenfeld &
Nicolson, 1993
Erickson, John and Dilks, David (eds), *Barbarossa, the Axis and the Allies*, Edinburgh,
Edinburgh University Press, 1994
Finkel, G., 'Red Moles', (unpublished manuscript), personal correspondence, Calgary
Halder, Franz, *Hitler as Warlord*, New York, Putnam, 1950
Harrison, Mark, *Soviet Planning in War and Peace*, Cambridge, Cambridge University
Press, 1985
Hinsley, Sir Harry, *British Intelligence in the Second World War*, abridged edition, London,
HMSO, 1993
Irving, David, *Churchill's War*, New York, Avon Books, 1987
Kahn, David, *Hitler's Spies: German Military Intelligence in WW2*, London, Macmillan,
1978
Philippi, Alfred and Heim, Ferdinand, *Der Feldzug Gegen Sowjet Russland*, Stuttgart, 1962
Polmar, Norman and Allen, Thomas. B, *The Spy Book*, London, Greenhill, 1997
Seaton, Albert and Barker, Arthur, *The Russo-Japanese War 1941–45*, London, Arthur
Barker, 1971
Wette, Wolfram and Ueberschär, Gerd R. (eds), *Der deutsche* Überfall *auf die Sowjetunion:
'Unternehmen Barbarossa' 1941*, Frankfurt, Fischer, 1993
West, Nigel, *Unreliable Witness*, London, Weidenfeld & Nicolson, 1984
Whaley, Barton, *Codeword Barbarossa*, Cambridge, MA, MIT Press, 1973

Chapter 4 Pearl Harbor, 1941
Beach, Ed L., *Scapegoats: a Defence of Kimmel and Short at Pearl Harbor*, Maryland, USNI
Press, 2000
Betts, Richard, *Surprise Attack: Lessons for Defense Planning*, Washington DC, Brookings
Institute, 1982
Burtness, Paul S., and Ober, Warren U., *The Puzzle of Pearl Harbor*, Colorado, Peterson,
1962
Clausen, Henry, *Pearl Harbor: Final Judgement*, New York, Crown, 1992
Elphick, Peter, *Far Eastern File*, London, Hodder & Stoughton, 1997
Kahn, David, *The Intelligence Failure at Pearl Harbor*, Foreign Affairs, Vol. 70, #5, 1991

Knorr, Klaus and Morgan, Patrick (eds), *Strategic Military Surprise*, New Brunswick, Transaction, 1984

New York Times article, 'William Friedman Dies; Broke Japanese Code; Truman Gave Cryptanalyst Highest Civilian Award; Marshall Said Work Saved Many American Lives', *New York Times*, 2 November 1969

Prange, Gordon, *At Dawn We Slept*, New York, McGraw Hill, 1981, and London, Viking, 1991

Rusbridger, James and Nave, Eric, *Betrayal at Pearl Harbor: How Churchill Lured Roosevelt into WWII*, New York, Summit Books, 1991

Shepherd, Peter J., *Three Days to Pearl: Incredible Encounter on the Eve of War*, Annapolis MD, Naval Institute Press, 2000

Stafford, David, *Churchill and Secret Service*, London, John Murray, 1997

Stinnett, Robert, *Day of Deceit*, London, Constable & Robinson, 2000

Toland, John, *Infamy*, London, Methuen, 1982

Chapter 5 Singapore, 1942

Allen, Louis, *Singapore*, London, Frank Cass, 1997

Bauer, Eddy and Barnett, Correlli, *History of WW2*, Monaco, Polus, 1966, and Country Meath, Galley Press, 1984

Crawford, Edward, The Malayan recollections of the late Brigadier V.R.W., Crawford MC, private correspondence to the author, November 1999

David, Saul, *Military Blunders*, London, Robinson Publishing, 1997

Elphick, Peter, *Singapore: The Pregnable Fortress*, London, Sceptre, 1995

Gilchrist, Sir Andrew, *Malaya 1941*, London, Hale, 1992

Kirby, Stanley, *Official History of the War against Japan*, Vol 1, HMSO, 1957

Lewin, Ronald, *The Other Ultra*, London, Hutchinson, 1982

National Archives, The, CRMC 34300 (G), 19 July 1938 (GOC Malaya, WO 106/2440)

— Defence of Malaya and Johore (GOC Malaya, WO 106/2440)

— 106/2432, 4/38

Owen, Frank, *The Fall of Singapore*, London, Michael Joseph, 1960

Shepherd, Peter J., *Three Days to Pearl*, Annapolis, US Naval Institute Press, 2000

Smith, Michael, *Odd Man Out: The Story of the Singapore Traitor*, London, Coronet, 1994

Stafford, David, *Churchill and Secret Service*, London, John Murray, 1997

Tsuji, Colonel Masanobu, *Japan's Greatest Victory, Britain's Worst Defeat*, Staplehurst, Spellmount Publishers, 1995

Young, Peter, *World War 1939–45*, London, Barker, 1966

Chapter 6 Midway

'Battle of Midway, 4–7 June 1942', Naval History and Heritage Command, 26 March 2015: https://www.history.navy.mil/browse-by-topic/wars-conflicts-and-operations/world-war-ii/1942/midway.html

'Battle of Midway, The', US Office of Naval Intelligence archive

Destination Point Luck: Voices from Midway, documentary film, US Navy Naval Media Center, 2008; includes interviews with Battle of Midway veterans

Friedman, William, William F. Friedman Collection of Official Papers, NSA archive:

https://www.nsa.gov/Helpful-Links/NSA-FOIA/Declassification-Transparency-Initiatives/Historical-Releases/Friedman-Documents/

Isom, Dallas W., *Midway Inquest: Why the Japanese Lost the Battle of Midway*, Bloomington, IN, Indiana University Press, 2007

Nimitz, Admiral Chester A., 'Battle of Midway', CINCPAC Report, 15 June 1942, Naval History and Heritage Command: https://www.history.navy.mil/research/archives/digital-exhibits-highlights/action-reports/wwii-battle-of-midway/commander-in-chief-pacific-fleet.html

Patrick, John; 'The Hard Lessons of World War II Torpedo Failures', *Undersea Warfare*, 2013: http://www.public.navy.mil/subfor/underseawarfaremagazine/issues/archives/issue_47/torpedo_2.html

'Recollections of Lieutenant George Gay, USNR', Naval History and Heritage Command, September 2015: https://www.history.navy.mil/research/library/oral-histories/wwii/battle-of-midway/recollections-of-lieutenant-george-gay.html

Weadon, Patrick D., 'The Battle of Midway: How Cryptology enabled the United States to turn the tide in the Pacific War', NSA archive: https://www.nsa.gov/portals/75/documents/about/cryptologic-heritage/historical-figures-publications/publications/wwii/battle-midway.pdf

Chapter 7 Dieppe, 1942

Atkin, Ronald, *Dieppe, 1942: The Jubilee Disaster*, London, Macmillan, 1980

Campbell, John P., *Dieppe Revisited: A Documentary Examination*, London, Frank Cass, 1963

Churchill Archive, Cambridge (Chu) 4/300a, f196, aide memoire to Molotov, 11 June 1942

— Chu4/292, WSC questions to Ismay, 21 December 1942

— Chu4/280A, Mountbatten's explanations to WSC, 1950

— private correspondence WSC to Mountbatten, Aug–Nov 1950 (various)

— private correspondence (Chu4/25A) WSC questions (many) on the Dieppe raid, March 1952

– WSC draft *ms* 'The Dieppe Raid', *The Hinge of Fate*

Coward, Nöel, *Future Indefinite*, London, Heinemann, 1954

Hough, Richard, *Mountbatten: Hero of our Time*, London, Weidenfeld & Nicolson, 1980

Maguire, Eric, *Dieppe, August 19*, London, Jonathan Cape, 1963

National Archives, The (PRO): CAB 79/22, COS, 234th meeting, 12 August 1942

– CAB 65/31, 115 of 42, 20 August 1942

– CAB 80/36 and 37, COS minutes (various), April to September 1942

Private Eye, 12 October 1979 (Grovel)

Royal United Services Institute Journal, article and correspondence, October 1999 to April 2000

Villa, Brian Loring, *Unauthorized Action: Mountbatten and the Dieppe Raid*, Toronto, OUP, 1989

Chapter 8 Korea

Appleman, Roy E., *South to the Naktong, North to the Yalu*, US Army Center of Military History, 1961 (reprinted 1992), https://history.army.mil/html/books/020/20-2/CMH_Pub_20-2.pdf

Birtle, Andrew J., *The Korean War: Years of Stalemate July 1951–July 1953*, US Army Center of Military History, 2000, p. 34. Retrieved 21 August 2021: https://history. army.mil/html/books/019/19-10/CMH_Pub_19-10.pdf

British Embassy Pyongyang, 'UK–Korea Relations', UK Foreign and Commonwealth Office, 9 February 2012

Li, Xiaobing, *A History of the Modern Chinese Army*, Lexington KY, University Press of Kentucky, 2009

Millett, Allan Reed, ed. (2001), *The Korean War*, Korea Institute of Military History, University of Nebraska Press. 2001

Parritt, Brigadier Brian, *Chinese Hordes and Human Waves: A Personal Perspective of the Korean War 1950–1953*, Barnsley, Pen & Sword, 2011

Topp, Walter S., 'Failures of US Intelligence During the Korean War', online review, 2017, https://wstopp.com/failures-of-u-s-intelligence-during-the-korean-war/

Weathersby, Kathryn, *Soviet Aims in Korea and the Origins of the Korean War, 1945–1950: New Evidence from the Russian Archives*, Cold War International History Project: Working Paper No. 8, Washington DC, Wilson Center, 1993

Chapter 9 The Tet Offensive, 1968

Bonds, Ray, *The Vietnam War*, London, Salamander Books, 1979

Braestrup, Peter, *Vietnam as History*, Washington DC, University Press of America, 1984

Colby, William, *Lost Victory*, Chicago, IL, Contemporary Books, 1990

Fall, Bernard, *A Street Without Joy*, London, Greenhill Books, 1994

Gilbert, Marc Jason and Head, William (eds), *The Tet Offensive*, Westport, CN, Praeger/ Greenwood, 1996

Gittinger, E. (ed.), *The Johnson Years: a Vietnam Roundtable*, Austin, TX, LBJ Library, 1993

Historical Division of the Joint Secretariat, *The Joint Chiefs of Staff and the War in Vietnam*, Washington DC, 1970

MACV (J2): Command briefing, 8 May 1972

— Command Intelligence Centre Study, Viet Cong Infrastructure, 1 April 1967

McMaster, H.R., *Dereliction of Duty: Lyndon Johnson, Robert McNamara, the Joint Chiefs of Staff, and the lies that led to Vietnam*, New York, HarperCollins, 1997

McNamara, Robert, *In Retrospect: The Tragedy of Vietnam*, New York, Times Books, 1995

Miller, Nathan, *Spying for America: The Hidden History of US Intelligence*, New York, Dell Books, 1989

Oberdorfer, Don, *Tet! The Turning Point in the Vietnam War*, New York, Da Capo Press, 1995

The Recollections of Colonel J. K. Moon, US Intelligence Corps, personal correspondence with the author

The Recollections of Colonel John Robbins, US Artillery, personal correspondence with the author

US Department of State, *Foreign Relations of the United States*, Washington, US Government Printing Office, 1994

Westmoreland, William, *A Soldier Reports*, New York, Dell, 1976

Wirtz, Colonel James, *The Tet Offensive: Intelligence Failure in War*, Ithaca, NY, Cornell University Press, 1991

Chapter 10 Yom Kippur, 1973

Agranat Commission, The, *A Report into the Failures Before and During the 1973 October War*, Tel Aviv, Government Printing Office, 1975

Badri, Hassan, Magdoub, Taha el, and Zohdy, Mohammed Dia el Din, *The Ramadan War 1973*, Dupuy Assoc., VA, 1974

Barnett, Correlli, *The Desert Generals*, London, William Kimber, 1960, and Bloomington, Indiana University Press, 1982

Bickerton, Ian and Pearson, Michael, *The Arab-Israeli Conflict*, London, Longman, 1993

Dupuy, Colonel Trevor, *Elusive Victory*, London, Harper & Row, 1978

Fraser, T. G., *The Arab-Israeli Conflict*, London, Palgrave Macmillan, 1995

Handel, Michael I., *Perception, Deception and Surprise: The Case of Yom Kippur*, Jerusalem, Leonard Daw Institute, 1976

Herzog, Chaim, *The War of Atonement: The Inside Story of the Yom Kippur War, 1973*, Mechanicsburg, PA, Stackpole Books, 1998

Perlmutter, Amos, *Politics and the Military in Israel 1967–1977*, Portland, OR, ISBS, 1978

Recollections of an Israeli intelligence officer (name withheld), private correspondence with the author, 2001

Chapter 11 The Falkland Islands, 1982

Arnaud, Vicente Guillermo; *Las islas Malvinas: descubrimiento, primeros mapas y ocupación. Siglo XVI*, Buenos Aires, Academia Nacional de Geografía, 2000, special publication 13

Clayton, Anthony, *Forearmed: A History of the Intelligence Corps*, London, Brassey's, 1993

Dolzer, Rudolf; *The Territorial Status of the Falkland Islands (Malvinas): Past and Present*, New York Oceana Publications, 1993

Franks, the Right Hon. The Lord, *Falkland Islands Review: Report of a Committee of Privy Councillors*, Cmnd. 8787, London HMSO, 1983

Hastings, Max and Jenkins, Simon, *Battle for the Falklands*, London, Michael Joseph, 1983, and Pan Books, 1997

Keesing's Contemporary Archives: Record of World Events, 1982

Middlebrook, Martin, *The Fighting for the 'Malvinas': The Argentine Forces in the Falklands War*, London, Viking, 1989, and Penguin Books, 1990

Moro, Ruben, *The History of the South Atlantic Conflict*, New York, Praeger, 1989

Official Report on the Campaign for the Malvinas and the South Atlantic, The (*The Calvi Report*), Buenos Aires, 1985

Rattenburg Report, The, Buenos Aires, Commission for the Evaluation of the South Atlantic Report, Circulo Militar, 1988

Thompson, Julian, *No Picnic*, London, Leo Cooper, 1985

Van der Bijl, Nick, *Nine Battles to Stanley*, London, Leo Cooper, 1999

Vaux, Nick, *March to the South*, London, Buchan & Enright, 1986

West, Nigel, *The Secret War for the Falklands*, London, Little, Brown, 1997, and Warner Books, 1998

Woodward, Sandy, *One Hundred Days*, London, HarperCollins, 1992

Chapter 12 The Gulf, 1991

Atkinson, Rick, *Crusade: The Untold Story of the Persian Gulf War*, Boston MA, HMH, 1994

Bellamy, Christopher, *Expert Witness*, London, Brassey's, 1993

Conduct of the Persian Gulf War: Final Report to Congress, Annex C (Intelligence), Washington DC, US Congressional Record, 1994

Cradock, Sir Percy, *In Pursuit of British Interests*, London, John Murray, 1997

Finlan, Alastair, *The Gulf War 1991*, Essential History Series, London, Routledge, 2003

Freedman, Lawrence and Karsh, Efraim, *The Gulf Conflict 1990–1991: Diplomacy and War in the New World Order*, London, Faber and Faber, 1993

New York Times article, 'Confrontation in the Gulf: US Gave Iraq Little Reason Not to Mount Kuwait Assault,' *New York Times*, 23 September 1990

Report of the Commission on US Intelligence, *Preparing for the 21st Century*, March 1996

Shukman, Harold (ed.), *Intelligence Services in the 21st Century*, London, St Ermin's Press, 2000

Simons, Geoff, *Iraq: From Sumer to Saddam*, London, Macmillan, 1994

Sultan, HRH Prince Khalid bin, *Desert Warrior*, London, HarperCollins, 1995

Trevan, T., *Saddam's Secrets*, London, HarperCollins, 1999

US Department of Defense, Superintendent of Documents, *Soviet Military Power*, Washington DC, US Government Printing Office, various years

Chapter 13 The Globalization of Terror/Chapter 14 The Biggest Blunder?

Given the global impact, there are inevitably more books and website articles on the events surrounding '9/11' than most people can cope with. These are the best that I have found and used for this book.

Baxter, Jenny and Downing, Malcolm, *The Day that Shook the World*, London, BBC, 2001

Bergen, Peter, *Holy War: Inside the Secret World of Osama bin Laden*, London, S&S, 2001

Bodansky, Yossef, et al., *Bin Laden, the Man Who Declared War on America*, New York, Random House, 2003

Channel 4, *Why the Twin Towers Collapsed*, TV documentary, November 2001

Cooley, John K., *Unholy Wars: Afghanistan, America and International Terrorism*, London, Pluto Press, 1999

Hoffman, B., *The Modern Terrorist Mind*, Centre for the Study of Terrorism, St Andrew's University, 1997

Ibrahim, Sa'd al-din, *The New Arab Order: Oil and Wealth*, Boulder, CO, Routledge 1982

Juergensmeyer, Mark, *Jihad! Terror in the Mind of God*, Berkeley, CA, Routledge 2000

Meltzer, Milton, *The Day the Sky Fell: A History of Terrorism*, New York, Landmark Books, 2002

Peters, Rudolph, *Islam and Colonialism*, Den Haag and New York, 1979

Reeve, Simon, *The New Jackals: bin Laden and the Future of Terrorism*, London, Andre Deutsch, 1999

Roy, Oliver, *The Failure of Political Islam*, London, Harvard University Press, 1994

RUSI, 'Weapons of Catastrophic Effect', Whitehall seminar, 2003

– 'Homeland Security and Terrorism', Whitehall seminar, 2003

Sinclair, Andrew, *An Anatomy of Terror*, London, Macmillan, 2003

Stern, Jessica, 'Terror's Future', *Foreign Affairs*, July 2003

The Encyclopedia of World Terrorism, New York, Armonk Publications, 1997

US Department of State, *Patterns of Global Terrorism*, Langley, 2001 and 2002

US Government Printing Office website, *Congressional Report into the Events of '9/11'*, 2002

Wilkinson, Paul, *Political Terrorism*, London, 1974

Chapter 15 Afghanistan

'US War in Afghanistan: 1999–2021', New York, Council on Foreign Relations, 2021

Andrews, Tom, 'Classified McChrystal Report: 500,000 Troops Will Be Required Over Five Years in Afghanistan', Huffington Post, 24 September 2009

Beaumont, Peter, 'Afghanistan papers reveal US public were misled about unwinnable war', *Guardian*, 9 December 2019

Bovenkerk, Frank and Levi, Michael (eds), *The Organized Crime Community: Essays in Honor of Alan A. Block*, New York, Springer, 2006

Cassidy, Robert M., *Peacekeeping in the Abyss: British and American Peacekeeping Doctrine and Practice After the Cold War*, Westport CT, Praeger, 2000

Doherty, Ben, 'Last man out: the haunting image of America's final moments in Afghanistan', *Guardian*, 31 August 2021

ISAF in Afghanistan CDI, Terrorism Project, 14 February 2002

Levine, Adam, 'What the numbers say about progress in Afghanistan', *Guardian*, 15 October 2010

Münch, Philipp, 'Creating common sense: getting NATO to Afghanistan', *Journal of Transatlantic Studies*, 2021

NATO report, 'Resolute Support Mission in Afghanistan (2015–2021)', last updated: 30 May 2022, https://www.nato.int/cps/en/natohq/topics_113694.htm#:~:text=Its%20 aim%20was%20to%20provide,was%20terminated%20early%20September%20 2021.&text=Resolute%20Support%20was%20a%20NATO%2Dled%2C%20non%2- Dcombat%20mission

Pedaliu, Effie G. H., 'The Taliban's victory proves the West has failed to learn the lessons of the past', LSE EUROPP blog, London School of Economics, 16 August 2021

Rashid, Ahmed, *Taliban: The Power of Militant Islam in Afghanistan and Beyond*, London, I. B. Tauris, 2022

Reuters report, 'NATO sets "irreversible" but risky course to end Afghan war', Reuters, 21 May 2012

Risen, James, *State of War: The Secret History of the CIA and the Bush Administration*, London, Free Press (Simon & Schuster), 2006

Stewart, Richard W., *Operation Enduring Freedom: The United States Army in Afghanistan, October 2001–March 2002*, US Army Center of Military History, 2004, https://history. army.mil/catalog/pubs/70/70-83.html

Thomas, Clayton, 'Afghanistan: Background and US Policy in Brief', Congressional Research Service report, 1 December 2022, https://sgp.fas.org/crs/row/R45122.pdf

US Congress, 'US Lessons Learned in Afghanistan', Committee on Foreign Affairs, House of Representatives, 15 January 2020, https://www.congress.gov/event/116th-congress/ house-event/LC64900/text?s=1&r=28

United Nations quarterly report S/2014/678 to the Security Council on the operations of the International Security Assistance Force (ISAF) operations in Afghanistan, 1 May to 31 July 2014, UN Secretary-General to the President of the Security Council, https://www.securitycouncilreport.org/atf/cf/%7B65BFCF9B-6D27-4E9C-8CD3-CF6E4FF96FF9%7D/s_2014_678.pdf

'What We Need to Learn: Lessons from Twenty Years of Afghanistan Reconstruction', eleventh report issued by the US Special Inspector General for Afghanistan Reconstruction, August 2021, https://www.sigar.mil/pdf/lessonslearned/SIGAR-21-46-LL.pdf. A most important source. The report examines the past two decades of the US reconstruction effort in Afghanistan. It details how the US government struggled to develop a coherent strategy, understand how long the reconstruction mission would take, ensure its projects were sustainable, staff the mission with trained professionals, account for the challenges posed by insecurity, tailor efforts to the Afghan context, and understand the impact of programmes.

Chapter 16 Ukraine

Since this is an ongoing war at the time of writing there are numerous reliable and not so reliable sources. Below is a list of useful ones.

Bangkok Post article, 'Russian Intelligence Mistakes, Ukraine', *Bangkok Post*, 22 September 2022

Bowen, Andrew S., 'Russia's War in Ukraine: Military and Intelligence Aspects', US Congressional Report, 14 September 2022: https://crsreports.congress.gov/product/pdf/R/R47068

Economist articles, 'Ukraine at War', *The Economist* (various), March 2022

Galeotti, Mark, 'The West Thinks Putin Is Russia's Spymaster. But Are the Spies Controlling Him?', *Guardian*, 20 June 2019

Guardian article, 'Russian intelligence officers and military commanders flee Crimea, Kyiv claims', *Guardian*, 14 September 2022

Hockenhull, General Sir Jim, Commander UK Strategic Command, 'How open-source intelligence has shaped the Russia-Ukraine war', RUSI members webinar, 9 December 2022

Lomas, Dan, 'Ukraine and Intelligence Prebuttal: A Quick Post-Mortem', London, RUSI, 24 February 2022: https://rusi.org/explore-our-research/publications/commentary/ukraine-and-intelligence-prebuttal-quick-post-mortem

MOD UK, updates on intelligence in Ukraine (various), February 2022–ongoing

Prince, Todd, 'Eyeing Ukraine, Putin Huddles in a Tight, Hawkish Circle', Radio Free Europe/Radio Liberty, 15 February 2022

Radio Free Europe, interview with Andrei Soldatov, 'How Russia's Intelligence Agencies Have Adapted after Six Months of War', Radio Free Europe/Radio Liberty August 2022

Chapter 17 Will It Ever Get Any Better?

Cukier, Kenneth, 'Big Data; Better Data?', *Economist*, 18 November 2011

Herman, Michael, *Intelligence Services in the Information Age*, London, Frank Cass, 2001

Shukman, Harold (ed.), *Agents for Change: Intelligence Services in the 21st Century*, London, St Ermin's Press, 2000

GLOSSARY OF TERMS

Abwehr German Military Intelligence (WWII)

Agency an organization that collects and disseminates intelligence collected by its sources (e.g. MI6)

AMAN Israeli military intelligence

BDA Bomb Damage Assessment

BfV Federal German Security Service

Bletchley Park British WWII code-breaking centre

BND Federal German foreign intelligence service

C3 Command, Control and Communications

CIA US foreign intelligence agency

CIG UK Current Intelligence Groups

CIR Critical Intelligence Requirements

COMINT Signals Intelligence

compartmentalized information protected by special internal procedures
    and restricted to a limited readership

CTC Counterterrorism Center

CYA Cover yo' ass!

DIA US Defense Intelligence Agency

DIS UK Defence Intelligence Staff

Double Cross UK WWII committee playing back turned MI5 double agents against the Germans

DSO UK Defence Security Officer

DST French Secret Service

EEI Essential Elements of Information

Enigma German WWII cipher machine

FAA Federal Aviation Authority

FBI US internal security service

FCO UK Foreign and Commonwealth Office

FHO and FHW WWII German military intelligence staffs

FISA Foreign Intelligence Surveillance Act

G2 General Staff Branch 2 – Military Intelligence and Security

GCCS WWII UK Government Code and Cipher School

GCHQ Government Communication Headquarters – UK sigint agency

GRU Soviet military intelligence service

HUMINT Human Intelligence – spies, interrogation and agents

IDF Israeli Defence Forces

INU/O WWII Soviet foreign intelligence analysts

INR US State Department policy advisory group

IRA Irish Republican Army

ISSB Inter-Services Security Board

I&W Indicators and Warning

J2 Joint military staff intelligence branch

J Stars US high-tech real-time radar surveillance plane

JARIC UK Joint Air Photo Reconnaissance Centre

JIC UK Joint Intelligence Committee

KGB Soviet secret intelligence and security service

LACIG UK Latin America Current Intelligence Group

LAKAM highly secretive Israeli 'technical' intelligence service (nuclear)

Langley CIA headquarters

LCS London Controlling Section – UK WWII deception staff

MACV US Military Assistance Command, Vietnam

Magic intercepted WWII Japanese high-level code

MI5 UK security service

MI6 UK secret intelligence service (SIS)

MI-8 US WWII code-breakers

MOD UK Ministry of Defence

MOSSAD Israeli overseas intelligence service

NGO Non-governmental Organizations

NIE US National Intelligence Estimate

NORAID Northern Irish Aid (US)

NRO US National Reconnaissance Office (satellite)

NKVD, NKGB forerunners of Soviet KGB

NVA North Vietnamese Army

NSA US National Security Agency (sigint)

ONE US Office of National Estimates

ONI US Office of Naval Intelligence

OOB Order of Battle

OP-20-G US Navy WWII code-breakers

OPEC Organization of the Petroleum Exporting Countries

PI Photographic Interpreter or Intelligence

PIR Party of the Iranian Revolution

PLO Palestine Liberation Organization

PR Photographic Reconnaissance

Purple US WWII code-breaking of Japanese top-level signals traffic

RCC Iraqi Revolutionary Command Council

RFU Radical Fundamentalist Unit

RVN-J2 South Vietnamese joint military intelligence

SIGINT Signals intelligence

SIS (UK) MI6

SIS (US WWII) US Army code-breaking office (Signal Intelligence Service)

SOE UK WWII Special Operations Executive

Source a device or individual for collecting information; sources are controlled by *agencies*

Techint technical intelligence

Twenty Committee UK WWII double agent controllers (hence 'XX' = 'double-cross')

UGS Unattended Ground Sensor

UNHCR United Nations High Commissioner for Refugees

UKUSA agreement UK/US secret treaty to share sigint

Ultra UK WWII code word for intercepted Enigma traffic

VCIGS Vice Chief of the Imperial General Staff

Venona Highly secret decoding operation of 1940s NKGB spy signals traffic

WIFJ World Islamic Front for Jihad against Jews and Crusaders

WMD Weapons of Mass Destruction

WTC World Trade Center

Y service general title for interception (*not* decoding) of unknown radio signals

INDEX